MIGRANTS

MIGRANTS

The Story of Us All

Sam Miller

abacus
books

ABACUS

First published in Great Britain in 2023 by Abacus

5 7 9 10 8 6 4

Copyright © Sam Miller 2023

The moral right of the author has been asserted.

Maps by Barking Dog Art

A CIP catalogue record for this book
is available from the British Library.

Hardback ISBN 978-1-4087-1354-9
Trade Paperback ISBN 978-1-4087-1353-2

Typeset in Bembo by M Rules
Printed and bound in India by
Manipal Technologies Limited

Papers used by Abacus are from well-managed forests
and other responsible sources.

Abacus
An imprint of
Little, Brown Book Group
Carmelite House
50 Victoria Embankment
London EC4Y 0DZ

An Hachette UK Company
www.hachette.co.uk

www.littlebrown.co.uk

To my Covid companions: Jane, Roxy and Fergus

And a special thanks to Heraclitus,
La Saggia Nuotatrice and the Butcher of Shillong

Contents

Prologue

Let me begin with a brief, extraordinary story: the tale of a migrant who survived a war and a terrifying journey across the Mediterranean to start a new life in Europe. I'm temporarily withholding, for what I think are good reasons, the nationality and religion of the migrant.

AT was a well-connected man in his thirties, who found himself on the losing side of a long-running war in an Asian country. He'd been a fighter in the war himself, and knew that he would be killed by the victors who were now streaming into the city in which he lived. These victors – who spoke the same language and practised the same religion as AT – had already murdered his father-in-law, a well-known figure in the city.

AT's own father could no longer walk and refused to leave the city, saying he would rather die at home than become a refugee. But eventually AT persuaded him to leave. AT would later describe how he carried his father out of the city on his back. Beside him, holding AT's hand, was his young son. The three of them managed to reach relative safety in a nearby valley. AT then went back to the city on his own to look for his wife, from whom he had been separated in the chaos. He learned that she had been killed.

He returned to his father and son in the valley. With some other refugees they travelled to the Turkish coast. From there they took a boat out into the Mediterranean. There was no clear plan, except to escape the violence, and to find a place where they would be welcome. The boat stopped at several ports that were unwelcoming, including a place on the Greek mainland to which AT's brother-in-law had fled. He learned that his brother-in-law had been killed. He prayed at his graveside and left.

The refugees continued westwards by boat. It was a harrowing journey. They had heard that the mainland of Italy would be a good place for migrants such as them, particularly the area around Rome. They landed briefly in Sicily – where AT's father died – but then were forced to travel back across the Mediterranean to Tunisia. They were then stuck in Tunisia for a year, where AT met a woman, herself a migrant from Lebanon, who fell in love with him. He was in two minds. He thought of staying there and marrying her, but he dreamed still of going to Italy, which had become a kind of Promised Land for him. Eventually he and his son, and others from his country, managed to get on a boat for Italy, and they eventually landed near Ostia, just to the west of Rome.

At the start, it was not easy for AT, his son, and their companions. They built a temporary refugee camp near the beach where they had landed. AT's son was accused of poaching, and the new migrants soon got caught up in local political feuds. But AT made clever alliances and became the right-hand man to a Roman dignitary. Eventually AT himself, by marrying the daughter of the dignitary, became an important figure in Rome.

AT, as some readers may have guessed, is no modern migrant. He is Aeneas of Troy, who lived in what is now Turkey. His murdered father-in-law was King Priam; his Tunisian girlfriend was Dido of Carthage. The Roman dignitary was called King Latinus, and according to Virgil, Aeneas' descendants ruled Rome for many centuries. For me the story is a reminder of how little has changed for would-be migrants over the last three thousand years, and how migration has always been, since the very beginning, central to the human story. And remains so.

We all need to talk about migration. Urgently and openly. And not just the insular country-by-country stuff; not only borders and passports and quotas and walls and visas. But something much deeper, more fundamental about who we are as human beings.

For everybody seems to have an opinion about migration. In fact, if you just dig a little, most people have several, sometimes contradictory, opinions. Some of us are very vocal on the subject. Others shy away from talking about migration, because the subject has become so toxic. No issue seems more emotive, more likely to create discord in a family, to set friends against each other, to divide a community or a political party. And many of us find it hard to look at the issue from the point of view of others, from the point of view of people who are not like us.

It's my contention that migration has, in fact, become a modern proxy for a whole range of other issues that impinge on our lives and our thinking: identity, ethnicity, religion, ideas of home, patriotism, nostalgia, integration, multiculturalism, safety, terrorism, racism. And that the reason migration plays this role is because, historically and culturally, migration is such an important element of the human story. We are all, of course, descended from migrants. And it is part of the story of each of us, whether or not we have been migrants ourselves.

I will argue here that the role of migration in human history has often been underplayed or overlooked or misunderstood.

There are a number of possible reasons for this. I suspect that the most important is a still-dominant narrative that sees the history of human beings as a story of continuing progress (with a few ups and downs), in which savages are transformed into citizens, and nomads become householders. The majority of us today have a home address and a nationality. Many of us own land or a home. We are sedentary. We belong to somewhere.

But all this has been true for just a tiny part of human history. Having a permanent home and a lifelong nationality are considered normal, as if they were part of the human condition. I think, in certain ways, that the opposite is true: we are almost unparalleled as a migratory species, able to thrive practically anywhere. And a wider recognition of this might encourage us to rebalance our view of the 'normal' world. Human history has usually been written by and for sedentary people, who claim an attachment to a particular location or country, or sometimes to justify an imperial adventure. And their accounts of their lives and of the past are more likely to have survived. And this, in my view, has gently skewed our understanding of our past.

My aim, here, is to restore migration to the heart of the human story, in a way that might also help us reset the modern discussion about migrants. This book sets out to question what might be called the 'myth of sedentarism', the popular modern notion that humans are naturally sedentary. And to conduct what can be seen as a series of experiments by viewing important periods in the history of humankind through the prism of migration, of people on the move, of societies in flux – rather than of stasis, of settled communities, of fixed ethnicity or nationality.

It is not essential to have been a migrant to see human history through this alternative lens, but it may help. I have been away from the country of my birth, the UK, for most of my adult years, for a range of reasons: as a spouse living in India, my wife's country; in order to work for the BBC, and to write books; and – quite simply – because I wanted to. And so, over the last ten years, while this project has been in gestation, I have lived (for at least three months, and sometimes a lot longer) in India, Tanzania, Nigeria, Tunisia, Afghanistan, Cambodia, Ethiopia and Indonesia – with several short spells back in the UK, usually in the London house in which I was born. And I am, for now, comfortable in not having a place I call home. It is important here that I also acknowledge my good fortune. In comparison to most migrants, I have it easy. My passport, my job, my background, my colour and my gender all combine to make it uncomplicated for me to live almost anywhere I want, for long or short periods, in ways that most migrants never experience. I am definitely not a typical migrant, though most of us would be hard pressed to identify someone who is.

There is no simple, uncontentious definition of a migrant. Many of those definitions are narrow in scope and are designed only to deal with migration in modern times. They often refer to nations or borders or citizenship. I've chosen, quite deliberately, a broad definition, borrowed from the work of the psychologist Greg Madison, according to whom,

> a migrant is someone who has moved from one culture to another, where the second [culture] is experienced as significantly different from the first, and for a sufficient duration that the person engages in daily activities and is challenged to undergo some adjustment to the new place.

I prefer this definition because there is no mention of nationality or ethnicity or frontiers. It therefore can be used to describe modern and ancient migrants, as well as those who migrate willingly and those who do not. It also emphasises the experience of the migrant, rather than the distance travelled or the border crossed. And it encompasses a broad spectrum: from those who freely choose to move to those who have it forced upon them, and everyone in between.

In practice, this means that the word 'migrant' clumps together people whose experience of migration is extremely diverse – slaves and spouses, refugees and retirees, nomads and expats, conquerors and job-seekers. It's a hypernym, an umbrella term which can be used to cover those who intended to migrate, and those who moved elsewhere for a short time and then just lingered on (like me), as well as those who are forced to move: driven or carried unwillingly into exile. It might apply to someone who moves just a few miles across an international frontier, or to someone who travels huge distances within their own country.

The language surrounding migration is often loaded and confusing, and in recent times has become increasingly bound up with ideas of the nation-state and its borders, as well as with race and racism. Immigrants and emigrants, arrivers and leavers respectively, are, obviously, the same people seen from distinct viewpoints, and yet are imagined quite differently. The two words carry very different connotations. In rich countries, emigrants are typically seen as adventurous risk-takers, while immigrants are often portrayed as parasites. Attitudes towards migrants can be deeply inconsistent. They are expected to assimilate and encouraged to remain distinctive; to defend their heritage and adopt a new one. They are sub-human and super-human, romanticised and castigated, admired and abhorred.

There is great modern-day concern over migration among the settled people of many nations. It is an issue that is deeply divisive, and one that frequently cuts across traditional party-political lines. Politicians will often attempt to outdo each other in their opposition to migration, particularly when times are hard. Attitudes towards many migrants have tended to be driven by economic cycles. At times of growth, foreign workers are needed, and employers and governments go out of their way to attract migrants. When a downturn inevitably comes, they are often expected to return 'home'. As the Swiss playwright Max Frisch once remarked, in relation to his country's immigration policy, 'We called for workers, and human beings came instead.' Migrants themselves are often dehumanised and unheard, their voices silenced by the controversies and vitriol that swirl around them.

The migration challenges of the next half century may be far greater than those of the recent past. Ageing populations in rich countries mean that many more migrants are needed to overcome labour shortages. And migration and the desire to migrate are set to increase dramatically as climate change begins to turn our world upside down. Coastal communities are disappearing, and fields will turn to desert – and frozen lands, far from the tropics, will become agriculturally viable. Migration, some are now arguing, will become the most important test facing humanity. Another reason, then, why we need to reset our view of migrants, and to recognise the pivotal role that migration has always played and will continue to play in the human story.

But it is also important not to become sentimental about migration, now and in the past. It can sometimes be deeply disruptive, and often destructive. And there are many cases in which migration has been far from benign or enriching. In the Americas, early European settlers brought disease and death. While the earliest human inhabitants of places as varied as Sri Lanka, the United States, Japan, Cuba and New Zealand have been reduced to tiny minorities by migration. But it's usually forgotten that these 'aboriginals' were also once migrants to a land where they were the first human settlers; migrants who often killed off previous animal migrants to the same place – and so on, in a backwards spiral, to the beginning of life on earth.

It's sometimes hard to know just how far back to go with migration – there is no natural starting point. I think it's useful, briefly, to go back to the most ancient of times, not only because this is one of those occasions where, as a species, we might benefit from some humility, but also because migration is a fundamental part of the story of our planet, and not just of humans but of our pre-human ancestors and their animal cousins. And a twenty-first-century discovery has made it possible to go back a very long way indeed, into an almost absurdly distant prehistory.

In the early years of this millennium, palaeontologists exploring a disused sandstone quarry near the Canadian city of Kingston came across a series of mysterious markings or indentations in the rock. Further investigation showed these markings to be fossilised footprints, the earliest ever found. They belonged to a group of long-extinct animals, described by the scientists as a cross between a lobster and a centipede, each about eighteen inches long. There were so many footprints that the scientists couldn't work exactly how many legs each of these animals had – but somewhere between sixteen and twenty-two – and they could tell from other fossilised markings that they dragged their tails behind them as they scuttled across the sand. These creatures had just emerged from the ocean and stepped onto land, at a time when all animals lived in the sea. Symbolically at least, these 'lobsterpedes' might be considered the first migrants, moving between two very different habitats about 530 million years ago.

It's not clear why these marine creatures were on land. They may have been there to search for food, or to escape from predators, or driven there by a changing climate or by overpopulation, or maybe they simply got lost. I would like to ascribe to them a sense of adventure or curiosity, but I have no evidence for this. What makes this feat so extraordinary

is that there were no other animals living on land – no dinosaurs, no ants, no rats, no cockroaches, and very little plant life.
So it's really the lobster equivalent of humans landing on the
moon. Like the moon landing, and unlike most migrations,
there was no one already there to take offence at the arrival of
the lobsterpedes, or to fear that these newcomers might cause
trouble. It was genuinely virgin territory. The newcomers
themselves probably weren't impressed; there was no food, no
shelter from the sun (though it might have been raining), and
they must have become dehydrated pretty quickly.

This was an almost unimaginably long time ago, long
before mammals or birds existed, when our own ancestors
were legless fish-like creatures swimming in the sea. We don't
know exactly what happened next, but it is possible that the
lobsterpedes, like the astronauts, simply returned whence
they came. Because it was at least another 150 million years
before animals began to build permanent colonies on land.
And among those early migrants were our own distant ancestors, who had by now evolved into small fish-lizards whose
four fins had become four very short legs, and from whom
every single one of us (along with all reptiles, mammals and
birds) are descended. By about 250 million years ago, some of
those fish-lizard ancestors had developed into animals known
as cynodonts who resembled a cross between a lizard and

a dog, and from whom all mammals are descended. Fossils of cynodonts have been found on every continent including Antarctica, showing just how successful they were as migrants – arguably the most successful until the arrival of modern humans.*

Primates only emerged about eighty million years ago, and in their early days some of them were also quite impressive as migrants, but our closest simian cousins were far less adventurous. Chimpanzees, our nearest relatives (closer to us than they are to gorillas, their next nearest cousins), never left sub-Saharan Africa except when forced to do so in modern times by human beings. The evolutionary line between chimps and humans split about five million years ago, and some of the earliest human skeletons – in South Africa and in Ethiopia – have been found in places where chimpanzees never lived. Chimpanzees are the distant relatives who stayed at home, in their ancestral habitat.†

Early human history is a scholars' battleground, particularly when it comes to migration. There is broad agreement that we are all originally from Africa – apart from a coalition of blind nationalists and evolution-deniers who consider that some groups of humans (usually their own) live where they

---

* The cynodonts' world was very different from ours, principally because there was just one enormous landmass now known as Pangaea – allowing the easy migration of these proto-mammals to all parts of the globe. Members of the rat family might also make a claim to be the most successful of mammal migrants – though their migration routes echo those of humans and may well have been driven by the opportunities of food provided by humans. Both rats and humans are descended from cynodonts. The most recent common rat-human ancestor lived about 100 million years ago.

† Some humans, of course, also remained in that ancestral homeland. And adult chimpanzees actually perform daily micro-migrations, almost always sleeping in a different tree, and often travelling for many hours – but never venturing beyond the forests and savannahs of Central and West Africa. While all bonobos, once known as dwarf chimpanzees, live south of the Congo River, other larger chimps all live to the north. Some other primates have migrated long distances, though not necessarily by choice. There's a mystery about how the lemurs of Madagascar first got there from Africa, because they needed to cross the 400-kilometre-wide stretch of the Indian Ocean known as the Mozambique Channel. Many scientists argue that they must have accidentally floated across on rafts of tangled vegetation.

have always lived. But as for the detail, much has changed in recent years.

Modern science – particularly the testing of modern and ancient DNA – has revolutionised the study of early human migration. And the overall picture that has emerged during the last decade is far more complex than anyone had previously anticipated. Almost all of us are more of a mixture than we thought we were. And those simple directional arrows that used to be placed on world maps to describe tens of thousands of years of history as humans settled the earth, are gross over-simplifications, and often wrong. In Europe and Asia more specifically, we now know that there were layers upon layers of overlapping, entangled movements of population – that look much more like a transport map for a megacity than a simple flowchart or a family tree.

Until recently there was a vague consensus that there were two significant human migrations out of Africa. The first of these took place more than half a million years ago, and helped explain the discovery of human-like Neanderthal skeletons in Europe and Asia. That migration was seen as a failure because the Neanderthals died out. The second migration, which began less than a hundred thousand years ago, was of what became known as 'anatomically modern humans' – that is, 'people like us'. This migration was deemed a success, because these migrants gradually settled the world – and everyone out-side sub-Saharan Africa is descended from them. But we now know that this older view of our evolutionary past is mislead-ing at best and, on one key point relating to the Neanderthals, simply wrong.

It now appears from studying the genomes of ancient and modern humans that there were in fact more than two major migrations out of Africa, and at least one possible migration back to the continent. And in Europe and Asia there were many layers of multi-directional, overlapping and interconnected migrations. Unpacking the research of the geneticists, and drawing up historical timelines based on their findings, reveals a species on the move like no other species. Of course, these acts of migration happened over long periods of time, and it's hard to know whether many individuals travelled huge distances during their lifetimes. But it is clear that, over the generations, humans gradually made their determined way – despite enormous barriers of geography and climate – to every part of the world, except Antarctica. We will never know exactly what made them do this – and there are probably a range of interconnected reasons, many of them familiar today – including getting away from other humans, climate change and the search for food. And a sense of adventure or curiosity or restlessness may be just as important. Indeed, there are scientists who have referred to the existence of what has become known as the 'curiosity gene', a genetic mutation found among about 20 per cent of humans.

But perhaps the most startling discovery made by the genetic scientists was about the Neanderthals, those supposedly brutish, stupid, humanoid distant cousins of ours who disappear from the archaeological record about forty thousand years ago. They did not, after all, become extinct. They are with us now, quite literally. For it turns out that the vast majority of modern humans are descended from Neanderthals.

CHAPTER ONE

Neanderthals, Sapiens and the *Beagle*

It's a short downhill walk along a leafy footpath from Neanderthal railway station to the elegant, curved glass building that houses western Europe's only museum dedicated to its aboriginal people. The museum stands near an area of well-tended young woodland that conceals the strange history of this German valley. For it all looked very different until the middle years of the nineteenth century. This part of the Neander Valley was once an enormous, dramatic limestone gorge, fifty metres high, beloved of Romantic painters and famous for its caves and waterfalls. But limestone became a valuable commodity in the construction industry – the raw material for the great municipal buildings of the nearby city of Düsseldorf. And a small army of miners flattened the gorge, destroying all its caves, transforming it into a quarry, and leaving behind a wasteland when the limestone ran out. In recent times, the valley has been landscaped, replanted with trees and developed as a well-signposted tourist destination for those who are interested in the deep history of humankind.

In the summer of 1856, two Italian migrant workers were searching for limestone deposits in the valley when they discovered the entrance to an ancient cave. And inside, as they scraped away at many centuries of hard sediment, to make sure that the floor of the cave really was made of limestone, they came across some old bones. They showed them to the landowner, who thought they were the skeletal remains of a bear. But because he wasn't absolutely sure he decided to take them to the local teacher, who also happened to be a fossil-collector. That teacher, Dr Fuhlrott, immediately recognised the bones as human, but also noticed that they were different in a number of significant ways from those of modern humans. Over the following decade, a separate subspecies of extinct humans was identified, and was given the name *Homo Neanderthalensis* after the valley. The Neanderthals were reborn.*

The Neanderthal Museum is built as a single helix, spiralling slowly upwards, steplessly, through our ancient history. It is popular with parties of teenage German schoolchildren, who can play the fool with replica skulls, pretend to dig for ancient bones in an indoor sandpit, and take selfies with life-sized naked early humans. The museum is a place of teasing, flirtation and laughter. There's even a Neanderthal

---

* Neanderthal bones had been found earlier than 1856, but not recognised as a different species or subspecies. I've opted for subspecies here because it makes it clearer that they are close enough biologically to interbreed. *Homo Stupidus* was originally considered as the name for the new subspecies, in obvious contrast to *Sapiens*, which means 'wise'. The discoveries in the Neander Valley took place three years before the publication of *The Origin of Species* and helped create a scientific climate in which evolution very gradually became accepted. There were lots of arguments among German scientists, one of whom, Professor August Mayer, said the 'malformed' bones found in the Neander Valley were those of a wounded horse-riding Cossack suffering from rickets who had climbed into the cave during the Napoleonic Wars. When the similarities were noticed to a Neanderthal skeleton found in Gibraltar, the British palaeontologist George Busk declared 'even Professor Mayer will hardly suppose that a rickety Cossack engaged in the campaign of 1814 had crept into a sealed fissure in the Rock of Gibraltar'.

man dressed in a suit and tie, leaning over some railings, waiting to be mistaken for a member of the public. And yes, looking like this, he would not draw much attention on the train back to Düsseldorf. But, gently curated, there is a more serious message here, part of an attempt to re-humanise the Neanderthals – both as Europe's aboriginals, and as our ancestors.

By the 1920s, the word Neanderthal had entered common parlance in several European languages.* It was used to describe oafish, dim-witted, backward-looking individuals. H. G. Wells, thanks to his 1921 short story 'The Grisly Folk', deserves some of the blame. He recognised Neanderthals as the original Europeans, but described them as stupid and ugly

---

* Neanderthal means Neander Valley in German. The word 'Neander' is taken from the Greek, meaning rather wonderfully in this context, but entirely coincidentally, 'new man'. The valley was named after a seventeenth-century German theologian called Joachim Neander, whose grandfather, following the intellectual fashion of the times, had translated his surname, Neumann, into ancient Greek.

and hairy, and running around like baboons. In his story, they are defeated, killed off by 'true men' who are like us, who are clever and handsome and who know how to work as a team. Neanderthals soon became the archetypal club-wielding, grunting cavemen of cartoon humour – often portrayed, quite absurdly, as co-existing with dinosaurs. 'Knuckle-dragging Neanderthals' has become a rhetorical insult, used to describe reactionary politicians and drunken football fans.

Neanderthals didn't drag their knuckles. They stood upright, and had fire and language and art – and larger brains than modern humans. They cared for their sick. They survived several ice ages, and they lived in a wide variety of climates – from the Atlantic to central Siberia, from the Arctic to the Middle East. Yes, their brows were thicker, and they were shorter and stronger than most anatomically modern humans. But they weren't really very different from the new migrants from Africa who supplanted them.

The Neanderthal Museum manages, fleetingly, to conjure up some fragmentary mental images of a lost world, a world that lasted an astoundingly long time. Remember: for almost half a million years, Neanderthals were probably the only humans in Europe; nearly ten times as many years as we, modern humans, have been on the continent. And it is increasingly possible, at the intersection of genetics and palaeontology, to learn something of the lives of Neanderthals, of where they came from, of how they were related to each other, of their diseases and diets.

And yet, there is so much more, beyond the purview of science, that we will never know. As I ended my visit, having flitted through the museum gift shop (with 'Neanderthal beer', 'Stone Age' lollipops, caveman jigsaw puzzles, and real fossils for just one euro), and out into the summer sun of the Neander Valley I tried to imagine something of the lives of the men, women and children who once lived here. Did they, for instance, return to stay in the same caves each year? Did they consider the caves to be their home; and did they have a sense of home similar to the way we use that word now? And what did they make of outsiders – other groups of Neanderthals, or the new migrants from Africa?

The voices of Neanderthals, though, like those of all early humans (and of so many migrants) are irretrievable. We know nothing of what they thought, of how they saw their world, of what they cared about most – and we never will. But that shouldn't be an absolute limit on our powers of imagination, and empathy. And novelists have tried – often more thoughtfully than H. G. Wells, who declared of the Neanderthals that we might as well try to imagine how 'a gorilla dreams and feels'.

William Golding, for instance, fresh from the success of his first novel, *Lord of the Flies*, but long before his Nobel Prize, depicted the decline and death of a Neanderthal community in his second book, *The Inheritors*. It's a strangely affecting novel, ahead of its time, and Golding's own favourite. It's also a deliberate response to Wells. A quotation from Wells is used as an epigraph – in which he refers to the 'ugliness' and 'repulsive strangeness' of Neanderthals. Golding's Neanderthals are quite different. The world is seen through their eyes in all but the last sad chapters of the book. They are the good people of Golding's story; thoughtful, loving, in tune with nature, gentle, innocent, living happily somewhere in northern Europe. They are seasonal migrants, forest-dwellers in the summer, who retreat to a coastal cave each winter – a life unchanging. And then, one terrible summer, the 'new people' turn up; *Homo Sapiens*, that is. They are hungry and desperate and cunning, and ready to kill. They have spears and boats, and knowledge of a wider world. And they think the Neanderthals are devils. By the end of the summer and the end of novel, the Neanderthals are wiped out, except for a baby boy carried off by the new people.*

The Neanderthals, as a separate subspecies, died out around forty thousand years ago. We don't know why. There's a range of possible explanations. It's plausible, at least, that the 'new people' were partly responsible. They may have been more successful in competing for scarce resources; they had better weapons; and may have carried diseases for which the Neanderthals had no immunity. If so, it would not be the only time in history that migrants have wiped out an existing population: in the modern era, Europeans bearing weapons and diseases destroyed entire aboriginal communities in the Americas and Australasia, and decimated many others.

And yet it's important to be careful with such comparisons. Neanderthals and anatomically modern humans probably coexisted in Europe for several thousand years – in which case, does it still make sense to refer to the latter group as migrants? And it seems likely that in this period – hugely long for us, tiny in prehistoric terms – Neanderthals and Sapiens were both migrating within Europe, probably quite large distances. And so the story is not as simple as Neanderthals simply being supplanted by new migrants.

In fact, both subspecies were migratory people, for whom movement – seasonal and permanent – was normal and necessary; and we can only presume that the questions 'when and where to move?' were major topics of discussion for all early humans. Simply put, humans did not, at this stage, build homes, and caves provided only temporary or seasonal shelter. Early humans were hunter-gatherers and scavengers. Prior to

---

* The most commercially successful example of Neanderthal fiction is Jean M. Auel's best-selling *The Clan of the Cave Bear*. There the Golding ending is reversed, and a young *Homo Sapiens* girl gets separated from her family and is adopted by a group of Neanderthals. The Neanderthals are portrayed as being barely able to speak; and unable to cry or laugh. Beyond this, the Neanderthals are not demonised, and Auel has positive and negative characters who belong to both subspecies.

the development of agriculture, about thirty thousand years after the extinction of the Neanderthals, there was little to be gained from staying put – so long as their food was on the move, or only to be found growing over a large area of land, or in the sea.

Additionally, even the notion that the Neanderthals are extinct is a nuanced one. For the simple reason that we now know that Neanderthals and Sapiens had sex with each other, and children were born as a result. And that most human beings are descended from these children. A small part of the DNA of most modern humans – between 1 and 4 per cent – is of Neanderthal origin. We don't yet know where and when Neanderthals and Sapiens interbred – but genetic scientists may soon be able to tell us. The mingling of these two human sub-species is a reminder of the very recent consanguinity of most of us. A reminder that peoples who are normally thought of as quite different from each other – from South Sea Islanders, through Indian farmers, Siberian nomads, Europeans of every description, to Native Americans – are inter-related not only through their Sapiens forebears but through their common Neanderthal ancestry.

The only exceptions – those among us who have no Neanderthal genes – are those with long unbroken lines of descent from sub-Saharan Africa; those, that is, who never left the continent on which humans originally emerged as a separate species. Africa – from where all humans come: Neanderthals and Sapiens, and any of those other subspe-cies* which have disappeared into the haze of prehistory. Everywhere else, and even in most parts of Africa, humans

---

* A number of other hominids have been identified, including *Homo Erectus* – often described as the ancestor of both Neanderthals and Sapiens. In 2010, the DNA of another subspecies, named the Denisovans, was identified from a finger bone exca-vated in a Siberian cave. Subsequent analysis showed that small amounts of Denisovan DNA were widespread among Asians. Other subspecies, *Homo Floresiensis* and *Homo Luzonensis,* have been identified from old bones found on islands in South-East Asia.

are relative newcomers – migrants and the descendants of migrants.

The prehistoric human journey was an extraordinary one. And those many ancient migrations to and within Europe – Neanderthal and Sapiens – were a small sideshow compared to what was happening in Asia, and then the Americas. To get to Europe, humans from Africa 'simply' needed to reach the Middle East and turn left, following the coastline of the Mediterranean or the Black Sea. The journey to other parts of the globe was far more complex. Some early migrants used a coastal route into Asia and beyond, island-hopping all the way to Australia. Others headed, blindly, inland to Siberia (or possibly along the coast of China), and then across the Bering Strait – and eventually down through the Americas to the southern tip of what is now Chile.

In recent years, as a by-product of the sequencing of the human genome and improved techniques of extracting DNA from old bones, we have learned a lot more about these ancient migrations. It's not always clear-cut, and for now it's probably wisest to let the scientists do battle (and they are in permanent mid-skirmish) over the dates and the routes by which humans peopled the world. But beyond those arcane battles it's impor-tant to remember that there is a consensus that it all undeniably happened; that *Homo Sapiens* achieved this astonishing feat, for better or worse, of peopling the earth long before they had what we would consider even the most basic technology. They had fire and language, and simple tools made from stone or wood or bone, and that was all.

The more important question, for my purposes, is not when or how, but *why* it all happened; and what the tentative answers to that question might say about us as a species. For here we enter the murky world of paleo-psychology, which in this context is really an attempt to understand the motivation for human migration to every corner of the planet. We have no human words, no texts, of course, to help us with this question, nothing until the third millennium BCE and the city-states of Mesopotamia, by which time it's far too late and almost all of the world that is currently inhabited had been settled.* And so we have to look elsewhere for answers. There is bound to be, in most cases, a combination of possible local reasons for migrating, including climate change, scarce resources and territorial disputes. But these could apply to any species, and no other land mammal apart from, possibly, the rat has shown such a disposition to travel the globe. And therefore I'm tempted by the idea that, for some humans at least (and perhaps some rats), there is a deep-rooted, ancient, instinctive, perhaps genetic desire to be on the move.

Remember that being sedentary, having a permanent home is, in deep historical terms, a relatively modern phenomenon, and that just four hundred years ago about a third of the world's population was nomadic. Even today, there are more than thirty million people† living a traditional nomadic lifestyle, and many millions more who might be called employee-nomads, or short-term migrant workers. And so I suggest that we may learn something about ourselves as a species if we put aside the notion that there is something innately normal or natural about staying in, or close to, the place where you were born. And remember, too, that given the timescales involved, and the absence of any prior information about the lands they were travelling to, the great prehistoric migrations probably

---

* Among the few places that had not been settled by humans at this time were a number of outlying islands including New Zealand, Iceland and Madagascar.
† Historical context is important here. That figure of thirty million modern nomads represents less than 0.5 per cent of the world's current population, but is far greater than the global population ten thousand years ago, when almost every human being was a nomad.

happened in ways that were more complicated than we can now imagine. With perhaps more failures than successes, more reversals and dead ends than we will ever know about.

The longest journey of them all was to the southernmost tip of South America, to the series of islands known as Tierra del Fuego, shared now between Argentina and Chile. There's a scientific consensus that humans first reached there around ten thousand years ago, migrants whose ancestors had come all the way from Africa to Asia and on to Alaska, and down through the Americas, until they ended up below the 54th parallel, the closest human settlements to the South Pole. Until recently, it was thought the earliest humans in North America were hunters drawn inland by the big game that roamed the great plains. But the most popular current theory is the Kelp Highway Hypothesis, which proposes that the first Americans were not big game hunters at all but fisherfolk travelling along the coast, following vast underwater forests of seaweed that supported a very extensive marine world full of edible sea creatures – 'a seafood buffet', according to one description.

And so it was, probably, that many millennia ago the most travelled of all early migrants, a group now known as the Yaghan, reached the southern islands of the wind-ravaged Tierra del Fuego archipelago, close to Cape Horn. And, having nowhere further to go, they stayed. The Yaghan thrived, building up quite astonishing resistance to the cold, unparalleled among other humans – living naked in sub-polar temperatures and adapting successfully to some of the harshest conditions anywhere in the world. They continued to lead a nomadic existence, harvesting shellfish, catching fish and sea lions, mixing only with other Fuegian communities, and not moving beyond the archipelago until a new set of travellers and migrants

The Yaghan Journey

appeared on the shores of Tierra del Fuego. And so this, perhaps the greatest migration story of them all, has a modern post-script, in which the Yaghan do not get to live happily ever after.

The earliest encounters between Europeans and the Yaghan did not go well. From the sixteenth century onwards, a series of Europeans made their way to the southern seas, to sail round the world and, of course, 'discover' land that had been already discovered and occupied by the Yaghan and others ten thou-sand years earlier. Magellan of Portugal sailed straight past, but was close enough to notice the many fires that had been lit by the Yaghan (perhaps as a warning to each other of the fleet's arrival) and gave the islands the name Tierra del Fuego or 'Land of Fire'. The English explorer and slave trader Francis Drake led the second circumnavigation, and briefly stopped to name part of the Yaghan archipelago the Elizabethides Isles after the Queen of England. Fortunately, this almost unpronounceable name was soon forgotten.

Then, in 1624, seventeen sailors from a Dutch fleet were killed when they disembarked on a Yaghan island. Some of the bodies were mutilated, and it was thereafter believed by Europeans that the Yaghan were the worst kind of cannibals: consumers of uncooked human flesh, lower even in Western eyes than those who cooked their humans before eating them. They became archetypal savages – naked, cruel, unkempt, ugly and stupid. A contemporary engraving, widely circulated, of the killings showed the Yaghan as savages tearing a Dutch sailor limb from limb, while other dead sailors were being dragged off to makeshift huts, presumably to be eaten. In fact, there is no convincing evidence that the Yaghan ate any human flesh – cooked or raw.

The most significant visitor of the nineteenth century was a British warship, HMS *Beagle*, sent on a series of surveying expe-ditions to the southern seas. When it went to Tierra del Fuego in 1829, under the command of a well-connected young man called Robert FitzRoy,* some Fuegians stole one of the *Beagle's* rowing boats. Captain FitzRoy took hostages in an attempt to get the boat back. This didn't work, and FitzRoy sailed to Britain with four of the hostages on board, who were given the names Jemmy Button, Fuegia Basket, York Minster and Boat Memory,† presumably because the crew weren't interested in calling them by their real names. Four descendants of that great migration to the southern tip of America were on the move again, unwillingly, roughly ten thousand years later.

On board and then back in Britain, the hostages were treated less as captives and more as scientific specimens or curiosities. They were clothed, their hair was trimmed; they were sent to boarding school, taught English, converted to Christianity, and presented to King William and Queen Adelaide. A little over a year later the three remaining captives (Boat Memory had died of smallpox soon after landing in Britain) re-boarded the *Beagle*, tasked with setting up a mission on Tierra del Fuego and converting the Yaghan to Christianity – and it was on board that FitzRoy drew the only surviving portraits of them.

FitzRoy also invited a twenty-two-year-old naturalist called Charles Darwin to join the return voyage of the *Beagle*. And so it was that Darwin befriended the teenage Jemmy Button, who laughed a lot, and showed great concern whenever the former felt seasick. Darwin later described the teenage Jemmy as 'very

---

* FitzRoy was of royal blood, just twenty-three, and was appointed because the previous captain had become depressed and killed himself. FitzRoy would later become an MP and then Governor of New Zealand, the founder of what became the Meteorological Office, as well as an outspoken opponent of Darwin's views on evolution.
† Button was bought in exchange for a mother-of-pearl button, while Fuegia Basket, who was thought to be nine at the time of her kidnapping, was given her name because she came over to the ship in a basket boat. Minster was kidnapped near a rock that the sailors thought looked like York Minster. Boat Memory was named in memory of the lost rowing boat. Their real names were O'run-del'lico (Jemmy Button), Yok'cushly (Fuegia Basket) and El'leparu (York Minster); Boat Memory's real name was unrecorded. Only Jemmy Button considered himself a full Yaghan, while Fuegia Basket was half-Yaghan. The other two were members of a group known as the Alakaluf.

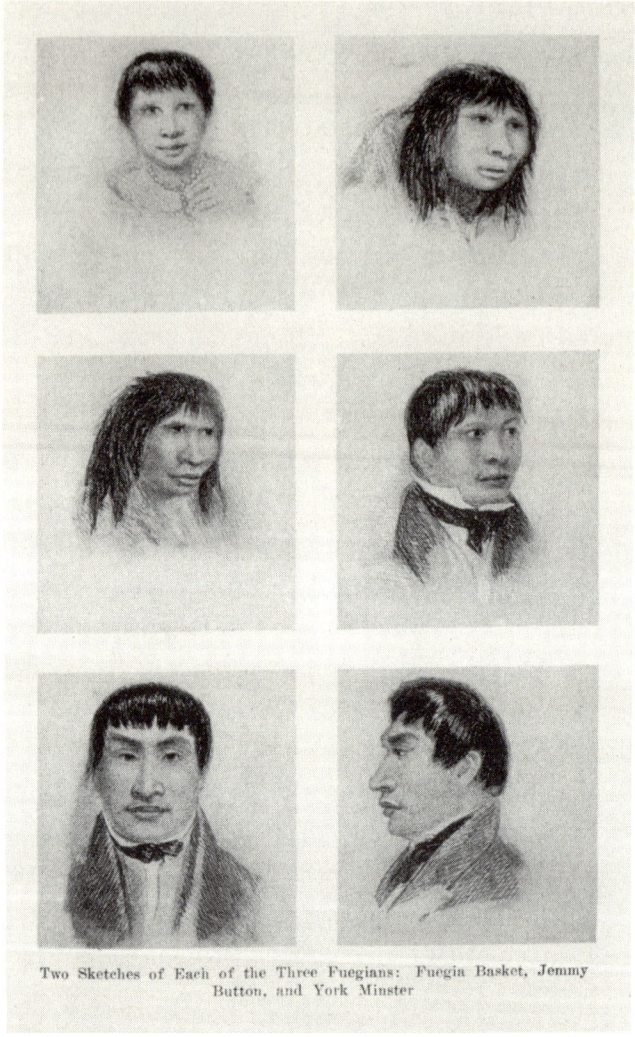

Two Sketches of Each of the Three Fuegians: Fuegia Basket, Jemmy
Button, and York Minster

fat, & so particular about his clothes, that he was always afraid
of even dirtying his shoes; scarcely ever without gloves & his
hair neatly cut'.

The three hostages were dropped off in Tierra del Fuego,
where Darwin was less impressed by Jemmy's people:

These poor wretches were stunted in their growth, their
hideous faces bedaubed with white paint, their skins filthy

and greasy, their hair entangled, their voices discordant and their gestures violent. Viewing such men, one can hardly make oneself believe that they are fellow-creatures, and inhabitants of the same world. It is a common subject of con-jecture what pleasure in life some of the lower animals can enjoy: how much more reasonably the same question may be asked with respect to these barbarians! ...

Their country is a broken mass of wild rocks, lofty hills, and useless forests: and these are viewed through mists and endless storms. The habitable land is reduced to the stones on the beach; in search of food they are compelled unceasingly to wander from spot to spot, and so steep is the coast, that they can only move about in their wretched canoes. They cannot know the feeling of having a home, and still less that of domestic affection ...*

This view of the Yaghan does not do Darwin much credit, though he does hint later on that he might have misjudged them. The *Beagle* and Darwin returned after a year to the place where they had left the three hostages, by which time Fuegia and York had run away together. There was no sign of the Christian mission, the vegetable garden for which they had brought seeds, and the Western clothes, the Bibles and the English crockery the Fuegians had worn and carried with them. And it took them some time to track down Jemmy Button.

'We could not recognise poor Jemmy,' wrote Darwin. 'It was quite painful to behold him; thin, pale, & without a rem-nant of clothes, excepting a bit of blanket round his waist: his hair, hanging over his shoulders.' But Jemmy, Darwin soon realised, was quite content. He had more than enough to eat, he was not cold, he had got married and, Darwin wrote in his

* Darwin's low opinion of the Yaghan was partly derived from the fact that he believed, incorrectly, that they were cannibals, who when faced with starvation in winter they would kill and eat the oldest women of the community.

diary, 'we were rather surprised to find he had not the least wish to return to England'. It was as if Darwin briefly allowed himself to consider that Jemmy might be happier as a homeless 'barbarian' than as an English gentleman. And that the Yaghan might be just as capable of domestic affection as anyone else in the world.

After the *Beagle* came the ravaging of Tierra del Fuego. Europeans brought missionaries, disease and weapons of war to the islands. Most Yaghan converted, many died of diseases introduced by Europeans, others were killed or driven off their lands. For Europeans also brought ideas of property, and soon the Yaghan discovered that their traditional lands were no longer theirs. A gold rush in the late nineteenth century meant more migrants, and was followed by a large influx of Croatians fleeing poverty and discrimination under the Austro-Hungarian Empire. The sea lion and seal population, on which the Yaghan depended for food and skins, had collapsed because of over-hunting by Europeans. The Yaghan were reduced to living off mussels. Some of them left Tierra del Fuego for elsewhere in South America, others married Europeans and identified with the dominant Spanish-speaking Christian settlers, and there was even a failed attempt to settle a group of Yaghan on the Falkland Islands. The Yaghan way of life, and ten thousand years of continuity, were coming to an end.

In February 2022, Cristina Calderón, the last native Yaghan speaker left in the world, died at the age of ninety-three. She hadn't been able to talk to anyone who was fluent in her mother tongue since the death, in 2005, of the second-last Yaghan speaker, her sister-in-law Emelinda (though as one Yaghan-researching journalist pointed out in 2004, the two women had quarrelled and weren't on speaking terms anyway). In recent years, Calderón had become something of a celebrity, the last 'pure-blooded' Yaghan, the symbol of a lost world, and of a vague regret at how self-proclaimed 'civilised' people treated the original human inhabitants of this region, and elsewhere. She was visited by journalists, anthropologists and cruise-ship tourists at her home on the outskirts of the world's most southerly town, Puerto Williams, and she responded phlegmatically to their questions about being the last of the Yaghan. And they wrote articles, or dissertations, or posted selfies with her on Facebook. She was even declared a UNESCO 'Living Human Treasure'; and pronounced a 'national heroine' as part of the celebrations for Chile's bicentenary in 2010.

There is a certain sad irony to the tale of the last of the Yaghan who, as the descendants of the greatest migration of them all, had seen their way of life destroyed by nineteenth- and twentieth-century migration. But it is a pattern that is repeated again and again through history; of peoples who have disappeared – some of them leave literature, or buildings, or archaeological remains, or genetic traces; others leave nothing.

The Yaghan have left a rich archaeological record of their nomadic life: thousands of middens, as archaeologists like to describe rubbish dumps, built up of shells and bones and vegetation. They have left their language, recorded in great detail for posterity; and one tongue-twisting Yaghan word took on a new life of its own. *Mamihlapinatapai*, appeared in the *Guinness Book of Records* as the world's 'most succinct word', was used as a title for a song, an exhibition and a short film, and made a memorable appearance in the 2011 cult movie, *Life in a Day*. The reason for such interest is that the word was said to be untranslatable, though this was usually followed by a rough translation: 'a look shared by two people, each wishing that the other would initiate something that they both desire but which neither wants to begin'. There's a touching, almost woeful, sensitivity to the concept of *mamihlapinatapai* and its anxieties that seems to appeal to millennials. It also makes Darwin's description of the Yaghan as savages and barbarians seems more absurd than ever.

Finally, the Yaghan have also left thousands of descendants, not 'pure-blooded' or Yaghan-speaking, like Cristina
Calderón, but children and grandchildren of mixed marriages.
Many of them identify themselves, to each other, to census-
takers, and to visitors as Yaghan – and so, through them, the
Yaghan live on. The notion of 'pure-bloodedness' is a woolly
one at best, and racist at worst. Especially when it refers to a
small group of people who have interbred for what seems like a
long period, but which is actually a very short one in terms of
our history as a species.

For, in fact, the Yaghan, like me, like the European settlers
of Tierra del Fuego, like most of the people who will read these
words, all have a common heritage. We are descended from
Neanderthals, and from modern humans who left Africa about
a hundred thousand years ago. Consanguinity, it should be
remembered, is far more ancient than pure-bloodedness. And
it's the loss of Yaghan culture, not the loss of Yaghan bloodlines, that should be mourned.

AN EARLY INTERMISSION

One damp October morning in 2018, I spent twenty-five minutes in my father's old study spitting into a small plastic tube. I was briefly in London, in transit between two jobs – the old one in Cambodia, and a new one in Tunisia – and was staying with my mother in the house in which I had been born more than half a century earlier. It's still the place I know best, the closest I have to a home – and it has a way of bringing out the child in me.

I had returned to that home briefly in March 2014 to be with my dying father, and when he died six months later, I was on the move again. I became something of a nomad, taking up a series of short-term jobs in Asia and Africa. My work – for the BBC's international media charity – has given me a greater chance to spend time with local people than most newcomers to a country. My visas, my flights and my housing are all organised for me. And I get paid. I feel more than fortunate. Yet when I return to London, I'm made to feel odd and stubborn by the questions and assumptions of some of those who have known me for most of my life. They ask me when I will settle down, stay in one place. I have no simple answer, and become petulant. Their questions make me feel as if I have chosen a lifestyle that goes against the laws of nature. That my lack of a home makes me less than human. That I am in some way impoverished by living out of two suitcases. That I am eccentric. That I haven't really grown up. That I don't quite belong.

I am bad at explaining myself to my contemporaries – for the simple reason that I don't know why I am like this and they are not. But it feels elemental, as if a desire to be on the move, to travel to new places, to be with people who are not like me is part of my being. There's undoubtedly a fear of monotony, and an excitement at novelty – at navigating the transport system in a new city, for instance, or working out what local dishes to eat for lunch – but it also feels much deeper. As if an excess of curiosity is part of my genetic make-up.

And, indeed, there are some people who think a curiosity gene exists. They've identified it, a string of markers in our genome known as DRD4-7R – an ancient genetic mutation present on a significant scale in all human populations, but particularly prevalent in the first inhabitants of the Americas. And, it's been surmised, that is part of the reason they travelled so far, that they migrated to the end of the world. It's impossible to prove, of course – genetics cannot provide answers to questions about the motives that led the Yaghan to Tierra del Fuego.

Nevertheless, DRD4-7R has taken on a virtual life of its own. Run a Google search of this combination of symbols and you quickly enter the strange world of popular and often unreliable genetic pseudo-science. There are dozens of articles about DRD4-7R, ascribing to it an absurdly broad range of extremely loosely connected behaviours and conditions: curiosity, risk-taking, adventure, drug use, wanderlust, novelty-seeking, adolescent delinquency, promiscuity, autism and attention-deficit hyperactive disorder.

'The "Wanderlust gene" – is it real and do you have it?' screams the headline in the *Daily Telegraph*. 'Do you Have The "Curiosity" Gene? (And Will It Make You More Successful?)'

is the question posed by the astrophysicist Mario Livio, who strays far from his normal subject of expertise on the *Excited Science* podcast, while the *Alternative Daily*, 'a health and wellness website', declares 'If You Love to Travel or Take Risks, You Have THIS Gene'.

There's even a travel blog with the catchy name *DRD4-7R: Posts from a Flashpacker*, which contains the 'musings, mishaps and thoughts of a vagabond 50+ mostly solo traveler' called Cindy Sheahan. Ms Sheahan explains her choice of blog name:

So DRD4-7R. WTF? I first heard about this concept about 6 months ago ... here's the premise: this is the name of the 'restless' gene, or the 'wanderlust' gene ... Now, I'm no scientist, but I am a bit of a romantic and I'm gonna embrace this theory and claim that I do have and may suffer from the effects of DRD4-7R.

The science is still uncertain. But there is, for instance, growing evidence of a correlation between some genetic markers including DRD4-7R, and how far particular groups travelled from Africa in prehistoric migration. This falls well short of providing an explanation for long-distance migration. And it certainly couldn't explain on its own why some individuals have the travel bug and others don't.

These caveats didn't stop me from being intrigued; curious, even. And so it was after reading several of these articles that I, in a whimsical moment, decided to test my DNA – which explains why I was spitting into that test tube on that October morning. And it wasn't just about the curiosity gene. I know quite a lot about my family, or I think I do. That my biological father was not who everyone thought he was; he was not the man who brought me up, the man whose surname I bear. And that he was half French. I was intrigued to see whether this would show up in my DNA. And I also wanted to know whether the genes of my maternal grandmother, descended from Jews who'd lived in Britain since the eighteenth century, would also make their distinctive appearance in my saliva. And would there be traces of other migrations? Best of all, I hoped, for largely sentimental reasons, to find out how closely related I was to the Neanderthals.

And so I sealed the tube of saliva and placed it in a well-padded box supplied by the testing company. Soon my DNA was on its meandering way, via a west London post office and a Dutch distribution centre, to a laboratory in North Carolina with the promise that in five weeks' time I would know a lot more – possibly too much – about my ancestry.

CHAPTER TWO

Babylon, the Bible and *Blazing Saddles*

In the early 1970s, as a London schoolboy, I learned to twist my lisping tongue around a new placename: Mesopotamia. We were being taught history, in sequence, from the beginning. Everything that came earlier than Mesopotamia was dismissed as fossils and guesswork. The Neanderthals and the first great migrations were unmentioned.

Mesopotamia, we were solemnly informed, in the first of a series of childbirth metaphors, was the 'cradle of civilisation'. It was, we learned, the 'birthplace' of agriculture and irrigation, property and cities, palaces and temples, writing and rulers, frontiers and laws, taxes and armies. The future of the human race 'in embryo'. And all because of an almost-miraculous technological breakthrough: humans somehow had managed to domesticate both wild plants and wild animals, and now all was possible.

Most historians would argue that this traditional narrative is incomplete, simplistic and inaccurate. I also think it underplays the most important part of this particular story. Namely, that, at the same time, humans began to domesticate themselves by spreading the idea that each of us has a place to which we belong. In practice, this meant that some of our ancestors became tied to a single location – a small tract of land on the globe – in a way that would later come to define us, to provide us with a central part of our identity. And by doing so we began to create a world in which it would one day no longer seem normal to be a migrant.

About twelve thousand years ago, before Mesopotamia, we were all migrants – every one of us, in the sense that no one seems to have had a permanent home.* But at about this time, a tiny percentage of the world's human population, first in the Middle East and then in several other parts of the globe, stopped moving. They became sedentary – the first non-migrants in human history. It's not entirely clear why these few humans stopped migrating. Historians once argued that early humans settled down and started living in villages because of scarcity of food, and that agriculture provided a solution to that scarcity. The opposite is now thought more likely. It's been shown that most of these first non-migrants lived in places of abundance – wetlands, for instance, or locations on the border of two climatic zones, where there was enough food naturally available nearby to sustain a fixed population of humans. And few of them found the time and the opportunity to cultivate wild grains – sowing the seeds, quite literally, of the agricultural revolution.

This tiny minority of the world's human population lived in little villages where they built themselves homes, out of wood or mud or stone, in which they lived all year round. For the

---

* It is impossible to prove this beyond reasonable doubt, but there is no firm evidence of long-term, year-round habitation of a particular place prior to this date. It's been suggested that some East Asian fishing villages, built on bamboo stilts above the sea water, may predate the earliest Middle Eastern settlements. However, there is no archaeological evidence of this, and none is likely to be found given the nature of the building materials used, as well as rising sea levels. There are also monumental buildings that predate sedentarism, such as Göbekli Tepe near Turkey's border with Syria, and it's possible that some people lived at such locations throughout the year, as well as in villages in Palestine that are of similar antiquity.

first time, humans could possess more than they could carry. They had somewhere where they could keep their belongings. And these sedentary humans had domesticated themselves in the literal sense of the word, by attaching themselves to a permanent location: a house, a *domus*, a home. And – over the millennia – those experiments with agriculture continued as they domesticated plants, and then wild animals, in ways that would make it possible for still larger numbers of humans to become sedentary.

As agriculture spread through Mesopotamia, and newly settled farmers cleared land to build homes and to plant their crops, some of them claimed a special relationship with the land they had worked, and which they now occupied. The crops were theirs, as were those houses – and so, by the logic of occupation, was the land on which their crops grew and their houses were built. It was probably a gentle glide from possession to ownership. The parcelling-up of the world into units of property had begun – a process that, by its nature, excluded those who were on the move.*

Those first homes in the first villages were single-room circular huts. These would later be replaced, mainly, by rectangular buildings, some of which had several rooms used for different purposes. And ruins of these, uncovered by archaeologists, have provided us with the earliest significant evidence of human inequality, in the form of the large, multi-roomed

---

* Of course, it's not a simple linear story, and sometimes it is hard to say who is settled and who is not. Some hunter-gatherers lived in villages, and some villagers returned to a nomadic lifestyle out of choice, or when their farmlands became less fertile. And the impact of the domestication of animals was complex and depended on the type of animal. The domestication of sheep, goats and cows, for instance, created a new intermediate kind of migrant: the pastoral semi-nomad, the shepherd, who travelled seasonally with grazing livestock, but who might have ties to a settled community. The later domestication of some less mobile animals – chickens and pigs, for example – reinforced a settled lifestyle; whereas the domestication of more mobile animals such as horses, camels and llamas actually encouraged a new kind of migratory lifestyle – in which nomads could travel at greater speed and take more possessions with them.

homes of the rich, and the smaller, simpler homes of the poor. In this context, it's possible to argue that the creation of immovable property was the greatest of all the changes brought about by these early sedentary people. For they introduced two great divides into human society, which overlap and which persist to this day: between those who own land and those who don't, and those who are settled and those who are not.

A few of the villages of Mesopotamia became towns, drawing in migrants from the countryside as the land available to hunter-gatherers shrank. Many continued to farm their fields, but others developed new skills including pottery, weaving and metalworking, and bartered their skills and products for food. These towns often had what we would think of as a municipal or religious building; some town-dwellers might become priests or rulers, or both. Property and status could be inherited, and a few individuals assumed the power of making laws and raising taxes. And some of these towns grew larger and richer and more powerful − and the first city-states emerged about five thousand years ago. They and their accumulated wealth needed to be defended, as did the farmland that provided them with food and with taxes. Walls were built, frontiers were marked and guarded, soldiers were trained. They feared attacks from other city-states, but even more they feared raiders − nomads who were often now landless, and were sometimes depicted by the city-dwellers as lawless savages.

Mesopotamia matters to this story in several ways. Not just because it was the first place where humans became permanently sedentary − as hunter-gatherers, and then farmers, and then city-dwellers − and not just because the notion of personal property in land seems to have been invented here. But also because it is at this time we see the emergence of several new categories of migrant. And, more important still to this narrative, we have the earliest surviving written accounts of human attitudes towards migration and migrants.

Prior to the 1850s we knew of Mesopotamia largely through semi-mythological accounts in ancient Greek sources and, even more so, from the Bible. Places and names like Babylon and Nineveh and Ur and Nebuchadnezzar would have been known to my Christian and Jewish ancestors, but they belonged more to a world of ritualised imagination than to human history. There was, then, not much evidence that they really existed. But since the 1850s, despite the disruptions of many wars and revolutions, archaeologists have been digging up the ancient cities of Mesopotamia – in Iraq, Syria, Turkey and Iran. They have found remarkable treasures including, most valuable of all, many hundreds of thousands of clay tablets, marked with the distinctive wedge-shaped lines of cuneiform script. A huge range of texts have now been translated: inventories, account books, prayers, hymns, schoolbooks, histories, letters and myths. And these writings, the earliest to survive from any-where on the globe, and breathtaking in their range and detail, have made it possible to recreate large parts of a lost world.

The writings of Mesopotamia provide a partial view, of course: a world seen through the eyes of the rich and the powerful who live in cities – and their scribes. But it is still possible to catch, like a glance in a mirror, something of the lives of others, of those who weren't city-dwellers and of those who were new to the city. For in these clay-tablet records we can trace the emergence of an impressive cast of usually silent extras who are all migrants – forced and free, and everything in between. These included invaders from the mountains, slaves captured in warfare, traders bringing lapis lazuli from Afghanistan or carnelian beads from the Indus Valley, commu-nities deported en masse to a distant land, and royal daughters traded in marriage as part of a new alliance with a distant king-dom. But the largest contingent of wandering people were no longer hunter-gatherers but nomadic pastoralists, mainly shep-herds and goatherds, who drove their herds of domesticated animals between summer pastures in the hills and winter pastures in the plains.

There is little evidence of what we would now refer to as racism in the writings of Mesopotamia – that came much later in human history. There is, though, a clear hierarchy of status, and a strong prejudice against those who were not settled: a general presupposition that city life is superior to farming, and that being a farmer is superior to being a nomad. Gods are often closely identified with individual cities, and the opening lines of the story of the water god, Enki, and the mother goddess, Ninhursaga, suggest that urban sedentariness is next to godliness: 'Pure are the cities – and you are the ones to whom they are allotted.'

These godly tales, though, are often rich with nuance and drama – and open to a variety of interpretations. Take, for instance, the *Marriage of Martu*, which has sometimes been portrayed simply as a dismissive sideswipe at the lifestyle of nomads, in this case one who migrates to the city in search of a bride.* Towards the end of the tale, a city woman talks with contempt of the would-be bridegroom, Martu, and his people:

> their features are those of monkeys; they never stop roaming about … He is clothed in sack-leather … lives in a tent, exposed to wind and rain, and cannot properly recite prayers. He lives in the mountains and ignores the places of gods, digs up truffles in the foothills, does not know how to bend the knee, and eats raw flesh. He has no house during his life, and when he dies he will not be carried to a burial-place.

---

* Martu is also a symbolic character. There is a god of that name, portrayed as a representative of the nomadic Amorites, who during the second millennium BCE ruled large parts of Mesopotamia. The Amorites were seen by the more sedentary Mesopotamian elite as outsiders and interlopers – which helps explain the wider context of the *Marriage of Martu*.

This city woman is trying to dissuade her best friend from becoming Martu's wife, and concludes this spiteful little speech with a question that is meant to be rhetorical: 'My girlfriend, why would you marry Martu?' If the story ended there, or if the cuneiform tablet had been broken (like so many of them), we might believe that Mesopotamian city-dwellers considered nomads to be subhuman. But there's a kick to this story, a final line, uttered by the would-be bride, who says just four words, three in ancient Sumerian: 'I will marry Martu.' And that is that – though we don't get to know if they lived happily ever after.

And so this story can be read quite differently, as preaching both the fundamental unity of humans and an early version of miscegenation. Nomads may have very dissimilar lives, but they are not a lost cause, not a race apart. There's a sense in this story both that nomads are quite different from city folk and that they can become 'civilised' and settle down to city life – and even marry a city girl. It's still patronising towards nomads (though Martu is portrayed as strong, generous and determined), but it also reflects what we would nowadays see as a multicultural inclusiveness in many Mesopotamian city-states. And there was, in some of these tales, and in other tales of the ancients, a shadowy recognition that once upon a time we were all nomads.

The wild man from the hills who becomes civilised in the city appears to be a trope of Mesopotamian writing. For there's a similar dynamic in the *Epic of Gilgamesh*, nowadays widely seen, for good reason, as the world's first great work of literature but still, sadly, more praised than read. It's a story with many themes – power, despotism, wisdom, mortality, sexuality – which speaks as strongly to modern audiences as any work of ancient times. But at the heart of the story is the tale of two men who are, at first glance, total opposites: Gilgamesh, the sophisticated and tyrannical ruler of the city of Uruk, and

Enkidu, a naked, hairy savage born in the wild uplands and raised by gazelles.

Near the start of the story, Enkidu is transformed, domesticated even, by an encounter with a woman with whom he has almost a full week of continuous sex ('for six days and seven nights / Enkidu was erect as he coupled with Shamhat'). She then covers him up with part of her own clothing and leads him like a tame beast to Uruk. There, Enkidu and Gilgamesh meet, and all are struck by their physical similarity. They become friends and lovers, and together they share great adventures. It is almost as if they have become one person, two sides of the same coin – in a way that leaves us, the readers, with the thought that we, and all human beings, might each be part Enkidu and part Gilgamesh. And then when Enkidu dies, the grief-stricken Gilgamesh seems to become an amalgam of the two of them, and wanders to the edge of the world in a futile search for immortality.

The *Epic of Gilgamesh* can be seen as a migration story – but one with a difference. It does not, like many such tales, seek to tell the story of the origins of a group or a community, or say that migration is a good or bad thing. Instead, it reaches deep down into the psychology of the human condition by examining why it is that we might not want to remain where we are; or why, more precisely, we might want to leave home. Migration for Enkidu and Gilgamesh is not driven by necessity; it is a life choice. Put simply, Enkidu migrates to become someone else, Gilgamesh to find out who he really is. Happily living in peace with nature, Enkidu was seduced by sex and friendship into another world – the teeming city of Uruk – in which he could assume a new identity. Gilgamesh, meanwhile, is desperate to leave Uruk in search of adventure and glory, and persuades an unwilling Enkidu to travel back through the wilderness in search of a mountain monster they could kill. So when Enkidu dies, Gilgamesh says he will let his hair become matted and wander in the wilderness – that is, he will become what Enkidu once was. And when he discovers that he cannot be immortal, that he cannot be both a god and a human, he breaks down in tears, and then returns to the city he rules as a wiser king, we are led to believe.

It is possible to find migrants in most ancient texts – from China, India and Egypt for instance – but they are usually transient half-drawn characters: slaves and prisoners; mysterious or untrustworthy people from beyond the frontiers; passing nomads portrayed as savages; or characters from prehistoric legend. Often they are no more than voiceless shadows. But there is one ancient text in which we hear the voices of migrants themselves, rejoicing at the walls of Jericho, weeping beside the rivers of Babylon.

One does not need to read between the lines to find migration stories in the Bible. Migrants are everywhere – driven out of Eden, repopulating the earth after the Flood, fleeing across the Red Sea, exiled to Mesopotamia. The Bible can be read as a migration handbook. And unlike most migration-related texts, ancient and modern, it was written by and for migrants. Even if many of the stories have little relationship to real historical events, they tell us a great deal about attitudes towards migration at the time the Old Testament was first written down about two and half thousand years ago.

The Bible begins with migration as both a fact of life – and, less promisingly, as a punishment from God. The first three human beings are all cast into exile. Because of their serpent-inspired disobedience, Adam and Eve are expelled from the luxurious abundance of the Garden of Eden and condemned to a life of toil. Then their murderous first-born, Cain, a sedentary farmer, is sentenced to wandering the world as a 'fugitive and a vagabond' for killing his brother. And that's just the first four chapters of the opening book of the Bible.

Then comes a major climate change event – always a primary cause of migration – in the form of the Great Flood, survived by just eight human beings, who had clambered, with a much larger number of animals, into a homemade wooden boat and spent six desperate months floating aimlessly in the water until they ran aground on Mount Ararat, in what is now eastern Turkey. We don't know how far this was from where Noah was supposed to have lived before the Flood, but his old home was certainly not on a mountaintop. And then God commands Noah and his three sons, Shem, Ham and Japheth, and their unnamed wives to leave their boat, and 'be fruitful, multiply and replenish the earth'.* It's a direct order from above to migrate, to repopulate the world.

The subsequent chapter of Genesis is now often referred to as the Table of Nations and amounts to a lightly disguised description of the post-Flood migration. It lists seventy descendants of Noah, most of whom are the founders of a particular community or 'nation' in what we would now call the Middle East and beyond. The names of most of these founders also become the source of a similarly named 'nation': Noah's grandson Canaan for the Canaanites; a second grandson, Ashur, is the founder of the Assyrians; and a third called Yavan is the first Ionian (or Greek). A great-great-grandson called Eber appears as the ancestor of the Hebrews.

It's a slightly confusing list, with some names repeated – and one which has been subject to controversial and often racist re-interpretation by more modern believers. And it is easy to

---

* Mrs Noah and her three daughters-in-law don't get mentioned by name but clearly the greatest burden of obeying God's command falls on them. However, they are named – as Emzara, Sedeqetelebab, Ne'elatama'uk and Adataneses – in the Book of Jubilees, which is canonical to the Ethiopian Orthodox Church and to Ethiopian Jews.

The Middle East in Ancient Times

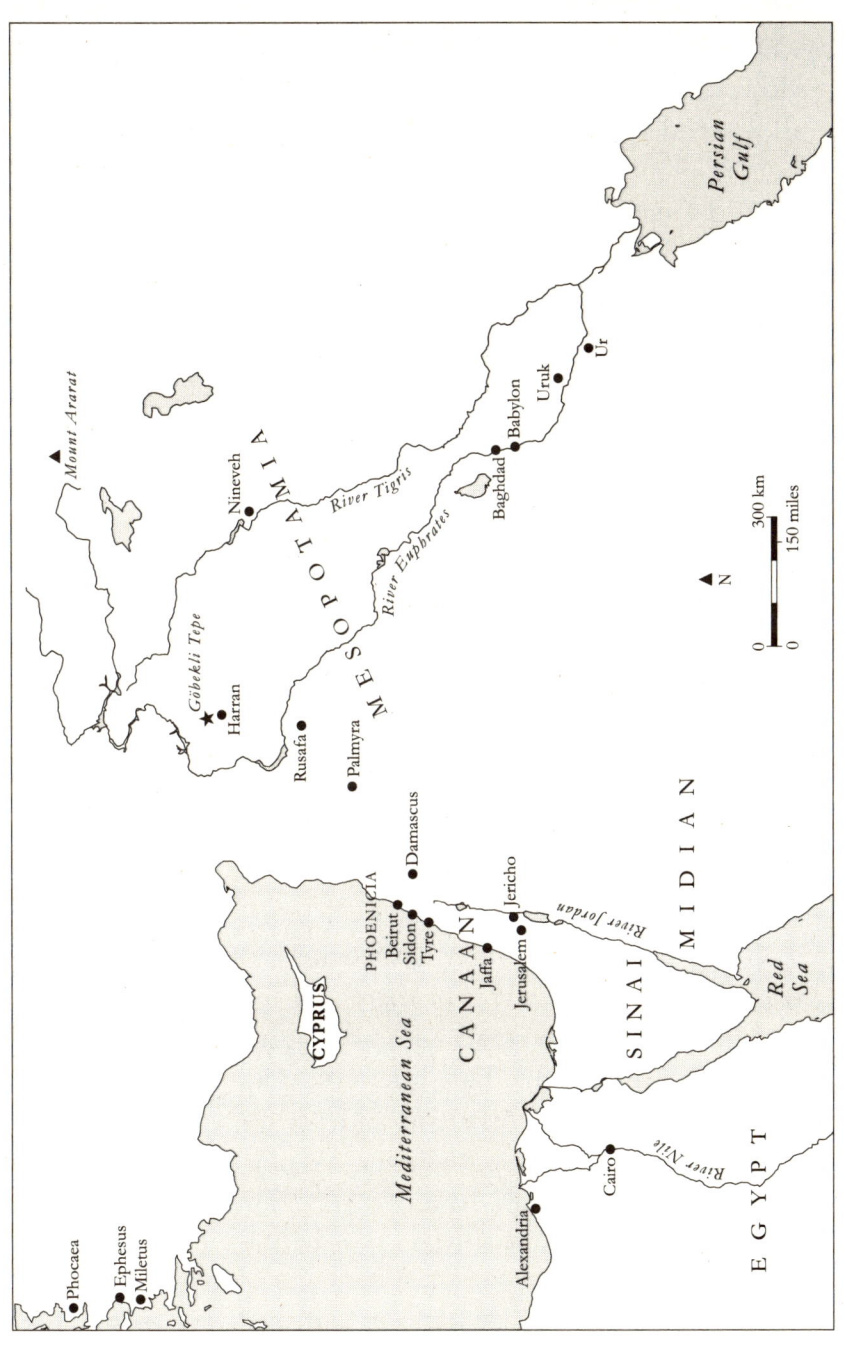

Phocaea
Ephesus
Miletus

CYPRUS

Mediterranean Sea

PHOENICIA
Beirut
Sidon
Tyre
Jaffa
Jerusalem

CANAAN

Jericho
Damascus

River Jordan

SINAI

MIDIAN

Red Sea

EGYPT

Cairo

River Nile

Alexandria

Harran
Göbekli Tepe

Rusafa
Palmyra

Nineveh

Mount Ararat

MESOPOTAMIA

River Tigris

River Euphrates

Baghdad
Babylon
Uruk
Ur

Persian Gulf

N

0 ___ 300 km
0 ___ 150 miles

see why the Table of Nations might become a tool for those
who seek to discriminate between people of different races.
However, its starting point is that we are all related; that we are
all descended from Noah (and Mrs Noah), and all descended
from migrants.

By the end of the following chapter of Genesis, attention
has turned to the Hebrews and more specifically Abraham,
the five-times-great-grandson of Eber, their legendary
founder. Abraham is living at home in Harran, in northern
Mesopotamia, when God appears to him and, apropos of
nothing in particular, orders Abraham to migrate. 'Get thee
out of thy country' is his bald command, at least in the King
James Version of the Bible. No explanation is given for why
he should leave Mesopotamia, and we are left assuming that
Abraham had been perfectly happy there but has no choice
other than to obey the word of God. Though God does help
to make it easier, enticing him to migrate with the promise of
land: 'I will make of thee a great nation, and I will bless thee,
and make thy name great.' And so Abraham leaves Harran
and heads to Canaan, the Promised Land, to territory already
occupied by other descendants of Noah, and that has been disputed ever since.

When Abraham gets to Canaan, he builds an altar and prays
to God – then leaves almost immediately, clearly disappointed
with the Promised Land. For there's a famine in Canaan, and
so Abraham and his small entourage just keep on travelling
until they reach Egypt. That brief visit is just the first of many
abortive attempts by Abraham and his descendants to settle
permanently in the Promised Land. Abraham does eventually
make it back to Canaan, having made a fortune in Egypt as a
migrant worker. And he settles there, battling against and ally-
ing with local chieftains.

The rest of Genesis is taken up with the story of Abraham
and his family, who have an increasingly complex relationship

with the Promised Land. And in the final chapters they leave again for Egypt – driven out once more by famine. It's a familiar tale, of course, and this new migration would provide, pretty precisely, the storyline for the 1970s hit musical *Joseph and the Amazing Technicolor Dreamcoat*. One of Abraham's great-grandsons, Joseph, went first to Egypt, under duress, having been sold into slavery by his jealous brothers. Joseph rises to become the Pharaoh's right-hand man while his brothers flee from Canaan during the famine. Eventually, the brothers are reunited and all is forgiven.

The Age of the Patriarchs is over, and the Israelites, as the Bible now refers to them, are no closer to living in the Promised Land. Instead, Joseph and his family and their followers flourish, having been granted fertile lands near the Nile by the friendly Pharaoh. And it's usually forgotten – because of what happens next – that the Book of Genesis ends with the descendants of Abraham happily settled in Egypt.

Two great migration set pieces dominate much of the rest of the Old Testament: the Exodus from Egypt and the Babylonian Captivity. These are touchstone stories; epics that have reached far beyond their Middle Eastern origins; painted, filmed, set to music and retold in myriad ways. As biblical narratives, they each involve great hardship and sadness and uncertainty and homesickness for the Israelites as the migrant community – and they each also involve ill-treatment by a host community. But in other ways they are opposites. In Exodus, the Israelites, led by Moses, are on the run, fleeing from persecution; in the Babylonian Captivity they are forced to move, carried away to a strange land.

The Egypt into which Moses was born was very different from the Egypt to which Joseph and his brothers had migrated four generations earlier. A new Pharaoh saw the Israelites as a threat, in ways that would come to encapsulate the paranoid majoritarian response to successful small-scale migration. He described them, absurdly, as 'more and mightier than we', and believed them to be in league with his enemies. Their right to work freely was taken away, and they became conscript labourers, building great cities for the Pharaoh. Still he feared the Israelites and ordered the killing of all their male children. It was time to leave.

Moses himself was a serial migrant. When he was just three months old, he went on his first solo trip, floating down the Nile in a basket, and was then brought up as an Egyptian not an Israelite, living in a palace with his royal foster mother. As a young man he fled a murder scene and escaped to Midian, in what is now Saudi Arabia. He lived there contentedly for many years, working as a shepherd for a local priest, whose daughter he married. Being an outsider is central to Moses' identity, and he proudly declared himself to be a migrant, a foreigner, 'a stranger in a strange land'.* Then one day, when he was wandering in the desert with his flocks, he saw a burning bush, from which he heard a godlike voice calling to him, persuading the unwilling, introverted, solitary Moses to return to Egypt and lead the Israelites to the Promised Land.

Back in Egypt, Moses had a double mission: first, to persuade the Pharaoh to let the Israelites leave; and second, to persuade the hesitant, beleaguered Israelites to migrate to Canaan, to the Promised Land, which he told them, repeatedly and misleadingly, flows with milk and honey. Ten plagues later, six hundred thousand Israelites and their herds of cattle and sheep

---

* He said this while explaining the special name he gave to his oldest son. Moses called him Gershom, which in ancient Hebrew means 'a stranger here', or possibly 'name of a stranger'. The word *ger* is most commonly translated as 'sojourner' in English-language versions of the Bible, but this implies, misleadingly, that the traveller is only there for a short period. Foreigner or stranger or migrant are more accurate translations, depending on the context.

were on the move eastwards. Canaan is only four hundred kilometres away, but it took them forty years. That's an average speed of just over one metre per hour, one of history's slowest and most determined migrations.

The books of the Bible that deal with the journey from Egypt to Canaan are rich in detail and hardship – and migration-related nuance. The Israelites were hungry, anxious and divided. They couldn't stop quarrelling. Some of them wanted to return to Egypt. Their leader kept wandering off without telling anyone, and at one point Moses' own siblings turned on him for having married a non-Israelite. Food, understandably, became an obsession. They all spent long periods in the wilderness living off desert herbs and nostalgically remembering how well they ate in Egypt. They'd list the food they missed most: meat, fish, cucumbers, melons, leeks, onions and garlic. And in these early years of their migration it is hard not to feel sympathy for the Israelites, fleeing tyranny for a dream, like so many in more recent times.

By about halfway through their journey to the Promised Land, the Israelites had been transformed by desperation and self-righteousness into fratricidal vagabonds more than happy to break that newly minted Sixth Commandment – 'Thou shalt not kill' – for the most minor of reasons. Moses himself turned on his former protectors, the Midianites, and had all the adults slaughtered, except the female virgins, whom he directed his people to 'keep alive for yourselves'. At the end of their journey – with only three of the adult male migrants who fled Egypt forty years earlier still alive – the Israelites had become a brutal invading army. The conquest of Jericho and most of the rest of Canaan was accompanied by slaughter. In Jericho itself every living being – including children and farm animals – was put to the sword; except for one woman and her family, who had spied for the Israelites. The city was burnt to the ground.

The dominant narrative of these early books of the Bible – from Exodus to Joshua – is a triumphalist one. The browbeaten, hesitant migrants who left Egypt became, more than four decades later, the proud, unbending masters of their Promised Land. But there is another less chilling, more conciliatory subtext, half-concealed, often unnoticed these days, for it is largely to be found amid long lists of laws and commandments about diet and rituals seen as so obscure that they are typeset in a smaller font in many modern Bibles. Moses ordains that migrants should not be oppressed, and the same laws should apply to everyone, including migrants. And, on several occasions, Moses reminds the Israelites that they have a special reason for treating migrants humanely, for 'ye were strangers in the land of Egypt'.

Not only is migration the subject of large parts of the Bible, but it is also its immediate historical context. Much of the Old Testament was written down and compiled during or soon after the Babylonian Captivity, an act of mass deportation, of forced migration – and a time of great sadness and reflection for the Jews. There is less of the narrative storytelling detail that accompanies the description of the Exodus; no in-depth description, for instance, of the miserable journey to Babylon, or the happy journey back two generations later.

Instead, we learn about the Babylonian Captivity episodically, as part of other stories, or through poems of lamentation – perhaps because it was all too recent to be told as mythology. The most famous of all the poems, largely because of the modern musical versions by the Melodians and Boney M, is Psalm 137, which begins:

By the rivers of Babylon
There we sat down, yea, we wept
When we remembered Zion
We hanged our harps

Upon the willows on the midst thereof.
For there, they that carried us away captive required
   of us a song
And they that wasted us required of us mirth, saying
Sing us one of the songs of Zion.
How shall we sing the Lord's song
In a strange land?

It's a poem that catches a mood of humiliation as well as of sadness and despair. They are forced migrants compelled to sing and play music in front of their captors, and, even worse, they have to pretend that they are enjoying themselves.

There were in fact several mass deportations to Babylon – each of them a ratcheting-up of the penalty for disobedience. And unlike the migration from Egypt, there are a range of non-biblical references and archaeological finds that relate to the Babylonian Captivity: even a ration book in the form of a tablet for the exiled Jewish king, Jeconiah. And we know, for instance, of other communities of migrants in Babylon – Egyptians, Phoenicians, Persians. Some of them, like the Jews, had been forced to migrate, others seem to have come there in search of opportunity, or fleeing a different enemy, or their own rulers. Babylon was probably the first great melting pot: a large multi-ethnic urban area where many languages would be heard on the streets and almost certainly the most populous city in the world. It's clear that there were restrictions on the movement of some migrants, such as the Jews, beyond Babylon, but we know from contemporary records that many of them were able to own property, sign contracts and employ staff; one Egyptian migrant even became a judge.

There was also a lot of intermarriage, which the Babylonians did little to discourage. But some Jews were very unhappy about this, for it was in exile that racial purity appears to have become a major issue. This became even more pressing when, about fifty years after the first deportation, the Jews were allowed to return home.* Among them was the priest Ezra, who on reaching Jerusalem became furious when he discovered that so many Jewish men had married foreigners. According to the biblical book that bears his name, he tore his clothes, and pulled the hairs from his head and plucked the beard from his chin, declaring the mingling of 'the holy seed' to be an abomination. The Jews then agreed to 'put away' or expel all the foreign wives, and the children they had with those foreign wives. These women and children were now homeless migrants themselves, and the Bible tells us no more about them.

There's a short sequence in the 1974 spoof Western *Blazing Saddles* in which a tribe of 'Red Indians' appear on horseback, whooping and waving their tomahawks – a typical scene in many dozens of cowboy-and-Indian films. But then the chief, played by the director Mel Brooks, wearing a ridiculously large feathered headdress, opens his mouth and starts talking to his underlings in broken Yiddish. It's an absurd moment in a film that delights in farce and in anachronism. But it's somehow made even more absurd when one realises how much effort has been wasted over the centuries attempting to identify Hebrew words in the native languages of America. Because there are many who once believed, and a few who still believe, that some or all Native Americans are descended from the Lost Tribes of Israel.

---

* According to the Old Testament, women who were married to Jews, and their children, were not allowed to join the 42,360 Jews who returned (along with, the Bible informs us, 7,337 maids and servants, 200 singers, 736 horses, 245 mules, 435 camels and 6,720 asses). Some Jews, pure-blooded or not, headed elsewhere. One of them, Esther, the great-granddaughter of an original Babylonian captive, stayed on and married the Persian emperor, who by then was also the ruler of Babylon.

For there was one other major forced migration in the Bible – and it took place prior to the Babylonian Captivity. It was an event that, two thousand years later, provided the raw material for one of the greatest of all migration stories; a legend that continues to capture the imagination. One that has been used as a foundation myth for a preposterously varied collection of communities: from the British to the Maori, from African Americans to the Japanese. In fact, the original event figures only briefly in a few chapters of the Bible, and plays a relatively minor role in the storytelling and the poetry of the Old Testament. Like the Babylonian Captivity, it was a mass deportation from what is now Israel to, once again, Mesopotamia.*

Despite (and perhaps because of) the underwhelming coverage this event receives in the Bible – the Assyrian Captivity has arguably played a larger role in the development of Judaism and Christianity over the last five hundred years than either the Exodus from Egypt or the Babylonian Captivity. And the

---

* And it's an event for which we also have considerable contemporary evidence from non-biblical sources. In particular, there's a cuneiform tablet which describes how the Assyrian ruler Sargon II carried away 27,290 people from Samaria, in what is now northern Israel, in about 720 BCE.

reason for this is the myth known as the Lost Tribes of Israel –
lost because the Assyrian captives, unlike those who were
taken to Babylon, were not allowed back. There were ten of
these lost tribes, out of twelve tribes altogether, each of them
named after a brother or son of Joseph, each of which had made
its home, temporarily, in part of the Promised Land.

There are still people searching for, or who claim to have
found, the descendants of these lost tribes. And the lack of biblical or historical detail about their fate has meant that the story
can easily be appropriated by or for anyone. Like the story of
Troy, the tale of the Lost Tribes provides malleable raw material for anyone trying to create a foundation myth out of an
ancient migration.

It was the 'discovery' of the Americas by European explorers
that marked the start of the post-medieval obsession with the
Lost Tribes of Israel, for it provoked a crisis among those who
believed that the text of the Bible should be interpreted as the
literal word of God. After all, the Americas are unmentioned
in the Bible. But how could an all-knowing God apparently be
unaware of the existence of an entire continent, teeming with
human beings? And how, more specifically, did the people of
this continent fit into the Table of Nations? How were the
Inca and the Aztec, for example, descended from Noah? Some
went so far as to suggest that there was a second ark that must
have drifted westwards, and whose fate until now had been
unknown. Others scoured the Bible for alternative explanations, often twisting the meanings of obscure passages so that
they could just possibly hint at the existence of the Americas.
But the mystery of the Lost Tribes provided, on one level, a
simpler solution.

It's not clear who was the first to suggest that Native
Americans were in fact descendants of the Lost Tribes. One
influential early Spanish colonist, the priest Bartolomé de
Las Casas, who moved to Hispaniola in 1502 and who will

reappear in this story, asserted that the island's inhabitants were of Jewish descent and spoke a corrupt form of Hebrew. 'Cuba', another traveller pointed out, meant 'helmet' in Hebrew, and therefore the earliest ruler of the island must have been an Israelite chief with particularly magnificent headgear. In the same spirit, the seventeenth-century Spanish historian Juan de Torquemada decided that the Haitian river Yunah had obviously been named after Jonah, and the river Yaqui after Jacob. Travellers to the New World collected huge quantities of such dubious evidence: tribes that practised male circumcision, or didn't eat pork, or chanted words that sounded like Hallelujah, or who, most frequently, seemed to fit in with antisemitic tropes about Jews having big noses and being miserly. Proof, they decided, that they'd found the Lost Tribes.

It was a myth that persisted, and then spread to the North American mainland. The early colonist William Penn described Native Americans in the state that would be named after him. 'Their eye is little and black, not unlike a straight-looked Jew,' he wrote, while

> their language is lofty, yet narrow, but like the Hebrew in signification; like short hand in writing, one word serveth in the place of three ... For their original I am ready to believe them of the Jewish Race; I mean of the stock of the Ten Tribes.

Others identified Hebrew words in a range of Native American languages including Cherokee, Creek and Mohican. And then came a series of nineteenth-century hoaxes – coins and other artefacts bearing Hebrew inscriptions supposedly dug out of American soil. In particular, there were the Newark Holy Stones, which included a piece of black limestone inscribed with a condensed Hebrew version of the Ten Commandments. A local dentist may have been responsible – probably a well-intentioned attempt to prove to white racists that all humans were of common descent, and that the Native Americans, whom the racists so disparaged, were human beings just like them, and indeed were descended from people of consequence.

It's easy to laugh at those who confidently declared that the Lost Tribes of Israel were to be found in the Americas. But beliefs of this kind were incredibly popular – and reassuring. It helped make sense of a changing world, and it connected the present with an imagined past. And it wasn't only 'newly discovered' peoples who were the subject of these claims. Until about a hundred years ago, there was a widespread belief that the British were also a Lost Tribe. And that the very word 'British' was derived from Hebrew, meaning 'People [*ish*] of the Covenant [*brit*]'.

The British Israelite movement, according to Tudor Parfitt, the doyen of modern scholars of the Lost Tribes, had about two million members in 1900. In some ways, British Israelism was both an offshoot of romantic nationalism and an exercise in nation-building. It helped to provide a previously inconsequential island off the north-west coast of Europe with an ancient identity, and a sense of self-importance and imperial destiny, based on a mythical act of migration by the Tribe of Dan. The journey of the tribe to Britain could be traced, according to the British Israelites, through places that had 'Dan' or almost-Dan in their name: the Dar*dan*elles, Mace*don*ia, the *Dan*ube, *Den*mark, *Dun*kirk, *Don*caster, *Dun*bar and *Dun*dee. Even Lon*don* and E*din*burgh. There was little attempt at rigorous argument.

The most influential text of British Israelism, *Forty-seven Identifications of the British Nation with the Lost Ten Tribes of Israel* by Edward Hine, was a Victorian bestseller, going into more than forty editions. It's a curious book, full of contrived readings of opaque passages from the Bible and some quite wonderful linguistic nonsense. The word 'Saxons', Hine asserts, is the short form of 'Isaac's sons'. There's a small chart of Hebrew words that he believes have survived into modern English, including 'garden' and 'kitten'.

ENGLISH.	HEBREW.	ENGLISH.	HEBREW.
Sever	Shaver	Crocus	CRoCuM
Sabbath	Shabbath	Balsam	Ba Sam
Scale	Shakal	Garner	Ga Kan
Kitten	Qui To N	Garden	Ge DaR
Goat Kid	Gi Di	Hob	Ha B
Doe	Tod	Tar	TaR
Gum	Ga M	Light	LaHT

The Coronation Stone, we're assured, is in fact the Pillow of Jacob described in Genesis, which had been carried to Britain by the Tribe of Dan; while Queen Victoria was unquestionably a direct descendant of King David.* The British are special, according to Hine: God's chosen people. The argument is circular – the British must be a Lost Tribe because they are special, and they are special because they're a Lost Tribe.

It's possible to brush off the British Israelites as inoffensively ridiculous evangelical Christians. But there is a darker side to it all. Hine's book is also very much a defence of the British Empire, whose growth he both explains and justifies in terms of the story of the Lost Tribes, and what he describes, not very accurately, as the ability of both ancient Israel and Victorian Britain 'to obtain decisive victories by the use of only a small force'. In one chilling passage he refers to the high death rates and near-extinction of some of the aboriginal peoples of Australia and New Zealand. 'It has,' he says, 'been observed

---

* There is in fact a high probability that Queen Victoria and millions of others are descended from King David, if he ever existed, and had more than a dozen children, as the Bible says he did. Many millions of us are also likely to be descended from Genghis Khan, Charlemagne, Cleopatra or, as we'll see, the Vikings.

that this is a cruel thing; but this is a wicked observation to make, because it is God's own design.' It is as if Hine believes the British Empire to be the Kingdom of God.

The British Israelite movement continued to flourish into the first half of the twentieth century – always seen as slightly cultish, but mildly influential. One of Queen Victoria's granddaughters was the patron of its umbrella organisation, the British-Israel-World Federation, until her death in 1981. The BIWF still exists, much-shrunken, no longer based in an office near Buckingham Palace but in the town of Bishop Auckland in northern England. It has become a right-wing 'educational society' holding to its belief that the British are descended from the Tribe of Dan, but now fiercely opposed to migration from the Middle East. The BIWF also became a fervent and often eccentric supporter of Brexit. At one point it called on its followers to fast for a day in support of the British departure from the EU, declaring that 'we need to pray that the LORD will deliver the United Kingdom completely from the Babylonish EU as the difficult negotiations proceed'. Even when discussing Brexit, the ancient Mesopotamian migration story has not been forgotten.

Britain was not alone in its nineteenth-century Israel obsession. There were similar, less influential movements in the Nordic countries, which sought to demonstrate the racial superiority of a white northern European nation based on the legend of an ancient migration by a Lost Tribe. In twentieth-century America, the notion that the USA and the UK were the home of the Lost Tribes of Israel was central to the Christian evangelism of the Worldwide Church of God, whose founder also declared that the Germans were descended from the Assyrians. It's a view of the world and the past that is going out of fashion, but there remain several American evangelical splinter groups who still repeat Edward Hine's biblical and linguistic evidence for Israelite descent. They're unmoved by the

DNA data that demonstrates no such descent, for the British or the Germans – or indeed for almost all the multitude of other contenders for the title of 'Lost Tribe of Israel', from Native Americans and the Maori of New Zealand to the Mizos of India and the Gogodala tribe of New Guinea.

And yet, there's a certain irony here. For even if these claims are wrong in all their details, they do help to remind us of the centrality of migration to the human story. And on the very broadest level they are not completely wrong. For everyone who has roots outside sub-Saharan African does have Middle Eastern ancestry. We now know from genetic evidence that all of these failed non-African contenders as possible Lost Tribes of Israel are of solid ancient Middle Eastern stock, for their ancestors passed through the Middle East after modern humans left Africa – and of course, they also all have Neanderthal ancestors who travelled the same way much earlier. And, as for the Lost Tribes, they were probably dispersed in the same way as so many tribes and communities mentioned in the Bible have disappeared. Just as we are all descended from many different prehistoric tribes, migrating and intermarrying, and almost all of them now lost in the fog of history.

A Second Intermission

My first cousin Kate got in touch with me recently. 'We are first cousins!' she declared, uncontroversially, on Facebook Messenger. 'We are!' I replied decisively. We had both had our DNA tested by the same company – and an automated email had informed us of something we have known to be true since we were toddlers.

Genealogy can be rather boring. Unless it's about you. And even then, it's not always scintillating. But there has been a quiet revolution in recent years – since the sequencing of the human genome in 2003. And another aspect to the genealogical story has emerged. As more and more people have their DNA tested, mainly to find out about their ancestors, it becomes possible to aggregate their data in a way that could begin to change how we look at the world. It's a change that may undermine many of our ethnic and racial certainties, and will help to build up a picture of millions of human migrations through history, of *Homo Sapiens* as a species on the move. And everyone's DNA, including that of the dead, helps to create that picture.

Five weeks after I'd spat into a test tube I got my results back. Sitting at my laptop in Tunisia, I opened the email with a sense of anticipation, as if I were about to learn something about myself that would alter my life. I'd signed up, unthinkingly, for everything: not just ancestry, but other tests that might tell me whether I had a life-threatening genetic disease and, most bizarrely, would predict a series of 'traits' such as whether I have dimples, my views on the taste of coriander and what time I normally get up in the morning.

There were no life-threatening diseases. The predictions were surprisingly accurate: I am tone deaf, I don't get vertigo, I don't have dimples, I can smell asparagus, my ring finger is longer than my index finger, I do have 'detached' earlobes, 7.12 a.m. is pretty close to my normal wake-up time. But not perfect: I do like coriander, and my second toe is not longer than its fatter neighbour.* The results failed to reveal whether I carry the curiosity gene – leading to a grouchy email exchange with the testing company. And yes, I have Neanderthal genes: the testing company detected 248 genetic variants in my DNA that come from Neanderthals. But that's slightly fewer than Kate, and well below the average for non-Africans who have been tested. In my romantic imagination, I had hoped for a more impressive Neanderthal ancestry. I was a little disappointed.

There were, to my further disappointment, no immediate surprises in relation to my ancestry, and no great intercontinental migrations for at least the last millennium. The results seemed to confirm what I already knew about my family – that I had a mixture of British, French and Jewish ancestry. My secret father's DNA was unmissable, in the form of French and more general north European ancestry. And the report described me as 24.3 per cent Ashkenazi Jewish, which fitted almost exactly with what was known about my maternal grandmother's ancestry. A lot was known – too much, according to my grandfather (who found the genealogical obsession of his wife's family rather tiring). And indeed some of my mother's relatives

---

* These are all well-informed guesses, of course, and are based on what people with similar genes have reported back. The key science behind these predictions and the ancestry results is statistics not genetics.

had taken a huge amount of interest in family history, trawl-
ing through old records, which revealed that my grandmother
was the great-great-great-great-granddaughter of someone
with the wonderfully unforgettable name of Israel Israel, who
died in London in 1817, and whose father had migrated from
Germany. I almost feel that my ancestor's epizeuxic name gave
me the right to claim descent from a Lost Tribe of Israel, or
indeed one that was only slightly lost.

There was a small mystery, however. And one that became
more evident when I looked at Kate's ancestry test. The results
email had provided us each with long lists of more distant relatives: third, fourth and fifth cousins. All of these other cousins
shared our Ashkenazi Jewish ancestry and almost all of them
live in the United States – and yet I could not work out how I
could possibly be so closely related to any of them, given how
much tedious detail I knew about our recent family history. Of
course, there might have been, as there had for me personally,
a case or two of what geneticists coyly refer to as 'misattributed
paternity'. But it was also striking that many of these supposed
cousins in America were not even closely related to each other.
So it would have taken multiple nineteenth-century Ashkenazi
Jewish infidelities and adoptions on an inter-continental scale
to produce these results. That seems improbable.

There is a more likely explanation – which suggests that the
DNA testing companies might need to refine their methodol-
ogy. It's a more technical reason, but it tells an important part
of the story. We know from genealogical evidence that the
historical levels of intermarriage within many groups of Jews is
much higher than in most other communities. Indeed, as I look
at the family trees drawn up by my genealogically obsessed
Jewish relatives in the early twentieth century, cousin-marriage
was very common. In one family of five siblings, three of them
married their own first cousins.

And so this means that those third cousins listed on my

test results are not, in genealogical terms, third cousins. But because there has been so much intermarriage among closely related Jews they are, in terms of shared genes, the equivalent of third cousins within the wider non-Jewish population.* It's another reminder that we are all related. And that, for instance, I must be related much more distantly to my cousin Kate, not just through the two maternal grandparents we have in common, but also, much more anciently, through our paternal ancestors.

We are never going to be able to complete a family tree for all humans who ever existed, simply because so many people have left no DNA trace – neither descendants nor skeletons. But powerful computers and an improved ability to extract DNA from ancient bones means that we can fill in many gaps. And already these enable us to know how much genetic material we have in common with Neanderthals. The same exercise can be carried out with other ancient groups, and from that we will be able to piece together some of the many forgotten migrations of the past.

---

* This is something borne out by genetic studies. As the Israeli American geneticist Gil Atzmon points out, 'the shared genetic elements suggest that members of any Jewish community are related to one another as closely as are fourth or fifth cousins in a large population, which is about ten times higher than the relationship between two people chosen at random off the streets of New York City'.

CHAPTER THREE

Phoenicians, Greeks and Aryans

About twenty minutes' walk from my temporary Tunisian home there is a deep hole in the ground, covered by a thick sheet of Perspex. It looks like the shaft of a well. But it's actually the passageway to an ancient Phoenician crypt, discovered accidentally in 1994 by a gardener. Inside the crypt was a sarcophagus containing the skeleton of a young man who had died more than two and half thousand years earlier.

The crypt is on Byrsa Hill, at the heart of what was once Carthage, in its time the richest and most powerful city in the Mediterranean, and now an upmarket suburb of modern Tunis. Carthage was founded, according to legend, by Dido – and visited by Aeneas not long after the Trojan War. Dido herself was not a local. She was, according to these same legends, a princess from the group of coastal city-states in modern Lebanon now usually referred to as the Phoenician civilisation. And Dido, like Aeneas, was on the run – her husband having been murdered on the orders of her brother. On and around Byrsa Hill, a new city was built – quite literally, because in the Phoenician language the word Carthage means just that: New City.

The skeleton of the Young Man of Byrsa was intact and undisturbed. His hands were crossed in front of his pelvis, and he was surrounded by grave goods – amphorae, a lamp, an ivory box of ointments and some food offerings. The discovery of the skeleton led to some late-Phoenician fraternal excitement in Tunisia and Lebanon. These two smaller Mediterranean countries – both of them proud of their ancient Phoenician heritage – shared a claim to the glories of a civilisation that invented the alphabet and once dominated the Mediterranean.

A forensic reconstruction was made of the Young Man of Byrsa. His bones were measured and a face modelled over the

shape of his skull. He was tastefully clothed and coiffed, and given the name Ariche, meaning 'beloved one'. The skeleton and the reconstruction became part of an exhibition, and in 2014 the Young Man of Byrsa 'returned' briefly to his Lebanese 'homeland' and was put on display at the American University of Beirut. While in Beirut, two fragments of bone were removed from his ribs and sent off to a laboratory. There, DNA was extracted from the bone fragments – the first Phoenician DNA to be isolated and tested. At the same time, DNA from forty-seven citizens of modern Lebanon – all possible candidates as modern relatives of the Young Man of Byrsa – was analysed. Everyone hoped, even presumed, that the sequencing of these genetic samples would demonstrate the Lebanese origins of the people of Carthage, and might even show which among Lebanon's many modern communities were the closest living descendants of the ancient Phoenicians.

Everyone was surprised, and a little disappointed. The Young Man of Byrsa did not after all come from Lebanon, and neither did his recent ancestors. He had none of the DNA variations that would mark him out as even being from the eastern Mediterranean. Instead, he had strong recent ancestry from somewhere completely different, a region close to the Atlantic coast of what is now Spain and Portugal.*

The Young Man of Byrsa no longer fitted neatly into one of those many uncomplicated narratives we have of the past: in this case that Carthage was a Phoenician settlement. Of course, the results didn't disprove anything of the slightest significance, for there is plenty of other undisputed evidence of the Phoenician connection with Carthage. But instead the young man and his unexpected DNA is a reminder that the past is not necessarily less complicated than the present, that our simplified notions of ancient migration, those broad arrows on a familiar map, are an approximation at best, and often deeply misleading. And they can never come close to capturing the

---

* The nearest genetic match was some ancient DNA found near Leon in northern Spain. There shouldn't really have been such surprise that the young man was not of Phoenician descent. The Phoenicians built settlements in many places along the coast of the Mediterranean and beyond, including major trading ports in Sardinia, Sicily and Malta. They went further west than the ancient Greeks, through the Strait of Gibraltar, building settlements in what is now Morocco. And they founded the city of Cadiz even before Carthage was built.

millions of individual journeys that made our ancient world, and continue to make our modern one.

The Phoenicians founded many dozens of settlements, around the Mediterranean and on the Atlantic coast of Africa and Europe, but we know almost nothing about their attitudes towards migration. They may have invented the alphabet, but they weren't great writers. And what they did write was almost entirely lost when the library in Carthage was destroyed by the Romans, along with the rest of the city, in 149 BCE. And so we have to rely on archaeology, and on sparse Greek and Roman accounts – which are often coloured by their rivalry with the Phoenicians. There is one stray reference in Aristotle's *Politics* to sending poor Carthaginians to new settlements as a way of preventing social unrest – but elsewhere we learn that trade was the main motivation for the spread of Phoenician power and influence into the western Mediterranean and beyond.*

For the ancient Greeks, the problem of sources is almost exactly the opposite. The range of historical, archaeological and literary information can seem daunting, with plenty of counter-examples to contradict any grand generalisations. It all suddenly feels less obscure and more obviously relevant, largely because of the undying influence of ideas and attitudes that can be traced back to ancient Greece.

It's important to note that migration doesn't seem, at first glance, to dominate the story of the ancient Greeks in the same

---

* Carthage has spawned other 'New Cities'. Cartagena in Spain was founded by a Carthaginian general in about 227 BCE and renamed Carthago Nova – meaning New New City – by the Romans. In 1533, the Spanish founded the Colombian city of Cartagena de Indias, or New City of the Indies. Modern Cartagena in Colombia has a sizeable Lebanese community, which has absolutely no connection with the Phoenician origins of the name of their city.

way that it does for the Israelites and the Phoenicians – or, indeed, the Romans. For instance, modern schoolchildren, in many countries, learn a fair amount about the Greeks: their gods and heroes, temples and oracles, tyranny and democracy, Athens and Sparta, the *Iliad* and the *Odyssey*, Greek theatre and philosophy, the Olympic Games and famous battles – both between the Greeks and against the Persians. But they learn very little about migration. And that, I think, is an omission and a mistake.

The enormous scale of Greek migration, and the enduring importance of Greek attitudes towards migrants, are well known among those who take their history seriously, but often unnoticed by others. During what are known as the archaic and classical periods, before Alexander the Great tried to conquer the 'known' world, the Greeks built no less than 270 new independent settlements: mainly coastal cities around the Mediterranean and the Black Sea, including Marseille and Naples.* And that's quite apart from all the other minor and major acts of migration. In fact, issues of migration and exile and homeland run like a thickly tangled thread, with many straggling loose ends, through almost everything we know about the ancient Greeks.

There's another reason that migration plays a minor role in our most basic accounts of ancient Greece. Much of what the Greeks did write about migration was negative, and individual migrants were often portrayed as either tragic or subversive or not quite human or not quite Greek. There was no clear place for nomads in the Greek view of the world. Humans in general, and Greeks in particular, were sedentary beings – or they ought to be. Aristotle, for example, writing in about 330 BCE, sought to paint most types of voluntary migration as abnormal,

---

* Naples was originally Neapolis (whence the adjective Neapolitan) which means, like Carthage, New City.

and depicted the idea of living permanently in a city, or its rural hinterland, as normal, as part of the natural and eternal human condition:

> It is clear that the city-state exists by nature and that, by nature, man is a being who lives in a city-state. He who is without a city-state by nature, and not by circumstance, is either a rogue or greater than a human being.

It's an important argument, which carried much weight and has many modern echoes. And also, in those last few words of Aristotle's, there's a shadowy recognition of a prehistoric past, a world of godlike heroes, greater than human beings – such as Perseus and Heracles – who might roam freely without contravening the laws of nature. But even these heroes were driven to wander by duty and the gods – and really would have preferred to settle down in a place they could call home.

Aristotle is providing a philosophical underpinning to a range of older Greek stories – in Homer, for instance – where migrants are usually cursed, and in which migration is a punishment from the gods. In the *Iliad*, Achilles declares:

> When Zeus the Thunderer bestows unmitigated grief upon a man, he makes him an object of contempt and drives him over the face of the earth, so that he wanders, honoured neither by men nor by the gods.

And in the *Odyssey*, the sea-god Poseidon curses Odysseus, who becomes a tragic figure roaming the Mediterranean. This is a disaster, for 'no life is worse for mortals than roaming', and Odysseus' sole aim is clear: to return home – nothing is more important. It takes him ten years. This original odyssey, and the other wanderings and migrations of Greek mythology, made great stories, but the heroes were almost always victims who would have preferred a sedentary life and dreaded that they would remain forever in exile.

By Aristotle's own time, exile had become a common and widely feared judicial penalty, imposed by one's own people or the ruler of one's city-state. One of Euripides' characters declared that being deprived of one's city is 'the greatest misfortune, greater than can be put into words'. Exile, for some Greeks and Romans, felt like a punishment worse than death. Socrates – who had taught Aristotle's teacher Plato – chose suicide rather that exile.

But there are traces of a counter-narrative too, particularly among historians. Herodotus, for instance, travelled widely in the Greek-speaking world and beyond – though perhaps not quite as widely as he claimed. We don't know how he earned a living, but he made wandering the world for reasons of curiosity seem like an attractive life choice. Migration stories play an important role in his *Histories*, and he was accused of showing too much partiality towards barbarians. And some minority philosophical traditions, such as Cynicism, proclaimed that those who had a wandering lifestyle would have greater wisdom. However, the most popular view, in the philosophical and literary writings that have survived, and particularly in Athens, was that migration was not a good thing, often dangerous and best avoided. And there's a deep tension between this idea, this adulation of a sedentary existence and what we actually know about the ancient world, Greek and non-Greek; a world that was very much on the move.

Ideas about individual and group identity are critical to understanding Greek attitudes towards migration, particularly in terms of building new settlements. In that context, it's instructive to look at the language they, and others ever since, have used to describe migration and migrants. Even the very notion of 'the Greeks', in this context, can be confusing and anachronistic. Most Greek-speaking migrants living in a new settlement would not have identified themselves primarily as Greeks, but as coming from a particular city-state: perhaps Corinth or Athens (the same was true of Phoenician migrants who came from a particular mother-city: usually Tyre or Sidon). Their natural loyalties were to their own original city-state, itself a ragged translation of the Greek word *polis* – ragged because it fails to convey the sense in which the *polis* is not just a place but a group of people.

The term that Greek migrants used for that original city-state was a word, *metropolis*, that is still in use today, but with new sets of meanings – one of those peripatetic words whose roots and variations and abbreviations have themselves travelled the world to appear in dozens of languages.* In ancient times, the *metro* part of *metropolis* meant, quite simply, mother, and therefore the whole word is best translated as mother-city, or motherland. The term for the place that they moved to from the *metropolis*, the new independent settlement, was *apoikia*, meaning 'home away from home'. Sadly, unlike *metropolis*, the word *apoikia* has been lost to history. This is largely because it was replaced in slightly less ancient times by a Latin formulation, *colonia*. And from *colonia* came the modern word 'colony', as does a series of other words in many languages beginning with the same first five letters, and which today – except in relation to nudists and ants – have negative connotations in most parts of the world. For that reason, over the last few decades many historians have stopped using the word colony

---

* *Metro* is the ancestor of the English word 'mother' and is similar to words for mother in almost every Indo-European language from Icelandic to Bengali. While 'metropolis' meant 'mother-city' long before it became a description of any large urban area (or the fictional home city of Superman), and long before its adjectival form became a kind of bishop or a London tube line, or whose abbreviated versions became shorthand for an urban transport system, a New York museum and the London police force. The French use the word *métropolitain* to mean the mainland of France. And *polis*, on its own, has had a similarly convoluted afterlife, giving us the words politics, policy and police.

to describe the Greek settlements – for most of them weren't colonies in the modern sense, in that they were independent of their *metropolis*.

Greek city-states had a range of different attitudes towards migration. Many of them had foundation myths in which they proudly claimed descent from migrants – often semi-mythical superheroes, such as Heracles or Pelops. But Athens, unusually, didn't. Its distinctive identity and its claims to superiority over other Greek city-states are partly drawn from the assertion that Athenians are indigenous, not migrants – that they are, in the words of the early Greek poet Pindar, 'born of the earth'. The legendary founder of the city was said to have quite literally emerged from the soil of Athens.* Herodotus repeats the boast made by an Athenian envoy to a Greek settlement in Sicily: 'We Athenians, the most ancient people in Greece, [are] the only Greeks who never migrated.'

The 'earth-born' trope is much repeated in Greek literature as a cause or explanation of Athenian exceptionalism. This matters in view of the long shadow Athens would cast over the ancient world and, more recently, over the development of what is loosely referred to as Western civilisation. Because it's from this period, in ancient Athens, that we can trace an early version of the idea that the world is divided into two types of people: those who claim to have been in a particular place for all eternity or a very long time indeed, and those who admit, or are proud of the fact, that they have come from elsewhere. It's a division that has endured.

In ancient Athens, then, the notion that its original

---

* According to Apollodorus, Erichthonius – the founder of Athens – was born from the spilled semen of Hephaestus as he tried to rape Athena. Athena wiped the semen from her thigh onto the soil of Athens with a piece of cotton. Elsewhere that Athenian claim to autochthony wasn't totally unchallenged. In Euripides' play *Ion*, a man from northern Greece, married to an Athenian, declares 'the earth does not bear children'. The punctilious Athenian historian Thucydides indirectly challenges the earth-born myth by saying that in ancient times no Greeks were settled.

inhabitants were not migrants was normalised, and so was its uncomfortable corollary, that migrants and their descendants could never become true Athenians. And, indeed, Athenian exceptionalism extended to the treatment of foreigners living there — creating a deep and permanent rift within the social structure of the city-state. For Athens had a large community of foreign migrants, known as *metics*, who settled there but could not become citizens. And neither, more significantly, could their descendants, even if they had been born in Athens. *Metics* could come from a wide range of social and economic classes — they could be newly freed slaves or among the richest men in Athens. They paid higher taxes than citizens, could not vote, and needed to have a patron who was a citizen, even if their family had been living there for several generations. A class of Athenians had been created who could not become full citizens because of their ancestry.

At one point, around 435 BCE, there may have been as many *metics* as citizens living in Athens. And *metics* were expected to conduct themselves better than citizens. In Euripedes' play *The Suppliants*, there is a telling description of a *metic*: 'He behaved as resident foreigners should behave. He did not make himself objectionable or troublesome to the city.' It's a description echoed by second- and third-generation descendants of modern migrants, many of whom feel they are always under greater scrutiny than the descendants of long-standing inhabitants, and that they are treated as if they only half belong to the country they were born in, and that their right to stay there might even be taken away.

There were also important differences among the Greeks in relation to emigration. The great settlement-builders of ancient Greece were not from the still-famous city-states of Athens and Sparta but from ones which have been largely forgotten:

Miletus, Eretria, Megara and Phocaea.* Miletus, on what is now the coast of Turkey, founded more settlements than any other city-state: at least thirty-six of them, mainly around the Black Sea. Greek is still spoken along parts of the coast settled two and a half thousand years ago by the Milesians.

Migrants from the city-state of Phocaea, now the small Turkish seaside town of Foça, travelled much further: to Italy, France and Spain. Among the settlements they founded was Massilia, which became Marseille, still often referred to in France by the nickname *La Cité Phocéene*, the Phocaean city. Marseille remains aware of its Greek heritage, and proud of its role in bringing 'civilisation' to western Europe. And there's a large metal plaque embedded into the paving stones of the Old Port, where the Phocaeans are believed to have landed, proclaiming that

IN ABOUT 600 BC,
GREEK SAILORS LANDED HERE,
COMING FROM THE GREEK CITY
OF PHOCAEA IN ASIA MINOR.
THEY FOUNDED MARSEILLE
FROM WHERE CIVILISATION
SHONE TO THE WEST

The Marseille story – largely ignored in Anglophone accounts – is a broadly benign and poorly sourced tale of two waves of Greek migration, in which, according to legend, the migrants were warmly welcomed by the people already living in the nearby countryside. The leader of the first group of

---

* The Athenians came late to setting up new city-states, and did not travel far. Sparta built no formal settlements, though one freelance group referred to as the 'Spartan bastards' did found the city of Taranto in southern Italy – today the country's main naval base. The bastards, or Parthenidae, were the offspring of Spartan women fathered by men who were not citizens.

migrants is said to have married the daughter of the local king, a side story that is echoed in several other foundation myths, including Rome's, and may be seen as a way of providing legitimacy to migrants who might otherwise be considered as land-grabbing invaders.

A few decades later, Phocaea, Marseille's distant *metropolis*, was overrun by the Persian army. Many Phocaeans fled their motherland and there was a second, much larger migration to the west. Marseille soon became a *metropolis* itself, creating settlements at Nice (*Nikaia*) and Antibes (*Antipolis*) and elsewhere. And it developed into a base for exploration and for new trading routes, particularly by land and river into northern Europe. In about 320 BCE, a Greek mariner from Marseille named Pytheas travelled still further, writing up his account of a journey to the cold northern seas, where he sailed round a large island he referred to as *Bretannikē* – the earliest known reference to Britain.

Trade undoubtedly played a key role in the creation of new Greek settlements. But there are a lot of other reasons why so many Greeks migrated to new or old city-states, or beyond into barbarian territory. It's a long list, and it is remarkably similar to one that might be drawn up to describe modern motives for migration. It includes overpopulation, drought, climate change, war, flight from tyranny, boredom and curiosity, and the search for land or power or a job. Others were forced to move – as slaves, exiles, convicts and prisoners-of-war.

There's little in the Greek sources about female migrants. What there is suggests that far more men than women migrated, and female migrants were often prostitutes or priestesses; though there is some sparse evidence of women joining later groups of migrants once a settlement had been established. In principle, at least, most Greek city-states did not object to intermarriage. And male migrants would seek wives in the indigenous population – though there's little evidence, as is so often the case, about how much choice local women were given in the matter.

There was no clear overall pattern as to how the native populations were treated by settlement builders. In Naples, like Marseille, relations were said to have been good, with non-Greek locals 'allowed' to become citizens and magistrates of the new city-state. Elsewhere, existing inhabitants were driven out by the new migrants, or enslaved – as happened in Syracuse. Occasionally, the Greek migrants were themselves enslaved. This happened in Posidonia, south of Naples, where according to a much later account, the new migrants were allowed to follow only one of their festivals, 'where they gather together and remember their old languages and customs, and after weeping and wailing with one another, they depart'.

Over time, an informal code of practice emerged about how to build a new settlement. So, for instance, it became customary before migrating to seek the advice of the gods, usually by consulting the oracle at Delphi. The leader of the new settlement would normally be appointed before departure from the metropolis, and the migrants – almost always young men – would swear allegiance to that leader. On many occasions the migrants would carry fire from the mother-city's sacred hearth. And when they arrived they would typically set up a makeshift temple to Apollo, and begin laying out a grid plan for the new city. In this way, one specific kind of migration – Greek emigration for the purpose of building new settlements – became normalised, subject to rules or custom. And those who followed these rules would be seen, in general, as good migrants.

There was one other migration-related activity, with strong modern resonances, that came to be codified in ancient Greece: asylum-seeking. The word asylum was closely associated with the idea of places of sanctuary, usually temples, from which individuals were, in principle, safe from the legal or illegal demands of their rulers. It's a powerful idea – and much argued over in antiquity. In many places, the right to sanctuary applied to everyone: criminals, political migrants, runaway slaves, women escaping an unwanted marriage, general travellers – though there were variations. Athens, for instance, ruled out the right of sanctuary for murderers and a range of other offenders, including those who had shown cowardice on the battlefield or mistreated their parents. Rulers who broke the code of sanctuary would be punished by the gods – with madness in the case of one Spartan king, who had executed refugees seeking sanctuary in a sacred grove.

In the 330s BCE, these two unwritten codes – over asylum-seekers and settlement-building – were undermined, if not shattered, by Alexander the Great. His army dragged old people, women and children from sanctuary temples in the Greek city of Thebes, where 'outrage without limit' was committed against them. And as he headed eastwards into Asia – with a brief foray into Egypt – he founded or rebuilt dozens of cities, naming many of them after himself. They were not independent like earlier Greek settlements, but part of Alexander's empire. And they were usually multi-ethnic cities from the start, garrisoned by his soldiers – Greek and non-Greek – and frequently with local rulers drawn from the old Persian elite, who continued to use old Persian titles such as *satrap*.

Alexander is a complex, elusive, transitory figure – both a hero and villain to his contemporaries, and ever since – and is an important figure in any attempt to look at the early history of attitudes towards migration. His legacy is still fought over, largely between modern Greece and the neighbouring country now known as North Macedonia. Alexander himself is an interesting early example of someone who doesn't quite belong to anywhere. He was born in Macedon, in the northern Greek borderlands. He was the son of the king, and his mother was a princess from elsewhere – another frontier kingdom – and there is plenty of evidence that this gave him an early sense of divided loyalty. At the age of twenty, Alexander took over from his murdered father as the ruler of a newly powerful Macedon, a kingdom that was often seen by other Greeks as not fully Greek. As one of Alexander's modern biographers argues, the attitude of the city-state Greeks to Macedon

> was one of genial and sophisticated contempt. They regarded Macedonians in general as semi-savages, uncouth of speech and dialect, retrograde in their political institutions, negligible as fighters, and habitual oath-breakers, who dressed in bear pelts and were much given to deep and swinish potations, tempered with regular bouts of assassination and incest.

For some, particularly those from the Greek heartlands around Athens, Alexander (and his father before him) was really an outsider, a barbarian who was also an invader and a foreign conqueror. And Alexander did little to disabuse them.

Alexander spent most of his short adult life on the move. He was a migrant of sorts, though an unusual one, given the size of the army he brought with him wherever he went. He was someone who, as it proved, would never stay still, who ultimately had no clear destination in mind, who was almost nomadic in his attitude towards home. And in Asia, when he adopted the dress and customs of locals, some Greeks saw this as further proof that he was not really one of them, that he had, as the Victorians would have said, 'gone native'. Even more so when he took local wives, and persuaded or forced others in his army to do the same. He continued eastwards, after conquering Persia, to the frontiers of India, against the advice of his generals, with no clear aim or motivation except perhaps curiosity and glory and a love of risk, until he was forced to turn back by his own soldiers. They wanted to go home or settle down somewhere. Alexander didn't.

He died in Babylon, more than two thousand kilometres from where he was born, at the age of just thirty-two. Among Alexander's papers were his short-term plans, which included the conquest of Carthage and the western Mediterranean, and the construction of a road along the coast of North Africa. And there is, most strikingly, a radical proposal in which he declared his intention

> to settle cities and transplant populations from Asia to Europe, and vice versa from Europe to Asia; to bring the largest continents – through intermarriage and ties of kinship – to a common harmony and feeling of friendship.

Alexander seemed to be proposing something quite extraordinary, a piece of social engineering on an inter-continental scale: a massive, two-way, state-organised migration and intermarrying of the people of two continents as a way of uniting the Greeks and the Persians, and the other peoples of his empire. And he spoke of Asians and Europeans as equals, who might be encouraged to end centuries of conflict with a mixture of migration and miscegenation.

Arguably, he'd already begun this by encouraging the settlement of Greek soldiers in newly conquered parts of the former Persian empire and urging or compelling them to marry local women. But that was small-scale and in one direction – from Europe to Asia. It's not clear how he would have gone ahead with the rest of his plan, and whether it would also have entailed the migration of women, and whether he would have settled Persians in Greek city-states. His successors, less keen to change the world, and more overtly proud of their Greek origins, had neither the intention nor the ability to implement his ideas. The plans for the largest organised migration of ancient times died with Alexander.

The Alexander legend would sprout wings, a benefit per-haps of dying young and undefeated, and became a source of twenty-three centuries of Western hyperbole. It was as if he'd conquered the world on behalf of the Greeks, or of Europe – when he'd actually conquered an area slightly smaller than that of the Persian Empire (at its height) that Alexander defeated. And it's useful to remind ourselves that he briefly controlled what was, in global terms, a long, narrow east–west strip of land, largely consisting of sedentary people – farmers and city-dwellers, at the meeting point of three continents, none of which he dominated. At either end of that strip of land were other unconquered sedentary people: the Carthaginians to the west, and the Indians and the Chinese to the east. But most of the inhabited world was far beyond his reach, and the vast majority of human beings knew little of cities, and nothing of the Greeks. They were farmers and nomads, and they left no written records. This makes it harder to include them in our narratives of the past, but that is no excuse for behaving as if they did not exist.

However, Chinese and Indian writings do survive from this period and provide some comparison with the Greek accounts. There's not a vast amount about migrants specifically. But as with Greece, there's a dominant narrative that proclaims the superiority of sedentary, city-dwelling humans; a narrative that also proclaimed their particular group of sedentary humans to be living, geographically and metaphorically, at the centre of the world. And this despite a very low level of interaction between these literate cultures. Sometimes, nomads intrude into the writings of these sedentary peoples, but only because they live in the borderlands, and they are usually depicted as either a cause of trouble, or a supplier of rare commodities, or a source of slaves, or all three. Beyond, in the far distance, according to many ancient writers, from very different places, are monsters, half-humans; a warning, perhaps, not to wander too far from home.

The ancient Chinese often compared their nomadic neighbours to real animals. The Rong-Di people, for instance, are described as 'wolves, to whom no indulgence should be given', while foreigners in general 'are like the deer, wild birds and the beasts – in that the young order their old around, while the old fear the able-bodied'. However, there are also complex narratives which suggest that foreigners are not irredeemably lost to the civilised world. There are references to a common ancient heritage, with the suggestion that nothing is wrong with the blood of those who aren't Chinese, just their behaviour. They can and should, according to some writers of this period, simply become Chinese by adopting Chinese culture; ancestry or appearance seem to play no important role here. Intermarriage was also therefore possible. And one Chinese writer argued that foreigners really wanted to be assimilated, were indeed queuing up for this to happen. But the voices of migrants themselves are unheard.

We know far more about migration in relation to India which was (and still is) more of a cultural mosaic. And its tales of ancient migration, as we'll see shortly, are a cause of extremely pugnacious modern political debates. From India we have, unlike China, accounts from both sides. For in the century that followed the death of Alexander, a traveller and a resident each described, inter alia, the treatment of migrants in Pataliputra, the capital of the Mauryan Empire and then probably the largest city in the world. The traveller was a Greek ambassador called Megasthenes, sent by the ruler of one of

Alexander's successor kingdoms. Megasthenes was impressed
by the size and orderliness of the empire. He also pointed out,
full of praise, how carefully the Mauryans look after all its foreigners, not just ambassadors:

> Officers are appointed ... whose duty is to see that no for-
> eigner is wronged. Should any of them lose his health, they
> send physicians to attend him, and if he dies they bury him,
> and deliver such property as he leaves to his relatives.

The second account, by an adviser to the Mauryan Emperor,
indicates that that these helpful government officers assigned
to assist foreigners were also spying on them. The writings of
Kautilya, who was probably a contemporary of Megasthenes,
were only rediscovered in the early twentieth century, and
provide an extraordinary level of detail about the Mauryan
Empire more than 2,300 years ago. A large part of his wide-
ranging book *Arthashastra*, or *The Science of Politics*, is about
the importance of building a network of spies, at home and
abroad, who, he says, should be 'of good family, loyal, reliable,
well-trained in the art of putting on disguises appropriate to
countries and trades, and possessed of knowledge of many languages and arts'. Spies were expected to

> find out the causes of emigration and immigration of per-
> sons of migratory habit, the arrival and departure of men
> and women of condemnable character, as well as the move-
> ments of spies.

Megasthenes, we can be pretty confident, was being
closely watched.

There's little reference to migration in early writing from
north India, at least not in the sense of large movements of population. But there was an expectation, at least in principle, that

Indians of a certain age would migrate. Several early works refer to four stages of life, usually translated into English as: student, householder, retirement and renunciation. The Sanskrit word for the retirement phase is *vanaprastha*, which literally means 'going to the forest'. The *Laws of Manu*, probably compiled about two thousand years ago, says that grandfathers must migrate: 'When the householder notices his wrinkles and greyness, and sees his child's child, then he should retire to the forest.' His wife should either come with him, or stay with their sons – though it is not clear whether she gets to make this choice.

Now this is not quite the equivalent of the British sun-seeking sixty-somethings moving to Spain, or Americans retiring to Florida, because these forest-dwelling Indian grandparents are expected to avoid luxury. They are supposed to spend a lot of time praying, and sleep on the ground, eat wild plants, nuts and berries, and generally lead a less materialistic life. It's a lifestyle that also mimics a nomadic one, both because it seeks to replicate the lives of existing forest-dwellers and because it envisages humans returning to our ancient nomadic roots towards the end of our lives. But it also suggests that nomadic lives are ones of hardship – which, as we've seen and will see, is not necessarily the case.

There's a two-syllable word that occurs repeatedly in the earliest Sanskrit texts, secular and religious, one that is often left untranslated in other languages. It's a word with a strange, contorted modern history; a word that became an important clue in a migration mystery, that would be imported into many Western languages, and given a new meaning which became more than contentious – particularly in the first half of the twentieth century. That word is *ārya*, better known in the west in a slightly modified form: Aryan. On one level, 'Aryan' is simply a descriptive label used by these ancient writers to

designate the dominant culture and people of northern India –
and, used as an adjective in Sanskrit, it can also mean noble. But
in more recent times, by several strange twists of etymological
misfortune, Aryan became a racially charged word for white-
skinned, blond-haired, blue-eyed north Europeans. And it all
harks back to an ancient migration that many modern Indian
nationalists insist never happened.

In the eighteenth century, several scholars noted the similarities between Sanskrit and Western classical languages. Soon
it was accepted that these languages did indeed spring from
a single source, and that therefore most of the languages of
northern India, Iran and Europe were also inter-related. Before
long, an ancient people had been imagined, called the Indo-
Europeans, who had migrated throughout Europe and large
parts of Asia, and whose legacy was a wide range of modern
languages that were cousins or second cousins, from Icelandic
in the west to Bengali in the east. But no one could agree on
the identity of the Indo-European homeland, and there was no
obvious historical or archaeological evidence of such a large-
scale migration, or proof that the spread of languages depended
on big movements of populations.

But some European scholars thought they had an answer.
They found some clues in those ancient references to Aryans.
They decided, on pretty flimsy textual evidence, that the
Aryans of the early Sanskrit texts, particularly the *Rigveda*,
were migrants or invaders from the west. Various putative
homelands were suggested for the Aryans including, critically,
Germany. The arguments for this were even more flimsy, and
suffused with racism, but large numbers of scholars from several
countries adopted the notion that the Aryans were originally
blond, blue-eyed, white-skinned Germans – and that these
traits had been diluted by intermarriage the further they had
migrated from their north European homeland.

Houston Stewart Chamberlain, a British-born writer living

in Germany, was key to bringing these notions to the attention of Adolf Hitler and his nascent National Socialist Party in the 1920s. And before long the Nazis had adopted the idea that the Germans were the original Aryans, the master race. They even borrowed the ancient Indian swastika symbol as an emblem of their party. Since the defeat of Hitler, the use of the word Aryan has largely died out in the West, except among neo-Nazi groups.* And the swastika, outside India, is almost unused.

But the argument about the origins of the Aryans lives on in modern India and is a matter of ill-tempered and often unpleasant debate. At the internet-trolling extremes are two theories known by almost-identical acronyms, AIT and OIT, standing for 'Aryan Invasion Theory' and 'Out of India Theory' respectively. Their supporters tend to shout at and curse each other on social media forums, often to the bafflement of outsiders. The old case for the AIT has been described above, but its more temperate modern supporters now suggest that migration would be a better word than invasion, and argue that, in fact, there was never evidence of a European origin for the Aryans, who probably originated in Central Asia or the Russian steppes. The supporters of the OIT, meanwhile, draw on ancient traditions, co-opted into modern nationalism, according to which Indians have always been in India. Megasthenes had asserted that India 'is peopled by races both numerous and diverse, of which not even one was originally of foreign descent', and indeed there are no clear references to any significant group migration in the earliest Indian writings. Therefore, by this logic, India must be the Indo-European homeland.

Far less dangerous than the Nazi claim to Aryan ancestry, though just as absurd, have been the more detailed arguments

---

* Genetically speaking, the most Aryan people in Europe were the Roma, formerly known as Gypsies, who were murdered in large numbers by the Nazis. Search for Arya on the internet and you get many pages of links to a character in *Game of Thrones* before anything that's connected with Sanskrit or India.

put forward by some supporters of the Out of India Theory. The forerunner here is P. N. Oak, an amateur Indian historian and author of *Some Missing Chapters of World History*, who argues that India's history has always been written by its enemies. The book reads, at times, like a brilliant spoof, making satirical mincemeat of white supremacists and their notions of European Aryanism. The chapter titles give a clue: 'Ancient England was a Hindu Country', 'Westminster Abbey was also a Shiva Temple' and 'Ancient Italy was a Hindu Country and the Pope a Hindu Priest'. The cathedral city of Salisbury, we learn, was originally Shaileeshpury, meaning 'town of the mountain god'. It goes on and on in this vein (Rome is named after Lord Ram, while Abraham was originally Brahma and Christ was Krishna). Sadly, it is not a spoof. P. N. Oak, who died in 2007, believed it all, and so did a tiny band of followers.

In their attempt to place the Indo-European homeland firmly in India, most Out of India supporters do not go nearly as far as Oak. And, fortunately, amateur linguistics plays a smaller role these days, on both sides of the Aryan argument. Archaeologists tried to resolve the issue by focusing on excavations at sites belonging to the Harappan civilisation that pre-date the early Sanskrit texts. The theory was simple: if these excavations show a continuity with Aryan culture, then this would prove the OIT; if they don't show a continuity, this would prove the AIT. In practice, it wasn't so simple, and the divisions deepened as part of an arcane journey into equine archaeology that deserves only a footnote here.* It feels as if

---

* The crux of the issue became, at one point, the uncertain existence of horses in ancient India. The earliest Sanskrit text, the *Rigveda*, mentions horses many times, but there is a mysterious absence of horses at the many Harappan excavations, either in the form of horse imagery or of equine bones. Except there are some images that are ambiguous or broken, that might just possibly, with a bit of imagination, be horses. And horse bones have been found at one late Harappan site – or they might be horse bones, or they might have been deliberately placed there to fool people into thinking that the Harappans had horses. And so the argument continues.

there's only one certainty now: if you are a Hindu national-ist, you are more likely to support the notion of India as the Indo-European homeland. While if you have a more secular, multi-cultural image of India, you are more likely to support the idea of large-scale migration into India.

Over the last few years, DNA evidence has been brought to bear on the wider question of the location of that supposed Indo-European homeland, and a potential resolution to the AIT/OIT dispute. As a result, there's a growing scientific con-sensus about ancient movements of population from the stretch of land usually referred to as the Russian steppes, covering east-ern Ukraine, parts of southern Russia and western Kazakhstan. This region's ancient nomadic inhabitants have been identified as the first Indo-Europeans – whose descendants can be found in large numbers throughout communities who speak Indo-European languages in Europe and Asia and, as a result of more recent migrations, in the Americas and Australasia.

A journalist called Tony Joseph has taken on the task of explaining to his fellow Indians that the Aryans almost cer-tainly came from the Russian steppes. He's not been given an easy time. His 2018 book, *Early Indians*, sets out how, accord-ing to the latest research, migrants, largely male, entered what is now India around four thousand years ago, introducing an early version of Sanskrit as well as new religious beliefs and practices – some of which play an important role in modern Hinduism. He was roundly condemned for this by many Hindu nationalists. His critics appear deeply threatened by the idea that migrants had contributed to their genetic stock, and to the languages, beliefs and customs of which they are so proud. The internet, as usual, incubates and exacerbates all this. And the tone of some online comments has been both desperate and vitriolic (though there has been some more thoughtful criti-cism). Tony Joseph was accused of writing 'propaganda' which will 'destroy the fabric of the country', of promoting 'racist

Eurocentric lies', of being 'deceptive, dishonest ... a leftist has-been', of assembling a 'hodge-podge of self-contradicting and incorrect claims' which should be consigned to the 'trash heap'.

For those who have never lived in India, it can seem bizarre that an obscure debate about ancient migration should become so emotional, so clouded by rage. But most of those involved would admit, at least privately, that the question about Aryans in India is only partly about the truth, about what may have happened four thousand years ago. Ancient migration has become a proxy for a whole range of other issues. It is part of a struggle over the identity of modern India, in which issues of caste, gender, language, religion, skin colour and, yes, migration play an important role. There are profound disagreements over that identity, and deep divisions on each of those issues. The Aryan debate touches on all of them – a subject that deserves a book of its own, not this skimpy paragraph. But it's worth noting that power in India remains largely, but not entirely, in the hands of paler-skinned, higher-caste male northerners who speak Indo-European languages. And they, if one trusts the geneticists, are more likely to be descended from people who migrated to India about four thousand years ago.

There's a broader issue raised by the recent history of the search for the origins of Indo-European language-speakers. And it's that very notion of an ancestral homeland, whether in the Russian steppes or anywhere else. It has become normal to suppose that we all had such a homeland, when, in fact, the opposite is closer to the truth. These possible ancient home-lands – whether identified through DNA or archaeology or linguistic analysis or cultural tradition – were all, at best, regions of the world that our ancient ancestors passed through, temporary residences in deep history.

Indeed, when we look at those putative first Indo-Europeans in the Russian steppes, one of the few things we know about them is that they too were not settled peoples but nomads on the move. There's a pattern here. And however hard we try to invent an ancient world in which some of us belonged to a particular place, we are all descended from nomads. If we really do need to identify an ancient homeland, if having such a prehistoric touchstone meets some deep psychological human need, then why can we not accept that our only true homeland is an entire continent, Africa, through which all our ancestors wandered, and from which we all came?

A THIRD INTERMISSION

Six months after I spat into a test tube, my daughter Roxy did the same. There was no paternity issue here: she looks and behaves in a way that is a gorgeous, unflustered version of a younger me. And sure enough, my Jewish, British and northern European DNA were all there, in half measures, in her genes. It was the other half of her DNA that Roxy and I were interested in.

Roxy's mother's grandparents and great-grandparents were all born in India, and yet we were not expecting to discover DNA from India in her genes. This is because her mother, Shireen, belongs to a tiny community who migrated from Persia to India many centuries ago, and who did not marry out of that community until very recently. They are Zoroastrians, the religion of Cyrus the Great, who released the Jews from Babylon, and of Darius III, defeated by the armies of Alexander the Great in 333 BCE.* Today there are probably fewer than two hundred thousand Zoroastrians in the world, and fewer than half of them live in India, where they are known as Parsis.

---

* My brothers-in-law, Bahram, Ardashir and Naoshirvan, are each named after Persian emperors from the Sassanid dynasty, who each fought against the Roman Empire. It's often forgotten quite how well the armies of some of the Sassanids performed against the Romans, capturing the Emperor Valerian at the Battle of Edessa in 260 CE (he died later in captivity), and killing the Emperor Julian at the Battle of Samarra in 363 CE.

The first Parsis arrived in India about a thousand years ago as migrants from Persia, which by then had a Muslim majority, and several more waves of migration followed. The Parsis are often held up, particularly within India, as an example of how a migrant group can integrate successfully into the host community but retain its distinctive identity. And there's a well-known foundation myth, a saccharine tale that describes their arrival in India. According to this tale, when the Parsis first arrived by boat in Gujarat, in the west of the country, they found they had no language in common with the population. The local king held out a jug of milk that was full to the brim as a polite way of saying there was no room for migrants in his land. The leader of the migrants, a Zoroastrian priest, poured a spoonful of sugar into the milk, which did not overflow. Rather, the milk was sweetened and enriched. They were allowed to stay.

It's a classic 'good' migration story, repeated with pride by Parsis and non-Parsis. And it's hard to find anyone in India who would suggest that this particular migration has been a failure. The tiny Parsi community has flourished in terms of status and affluence, particularly in the British period, but also since independence. That's not quite the whole story. Parsis – unlike Muslims and Christians who came to India – did not attempt to convert other Indians to their religion, and so because of this, and a low birth rate, the Parsis have remained unthreateningly small in number. And Parsis have occasionally faced violence at the hands of more powerful communities, with at least five anti-Parsi riots over the last two hundred years.

There's another version of the Parsi community's foundation story, known as the *Qissa-i Sanjan*, which is slightly less sugary, and refers to some of the real decisions that are forced on modern and ancient migrants, particularly in relation to language, and to what women are allowed to wear. For in this rendering of the story, the Zoroastrian priest was told that if the Parsis were to be allowed to settle in Gujarat they would have to stop using their old language and speak only in Gujarati, and that Parsi women (but not men) would have to dress in the same manner as local women. The priest agreed, and the Parsis obeyed.

As for my daughter's DNA – the results indeed showed that Iran, not India, was her maternal homeland. The laboratory analysis of her spittle revealed that more than 85 per cent of the DNA she inherited from her mother came from what used to be known as Persia. This suggests that there has been little interbreeding between the Parsis and other much larger communities in India. But the results did throw up one surprise: a huge number of previously unknown distant Parsi cousins living all around the world. It's a reminder that many Parsis have left their second homeland, India, and are on the move again. The modern world's most famous Parsis have been life-long migrants: the singer Freddie Mercury, born in Zanzibar, schooled in India, lived (and died) in Britain; and the composer Zubin Mehta, born in India, trained in Austria, who has lived in the UK, USA, Italy and Israel. The number of Parsis in India continues to fall, because of low birth rates, but also because so many Parsis have over the last fifty years been on the move again, with large numbers leaving India and migrating to the USA, the UK, Canada and Australia.

CHAPTER FOUR

Exiles, Romans
and Vandals

He stands, toga-wrapped, high on a plinth in the main square, looking eastwards, out to sea. Fresh white streaks, a gift of the gulls, blotch his bronze hair. His left hand, holding a book without a name, is clasped to his chest. On his other hand he rests his chin with an air of sad, contemplative dignity. He would, one senses, rather be somewhere else. Down below, tourists gather, rarely looking at him – he's too high up and too morose for a selfie. But around his plinth is where they meet, and screech and snack and smooch in the summer evenings, after scorching themselves on the broad sandy beaches of the Black Sea. For they are on holiday in Constanta, at the heart of what travel companies call the Romanian Riviera, host to hundreds of thousands of tourists every summer – with daily Wizz Air flights from Luton, London's forlorn fourth airport.

Nowadays, Constanta is a place of middle-income pleasure, but it is also remembered as ancient Tomis, a place of forced

migration for one man.* For it was here that the Roman poet
Ovid, who stands despondently on that plinth, was sent to live
out his days. And surely there is no one who has ever disliked
exile more, who was more sorry for himself. Several famous
exiles predate him, but he was the first to turn self-pity and
homesickness into an art form. And that matters here because
Ovid may have been the first to depict the notion of staying at
home, of not migrating at any cost, as a revered human attrib-
ute – and exile as the worst of fates. Ovid came to personify
a fear and hatred of migration that can seem a little extreme.
After all, one of the key messages of *Tristia*, or *Sorrows*, the
book-length poem of his later years, was that it would be better
to be dead than in permanent exile.

Ovid hated Tomis. Or he said he did. He portrayed it as a
hellhole. He hated the weather, the landscape, the lack of company, the lack of appreciation for a great poet: 'Writing a poem
you can read to no one / is like dancing in the dark.' He asked
if any exile has 'been dumped in a more remote and nastier
spot' and listed, with envy, those who were exiled to better
places than him. But there is also purpose to his moaning. For
he hoped to persuade the Emperor Augustus to let him return
to his beloved Rome.

There's an unsolved mystery at the heart of Ovid's exile.
He declared in *Tristia* that there were two reasons for his
punishment. The first was his love of poetry, considered
too indecent for Augustus, and the second – well, he chose
to keep that a secret, never to be revealed, but for which he
believed he might be forgiven. And he hoped his words,

---

* Constanta's more recent claim to fame is as the birthplace of the Grand Slam
winning tennis player Simona Halep. She's of Aromanian heritage, a descendant
of recent migrants to Romania from the southern Balkans. Aromanians were previously referred to as Vlachs. Romania's greatest footballer, Gheorghe Hagi is also
of Aromanian heritage, and was born just outside Constanta. In 2009 he became
the owner of a football team called Ovidiu, after (indirectly) the Roman poet, and
changed its name to Viitorul Constanta.

sometimes barbed, sometimes pleading, would encourage the Emperor to let him return. And so he made out that Tomis was far more unpleasant than it was, referring, for instance, to perpetual snow, to a treeless, birdless landscape, to barbarian inhabitants, and to frozen wine that had to be hacked into chunks and thawed. In fact, Tomis is further south than Venice or Genoa, was a Greek settlement dating back six centuries, and there was usually less than a week of snow each year. As for the birds, they take their revenge on poor Ovid's statue every day.

Augustus did not pardon Ovid, who died in Tomis in 17 CE.* And Ovid's later writings, the *Letters from the Black Sea*, suggest a greater acceptance of his exile, a partial reconciliation with the shortcomings of the place. He wrote poems in the local language. He described how people treated him with kindness, paying tribute to him as a poet and exempting him from local taxes. And there's even a half-apology, as he describes his 'tactless talent' of upsetting his hosts, who had heard of how Ovid had described Tomis in *Tristia* to his friends in distant Rome:

> But I've done nothing wrong, men of Tomis,
>   I've committed
> no crime: you, I love, although I loathe your land.

And there are other ways of reading Ovid's self-pity. It's not really about the climate, or the locals, or the wine, or anything tangible, but his loss of freedom and the psychological impact of being forced away from what is familiar. Homesickness is the closest word for what he feels, but it's also nostalgia, and a regret for choices he made earlier in his life. The British travel

---

* Precisely two thousand years later, in December 2017, Ovid's sentence was formally and unanimously revoked by Rome's city council.

writer Jan Morris declared that 'Ovid writes for millions of us today, whether we are languishing in Guantànamo Bay or beginning to wish we hadn't bought our retirement home in the Dordogne'. That's a pretty broad spread of experience, and I would place Ovid slightly closer to the Dordogne end of that spectrum. Maybe this is a failure of empathy on my part, but I can think of many worse fates, for a poet at least, than spending one's later years writing autobiographical lyric verse in a villa on the Black Sea coast.

Ovid did not, in fact, come from Rome. He was born in the sparsely populated Abruzzo hills of central Italy, more than a day's journey away, and had been sent to Rome by his father to get a good education. He grew to love his adopted city, in which he was a poetic star. Rome had become, in Ovid's lifetime, the headquarters of a growing empire, and home to a multitude of migrants – and Ovid was one of the first to call it the 'capital of the world'. Modern studies of the inscriptions on ancient tombstones, and the scientific analysis of excavated bones and teeth, tell us that the city's inhabitants came from every part of the empire, and beyond. The poet Martial, born in Spain, would later ask a Roman emperor 'what people is so remote, or so barbarous that it cannot be found in your city, O Caesar?'* No answer was needed. And most Romans – though always wary of those living on their borders – were proud of their own complex migrant history.

The story of Rome usually begins, as did this book, with the unhappy wanderings of a Trojan prince. Aeneas does have a

---

* Unlike the Athenians, no one seems to have claimed that Romans were born of the soil. The first-century CE philosopher Seneca saw migration as an undeniable part of the history of all humans: 'What is beyond doubt is that there exists no people which has remained in its place of origin.'

rival here, in the form of wolf-suckled Romulus, who gave the first third of his name to Rome, and who is also said to have founded the city. Perhaps it is best to think of Rome beginning in the imagination, through various versions of its two foundation myths, often clumsily combined, by Virgil, Ovid and a host of writers of the early years of the Roman Empire.

The story of Aeneas can comfortably serve as a universal tale of migration, ancient or modern. There are, though, many versions, and in most of them we can detect the more specific concerns of individual storytellers. In the *Iliad*, Aeneas was a minor character who mattered because he was, according to Homer, the only Trojan destined to survive the war.* By Ovid's time, many centuries later, Aeneas had been transformed into a mythical migrant from the east whose descendants had civilised the badlands of central Italy, and who had begun the process of turning Rome into the 'capital of the world'. Undoubtedly, Aeneas – of royal and divine ancestry – was what some modern governments would term a high-value migrant. He would have been far less valuable to the Romans, symbolically, if he'd been a commoner, or Greek or Phoenician or Persian. The Trojans had become extinct, and Aeneas had brought with him only a small band of fellow migrants. And so, because of their rarity, the Trojans of Rome could contribute to rather than distract from the notion of Roman uniqueness.

Aeneas came to matter even more with the end of the Roman Republic and its replacement by an empire in 27 BCE.

---

* It's for this reason, in Homer's version, that Aeneas is saved by the gods from certain death at the hands of Achilles. As for Aeneas' post-war future, Homer makes no mention of any great journey (that's Odysseus' fate) or of anything that could be interpreted as vaguely Roman. But he refers to Aeneas' destiny, saying, cryptically, that he will become 'the Trojan king, as will his descendants in time to come'. Thereby, Homer provided later writers with the hint of a 'new Troy', or a hook, perhaps, upon which they could hang their stories.

This was because the first Emperor, Augustus, whose descendants – biological and adopted – would rule Rome for almost a century, came from a family that claimed direct descent from Aeneas, and thereby his mother, the goddess Venus. In the *Aeneid*, composed in the early years of Augustus' rule, Virgil describes how his hero, on arriving at the site of Rome, was given a magical shield by his mother. The images on that shield came alive and Aeneas was able to witness scenes from the city's future. The final images he sees are of his heir, Emperor Augustus, seated outside the Temple of Apollo, presiding over the glory of the city of Rome with conquered peoples – 'as various in their dress and weapons as in their speech' – queuing up to present gifts and pay homage to their ruler. Augustus, meanwhile, was very happy to encourage the notion that he was a descendant of a migrant from Troy, though he may have been even more pleased to have a goddess as his ancestor.

In many of the stories that survive, Romulus is a troubled, troubling figure, who kills his twin brother, Remus, and, arguably, encourages rape. He is also a proponent of what some would now refer to as uncontrolled migration. Romulus and Remus are born close to the site of Rome. They are heirs to a royal throne, descendants of Aeneas, sons of the god Mars and victims of a violent family power struggle. As a result of the latter, they are left to die beside a flooding river, but saved by a wolf who suckles them in a cave.

Eventually, in 753 BCE, Romulus founds, or re-founds, Rome. And he needs people for his city. He turns part of Rome into a place of asylum, where fugitives can be safe. And what this means, as spelled out by later Roman writers and their modern translators, is that he lets a 'miscellaneous rabble', 'a rag-tag-and-bobtail of neighbouring peoples', 'a promiscuous crowd of freemen and slaves' settle within the newly built walls. They came 'wanting nothing but a fresh start'. They were what many modern governments would refer to as low-value migrants. The newcomers were all men, and that created a problem for Romulus, which he resolved in a way that would bring him considerable notoriety.

The Rape of the Sabine Women has been the subject of many well-known paintings over the last five hundred years – all of them, as far I can tell, the work of male artists. Most of them show women, in various states of undress, being chased and groped by men, against the backdrop of a great city full of fine architecture. This was not quite how the story of Romulus and the Sabine women was told in Ovid's day. First, Ovid and his fellow writers imagined early Rome as a rough sort of place, full of wooden huts and animals – not a great city. Second, there was no suggestion that, whatever actually happened to the Sabine women, it involved them being naked in public in the centre of Rome. Third, there is a problem with the word 'rape'. The Latin word they used was *raptio*, which is best translated here as 'abduction' – which doesn't exactly let the new migrants off the hook, but indicates that they may not have been responsible for mass rape.

Ovid, for instance, tells the story of the Sabine women in his pre-Tomis *Ars Amatoria*, or the *Art of Love*, a three-volume guide to seduction techniques for men and for women. He is not interested in the context to the story, and whether the men are migrants or not, but only in how the men persuade the women to agree to sex and marriage. Ovid's contemporary Livy treats the story as if it were a real historical event and sets it in a broader political context. He explains that the elders of the neighbouring tribes had decided as a matter of principle not to let their daughters marry the 'fugitives and vagabonds' who had gathered in Rome. And so Romulus, in order to ensure the survival of Rome into the next generation, and to allow the possibility of true love taking its natural course, organised the abduction of the Sabine women.

This, in Livy's account, led to a lengthy war between the Romans and Sabines, which ends only when the Sabine women, now mothers, appeal to their fathers and their husbands to stop killing each other. It's the only point in the story when the voices of the women themselves are heard. And those voices bring peace. The fighting ends, and Romulus and the Sabine king agree to share power. By now, the Sabine women have converted their rough-spoken, ill-mannered consorts into good citizens, who raise families and are respectful towards their in-laws.* Fugitives have become fathers, migrants have been transformed into householders. And Rome is born.

Rome remained insignificant for many centuries, its existence barely noticed by contemporaries elsewhere at a time when Greeks and Carthaginians dominated southern Italy, Sicily and the Mediterranean. But there is one other early story, involving migrants from what is now France, that was widely believed in Ovid's day. It's a story that is far less positive towards migrants than those of Aeneas and Romulus. A story that conjures up images of barbarians at the gates and helps explain the deep, half-excavated complexity of Roman attitudes towards those who came from beyond its frontiers. And why later Romans placed such an emphasis on military power.

In 390 BCE, Rome was, according to its later historians,

---

* A century later, Plutarch echoed Livy's narrative, explaining that for Romulus the abduction took place with 'the fixed purpose of uniting and blending the two peoples in the strongest bonds'. Plutarch recognises that the abducted women were 'indignant' about being kidnapped but suggests that there was no rape. This version became the basis for a 1920s short story, 'The Sobbin' Women', by Stephen Vincent Benet, which in turn inspired the hit 1950s musical *Seven Brides for Seven Brothers*, set in the hills of Oregon. The seven brides are seven town-dwelling women who overcome their initial reluctance, and that of their families, to marry seven hillbilly brothers. At one point the oldest of the brothers, played by Howard Keel, appears carrying a book by Plutarch, and sings these immortal lines: 'Tell ya 'bout them sobbin' women / Who lived in the Roman days. / It seems that they all went swimmin' / While their men was off to graze. / Well, a Roman troop was ridin' by / And saw them in their "me oh my", / So they took 'em all back home to dry. / Least that's what Plutarch says.'

sacked by Gaulish tribesmen, who were said to be in search of good wine and fruit. Livy describes them as 'savage Gauls', 'outlandish warriors armed with strange weapons' chanting 'barbaric songs', who turned Rome into a 'heap of smouldering ruins'. The Gaulish invasion is represented as a nightmare, a great early trauma for Rome. It became a 'never again' moment: the city was rebuilt with high walls, and over the next century it became the dominant power in the Italian peninsula. Rome would be threatened – particularly by the Carthaginian general Hannibal and his mountain-climbing elephants – but not conquered. Or at least not for more than eight hundred years after that Gaulish sack of Rome. And Rome took its revenge on Carthage, destroying the city and burning its library in 146 BCE, the same year it also destroyed Corinth, the last of the great Greek city-states to hold out against Rome. Rome had become a great power.

One hundred and twenty years later Rome was also an empire, born from the ashes of a civil war that ended the Roman Republic. By this time, there is a problem with the word 'Rome'. It denotes a city, then and now, of course. But as Rome grew beyond its hinterland it came to mean much more than a city. It became an imperial capital, a template for civilisation, a source of military and religious power. And Rome came to be defined not by its city limits but by its distant frontiers. All of those living within its borders were, in some senses, Romans, even if most of them didn't have the rights of full citizens.

Much later, Rome the idea could survive without Rome the city. It was as if Rome was really an imaginary city on wheels, that could be trundled off to wherever self-proclaimed Romans wished it to be. But in Ovid's day Rome extended from the North Sea to the Sahara, and from the Atlantic to the

Black Sea.* There were already plenty of Roman citizens who had never set foot in the city itself, who had perhaps bought Roman citizenship or earned it through service, or were soldiers who'd been given land to settle in new colonies, or who were simply children of a Roman citizen.

Take the case of a well-travelled Jewish fifty-something former tentmaker called Paul, or sometimes Saul, who was born in what is now Turkey, and who was arrested in Jerusalem in 57 CE. The exact charges against the man now known as St Paul were not recorded but he was probably accused of defiling a place of worship. This was a serious offence, which might have carried the penalty of death by crucifixion – a fate suffered by a thirty-something carpenter's son named Jesus in the same city two decades earlier. However, unlike Jesus, Paul was a Roman citizen. There's a brief, revealing conversation in the New Testament in which the local commander of the Roman troops asks Paul if he is a Roman citizen. Paul says 'Yes'. The commander is clearly irritated, and tells Paul that it had cost him a lot of money to become a citizen. Paul simply replies, without further explanation, that he had been born a Roman citizen. The point of this is that, by the laws of Rome, Paul could not be crucified, a particularly cruel form of the death penalty considered by the Romans only suitable for slaves and barbarians. And additionally, by uttering the words 'I appeal unto Caesar', Paul could insist on being tried in Rome.

Paul had travelled widely in the eastern Mediterranean, trying to persuade anyone who would listen that Jesus was the son of God. But he had never been to Rome. He left the shores of Palestine by ship, escorted by a friendly centurion called Julius who allowed him to preach wherever they landed, and he was taken on a long, eventful journey via what are

---

* If only he'd been exiled to one of the Roman client states in Palestine, Ovid might have met a teenage carpenter's son called Jesus.

now Lebanon, Cyprus, Turkey, Greece and Malta to Rome, where he lived for two years under house arrest, preaching the gospel, while awaiting his trial. The New Testament account of St Paul the Apostle ends there, but we learn elsewhere that he was executed on the orders of Emperor Nero.* And so died in Rome, a Roman citizen who was also a long, long way from home.

By the time of St Paul, the definition of who was a Roman went beyond language, ethnicity or common descent. It was still undoubtedly an advantage in life if you were born in Rome to an old, rich family – but far less than it had been. The key qualification for being considered Roman was now the ability and willingness to adopt Roman behaviour, to live in a way that was recognisably Roman.

Throughout the provinces of the empire, many dozens, perhaps hundreds, of mini-Romes were built; towns that were inhabited by Romanised local elites, often descend-ants of soldiers from Italy and elsewhere. There were similar buildings and street plans in each of these towns: a public bath, the forum, temples, a theatre and an amphitheatre; there were statues of the emperor, along with roads and a water supply, often from an aqueduct. And there was a simi-lar cast of key individuals: often a governor who might have lived at some point in Rome, and, just as important for the smooth running of the empire, soldiers and tax collectors. Wine drinking was encouraged, and so was the use of Latin, particularly in the western empire, while Greek remained the most important language in the east. Local religions and customs were allowed to survive so long as they did not seek

---

* According to the Apocrypha, Paul was found guilty and decapitated, in the Roman fashion, with a single sword-blow. Milk spurted out of his neck, while his severed head bounced three times down the street, and on each bounce a fountain of water sprang from the ground, at a place marked today by the Church of St Paul at the Three Fountains.

to undermine Roman values. Rome had been brought to the provinces. And before long migrants from the provinces would rule over Rome.

One early example of these provincial mini-Romes was the town of Italica, a few kilometres outside the modern Spanish city of Seville. It dates back to 206 BCE, where it was founded as a settlement for Roman veterans of the war against Carthage and named in honour of the Italian origins of its earliest inhabitants. Italica was not special or unusual, except that more than a quarter of a millennium later it became famous as the birthplace of Trajan, the first Roman emperor who didn't come from Italy. Trajan was a soldier and the son of the soldier, who spent much of his life on the edges of the empire, largely in Syria and along the Danube. He was adopted as the successor to the previous emperor principally because he had the loyalty of many legions of the Roman army.

If there was any criticism of Trajan's appointment on the grounds that he was from Spain it hasn't survived. It's possible of course that no one dared to comment negatively on his origins. However, later on, when the histories were written, Trajan was seen as just the first of dozens of Roman emperors who were born a very long way from Rome. Because, by the third century, it had become quite normal for Rome to be ruled by a migrant.*

Trajan liked to model himself on Alexander the Great, another outsider. And Trajan too led his armies into battle in Asia – though he was in his sixties by then, twice Alexander's age. He conquered Armenia, Mesopotamia and parts of Persia, but lamented that he was too old to continue to India. He turned back and, like his hero, died on the return journey, in southern Turkey, far from either of his putative homelands.

---

* In the third and fourth centuries, fewer than 10 per cent of Roman emperors (there were about fifty of them) were born in what is now Italy. The most common country of origin in this period was modern-day Serbia, with eleven emperors.

Under Trajan, the Roman Empire was at its largest, similar in size to Alexander's. He is remembered, as was intended, for his priapic monolith in the Mediterranean sun, a thirty-metre marble column that bears his name and still stands in the heart of Rome, and whose helical carvings depict the expansion of the Roman Empire beyond the Danube. His successor Hadrian, also from Italica, let the empire shrink a little, and so it is perhaps appropriate that he is best remembered for a distant wall, seventeen hundred kilometres from Rome, in northern Britain.

The precise rationale for Hadrian's Wall is unclear – as has been true with many walls before and since. Some historians argue that it was aimed at keeping out invaders from the north; others that it was a means of controlling more general population flows, or that it served as a rather intimidating customs post, or was simply designed to mark the Roman Empire's northernmost border. What is interesting here, ironic even, is that the very presence of the wall, and, before that, of the older military camps along its route, actually had the effect of drawing significant numbers of migrants from elsewhere in the empire to this part of Britain, for the purpose of guarding the frontier.

Modern excavations at Vindolanda, for instance, a Roman military settlement deep in the Northumbrian countryside, have thrown up some surprises for those, like me, who are searching for the unmediated voices of migrants. A large number of fragments of writing were found, all written in ink on thin pieces of wood. They provide rare glimpses into the routines and excitements of frontier life for people from elsewhere in the Roman Empire, most of them soldiers and their families.* Among the Vindolanda fragments are letters, lists,

---

* The Vindolanda writers would have all claimed a Roman identity, and they wrote in Latin. Many of them have names indicating that they come from what are now Belgium and Germany, and possibly Spain, but not from Italy.

accounts, notes and leave requests. One letter-writer refers dismissively to the *Brittunculi*, or little Britons, who are then ridiculed for throwing their javelins without getting on horseback. And there's a note to a soldier that seems to refer to an accompanying package containing 'some socks and two pairs of underpants' sent by a friend or relative living far away.

But perhaps the most interesting find of all, and one that tells an unexpected migration story, was made not at Vindolanda but near the eastern end of Hadrian's Wall. For here a tombstone was unearthed, with an inscription in two languages – Latin and Aramaic – and a carving of an elegantly dressed woman seated on a wicker chair, a jewellery box at one side, a basket of wool at the other. Her name was Regina (modern writers have been quick to nickname her Queenie), and from the brief Latin inscription we learn quite a lot about her: that she belonged to the Catuvellauni tribe, which dominated the area just north of London and that she had once been a slave. She was purchased by a man called Barates, who set her free and married her, before Regina died at the age of thirty.

It is the identity of her husband that makes this story even more intriguing. Barates came from the other end of the Roman Empire, from the city of Palmyra in the middle of the Syrian desert, almost four thousand kilometres from Hadrian's Wall. And at the end of the Latin inscription on Regina's tombstone, a few extra words have been carved in the cursive Palmyrene script of Aramaic. They say simply: 'Regina, freedwoman of Barates, alas!' It's hard not to be touched by the sad Syrian–British love story of Regina and Barates. But what is also striking about the wording of the inscriptions is their directness. There is no pretence of self-importance, or high lineage. And there is no embarrassment about being a migrant, or about using one's mother tongue, or about the mixing of people from different continents and social backgrounds. These are matters to be recorded, as a matter of fact, for posterity.

Barates was not the only Syrian in Britain in the early years of the third century CE. For there was also Julia Domna, the wife of the Emperor Septimius Severus, who spent two years in Britain while her husband attempted, unsuccessfully, to subdue what is now Scotland. Julia and Severus were a well-travelled couple with an impressively intercontinental range of ancestors. And neither of them came from Europe – though each did claim a sprinkling of ancient Roman ancestry. Julia was born into the priestly royal family of Arabic-speaking Emesa, now Homs, in Syria. Severus, born in Libya, is often described as the first African emperor (there were at least two others). He was also probably the first not to have Latin as his mother tongue.

Severus had lots of enemies, but none, as far as we can tell, on account of his origins. Apart from a later reference to his non-Roman accent in speaking Latin, there's nothing to suggest that his contemporaries saw any great significance in his North African heritage. By this time, it was quite normal for men (and occasionally women) from a very wide range of ethnic backgrounds to be in positions of real authority – and often a long way from their place of birth. Second-century Britain had at least three governors from North Africa and two from what is now Croatia, while the four emperors who followed Severus were born in what are now France, Algeria, Lebanon and Bulgaria.

This certainly didn't turn the Roman Empire into some kind of multicultural utopia. To be emperor you needed soldiers and money and good fortune and ruthlessness, and you would then get to rule what was a slave-owning, heavily militaristic despotism – and then there was a good chance that you would be killed on the battlefield or murdered in your own bed. But it is noticeable that Rome does seem, certainly by the standards of today, to have been colour-blind, in the sense that skin pigmentation is barely mentioned. And any disadvantage that might come from having a different appearance, from speaking Latin with an unusual accent, from not having spent one's childhood in Rome, could be easily overcome, especially if there were a few legions at one's side.*

Gradually, then, a small elite of Roman citizens drawn from the provinces had come to play an increasingly large role in the running of the empire. But the vast majority of people living in the empire beyond Italy were not Roman citizens. That changed in 212 CE, when the Emperor Caracalla, the son of Severus and Julia, born in Lyon of Syrian-Libyan heritage, introduced a law which decreed that all freemen living within the frontiers of the empire should become Roman citizens, and similarly that all freewomen of the empire should have the same status as freewomen in Rome. One modern historian believes this may have been the biggest grant of citizenship in the history of the world, affecting more than thirty million people. The old hierarchy of citizenship rights and privileges was swept away (though new ones soon replaced them). It's not clear why Caracalla took this step. It may have been to increase tax revenue, or to please the majority of Roman soldiers, who served in the auxiliaries. It meant that large numbers of people who didn't speak Latin or Greek, who had not in any real sense been 'Romanised', who were once considered barbarians, were now citizens of the Roman Empire.

---

* One much later writer, the sixth-century John Malalas of Antioch, said Septimius Severus was dark-skinned. He was also said to have been embarrassed by the fact that his sister hardly spoke any Latin. Severus died of an infection in York in 210 CE, and became the first of two Roman emperors to die in that city (the other was Constantius, the father of Constantine, in 306 CE). Julia Domna died much closer to home, killing herself in Antioch shortly after the assassination of her son Caracalla. He was killed by a centurion while having a pee outside Harran in modern Turkey, the city where the biblical patriarch Abraham spent much of his youth.

About sixteen hundred years ago, a man called Gaiseric, who was probably born in modern Hungary, but whose ancestors came from further north, crossed the Mediterranean near Gibraltar with a large army. He then travelled along the coast of North Africa and captured Carthage, which had been under Roman rule for almost six hundred years, and made it his home. Gaiseric and his descendants ruled Carthage for ninety-four years. They were Christians, and the remains of the churches at which they prayed can be explored amid the ruins of old Carthage in the northern suburbs of Tunis. Gaiseric was also a Vandal, indeed the king of the Vandals, a group of people whose reputation, carried by their name, has been sullied by time.

The Vandals are key players in the final part of this Roman narrative, in which, according to the traditional telling of the story, Rome, the greatest empire of them all, was destroyed by migrants from the north and east. Huns and Goths and Lombards and Alans and others are also part of this story, and they are usually imagined as unlettered barbarians intent on destruction. In fact, much of this story is either untrue or misleading, and perhaps represents the greatest demonisation of migrants until modern times. But to place what became known as the 'barbarian invasions' in context, it's helpful to zoom out a little, in time and in place, before returning to the Vandals.

The notion of the barbarian is a complex one, in antiquity and more recently. It would ultimately spawn a broad collection of other terms: mostly pejorative, such as barbaric and barbarism, but sometimes descriptive – the Berbers, the Barbary Coast. It is a word and a notion that is critical to understanding the changing Roman worldview, and more specifically how the Romans imagined those who lived close to their frontiers. It's Greek originally, onomatopoeically describing the sound of someone speaking an incomprehensible language. And the earliest Greek writers, such as Herodotus, used it neutrally, without judgement, to describe those whose speech could not be understood. But by the later Greek period it had become a negative term, with implications of savagery and stupidity, and that's largely the meaning that was carried forward into Latin (and other languages). But just as 'Roman' is a word whose meaning changes as the Empire grows, so too does the meaning of 'barbarian'. The word 'barbarian' becomes, more often than not, the antonym of 'Roman'.

Despite this, there was no monolithic Roman view of barbarians. Indeed, Roman accounts of them are full of local stereotypes: that the Gauls were war-mad, while the Irish were promiscuous and the Ethiopians were crafty and cowardly. Occasionally Roman writers would even turn the description on themselves: Ovid, always glorying in self-pity, declared from exile 'here I'm the barbarian, understood by nobody'.* During the empire, barbarians tended to be identified more specifically with northern and eastern Europeans, and with tribal groups who were also a source of slaves and soldiers for Rome.

For the historian Tacitus, writing his *Germania* at the end of the first century, all Germans were barbarians – but this was not an entirely negative judgement. By the standards of his time, Tacitus was friendly towards barbarians, and it is possible to trace in his writings an early version of the idea of the uncorrupted noble savage, contrasted favourably with a corrupt Roman imperial administrator. There are occasional barbarian generalisations – Tacitus tells his readers that Germans 'are almost unique among barbarians in being satisfied with one

---

* The Roman orator and philosopher Cicero, meanwhile, was wise enough to recognise that the Greeks would have seen early Latin speakers as barbarians. In the *Republic*, he has Scipio Aemilianus, the man who led the final assault on Carthage, ask 'Now tell me then, was Romulus a king of the barbarians?' Scipio later answers his own question, suggesting that being a barbarian is a matter of character, not race.

wife each' – but more generally he questioned the stereotyping of Germanic barbarians by pointing to the differences among them – in customs, beliefs, behaviour, weapons, hairstyles and attitudes towards Rome.

In fact, Tacitus probably never visited the areas he described – the lands east of the Rhine and north of the Danube, an area much larger than modern Germany – and relied on often fanciful tales from other travellers and writers. But the text of *Germania* became influential as a model for what much later would be called ethnography, as well as for its invention of a proto-German identity – and, thereby, for its purported influence on Nazi ideas.

Most of the tribes mentioned by Tacitus soon disappear from the historical record, and some may never have existed in the first place. But buried deep in the text are early mentions, in passing, of three groups who live in Germania: the *Anglii*, the *Gotones* and the *Vandilios*, whose later migrations will form part of this and many other stories, and who are better known now as the English, the Goths and the Vandals.

Tacitus had a very Rome-centred view of the world, and of Germania. Those Germans who lived closest to the Roman Empire were most like the Romans. They were sedentary and more likely to accept Roman rule and follow Roman customs, while those who lived further away were strange, often sub-human and sometimes monstrous. For instance, the Fenni, possibly the modern Finns, are described as 'astonishingly wild and horribly poor; they have no weapons, no horses, no homes; they eat grass, dress in skins, and sleep on the ground'. And Tacitus says he has heard that beyond the Fenni there are tribes of people 'with the faces and features of men, but the bodies and limbs of animals'.

He's not the first to tell such stories of monstrous humans living far away, and it is a common trope in early Greek and Chinese writings. But it is also a reminder that the Romans, for all their learning,* knew almost nothing about the distant lands far beyond their borders. They had little interaction with nomads, the majority of the world's population, until large numbers of them appear in eastern Europe in about 370 CE.

The Goths and the Vandals (but not the English) played an important role in what befell the Roman Empire. They each sacked Rome, forty-five years apart, in the fifth century – two events that elevate them to the position of prime suspects for a crime that is not always easy to classify. After all, this was no murder, for Rome did not die. Rome remained the home of the pope and of the Catholic Church, even if it was no longer the most important city in the empire to which it gave its name. And a large part of that empire continued to flourish, still calling itself Roman, with its capital in Constantinople, and surviving until 1453 – while the Holy Roman Empire, a reborn version of the western part of the empire, survived in name until 1806.

Undoubtedly, the Roman Empire was by then very different from the one ruled by Augustus, or Hadrian or Severus, but that transformation had begun long before the Goths and the Vandals and Huns moved into southern Europe. The administrative partition of the eastern and western parts of the Roman Empire took place in 285 CE, and the conversion to Christianity less than thirty years later. A modern German historian of ancient Rome, Alexander Demandt, has

---

* This is a feature of much ancient writing, and is often echoed in more recent narratives about outer space. The world (or universe) is imagined as a series of concentric circles, with the imperial city, or the city of the writer, at its centre. As you pass through each circle, its inhabitants become progressively more savage, more barbarous, more animal-like – until, in the outer circle, are humans who share body features with other animals.

pulled together 210 reasons, from a variety of sources, for the decline of the Roman Empire. It's a wonderfully eclectic and inclusive list (gout, soil erosion, lethargy and childlessness are among the reasons), but it would be foolish to pretend that migrations from northern and eastern Europe didn't play a major role in the transformation of the Roman Empire. Just as it would also be foolish simply to blame migrants for that transformation.

Take the devastating events of 376–8 CE, often referred to as the start of the 'decline and fall' of the Roman Empire, and most instructive in terms of the history of telling migration-related stories. Here are two two-sentence versions of the same events, both of them factually accurate, each of which show the same group of migrants in a very different light.

1. A Roman emperor allowed a large group of migrants to enter his territory. They murdered him.
2. A Roman emperor allowed a large group of migrants to be treated with great cruelty. They murdered him.

Now here's my own one-paragraph, studiously neutral version, based largely on an account by the contemporary Roman writer Ammianus.

A large group of migrants gathered on the northern bank of the River Danube. They received permission from Emperor Valens to resettle in Roman territory, as he saw the migrants as a source of new recruits for his army. These migrants entered the Roman Empire in small boats, or by swimming, though some of the swimmers drowned. The migrants, perhaps ninety thousand of them, were herded into make-shift camps, where there was no food. The Roman military authorities sold them dog-meat at the price of one person given up into slavery in exchange for one dog. Eventually the migrants broke free of the camps and joined up with other migrants from the same community forming armed bands of men who headed southwards. There, some time later, they met the forces of Emperor Valens on the battle-field, and Valens was killed in the fighting.

Already, the story has become more complex, and it is harder to assign blame.*

However, this version still fails to include the wider context, which relates critically to the identity of the migrants and why they were on the move. These migrants were Goths, who had been living in what is now Ukraine, and they were fleeing another group of migrants, the Huns. Ammianus is critical of everyone involved, but is, on the whole, more sympathetic to the Goths. They are portrayed as savage, but also, particularly while staying in the camps, as victims. Ammianus refers to the dog-selling, slave-buying Roman generals as 'hateful' and their actions as 'disgraceful' and 'atrocious', while the Emperor Valens is described with a series of harsh adjectives: irresolute, unjust, uneducated and hot-tempered.

Ammianus reserves his strongest and more eloquent criticism for a different group of migrants: the Huns, invaders from the east, in terms that almost deny them their humanity. They are, he says

> so monstrously ugly and misshapen, that one might take them for two-legged beasts ... they are so hardy in their mode of life that they have no need of fire nor of savoury food, but eat the roots of wild plants and the half-raw flesh of any kind of animal whatever, which they put between their

---

* Mary Beard, the modern historian of Rome, does draw a clear message from these events: 'Cruelty to refugees can have terrible consequences. And that probably is a lesson.'

thighs and the backs of their horses, and thus warm it a little. They are never protected by any buildings ... For not even a hut thatched with reed can be found among them. But roaming at large amid the mountains and woods, they learn from the cradle to endure cold, hunger and thirst. When away from their homes they never enter a house unless compelled by extreme necessity; for they think they are not safe when staying under a roof. They dress in linen cloth or in the skins of field-mice sewn together, and they wear the same clothing indoors and out.

Ammianus' description of the Huns is remarkable partly because it shows how unfamiliar Romans were with nomadic lifestyles, and how disparaging they were about them. The empire was ringed by 'barbarians' who were largely settled and, to a significant degree, Romanised. But the Huns – to many Romans – were the stuff of nightmares.

These events matter, because they represent the start, in Roman and later accounts, of great new convulsions in Europe – an age in which the movement of large communities, often tens of thousands of people, became normal. The migration of Huns from Asia had a kind of domino effect, with consequences for almost every part of the continent, and for North Africa. It was at school that I learnt to call these events the 'Barbarian Invasions'* and I remember being spellbound by a multicoloured map with that title, covered in long thick arrows, many pointing at Rome, and the name of a particular groups of 'barbarians' written on each arrow.

The Huns, for instance, swept westwards across the centre of the map, but never quite made it to Rome or to the

---

* Historians now tend to use the less evocative, and less tendentious, description 'The Migration Period' to describe the time from about 386 to 568. The older phrase has its defenders, particularly among those who argue that barbarians, then and now, threaten the destruction of great civilisations.

Atlantic, though they did reach northern Italy and central France. The Goths – often chased by the Huns – did reach both Rome and the Atlantic, and at one point controlled much of the northern Mediterranean coast. The Vandals appeared to take the most convoluted route, westwards from central Europe via Spain, then south to Morocco and eastwards to Carthage, which became their capital, before travelling north to Sicily and Rome. Meanwhile, the Angles, from what are now the Danish–German borderlands, had one of the shortest trips, across the sea to lands that would later be named after them.*

As a schoolboy, I delighted in the fact that so many of these barbarian groups had an afterlife, and not just as place-names. That the word 'Hun', for instance, became a pejorative twentieth-century nickname for Germans; most inappropriately, I now know, because they were one of the few migrant groups who definitely weren't Germanic. Gothic came to describe a kind of medieval architecture – despised at first and then much loved, often contrasted with Romanesque – as well as a style of handwriting, a genre of fiction, a kind of rock music and, most recently, a gloomy dressed-in-black youth subculture.

And the Vandals? Well, they pulled the shortest straw, and spawned the word 'vandalism' and a host of similar terms in a wide range of modern European languages. And the Vandals themselves have been largely forgotten. I've been asking friends and strangers, and discovered that there are lots of well-educated non-historians in different countries who are aware of the Huns (Attila!) and the Goths. But many had never heard of the Vandals ('a rock band?'), who were

---

* Whereas the Lombards headed south into Italy, and the Franks westwards, also into lands that would come to bear their names. Some Saxons headed across the Channel to Britain, and their place of origin would survive in the names of three English counties: Essex, Sussex and Middlesex.

among the best-travelled migrants of the ancient world, whose kingdom ruled North Africa and many of the islands of the Mediterranean for longer than any of Rome's imperial dynasties. And no one seems to know about Gaiseric, the King of the Vandals for forty-nine years.

Now, the Vandals led by Gaiseric undeniably looted Rome in 455 CE but they didn't, it seems, vandalise anything. Indeed, they did not kill or rape or burn (as other 'barbarians' had in Rome and elsewhere), and they may even have been invited into the city by the widow of the emperor. As for specific acts of vandalism, there is just one uncorroborated story of an unsuccessful attempt to remove the gilded bronze ceiling of the Temple of Jupiter, and that's all. Unlike the Goths and the Lombards, no history of the Vandals has survived from ancient times, and this perhaps has made them easier to demonise. Modern historians have had to piece together their story from other writings and from archaeology. From what evidence survives, it appears that the Vandals were not stereotypical barbarians. There was a striking continuity with the Roman period in North Africa in terms of administrative structures, key personnel, fashion, the continuing use of Latin and the Christian religion. And through intermarriage the Vandals began to merge with the older Roman elite.* They were not agents of destruction, and more generally there is no real basis for the notion that the Vandals were vandals.

They almost disappear from the historical record until the sixteenth century. When they reappear, in the inventive minds of early European nationalists, the Vandals are barely recognisable. They became heroes in Germany and villains in France. Neither version bears much resemblance to the

---

* The great Roman general Stilicho had a Vandal father and a Roman mother, while Hilderic, the penultimate King of the Vandals, had a Roman emperor, Valentinian III, as his maternal grandfather.

ancient Vandals. The heroic version was born in the Duchy of Mecklenburg, on Germany's Baltic coast, where it was decided to adopt the Vandals as ancient and glorious ancestors; a piece of historical fiction soon appropriated by other Baltic states. While the villainous version spread by the French, with some English support, blamed the Vandals, on skimpy evidence, for devastating attacks on Gaul in 406 CE, almost fifty years before they plundered Rome.

It was the villainous version that won out, almost by accident, with the coining in 1794 of the word *vandalisme* by a revolutionary French priest called Abbé Grégoire, who used it to describe and condemn the actions of fellow revolutionaries who defaced or destroyed works of art. It's a meaning that soon caught on, despite criticism from some German scholars who claimed that the word was 'an insult to their ancestors, who were warriors and not destroyers'. Grégoire failed to say why he chose the term 'vandalism'.*

I, meanwhile, seem to have developed a soft spot for the Vandals, a sentimental obsession with this group of migrants who have been maligned by their own name. The reputation of the Neanderthals has suffered similarly, but it is not as if their existence has been relegated to a footnote. The word 'vandal' has become like quisling, or boycott or sandwich – terms for which only pedants and pub quizzers know the origins. I have to hold myself back from objecting when anyone uses the word 'vandalise'. And I may have become boring on the subject.

---

* According to modern experts on the Vandals, it may just have sounded better than the slightly more appropriate alternatives: Gothicism or Lombardism. Others have pointed to the stories of Vandals persecuting fellow Christians from a different sect and destroying their churches, though there's little evidence of this either.

I find myself searching in obscure places for vestiges of the Vandals, but there are usually none. These European migrants to North Africa left no great buildings, and almost no minor ones – there's one in southern Tunisia, consisting of the ruined arcades of a forgotten church. There have been a few other finds: jewellery, bronze and silver coins, grave goods, ancient land records, inscriptions. Some household mosaics in Carthage and elsewhere have been dated to the Vandal period, including one now in the British Museum, with a man waving as he leaves a city on horseback. I have taken to wandering around those parts of ancient Carthage closest to my home in Tunis, seeking out the untended ruins of the churches where the Vandals once prayed. There are three churches near me: one high on a cliff top, windswept, looking out to sea; another beside a major road, the full out-line of the nave and the apse visible from a passing car, and my favourite: a few sad fallen columns and the remains of a crypt in the middle of a field, only visible when the wheat has been harvested.

I'm still on the lookout for Vandal memorabilia, but a recent discovery taught me to laugh at myself, to take this obsession a little less seriously. With a friend, I visited Cap Bon, a long peninsula to the south-east of Tunis, in order to swim in the sea and search for more ruins – Carthaginian and Roman and Vandal. Cap Bon was the site of one of the great battles of ancient times, when a Roman force of more than a thou-sand ships was defeated by a smaller Vandal navy, which sent unmanned burning boats into the midst of the Roman fleet. But I could find no trace of the Vandals, not even a modern-day mention on a museum signboard. Proof, I lamented, that once again the poor Vandals had been forgotten.

And then as I walked down a backstreet in the town of Klebia, having located all its Roman ruins, I saw some-thing that made me laugh out loud, embarrassed by my own

pompous sentimentality, and delighting in the ingenuity of a graffiti artist. It was an understated postmodern joke, written in white paint on a half-built wall. And the graffiti took the form of just one word. Vandals.

A FOURTH INTERMISSION

Soon, I shall be leaving Tunis. It's been my home for more than a year, and is the place where most of this book – so far – has been written. My impending departure has put me in an introspective mood, thinking about where I might move next, and reflecting on these early chapters and the authorial decisions I have made. Because living here, on the southern shores of the Mediterranean, close to the ruins of Carthage, has undoubtedly affected the migration stories I have chosen to investigate, and coloured my views of the distant past. All of us who write have our backstories, our motivations, our dilemmas. Some of us try to hide them away or judiciously claim that we've put them to one side, fearing perhaps we will lose authority by being open about our quandaries and our choices. I prefer to be overt and unashamed about mine, and let readers know and judge. And so, yes, there is more of Carthage and the Mediterranean than might otherwise have been the case. And for those who've read anything else I have written, there's far less of India, once my home for more than decade, than they might have expected.

I am now faced with fresh choices. And not only over where to live. As I speed through the millennia, moving closer to the present, I am dealing with a series of dilemmas. Let me explain. This book does not aim to be a comprehensive history of attitudes toward migration. But it does seek to tell what I think of as important stories from the past in a slightly different way; through a prism in which migration is a normal activity, and in which migration may even serve as a key to making greater sense of the human condition. Now those two words, 'important stories', are becoming just a little imprecise for my purpose as I prepare to plunge into the post-Roman period. Because, quite simply, there are many dozens of stories that might be described as important, and for which there is at least some literary and archaeological source material. However, I will have to leave out many of them.

This isn't an entirely new dilemma: I am aware that I have already excluded stories that I might have included – from Japan, South-East Asia, Egypt and sub-Saharan Africa for instance. But it is one that has become more tangible, more pressing as I start to consider medieval migration. And for that reason, I feel the need to spell out my purpose more clearly, and to explain what I am trying to achieve.

It's a huge simplification, but the central dilemma runs something like this:

Do I choose those migration episodes that have been underplayed or overlooked, which are little-known and deserve attention, and which have largely been excluded or eclipsed by those grand, dominant Europe-centred historical narratives?

or

Do I directly confront those dominant narratives, the ones that Westerners, and many others, learn at school, by con-centrating on the better-known migration stories?

I have chosen the latter course. That feels to me like the need of the hour – because, by its very nature, it challenges, by stealth and implication and sometimes more directly, many of our modern assumptions about migration, at a time when the migration debate has become so toxic.

And in choosing this course my task has become clearer. As I head into what is known (in Europe, mainly) as the Middle Ages, I will resist the temptation to go global. And so I will ignore, in this book at least, the great migrations that followed the collapse of the Mayan Empire in Central America in 900 CE, or the dispersal of the Fulani people across a broad stretch of Africa south of the Sahara, or the nomadic empires of the Mongols, or the arrival of the first humans in New Zealand in the thirteenth century, or the displacement of the indigenous Ainu from large parts of Japan. Instead, migrants from the European periphery – first Muslims and then Vikings, with the briefest of overlaps – will appear centre stage. And I will set the scene by skipping around the fringes of Europe and the Middle East on the medieval coat-tails of those most mobile of religions, Christianity and Islam. Two religions whose theologies were always intertwined, and whose empires and conquests and triumphs and failures continue to dominate so many political and historical narratives – and, I will argue, the way we think of migration, now and in the past.

As for me, I do not know where I will live next. My time here in Tunis has run its course. My work, my day job at the BBC, is almost complete. I will miss this city, and my friends here. At times, it has felt like the perfect place for me: it is warm, by the sea, tolerant, intriguing, a throwback perhaps to a calmer world of seasonal food and siestas. And I did think of staying on, dropping anchor on the southern shores of the Mediterranean. But something else impels me to leave. A sense that I need to be on the move, to explore the world I do not know, as a way of feeling alive and human. And so I will briefly return to London, the city of my childhood, and stay in the house of my birth, still occupied by my mother, and visit old friends and flames and family – and draw breath before I set off again.

CHAPTER FIVE

Arabs, Vikings and Neo-Trojans

Let me resume with another brief, extraordinary story: the tale of a migrant, a second Aeneas, who survived a war and a terrifying journey from Asia to start a new life in Europe. I'm temporarily withholding, once again, the nationality and religion of the migrant.

AR was a well-connected man of about twenty, who happened to be on the losing side of a civil war. The victors in the war, who spoke the same language and practised the same religion as AR, had captured the great city in which he lived. They killed almost every member of his extended family. AR escaped with his thirteen-year-old brother, both of them trying to swim across a wide river to avoid capture. Their pursuers called from the riverbank, promising they would be safe if they returned. AR's younger brother believed them and swam back. He was beheaded. AR continued to the far side.

Eventually, AR reached North Africa, and in Tunisia he stayed with people whom he thought were friends. But they turned against him, and he only escaped by hiding beneath the skirts of the wife of a local chieftain as they searched for him. He then travelled further west, reaching Morocco, where he rested and where he was joined by others who had fled from his city. And he made plans to cross to the Spanish province of Andalusia, where his family had owned large tracts of land.

AR landed in Europe near Malaga, and gathered a small group of supporters. The ruler of Andalusia feared him, and tried to buy him off by offering him a comfortable estate and his daughter in marriage. But AR believed it was his birthright to recover his family's lost land. He defeated the ruler in battle and took control of a large swathe of southern Spain, based in his capital Cordoba. AR and his heirs ruled Andalusia for the next 275 years.

Aficionados of Arab, early Islamic and Spanish history will have guessed the identity of AR. He was Abd al-Rahman, prince and poet, a Muslim Arab with a Berber mother, often referred to by his Arabic nickname 'Dakhil', or 'the Immigrant', and who was born and raised in what is now Syria. He was said to have been the only adult male heir to survive the massacre of the Umayyad dynasty in and around Damascus in 750 CE, after which he fled eastwards, swimming across the Euphrates, where his brother was murdered. He then doubled back into Palestine and across North Africa, before crossing the Mediterranean and establishing himself and his descendants as the rulers of what had been an outlying part of his family's empire in Andalusia.*

Abd al-Rahman ruled for thirty-two years. He and his successors helped create a multicultural Arabic-speaking empire in Europe, famed now and then, fairly or not, for both its tolerance and learning. But despite his extraordinary success in

* One possible and much quoted source of the name Andalusia is Vandalusia – or land of the Vandals. The Vandals ruled much of southern Spain in the early fifth century. Others argue that Andalusia was a corruption of 'Atlantic'.

creating a new realm for himself (and driving off the forces of the French emperor Charlemagne), Abd al-Rahman was never really happy in Spain and wished he could return to his homeland. He named his favourite Spanish palace Rusafa, after the walled Syrian city in which he spent much of his childhood, and one day wrote a poem, a paean to homesickness, when he came upon a single sad palm tree that reminded him of home.

> A palm tree stands in the middle of Rusafa,
> Born in the west, far from the land of palms
> I said to it: How like me you are, far away and in exile,
> In long separation from family and friends.
> You have sprung from soil in which you are a stranger;
> And I, like you, am far from home.

Abd al-Rahman was unusual among Arabs – of this and earlier periods – in making such a public proclamation of his homesickness. For there is a longer, deeper, pre-Islamic tradition among many Arabs of the opposite, of exaggerating their mobility, of mythologising their nomadic past, and of romanticising desert life. And it's that tradition that helps explain why both the camel and the tent remain important symbols of Arab identity. Some etymologists argue that the word 'Arab' originally meant 'nomad' and carried with it the sense of a shared mobile lifestyle. It's become one of those unresolvable circular linguistic debates, since, at the time when we first have a record of the word Arab being used, by sedentary Mesopotamians in 853 BCE, most Arabs were nomadic. And that very first reference is to a named Arab, Gindibu, who, we are informed, owned a thousand camels.

Many of these earliest references are to Arabs as camel-riding nomadic warriors or traders. And when we begin to read the words of Arabs themselves – more than half a millennium later – camels and tents play a central role, as do tribal genealogies, goats, horses and bawdy humour. Now, not all pre-Islamic Arabs were nomads, and the town of Mecca was an important centre of trade and pilgrimage long before the Prophet Muhammad was born there in 570 CE. But pre-Islamic Arabic identity seems to converge around a culture of wandering or migration of various kinds, which took the form of nomadic pastoralism – and of long-distance trading and raiding.

There were also, for instance, the so-called 'brigand poets', *su'luks* in Arabic, who flourished in the century before the birth of the Prophet. They were young men of the desert, often from princely families, who played the role of risk-taking romantic vagabonds, living off the land, writing poetry, almost dying, getting drunk, seducing women and rejecting the conventional ties of tribe and village. Typical was the hard-drinking libertine Imrul Qays, whose love-in-the-desert poems are still widely read in the Middle East. Bosoms and tent-flaps and camel metaphors feature liberally – and one slender girlfriend had, he claims, a waist as 'thin as the twisted leather nose-rein of a camel'. Imrul Qays was, like Abd al-Rahman, a princely poet, but one who wandered freely by horse and camel – 'Have I not worn out my mounts, in every wind-blown waste?'*

It is also possible to detect something deeper here, in all this romantic desert-talk: real wisdom, perhaps, in the form of what was almost a philosophy of nomadism. An unnamed Arab at the pre-Islamic court of the Persian king Khusrow declared that his people 'own the land without it owning them. They are secure from the need to fortify themselves with walls.' This

---

* Imrul Qays died near Ankara – killed, legend has it, by a poisoned jacket given to him by the Byzantine Emperor Justinian, whose daughter he is supposed to have seduced. In fact, Justinian – whose armies reconquered the Vandal territories of North Africa – didn't have a daughter. It's more likely that Imrul Qays died of plague on his way back from meeting Justinian in Constantinople.

same man also talked of the great danger of cities and of sedentary lifestyles, saying that his people had

> weighed up the matter of cities and buildings and found
> them not only wanting, but also harmful – for places suffer
> illness as do bodies ... So they dwelt in the far-spreading
> lands which are free from pollution, full of fresh air, and
> insulated from plagues.

These judicious words would soon be ignored, and in the following centuries – the first centuries of Islam – Arabs began to
pride themselves on being great city-builders.

Before long the centre of gravity of the overlapping Islamic
and Arab worlds had shifted away from the deserts and small
towns of the Arabian peninsula to new and reconstructed
cities in the Middle East and beyond: Damascus, Baghdad,
Samarkand, Cairo, Kairouan and Cordoba. And so it was that
Abd al-Rahman, when he fled Damascus, did not seek shelter in the desert lands of his ancestors, but travelled instead
far to the west, to another city. His destination, the capital
of his new empire, Cordoba, became, by the tenth century,
one of the most populous cities in the world, possibly rivalled
by Baghdad, each of them controlled by competing Islamic
caliphates. These were sophisticated cities, bigger than any in
Christian Europe, and understandably proud of their power
and affluence, their palaces and libraries.

From this perspective, then, it seems almost obvious that the
rise of Islam might be depicted as a triumph of sedentarism and of
urbanism; a tale of nomads and traders who had become householders and palace-dwellers. But it is also possible to develop an
alternative narrative, which allowed and encouraged and even,
occasionally, glorified the act of migration. Let me explain, in
a version that incorporates stories from the life of the Prophet
Muhammad and his well-travelled companions and successors.

Muhammad himself came from a trading family based in Mecca, already a centuries-old place of pagan pilgrimage, as part of a society that was far more multicultural than modern Saudi Arabia, with large communities of Christians, Jews and worshippers of other gods. After his mother died, he was cared for by a woman from Ethiopia. His immediate family members were not nomads but were quite comfortable travelling long distances for work. Two of his uncles were traders, using the old caravan routes that passed through Mecca. One of them went regularly to Yemen to buy perfumes, which were then sold to pilgrims. Another, his guardian after he was orphaned, took the young Muhammad to Syria on a trading expedition. And as a young adult he worked for a merchant called Khadija. She sent him to Syria, and they were later married.* Muhammad then settled down to a more sedentary family life in Mecca, and when he was about forty, he began disappearing off to the nearby hills to meditate. It was there, in a cave, that he first heard the words of God, revealed by the archangel Gabriel and later transcribed as the Quran.

Two migrations mark the very early history of Islam between the revelation of the Quran in 610 CE and the death of the Prophet twenty-two years later. Both were driven by a mixture of necessity and prudence, in the face of intense opposition to the new religion from the old ruling families of Mecca. That first longer migration began in 615 CE, when Muhammad sent more than eighty of his followers by land and sea to the Christian kingdom of Aksum in what is now northern Ethiopia. There, they sought and received protection. It is too often forgotten in telling the story of the early triumphs

---

* According to some accounts, a young Muhammad was sent away to live with nomadic Bedouins outside Mecca: to immerse himself in desert life, to toughen him up and to improve his Arabic. This was a common practice then, not so different from British aristocrats sending small children to boarding school, but which in this case did not entrench class divisions but instead created lifelong ties between nomadic and sedentary families.

of Islam that the first community of Muslims outside Mecca was formed by a small group of migrants to Africa, who settled there, temporarily, under the protection of a Christian ruler.

The second migration, known as the *hegira*, took place in 622 CE, when Muhammad and all his followers left Mecca – fearing for their lives and the eradication of the new faith. The migrants regrouped in Yathrib, soon to be renamed Medina, which simply means 'city' in Arabic. They received a mixed welcome in their new home, which had large polytheist and Jewish communities and just a few very recent converts to Islam. However, the number of converts grew, as did the number of their non-Muslim allies, and seven years later Muhammad was able to return in triumph to Mecca. But Medina remained his capital city, where he was proud to be referred to as a *muhajir*, a migrant, as were all Muslims from Mecca.*

But there's another deeper, symbolic significance to the migration to Medina. For the *hegira* marks the start of Year One of the Islamic calendar, still used in many parts of the Muslim world. Read any newspaper from a Muslim country, and there on the masthead is the Islamic date with the letters AH after it. That letter H (and the Arabic letter ه) stands for *hegira*, and so AH, glossed either as *Anno Hegira*, or 'After *Hegira*', has become the equivalent of AD or CE. The Islamic era, then, began not with the revelation of God's word, or the birth or death of the Prophet, but with a simple act of migration – placing the reality or possibility of migration at the heart of the story of Islam.

The Islamic era would continue with more migrations, and many conquests. Within a hundred years, Arabs controlled an empire that was probably larger than Rome's at its height. It extended from the Atlantic to the Indus, reaching in the same year, 711 CE or 92 AH, what are now southern Spain

* Partly for this reason, *muhajir*, still used in Arabic as the word for migrant, usually has positive connotations. *Hegira*, meanwhile, is a medieval Latin version of the related Arabic word *hijra*, meaning 'migration'.

and southern Pakistan. And these new Islamic territories were ruled, in name at least, by one man, the caliph, living in Damascus. It was an astonishingly successful start for these early converts to a new monotheistic religion – in sharp contrast, for instance, to the centuries of persecution faced by early Christians. And the success of Islam is explained in large part by the role of migrants – soldiers, administrators and preachers – who travelled from the Arabian heartland and elsewhere to the borders of the new empire, and beyond.

It's worth stopping, briefly, to look at other comparisons to be made with early Christianity – in which the similarities are more striking than the differences, especially over migration. Yes, undoubtedly, it took Islam a much shorter time than Christianity to build its first earthly empire. But both religions were, in their theology and their practice, highly mobile faiths, migratory even. Neither was tied to a particular territory or ethnic group, despite the early significance of their holy places and of their founding fathers. They do not, in any formal sense, belong to a specific community or place, in contrast, say, to Judaism or Hinduism. And their founders may not have been long-distance migrants themselves, but smaller migrations were very much part of their stories – Jesus, after all, was born on the move, a homeless migrant in Bethlehem and a refugee in Egypt, while Muhammad went to Medina to escape persecution. And they both encouraged their followers to migrate, in order to spread the new word of God.

And so the growth of each religion was shaped by the desire to convert non-believers, and this meant travelling away from their holy places, the places where their founders were born and died. Early Christians and early Muslims were proud of those first outsiders, non-Jews and non-Arabs respectively, who joined their faith – though all of those who followed Jesus in his lifetime were Jewish. Cornelius, a Roman centurion, is usually referred to as the first non-Jewish Christian, though there's another possible candidate, an unnamed Ethiopian eunuch mentioned in the New Testament. As for Islam, there's a list of at least two dozen non-Arabs – Africans, Persians, Romans and others – who became Muslims and companions of the Prophet. Both religions made a point of welcoming former slaves, and had an early commitment to equality, among men at least, which was always more visible in theory than in practice, and which has dissipated over time. And both religions seemed content in principle with intermarriage between different racial and linguistic groups, though male bloodlines were more important than female ones.

It was the speed, then, of the early growth of Islam that provides the most striking difference between the two religions over migration. For there were lots of reasons why early Muslims migrated, not only to spread the new faith. Many of them were searching, like so many migrants, for wealth and power and land, or excitement, or simply to visit lands they didn't know. It was men from Muhammad's own tribe who led the first wave of migration out of the Arabian peninsula, often over long distances; they conquered new lands and settled there, usually marrying local women. Indeed, the two most important imperial families of early Islam, the Umayyads (based in Damascus and then Cordoba) and the Abbasids (based in Damascus and then Baghdad), were originally from Mecca and members of that tribe. Muhammad's uncle Abbas, after whom the Abbasid Empire would be named, and whose children settled far and wide, was said to have thirty-three thousand descendants less than two hundred years after his death.

And so it was that even before the arrival of Abd al-Rahman there was an undoubted hierarchy of Muslim migrants in Islamic Spain. Those who came from the Prophet's tribe were at the top. But others, including non-Arabs, could rise to powerful positions. Take, for instance, Tariq ibn Ziyad, whose 'Arab' army had landed near Gibraltar in 711, and so began an

almost eight-hundred-year Muslim presence in southern Spain.
However, Tariq himself and most of his army were not Arabs
but Berbers, new North African converts to Islam for whom
Arabic was a second language. Berbers were the foot-soldiers,
horsemen and tax collectors of the new regime, who settled
many of the border regions of the new empire, while Arab
migrants tended to head for the imperial court in Cordoba and
the other great cities of Andalusia. Abd al-Rahman himself,
the 'Immigrant', the first Umayyad ruler of Spain, for all his
grand Meccan ancestry had a Berber mother. It was her tribal
connections that made his escape across North Africa possible,
and helped smooth the way for him among Berber migrants to
Spain as he assumed the leadership of a new empire.

In fact, those early migrants – Berber and Arab – were few
in number, and the new rulers of southern Spain relied on alliances, sometimes marital, with the old pre-Islamic aristocracy,
which was largely of Gothic origin. They also drew on support
from Muslim converts from the local population, as well as a
larger number of Christians and Jews who chose not to convert.* However, the success and affluence of Umayyad rule in
Cordoba soon led to the arrival of many long-distance Arab
migrants, particularly from Syria and from Yemen. Berbers
also came in large numbers, to work or to settle, as farmers,
soldiers and preachers – and, much later, with the collapse of
Umayyad rule in the eleventh century, as conquerors. There
were even a few Muslim Vikings, of whom more in a moment.

But there were also a large number of non-Muslim migrants,
turning Cordoba into what was probably the most cosmopolitan and ethnically diverse city of its time. These included many
foreign Christians: Frankish traders, Italian merchants from

---

* There was also some intermarriage between the Christian and Muslim royal
families of Spain. The Basque Princess Onneca was the grandmother of both Abd
al-Rahman III, Caliph of Cordoba, and King Garcia Sanchez of Pamplona, as well as
the great-grandmother of Sancho the Fat, King of Leon.

the Amalfi coast, European diplomats – among them a future Christian saint by the name of John of Gorze, who stayed in Cordoba for three years – while the future Pope Sylvester II is also thought to have visited. Jewish scholars from the rest of Europe and the Middle East flocked to Andalusia, helping to set off a rebirth of Hebrew studies and transforming Cordoba into a major centre of Jewish learning. Southern Spain was also a major destination in the slave trade. In particular, there were large numbers of Eastern European slaves, known as Saqalabi, many of them eunuchs, castrated as children, who became the mainstay of the Andalusian bureaucracy. It was a time of great mingling, when ideas of racial purity or skin colour played far less of a role in political and social life than they would in later times.

In Andalusia, it was even possible to meet a few unlikely representatives of those distant northern Europeans who were the greatest migrants and explorers of the western hemisphere during the last centuries of the first millennium. For in southern Spain there lived a small group of those Scandinavians whom we now know as Vikings. They, or their ancestors, had taken part in a Viking raid on Seville in 844 CE, which was successful at first, but which was eventually beaten back by the Andalusians. Many Vikings were killed, but others were captured and converted to Islam, and allowed to settle outside Seville, where they were said to have worked as cheesemakers.

There are several modern stereotypes of the Vikings, none of which conjure up images of Muslim cheesemakers in southern Spain, nor – more significantly – do justice to the extraordinary scale and range of Viking migration. The common thread in these views of the Vikings is the notion of northern Europeans on the move, more specifically Scandinavians travelling long distances by boat to other lands. But beyond this, the stereotypes vary from the extremely negative to the boisterously positive, depending largely on one's age and country of origin.

The more positive views of the Vikings tend to depict them as free and fearless, as having exceptional determination, ingenuity and adventurousness. They are often held by people who come from Scandinavia, for whom the Vikings were emigrants, not immigrants – and there is often friendly competition among Norwegians, Swedes and Danes over who has the strongest claim to the best of the Viking heritage. For me, it was all very much the opposite. As a child, the dominant image of the Viking Age was of rape and pillage, of dim-witted, unwashed, muscle-bound men in horned helmets blundering about committing random murders, rapes and robberies. This was largely nonsense, and schoolchildren in Britain are nowadays presented with a more nuanced portrayal of the Vikings.*

In recent decades, slightly apologetic Anglophone historians have also been setting the record straight, particularly in relation to the complex story of the Viking Age in England. And a wider story has also begun to be told, both of the remarkable ability of some Viking migrants to assimilate themselves into Europe's ruling elite and more broadly of the astonishing geographical scale of Viking raiding, trading and migration. These journeys took the Vikings, by sea and river, more than two thousand kilometres from home in three directions: northwest across the Atlantic to Iceland, Greenland and the coast of

---

* The Viking Age, usually dated 793 to 1066, is a modern creation whose dates relate to events that took place in Britain – namely the Viking raid on Lindisfarne in 793 and the defeat of Harald Hardrada at Stamford Bridge in 1066. And the modern use of the word Vikings, to describe Scandinavians of that period, is an early nineteenth-century invention, though it can be traced back, as a description of raiders, to 'Viking' times. We now know that Vikings washed frequently, they didn't have horned helmets and they don't seem to have been more violent than their contemporaries. Those misleading views were largely drawn from Victorian literature and Hollywood films, in which the Vikings were little more than pirates. An English friend of mine, born in the once-Viking county of Lincolnshire, grew up with a much more benign view of the Vikings than I did in London.

The Viking Migration

Canada; south-west to Britain, France and Mediterranean; and south-east through Russia to the Black Sea and Constantinople.

Historians can't quite agree on what drove the Vikings to make these journeys. Over-population at home seems to have been an important reason. And as outstanding shipbuilders and navigators, the Vikings undoubtedly had the means to travel greater distances than their contemporaries. But beyond that, there are a multitude of other factors, including the possibilities of wealth and power, land and status, but also a desire to escape tyranny and a deep sense of curiosity – and it's a varying combination of these factors that helps explain the huge differences between each of the three great Viking migrations, as well as the life choices of so many individual migrants. There's plenty of evidence, written, archaeological and genetic, to help bring some much-needed detail to our modern understanding of the Vikings, though the Vikings themselves, like so many migrants, are almost silent.

First, those forays across the Atlantic – which reached the coastline of what is now Canada in the early years of the second millennium. In the 1960s, Norwegian archaeologists unearthed a ruined Viking settlement on Newfoundland large enough to support a community of 150 people. Its discovery proved that, about half a millennium before Columbus, Europeans reached the Americas – and that the Icelandic sagas' description of ships making landfall a few days' sailing west of Greenland was not a fantasy. The archaeological evidence suggests that the Vikings didn't stay long, probably less than twenty years, but gives very few clues about what motivated them to build settlements there in the first place, or why they left. For this, the sagas and other written sources provide much more evidence.

Two Icelandic sagas, written down after the end of the Viking Age, tell slightly different versions of the story of Erik the Red and his children, who were the key figures in the settlement and exploration of Greenland and North America. Erik himself was a man on the run, sent into exile three times – first as a youngster from southern Norway, and twice more from his new home in Iceland. In each case, he was accused of involvement in the killing of fellow Vikings or their slaves. As a result of that third expulsion, Erik and his family crossed from Iceland to Greenland, where they were the first Viking settlers. And it was Erik who gave Greenland that most misleading of names, so say both sagas, simply because he thought it would mean 'that people would be much more tempted to go there'.

The search for wealth seems to have played less of a role in Viking migration across the Atlantic than in their travels elsewhere. Curiosity, fame and the desire for new land to settle seem, according to the sagas, to be the primary reasons for the Vikings' continuing journey westwards. 'There was great talk of discovering new countries', says the *Graenlendinga Saga* of the decision to sail beyond Greenland. Erik was unable to travel, having fallen off a horse and hurt his leg. And so it was his sons Leif and Thorvald who led a series of expeditions to the coast of Canada, where 'they found the country there very attractive, with woods stretching almost down to the shore and white sandy beaches'. They named it Vinland after the wild grapes that grew there. And Thorvald declared, simply, 'it is beautiful; I should like to make my home here'.

But the Canadian adventure soon ended, and the migration failed. The land was already occupied. Thorvald was killed by an arrow shot by a Native American, probably an Inuit. A survivor said the Vikings 'could never live there in safety or freedom from fear, because of the native inhabitants'. We do not know what the Inuit thought of these interlopers. Europeans did not return to the Canadian coast until 1497; they called the island where the Vikings had settled Newfoundland, a name that, in these circumstances, seems even more wonderfully inappropriate than Greenland.

The Viking migrations to Greenland and Iceland endured

much longer, though they each provide us with very different modern narratives. In Greenland, the migrants built three stretched-out coastal communities, consisting of fewer than five thousand people at their most extensive. There had been earlier human settlers there, from North America, but they had left by the time the Vikings arrived. And so the new migrants only had to fight the climate and famine. For several centuries these small groups of Scandinavians clung to plots of land close to the sea: farming and hunting – and keeping some contact with Iceland and beyond. But theirs was always a marginal existence, and became still more demanding when Inuit crossed to Greenland from the islands of northern Canada. By about 1450 it was all over. The last Scandinavians had died out or fled – the full circumstances are still unclear. There were stories that a few Greenlanders had survived, perhaps in the ice-bound interior, and later explorers searched in vain for them, but only found the ruins of their farms and houses and churches.

Iceland, however, was and is a case apart; an outlier in the story of human migration. It was one of the last significant landmasses on the planet to have no pre-existing permanent human population, and after the initial settlement that began in the 870s there was no subsequent major influx of migrants. Within less than a century late-comers were complaining that all the best farmland had gone. Because of Iceland's isolation, and those low levels of later immigration, there has been an unusually high level of genetic and cultural continuity.*

---

* New Zealand, first settled in the fourteenth century, and Antarctica were the other uninhabited large territories. There are thought to have been some Irish Christian hermits on Iceland before the Vikings, but no families, and no permanent settlements. By the time Erik the Red turned up in Iceland a century later there was very little good land left. Since then not much changed, genetically speaking, until very recently. There was some further Danish migration, but no invasions – until the Second World War and the bloodless occupation of the island by the Allies, and the birth of several hundred half-American Icelanders. The last twenty years have seen a large influx of migrants, with by far the largest foreign-born population coming from Poland.

It was in Iceland that parliamentary democracy – for free men at least – was first practised, in 930 CE, and also where almost all the Norse sagas were written down. That has helped form a romantic migration narrative, partly aimed at tourists, in which Iceland, not the countries of continental Scandinavia, is the inheritor of the best of Viking culture. What is usually forgotten is that those first settlers, who arrived from the 870s, were not all Vikings. They were undoubtedly led by Viking men from what is now Norway, but they brought with them many others abducted during raids who became wives or slaves, or both. Indeed, DNA studies of maternal ancestry among Icelanders, dead and alive, suggest that a majority of female migrants to Iceland were not Scandinavian but of Celtic origin, from Scotland and Ireland.

There's a solid logic of proximity that explains the direction of the great Viking migrations. Just as Norway contributed most migrants to the Viking settlements of the north Atlantic, so Swedish Vikings headed east through the Baltic and south through Russia. Their experiences could hardly have been more different. The people now usually referred to as the Volga Vikings did not explore new lands; they left no significant genetic trail in the wider population, no communities of former Vikings. They went in search of silver and became traders, racketeers and mercenaries in the service of the Byzantine emperor and, as if this wasn't enough, the founders of an embryonic Russian monarchy.

Scandinavia had very little silver of its own, and the Vikings needed it, as the main form of portable wealth. The principal source at that time was the Abbasid Empire, whose silver dirhams were the medieval world's approximation to an international currency – which is why dirhams continue to be dug up by treasure-seekers in northern Europe, thousands of kilometres from the Abbasid capital in Baghdad. The Vikings

first set themselves up as traders, selling slaves and furs, building small settlements, often at places where they needed to
drag their boats across the countryside in order to reach the
great rivers of southern Russia: the Dnieper, the Don and the
Volga. They then built bigger trading posts: Novgorod as their
northern headquarters, and then Kiev in the south. These were
ruled as princely states by the family of Rurik, a Viking – and
the Vikings in this part of the world were known as the 'Rus',
a term of disputed origins that almost certainly was the source
of the word Russia.

In the same way that Vikings turn up as invaders (and
cheesemakers) in Muslim-ruled Andalusia in the far west of
Europe, so they also reached Muslim territories to the east of
Europe, near the Caspian Sea. A northern crescent of Viking
influence overlapped at each end with a southern crescent of
Muslim domination. And in Arabic writings of the period,
Volga Vikings appear in minor roles as slave-traders and exotic
extras from the mysterious north. So Ibn Fadlan, a tenth-
century traveller from Baghdad, for instance, chanced upon a
Viking camp on the banks of the Volga and declared 'I have
never seen bodies more perfect than theirs; they were like palm
trees'. But that was Ibn Fadlan's only Viking compliment, and
he goes on to say that they are the 'filthiest of god's creatures':

> They do not clean after urinating or defecating, nor do they
> wash after having sex. They do not wash their hands after
> meals. They are like wandering asses.

He then describes how they have sex with slave girls in public,
and provides a detailed account of a particularly cruel Viking
death ritual – unattested elsewhere – involving the gang rape
and murder of a slave woman.

However, Ibn Rustah, a Persian contemporary of Ibn
Fadlan, has a rather different story. He too admires the Vikings

for their height and physique, but insists that they 'treat their slaves well and dress them suitably, because for them they are an article of trade'. He says the Vikings 'never go off alone to relieve themselves, but always with three companions to guard them, sword in hand, for they have little trust in one another'. He says nothing about their washing habits, but does point out that 'their clothing is always clean'. It's hard to reconcile these accounts, but there's surely some irony to be extracted here, in the resemblance in tone and content of these descriptions to nineteenth-century European descriptions of desert-dwelling Arab nomads. The Vikings, strange northerners with even stranger rituals, have been Othered.

And the Vikings went further south still, with a small community of mercenaries living in Constantinople by the tenth century – and just occasionally we come across a word or two from the Vikings themselves. Just a single word, in the case of one of these soldiers, who scratched graffiti on a marble balustrade in an upper gallery of Hagia Sophia, once Constantinople's cathedral. They're Old Norse runes, too worn to be fully legible, but the name Halfdan can be made out, and it's generally supposed that the whole of the inscription once read 'Halfdan was here'. It's easy to imagine Halfdan as a bored member of the Varangian guard – Viking soldiers in the service of the Byzantine emperor. They fought in Georgia, Syria, Crete and Italy, but also spent a lot of time hanging around in the imperial capital. They'd come via Kiev, thousands of them over more than two centuries, and many would never return.

Back home in Sweden more than twenty memorials to those who were killed fighting for Byzantium have survived, standing stones inscribed with the names of those who died far away, and just a few who returned from Constantinople as rich men. And on one of these stones, found on the Swedish island of Gotland, was the tersest of testaments to Viking wanderlust: just six words, the first two being the names of the travellers,

Ormika and Ulfhvatr, the next four words their destinations, Greece, Jerusalem, Iceland, Arabia. It's hard to avoid seeing this as a masterpiece of succinct boastfulness, that Ormika and Ulfhvatr were just showing off, like modern travellers who try to visit every country around the world.

For those Vikings who preferred shorter journeys and quicker rewards, the coastlines of what are now Germany and the Netherlands, and of course Britain, were particularly attractive. The first Vikings to come to Britain were not migrants at all, but raiders, murderers, pirates and thieves, closest perhaps to that traditional Anglophone stereotype of the Vikings. Indeed, I was taught at school, with predictable Anglocentricity, that the Viking Age began in 793 with a raid on the monastery on the Holy Island of Lindisfarne off the north-east coast of England, in which many monks died and much treasure was taken.

The negative attitudes towards Vikings in Britain emerged largely from the retelling of the story of this and other raids, rather than the more complex tale of how Vikings controlled and colonised large parts of Britain and Ireland. After all, Viking migrants ruled Dublin for almost three hundred years, and the Orkney Islands for much longer – and the last Orcadian speaker of Norse only died in the nineteenth century. While in England, the Vikings attempted to supplant an older group of north European migrants, the Anglo-Saxons, and when they failed the leaders of the two communities reached an agreement to share the country between them.

That agreement, reached in about 886, was between two warlords – Alfred the Great and Guthrum – who partitioned the country we know now as England. Guthrum was a recent migrant, a Danish prince. Alfred, meanwhile, proudly proclaimed his migrant origins by using 'Anglo-Saxon' in his royal title. Alfred's family probably came from the borderlands of modern Germany and Denmark, and had been in Britain for almost four hundred years,* but the Anglo-Saxons had kept their language and did little to integrate with the older British population. Indeed, the two peacemakers spoke closely related Germanic languages, and Alfred's ancestors worshipped the same gods as Guthrum.† Perhaps the biggest difference between them was that Alfred was a Christian, and Guthrum was not. But that soon changed. As part of their peace treaty, Guthrum converted and was baptised, with Alfred as his god-father. And so began the first period of settled Viking rule over half of England, a huge tract of land north and east of a diagonal that ran, roughly, from London to Liverpool, with York as its capital. The Danelaw, as the territory ruled by Viking migrants became known, lasted for ninety years.

Late twentieth-century archaeological excavations in York's city centre have helped turn England's Viking heritage into a major tourist attraction. A visitor centre has been built on the site of the excavations, beneath a shopping mall, and it's possible to travel in an underground cable car through a reconstruction of the sights and smells of Viking York, complete with a wide range of robotic Vikings, their pets and a few hungry rats. It's all part of a gentle softening of English attitudes towards the Vikings. There are no horned helmets here; no rape, no pillage. Just busy craftsmen and shopkeepers and householders.

The actual excavations in York suggest that during the Danelaw period there was a dramatic growth in the city's population – as well as in diseases associated with urbanisation. Foreign trade increased, and Viking fashions in jewellery and hairstyles spread beyond the migrant community. Many places

---

* The *Anglo-Saxon Chronicle*, begun in the reign of Alfred, clearly establishes him as a descendant of conquering migrants, declaring that his accession took place '396 years from when his race first conquered the land of the West Saxons from the Britons'.
† The names of the old gods remained in the Anglo-Saxon and English words for the days of the week. According to King Alfred's first biographer, Asser, the king was descended from Woden, whose name gave us Wednesday, and who can safely be identified with the Norse god Odin.

in the north and east of England still have Viking names, such as those ending with -by or -thorpe, and it's in this period that a large number of simple words entered the English language: bag, cake, dirt, egg, fog and gift all come from Old Norse.

The tug-of-war over England continued well into the new millennium. The Vikings had been driven out in 954, and then were back again sixty years later, as the Danish prince Canute captured almost the entire country. Indeed, Canute was probably the first to use the title King of England, rather than King of the English, and his son was only overthrown by the Anglo-Saxons in 1042.* And this wasn't the end of Viking interest in England. In just one well-remembered year, there was one, or arguably two, Viking invasions. That year was 1066, and marks what is described, usually by Anglocentric historians, as the end of the Viking Age. In fact, it's possible to argue that it simply marked a new phase of Viking power and influence, as well as a deep entanglement with the royal families of Britain and the rest of Europe.

This version of the story of 1066 places a greater emphasis on the Viking roots of the protagonists. It begins with King Harald of Norway, most obviously a Viking, who would die in battle, an arrow through his throat, on English soil in that year — not to be confused with King Harold who would also die on English soil in 1066, an arrow in his eye. For King Harald, best known as Harald Hardrada, had a quite extraordinary life, told in one of the most action-packed of all Icelandic sagas. He was a prince, a poet, a fugitive, a mercenary, a trickster, a despot, a migrant and one of the best-travelled men of his age. Harald had lived in Constantinople, where he served in the Varangian guard, and in Russia, where he married a Viking princess, — before returning to take the throne of Norway, where he

---

* And he ruled much more than England. In a letter written in 1027, Canute, or Cnut, described himself – pretty accurately – as King of all England and Denmark and the Norwegians and some of the Swedes.

ruled for almost twenty years when he decided, unwisely, to invade Britain.*

When Harald met Harold at the Battle of Stamford Bridge just outside York, that graveyard of emperors, it was Harald of Norway who perished. And there ended what has been described as the last Viking invasion of England. But there's still a Viking twist or two to this tale. For less than a month later, another better-remembered battle was fought on English soil, at Hastings on the southern coast. With two protagonists: Harold once again, his forces much weakened, and William the Conqueror, fresh from France. And yes, both Harold and William might also both be considered Vikings. Harold first, who is always heralded as England's last Anglo-Saxon king, as if his mother's Viking origins were of no consequence. For she was the thoroughly Scandinavian Gytha Thorkelsdóttir, a Danish princess and aunt of King Sweyn II of Denmark, who twice attempted to invade England after the Norman Conquest. So on this matrilineal evidence we might even describe Harold as the last Viking king of England – if it wasn't for the fact that there's a very strong patrilineal case for describing William the Conqueror as a Viking too.

The most obvious clue to William's Viking ancestry is in the words Norman and Normandy. The Normans were once *nortmanni*, or men from the north, cognate with the English word Norsemen. William's great-great-great-grandfather was a Viking raider called Rollo, who was recruited by a Frankish king to defend Paris from other Vikings, and in 911 he was given territory on either side of the River Seine that soon became known as Normandy after the homeland of its new

---

* Harald was the half-brother of Olaf, a king who later became the patron saint of Norway. When his saintly brother died on the battlefield, the fifteen-year-old Harald was wounded and taken to recover in a secret place in a forest. He then fled his Norwegian homeland and travelled to Sweden, Russia and the Byzantine Empire. He returned to Norway an extremely rich man, who took the throne after his nephew died and ruled – harshly – for almost two decades.

ruler. That name has lasted, as have hundreds of other place-names of Scandinavian origin in Normandy. The Viking connection is often forgotten, only because Rollo and his descendants and compatriots soon adapted to local ways, converting to Christianity, speaking French and marrying into royal families.*

Thus, by this same logic, not only was the new King of England a Viking, but so were Norman rulers elsewhere. And the Normans certainly travelled – to rule new kingdoms in southern Europe and the Middle East. It's hard to keep up with Norman ubiquity, and their complex family trees. By the time William the Conqueror had become King of England, his fellow Norman Robert Guiscard, a former mercenary, was the ruler of most of southern Italy. Robert's son Bohemond fought in the First Crusade, and so became the ruler of Antioch, now in eastern Turkey, and Bohemond's descendants ruled Tripoli, now in Lebanon, until the late thirteenth century.

The Viking diaspora, if it deserves that name, had become widespread, and very royal. Take those Russian Viking rulers who, like the Vikings of Normandy, adopted local ways, and who had, by the third generation, taken Slavic names. Three of the daughters of Yaroslav the Wise, Grand Prince of Kiev, fourth-generation descendant of Rurik the Viking, married the Kings of Norway, Hungary and France, while a grand-daughter married the Holy Roman Emperor. The descendants of a Viking migrant to Russia had made it to the top, and most of the modern royal families of Europe can trace their ancestry back to Rurik.

On one level, this intricately tangled web of genealogy is of little real significance, and the dispersal of Viking genes is

---

* Most strikingly, Emma of Normandy, the great-granddaughter of Rollo, married two unrelated kings of England (Ethelred the Unready and Canute) and was thereby the mother of two more English kings by these husbands (Hardacanute and Edward the Confessor). She was also the great aunt of William the Conqueror.

of passing interest, for it doesn't ultimately matter whether we think Yaroslav or Bohemond or William the Conqueror or Harold of England were really Vikings, or what percentage of their DNA might be Scandinavian.* But there are, half-disguised, two other important migration stories here.

First: the Vikings and their descendants became a central part of what has been called the aristocratic diaspora of the Middle Ages, in which it became normal for queens to be foreigners, and quite common for kings as well. And for would-be kings, the greatest opportunities were on the borderlands of Christendom, in eastern Europe, or following the reconquest of Spain and Portugal. The Crusades deepened those opportunities for men, particularly for second or illegitimate sons, who headed to the Middle East, often with motives that are hard to unravel. Most of them seem to have genuinely believed in the importance of driving Muslim rulers out of Christian Holy Lands. But once they were there, it became more of an ugly land-grab, with the establishment of several Crusader kingdoms ruled by western Europeans who spent much of their time conspiring against each other.

The second migration story is more specifically about the Vikings, but it also can be seen as reflecting a wider migrant experience. For at its heart is a group of people, pagans from the north, depicted as uncivilised and brutal barbarians, equally despised and feared in Christian Europe, who were then co-opted into the European elite and became part of the backbone of the aristocracy. The military abilities of the Vikings and their descendants were undoubtedly important to their success in doing so, but so was assimilation. They gave up Odin and

---

* There's also a significant irony buried in this tale. Vikings are often referred to as the original Nordics, a category used by twentieth-century white supremacists as the highest, least-sullied category of whiteness. While the real Vikings, of course, showed little interest in ethnic purity and put an enormous amount of energy and emphasis on mingling their bloodlines with those of non-Nordics.

Thor, all their old gods, along with their Scandinavian names, their language and their customs, almost everything, as they rose to power.

But these erstwhile Vikings didn't entirely forget their history. They remained proud of their migrant past, happily commissioning court histories that told the story of their ancient, northern, pagan roots. So the twelfth-century Anglo-Norman monk Orderic Vitalis, admiringly describes the Normans – by which he includes the ruling elite of Sicily and Antioch, as well as England and Normandy – as 'an untamed race', who are 'innately warlike and bold'. He explains to his readers that the word Norman means 'man of the north', and specifically refers to Rollo of Normandy as a Dane. And then, as if he is performing a conjuring trick, he adds another even older layer of ancestry by giving the Danes, and thereby the Normans, a Trojan origin. Orderic declares the Danes to be descendants of Danus, a previously unknown son of Antenor of Troy, mythical founder of Padua, who had played a minor role in both the *Iliad* and the *Aeneid*.[*] And so, with this act of fantasy these northerners – Danes, Normans, Norsemen, Vikings, call them what you will – have been transformed into respectable members of the community of ancient nations, who also happen to be migrants from Asia.

What's happening here is that Rollo and the Normans, and their imagined Trojan ancestors, have been squeezed into an existing royal template, almost a cliché of its time, in which it had become normal for new rulers to proclaim their descent from mythological migrants. The post-Virgil medieval additions to the story of Troy served as exercises in nation-building and self-aggrandisement, in which new rulers and dynasties

---

[*] It was Virgil who claimed that Antenor founded Padua. And later writers would extend this role of Antenor's to nearby Venice. Padua has a 'tomb of Antenor', actually a late Roman sarcophagus, raised up high above the ground in a public square in the heart of the city, so that it provides a rain-shelter for cigarette-smoking students.

could share their ancestry with the first rulers of the Roman Empire. So just as Aeneas is said to have founded Rome and Antenor founded Padua, so many more Trojans were identified or invented as founders for other places and other people – often, as with Danus, bearing names that matched.

The French emerged as would-be Trojans from the seventh century onwards. Their Trojan ancestor was given the name Francion, or Francus or Franco – sometimes a nephew of Aeneas, elsewhere a grandson of Priam – who is supposed to have travelled across the Black Sea and then through northern Europe by land, or alternatively westwards by boat in the Mediterranean like Aeneas, and founded France. One twentieth-century researcher counted fifty-five French variations of the story from the early Middle Ages to the late Renaissance.

Others followed suit. Particularly the rulers of smaller north European principalities: Hainaut, Brabant, Burgundy all claimed Trojan ancestry. Geneva as well, with Lemannus the Trojan appearing as founder of the city that overlooks Lake Leman. So did the Ottomans, who at least could argue for a close geographical proximity to Troy. After sacking Constantinople in 1453, the Ottoman sultan is said to have travelled to the site of the Trojan War and declared himself the avenger of Troy. My favourite of these neo-Trojan fantasies is the simplest – one put forward by the fifteenth-century Corsican historian Giovanni della Grossa, who explained that Corsica was founded by a Trojan called Corso, who married a niece of Dido, called Sica.

The British, too, claimed Trojan heritage, and clung on to the story longest; it even reappeared recently, like the ghost of a ghost, during the Brexit debate. The British version is more elaborate than most of the fantasies about Trojan ancestry, and first appeared in the ninth-century *History of Britain* compiled by a Welsh monk called Nennius, who explained that Britain was

named after Brutus, a hitherto unknown grandson of Aeneas.*
It was a story that would swell and grow, until by the twelfth
century it had become the first part of an epic retelling of British
history by the cleric Geoffrey of Monmouth, a fantastical story
that starts with the life of Brutus and moves on to King Lear,
Cymbeline, King Arthur and the arrival of the Anglo-Saxons
(but stops short before the appearance of any Vikings).

At first, in Geoffrey's version, Brutus the Trojan seems
cursed. Born in Rome, he is accidentally responsible for the
death of both of his parents and sent into exile. He travels
around the Mediterranean and into the Atlantic, gets married
to an unwilling Greek woman and magically encounters fellow
Trojans, including his new best friend Corineus. By now they
are heading north from France, to 'the best of islands', uninhabited 'except for a few giants'. They land, kill all the giants
and name the island Britain after Brutus, while its south-west
corner becomes Cornwall in honour of Corineus. Brutus
builds his capital on the Thames, and calls it Troia Nova or
New Troy, now better known as London. Brutus rules Britain
for twenty-three years, and his three sons each inherit part of
his kingdom which roughly correspond to England, Scotland
and Wales.

There would be many dozens of versions of this story, all
based ultimately on Geoffrey's. Most of them were keen to
pick up on the notion that Britain was uninhabited, apart
from giants, before Brutus turned up and to reclaim a British
identity that pre-dated later migrants: the Romans, the
Anglo-Saxons and the Normans. Among the earliest versions

---

* Nennius' account may have been prompted by a notorious seventh-century remark
of Isidore of Seville. St Isidore, often described as the last scholar of the ancient world,
referred to a belief that Britons were so called 'because they were brutes' (*eo quod bruti
sint*).

were the Old French *Roman de Brut* by Wace of Jersey,* and a sixteen-thousand-line Middle English poem by a priest called Layamon, which he chose to call, with unexpected brevity, *Brut*. The story of Brutus also appears in Spenser's *Faerie Queene*, and in a lamentable play called *The Lamentable Tragedy of Locrine*, bizarrely ascribed to Shakespeare for many years. And there's even a proto-imperial contribution from Milton in the form of a prophecy by the goddess Diana:

> Brutus, far to the West, in th' Ocean wide,
> Beyond the Realm of Gaul, a Land there lies,
> Sea-girt it lies, where Giants dwelt of old,
> Now void, it fits thy people; thither bend
> Thy course, there shalt thou find a lasting seat,
> There to thy Sons another Troy shall rise,
> And Kings be born of thee, whose dreaded might
> Shall awe the World, and Conquer Nations bold.
> That to the race of Brute, Kings of this Island,
> the whole Earth shall be subject.

While Alexander Pope contemplated writing a *Brutiad*, on the epic model of the *Aeneid*, that task was eventually undertaken by two lesser, long-forgotten poets. William Blake, who famously wondered if Jesus had ever visited England,† was also taken with the story of Brutus of Troy and contributed a distinctively romantic vision of Britain's origins in his poem 'O Sons of Trojan Brutus', as well as a drawing of Brutus and his comrades landing on British soil.

---

* He also wrote the *Roman de Rou*, an account of the origins of Rollo the Viking. Rou was a French version of his name, which helps turn him into the founder of the city of Rouen.
† It's a question he raised in the poem now known as 'Jerusalem', which was set to music in 1916 and has since become England's unofficial national anthem: 'And did those feet in ancient time, / Walk upon England's mountains green: / And was the holy Lamb of God, / On England's pleasant pastures seen!'

In more recent times, the story – like that of the British Israelites – has remained popular only with a small group of eccentrics and fantasists. The myth of Brutus, and the story of the Trojan ancestors of the British people, has been largely ignored or forgotten. It's rarely mentioned in history books, which is a shame and a loss. Not because there's any evidence whatsoever that it is true, but because of what it tells us of older attitudes towards migration. It is another reminder of how normal it once was to eulogise rather than deny one's migrant past. There could be real pride in the notion, however daft, that the British people were descendants of people who came from what is now Turkey.*

There is one small part of this story that lives on, but only just, and it relates to the place where Brutus is said to have landed. Geoffrey of Monmouth is quite clear: 'With the wind behind him he sought the promised island, and came ashore at Totnes.' And so is a far more modern couplet supposedly spoken by Brutus:

> Now here I sit, and here I rest
> And this town shall be called Totnes.

The town of Totnes, population eight thousand, is in south-west England, and is not actually on the sea but eight miles upstream on the River Dart. The Dart is broad and navigable, and tidal beyond Totnes, and so it's just possible that some ancient boats did make their way up the river.

---

* In fact, they probably did. The most likely migration route out of Africa into Europe does go through Turkey, though this would predate the probable date of Troy by several tens of thousands of years, and for Neanderthals by several hundred thousand years. There are of course other important Anglo-Turkish connections, including St George, who was born and died there, as well as Boris Johnson, a recent prime minister of the United Kingdom, whose great-grandfather, Ali Kemal, was an Ottoman Minister of the Interior, and who was lynched in the early days of the Turkish republic. His son Osman (later known as Wilfred), living in England, took his mother's maiden name, Johnson.

Totnes sits on a hill beside the river, and halfway up that hill, on the high street, there's an inconspicuous stone embedded in the pavement marking the spot where Brutus is said to have landed. There's a sign painted on the wall, pointing out the Brutus Stone, but I'd have missed them altogether if I hadn't looked behind a dustbin that was covering both the sign and the stone. A friend who has spent all his life in Totnes did not know of its existence, and it's hard to avoid the conclusion that the Brutus Stone is a strong contender as Britain's least impressive visitor attraction. Totnes was once proud of its Trojan connection, but now Brutus has been all but forgotten. Today, the town enjoys a more modern reputation as the counter-culture capital of the south-west, with drop-in meditation, 'new moon manifesting ceremonies' and 'yoni love workshops' advertised

on billboards around the town. Totnes, they like to say, is twinned with Narnia.

Totnes was back in the news recently. Jonathan Cooper, a local lawyer and opponent of Brexit, declared Totnes an independent city-state, which unlike the rest of the United Kingdom would stay in the European Union. He stood in the street, handing out Totnes passports to any passers-by who would swear an oath to the European Union. There was a special passport for pets, too – with the hashtag #PooToBrexit.

The Totnes passport helped return Brutus to the story of Britain. For on the inside pages of each passport – more than a thousand were issued – was an image of a bearded warrior with a fabulously ornate helmet, and printed in faux-Latin script next to the warrior was the single word BRVTVS. Cooper's claim of independence was based, you see, on the argument that because Totnes was founded by Brutus of Troy, the people of Totnes are in fact residents of Troy and can therefore break away from the United Kingdom and remain part of the EU. All nonsense, of course, but mischievously subversive, and it brought lots of publicity to Totnes, and to Brutus of Troy, the legendary founder of Britain.

A FIFTH INTERMISSION

Placenames conceal and reveal. And behind many of them are tales of migration, half-forgotten. Some are obvious, though strangely unnoticed, as if daily repetition drives out that older meaning: New England, Newfoundland, New South Wales, New Jersey, New Caledonia. Others need greater unravelling: Normandy, Russia, Lombardy, Cartagena. For each of these placenames there were accompanying migrants, nostalgic for their old country, and usually powerful enough to impose that nostalgia on the existing population. That's not always so, of course: the inhabitants of most Chinatowns and Jewtowns, of Little Indias and Italys, are much less powerful – and those place-names have sometimes been used to describe ghettos. These names should help remind us how, since ancient times, human beings have either wanted or been expected to define themselves in relation to their place of origin, or that of their ancestors.

Modern migrants and their descendants are often asked where they come from, and when they reply 'London' or 'Paris' or 'New York', they are sometimes asked 'But origi-nally?' Once upon a time, I too asked this type of question, out of naive curiosity and a wide-eyed old-fashioned delight at the mingling of peoples. Sadly this question has been weaponised, especially when the questioner is white and the respondent is not. For it can be the question of a racist, someone who wishes to elicit this information in order to tell the respondent to 'go home'. And so I bite my tongue, or find another way of finding out what I want to know.

I too am asked this question on my travels. But my experience here, as a white man, who has not faced significant racial prejudice, is very different – and it's most unlikely that someone would be posing this question to me in order to make a racist point. And yet, for reasons that I need to explain, it's a question that makes me anxious.

You see, it's not easy being British, semantically speaking. And I struggle, foolishly, when I am asked where I am from – and find myself giving a variety of answers. Because all of the many words that might be used to describe the land of my birth – Britain, Great Britain, England, the UK, and the British Isles to mention just five – are triumphs of inexactitude and carry associations that can twist their meaning in particular contexts.

Take the words 'England' and 'English', which have wandered far, in time and distance, from their ancient Germanic homeland. There's that first mention of the *Anglii* tribe, in Tacitus' *Germania*, only to reappear several centuries later as the Angles, part of a migration across the North Sea alongside the Saxons and Jutes. The Jutes were soon cast aside, lexicologically, and the Saxons would be fossilised in what became 'English' history, remembered as the back half of the Anglo-Saxons, and in old place names like Sussex.* The Angles

---

* But the Jutes are remembered elsewhere. There's the Jutland peninsula, which forms continental Denmark and juts down into northern Germany, as well the common Finnish surname Juutilainen, which is thought to refer to the descendants of migrants from Jutland. And apart from three English counties, and a former kingdom and current duchy (Wessex), the Saxons live on in Britain in the word Sassenach, the old, vaguely derogatory Scottish Gaelic name for the English. It also appears as part of the name of the Saxe-Coburg-Gotha dynasty which, as recently as 1909, was the ruling house of four European countries: the UK, Portugal, Belgium and Bulgaria. Three modern German states, stretching from the North Sea to the Czech border, have Saxony as part of their name.

triumphed in matters of language over their migrating compatriots, and Angle-land became England.

'English' meanwhile became an adjective – as well as the name of a new language with wholesale borrowings from French and Norse. By modern times, the English language had spread far and wide, so that now only a small minority of English-speakers are English. And all this has been a cause of some irritation and confusion. It's particularly annoying for those mainly English-speaking people who share an island with the English, namely the Scots and the Welsh, and who incessantly get called English, and when they object are then informed that being Scots or Welsh is somehow a subset of being English.

My father was from Scotland, which is just one of several reasons why I don't describe myself as English. The other reasons are more complex and cultural and psychological. In part it is because I've never really felt at home in England, as if I didn't belong there, that I was born into the wrong nation, almost as others feel they are born into the wrong gender. I have also become uncomfortable with some of the modern chauvinism associated with Englishness, as the far right has attempted to hijack English identity and its symbols.

And it's in this political context that the word English causes further confusion. What, for instance, is the English Defence League? It might be mistaken for an organisation that aims to fully eradicate grammatical mistakes – the split infinitive perhaps, or paragraphs that start with a preposition. In fact, it's a far-right, Islamophobic, anti-migrant political group. And the same often applies to the symbols of England. How about the League of St George? St George, after all, is the patron saint of England – and Ethiopia, and Genoa and Georgia and Catalonia, and the saint himself was from Turkey, and never visited England – so the League of St George might be a good name for an international, multicultural organisation;

a Christian charity providing support to migrants, perhaps. It's not, of course. It's another rabid far-right group, which sells *Mein Kampf* from its website, declaring it to be an 'excellent book'.

What about Britain, then? This is where it gets even more confusing. Now, according to my passport I am British. So you might assume that I come from Britain. Well, yes and no. It really is a bit of a mess. The problem is that Britain doesn't really exist, either in law or as a useful description of a geographical or political entity. Britain is a vague concept, whose meaning has wandered over the ages – and which has become semi-detached from its adjective, 'British'. A version of the word Britain first appeared in the now lost, but well-quoted, work of Pytheas of Marseille, and included both of the large islands off the north-west coast of Europe. Later writers of the classical period such as the Greek-Egyptian geographer Ptolemy distinguish between Great Britain, or *megale Bretannia*, which refers to the largest of the islands ('great' was a description of size not magnificence) and *mikra Bretannia* or Little Britain, which referred to Ireland.* But by the time of Geoffrey of Monmouth, it's no longer Ireland that's known as Little Britain, but the French region of Brittany.

Great Britain survives as a geographical description of the largest island, but it is not a political unit and has no adjective of its own – no one would claim to be GBish or Great British. It has no parliament, no sports team, no official status.† It is often used as a shorthand for the United Kingdom, the political unit, the nation state, whose official name is the United Kingdom

---

* Elsewhere Ptolemy referred to the two islands as Albion and Hibernia, ancient usages which live on in poetry, the Romantic imagination and the names of football teams.
† Though it did exist as a sovereign state for most of the eighteenth century. Great Britain was formed by the Act of Union between Scotland and England (which included Wales) in 1707 and was replaced by the United Kingdom of Great Britain and Ireland in 1801.

of Great Britain and Northern Ireland. Sometimes this has run into controversy, notably when the UK's team at the Olympics was rebranded as 'Team GB', which drew some stern criticism from Northern Ireland.

What about British, then? Well, it's widely used as a descriptive word, to be placed before Empire or Grenadiers or Airways or passport or government, but in truth it has become, in most cases, a hand-me-down adjective – not for Britain, nor for Great Britain, but for the United Kingdom. Occasionally there are attempts to give British a wider, all-islands meaning, as in the 'British Isles'. But that, for reasons of history and logic, is not acceptable to many people in Ireland – and it seems right to me that the Irish should have a veto over a term that seeks to include them. And so there isn't in fact a word in common use for the group of islands that many British people call the British Isles. Some academics have begun using 'Atlantic archipelago', others use 'Britain and Ireland'. I'm finding it quite difficult to write this intermission without such a phrase.

One final problem, of the 'what am I?' variety. For most countries there is an English-language noun to describe an inhabitant: a Spaniard, a Russian, an Indian. There are three such words for the people of the UK, all of them connected to that borrowed adjective 'British', and all of them in different ways unsatisfactory. First, there's the word 'Briton', which is usually used to describe the ancient British people and sounds both archaic and pretentious. Then, there's 'Brit', used by many Americans (there's more to be said about that word too) but which has never quite caught on back home, except in an informal or self-deprecatory context. And finally 'Britisher', which always makes me smile, and is still widely used in South Asia.

So what do I say? Well these days, I tend to say I'm from London, which is true, since I was born there. And London is famous enough and specific enough for no further explanation to be needed. Except, strangely enough, in India. When I tell Indians of an older generation that I come from London, I'm often asked 'London proper?' To which I answer, simply, 'Yes.' But I now realise that I'm not quite sure what they are asking me. Do they want to check that I am not using London as a metonym, as a substitute word for England or the UK, just as people refer to Brussels when they mean the European Union, or Scotland Yard to mean the London police force? Or are they checking I don't come from the suburbs?

CHAPTER SIX

Genoa, Columbus and the Taino

The port city of Genoa, in the western armpit of Italy, was the birthplace of Christopher Columbus. A man whose Atlantic wanderings would ultimately lead to possibly the greatest of all modern human migrations: that of millions of people, willing and unwilling, who crossed to what became known, imprecisely, as America. And in Genoa, it's possible to visit Columbus' house, which is almost as unimpressive a tourist attraction as the Brutus Stone. It's a run-down two-storey building (three euros to enter) near the old city walls, with nothing inside except a couple of underdressed mannequins and a table covered with fake fruit. And the house is a fake too, built in the eighteenth century on the site of what might, just possibly, have been where Columbus was born. This sad old building was chosen in 1892 to 'represent' his home, as part of the four hundredth anniversary celebration of his first voyage across the Atlantic.

The house of Columbus, and its contents, are not the only fakes in Genoa – and they are certainly not the oldest. In the crypt of the medieval cathedral one can find the bones of John the Baptist, the plate on which his head was offered to Salome, a piece of the wooden cross on which Jesus was crucified and some strands of the Virgin Mary's hair. Best of all, there's the Holy Grail, a hexagonal green bowl from which Jesus and the Apostles drank wine at the Last Supper. The Holy Grail and many of the other relics were taken from the Holy Land during the First Crusade – sold to or stolen by Genoese merchant-warriors, who may just have been ever so slightly gullible.

The First Crusade (1096–99) is really the start of the story of Genoa as both a place of importance and a place to leave. The city – and the long narrow sliver of coastline to its east and west – is hemmed in by hills, and the best opportunities for many Genoese were as traders and pirates on the seas, or as settlers in a new land. They soon discovered that they could get rich very quickly. And so in the later Middle Ages the people of Genoa and its coastal hinterland built a prosperous trading empire in the Mediterranean and the Black Sea, which would play a leading role in both the slave trade and in the arrival of the bubonic plague in Europe. The Genoese experimented with different forms of colonial control, and they appeared, as citizens of Genoa or lightly disguised by an adopted nationality, at almost every major event of the period from the Crusades to the European conquest of the Americas.

The city of Genoa existed before the First Crusade; indeed it was said to have been founded by yet another Trojan migrant, by the name of Janus.* But Genoa played no important role in the Roman Empire, and only fully emerged from the gloom of history in the eleventh century. And it was the key financial and naval role it played in the First Crusade that transformed it into a European power. For Genoa joined the Crusade before its main local rivals, Venice and Pisa – and gained territorial footholds and religious relics as its reward. That highly suspect Holy Grail,† for instance, was presented to the city by a Genoese merchant called Guglielmo Embriaco, the recently ennobled Lord of Giblet. Embriaco had let his ships be taken apart to build siege towers for the capture of Jerusalem and was rewarded by his fellow Crusaders with the fiefdom of Giblet on the Lebanese coast, where he and his descendants lived for the next two hundred years.

Sections of several Middle Eastern cities, including Jerusalem and Antioch, were set aside for the Genoese – each of them miniature colonies that served as trading posts and homes for a small group of migrants. In Antioch, for instance, they were given a church, a warehouse, a well and thirty houses by the new Norman overlord, Bohemond. In Jerusalem and Acre, the Venetians and the Pisans also had

---

* Not that Janus, the two-faced god. Though it was often said that Genoa faced in two directions: east and west, or alternatively out to the sea and towards the land.
† The ancient provenance of the Holy Grail or *Sacro Catino* is spectacular. No existing work of art can have such an impressive or improbable backstory. It was said to have been carved from an emerald that fell from the turban of Lucifer as he was cast out of Heaven. It was then used by Adam and Eve in the Garden of Eden and given by the Queen of Sheba to Solomon before turning up at the Last Supper and eventually making it to Genoa. More prosaically, it was taken to Paris by Napoleon's troops in the early nineteenth century to be examined, and found to be made of glass. It broke into many pieces on the way back to Genoa and was then clumsily reassembled with one big piece in the middle missing. It has recently been restored, and the missing piece replaced. Recent chemical analysis of the glass indicates that it was made in Mesopotamia.

their own small clearly defined enclaves within the city, as the Italian city-states entered a bitter and often violent competition to dominate trade in the Mediterranean, which lasted for several centuries.

And over those centuries, the Republic of Genoa gained and lost many slivers of territory. Its most significant and long-lasting medieval settlements were along the trade route the Volga Vikings had known well, from what are now Russia and Ukraine to Constantinople and beyond. Kaffa, for instance, once the most important of Genoa's Black Sea possessions, is now the down-market beach resort of Feodosia, its harbour still overlooked by the crumbling battlements of a Genoese castle. The hard-to-impress and extremely well-travelled Berber Muslim scholar Ibn Battuta passed through Kaffa in the 1330s. It was, he declared,

> a great city along the sea-coast inhabited by Christians, most of them Genoese . . . we saw a wonderful harbour with about two hundred vessels, both ships of war and trading vessels, small and large, for it is one of the world's celebrated ports.

Fifteen years later, Kaffa was at war – under siege by an army of sickly Mongols, who had brought with them the Black Death. This version of the plague had probably originated further east, carried by flea-ridden rats, and was already devastating large parts of Asia. Before long the rats and their fleas – and the Black Death – were heading through the Mediterranean in Genoese ships, first to Sicily and then the rest of Europe, where between a third and half of the population would die.

Kaffa itself survived the siege and recovered from the plague, and in the 1430s the Andalusian traveller Pero Tafur declared the city to be 'as large as Seville, or larger, with twice as many inhabitants', and was amazed that the plague hadn't returned, given how many nationalities he found there. He declared that in Kaffa the Genoese sell more slaves, both male and female, than anywhere else in the world. He was shocked that

> the sellers make the slaves strip to the skin, males as well as females, and they put on them a cloak of felt and the price is named. Afterwards they throw off their coverings and make them walk up and down to show whether they have any bodily defect.

This didn't stop Tafur buying three slaves for himself, two women and a man, and telling his readers they were now at home with him in Cordoba. We do not learn their names, nor anything more of their lives.

Slaves, fur and wheat — as well as caviar, a new luxury for Europe — were brought to the markets of Kaffa and Genoa's other Black Sea colonies. There they were sold to merchants who took them by ship via Constantinople, where, in the northern suburbs, across the river known as the Golden Horn, Genoa had another colony, thirty-seven hectares of land called Pera. Then out into the Mediterranean, where, once again, there were long-term Genoese colonies — at Phocaea on the mainland, and the nearby island of Chios. And from there on to Genoa, or one of many dozens of ports in the Mediterranean, on the Atlantic coast, or onwards through the Channel into the North Sea.

These Genoese colonies and settlements (the distinction is not always obvious) had a range of different relationships with their motherland — often closest to the loose model provided by ancient Greece. Many of them had a large degree of independence from Genoa and were ruled by a prince or a group of Genoese notables.* What's important here is that it became

---

* The island of Chios, for instance, was run as a company, in which the stock was owned by a group of Genoese investors, a similar model to the one later used by the English East India Company.

normal for ambitious young Genoese men to migrate, either permanently or with the aim of returning to Genoa with a fortune – a life choice that would be echoed repeatedly when European colonialism began to develop in earnest in the sixteenth century. But unlike, say, the Vikings, they were less likely to assimilate into the local population. From what we know of their settlements, these migrants tended to set up little Genoas wherever they went, an idea captured in a thirteenth-century rhyme, written in Genoese dialect:*

E tanti sun li Zenoexi	And so many are the Genoese
e per lo mondo si distexi	And so spread out around the world
che und'eli van o stan	That wherever they go and stay
un'atra Zenoa ge fan	They make another Genoa there

The little Genoas could take different forms. Not only as colonies, where the Genoese lorded over the locals, but sometimes simply as tiny merchant communities that sprung up all over the place, from London and Bruges to Cadiz and Tunis, Alexandria and further to the east. The Genoese were almost everywhere – but in this they were not quite unique. There was an even broader trading network of Jews, for instance, and the Genoese would sometimes step into the vacuum left when Jews were massacred or expelled from particular territories, which took place repeatedly in western Europe in the Middle Ages.

Venice, too, had many similar settlements in the eastern Mediterranean, and it was a Venetian merchant called Marco Polo who became the most famous European explorer of the period, reaching China in the thirteenth century. But we know from the accounts of travellers heading eastwards – as traders, missionaries or diplomats – that they often found that the

---

* The same poet, known as The Anonymous of Genoa, also recommended that travellers write their wills before they left Genoa.

Genoese were already there. Marco Polo encountered Genoese merchants in the Persian city of Tabriz, while the missionary-bishop Andrew of Perugia mentions merchants from Genoa in the Chinese port now known as Quanzhou.

The Genoese went westwards too, some of them into the unknown. In 1291, two hundred and one years before Columbus began a similar journey, the Vivaldi brothers took two ships into the Atlantic in an attempt to reach India. They were never heard of again. A generation later, Lancelotto Malocello 'discovered' the island of Lanzarote – which was already inhabited by descendants of Berber migrants – and gave it a mangled Spanish version of his own first name. He was said to have been searching for the Vivaldis. And an early fifteenth-century Genoese traveller to the Malian Empire in West Africa believed he had identified a descendant of the Vivaldis on the African coast while Columbus, growing up in Genoa, would have been told the story of the Vivaldis.

By the late fifteenth century, the most influential community of Genoese migrants was in the Spanish city of Seville, where they had, over time, assimilated. Seville, on a navigable river almost seventy kilometres inland, managed to control much of the sea traffic between the Mediterranean and the Atlantic – so critical for northern Europe, and then in the fifteenth century for Africa and the Americas too. The Genoese had been in Seville for a long time: since the thirteenth century, under the last Muslim rulers of the city. And when Christian rule returned to most of Spain, the Genoese were given special privileges in the city, to the irritation of other groups of for-eigners, from France, England and Catalonia.*

---

* The Genoese were provided with their own area, or *barrio*, with a trading-house, a quay, a church, a bathhouse and a communal oven. They were given tax exemptions, and allowed to govern themselves, except in cases of serious crimes such as murder, and they had immunity from retaliation should other Genoese citizens commit acts of piracy.

Members of more than a dozen well-known Genoese trading families settled in Seville, some of them marrying into
local families, and they took up other professions: as bankers,
admirals, city officials, even a royal treasurer. Here they inte-
grated more than elsewhere and ultimately, according to one
modern historian, three-quarters of the nobility of Seville had
Genoese surnames, and their influence had spread throughout
the country, to all the major port cities and to the royal court
with its married co-monarchs, Isabella of Castile and Ferdinand
of Aragon. The presence of powerful Genoese migrants at the
heart of the political and economic elite of Spain made it easier
for the son of a weaver from Genoa to attract royal support for
his ambitious plans to sail across the Atlantic in search of India.
And the long-standing Genoese presence also made it slightly
easier for the monarchs to expel other successful minority
communities.

Spain had been in flux in the second half of the fifteenth
century, finding a new identity, emerging both as an idea and a
political reality after centuries of division. And the new rulers
of what had once been Europe's most multi-cultural state
began to demand a uniformity which forced many – mainly
Jews and Muslims – to convert or migrate. Queen Isabella
and King Ferdinand were the heirs to the two largest Spanish
kingdoms, and longed to expand their realm and to spread the
Roman Catholic version of Christianity to new lands. In this
they were supported by a series of popes – two in a row who
were born in Genoa followed by a Spanish-born pope – who
were friendly towards the monarchs' plans.

1492 is a key year in the history of Spain, and in the history
of migration. And not just because of Columbus and those
three ships – the *Niña*, *Pinta* and *Santa Maria* – which set sail
that August from Palos, just west of Seville. For by then two
major events had taken place, the consequences of which
would endure for centuries. In January, the last Muslim outpost

in western Europe, the Emirate of Granada, had surrendered to the armies of Isabella and Ferdinand, 780 years after the first Muslims arrived in Spain. The Emir, Muhammad XII, a descendant of ancient migrants from Medina and remembered in the Christian West as Boabdil or the Last Moor, was overthrown and went into exile in Morocco. Many thousands of Muslims fled from Granada or converted to Christianity.

Even more dramatic was the expulsion of the Jews of Spain, who had once had a privileged position similar to the Genoese. But in May 1492, following decades of persecution, they were ordered either to convert or leave Spain. About 150,000 Jews are thought to have fled, and an even larger number converted, though they remained, as *conversos*, targets of persecution. Those who left were only allowed to carry their personal belongings, and they headed off, in panic, in every direction.

The Jews who went to Christian countries often fared particularly badly. The large number who went to neighbouring Portugal faced further persecution, including forced conversion and enslavement. The children of Jewish refugees in Portugal were converted en masse to Christianity, and hundreds of them became forced migrants, as juvenile settlers shipped to the previously uninhabited African island of São Tomé. The Jews of Spain received their warmest welcome in North Africa and the Ottoman Empire, establishing themselves as part of Sephardic Jewish communities that flourished in these majority Muslim countries until the second half of the twentieth century – when once again most of them left, many of them for Israel.

And so to that other event of 1492: the first crossing of the Atlantic and the arrival of three small Spanish ships in the Caribbean on 12 October, where they were greeted by charming, friendly locals. It's possible to see this as the

benign – idyllic, even – opening scene of what would become
a quite hideous migration tragedy. For on the broadest level, it
was the prologue to a multi-century inter-continental historical drama series in which, during Season One, the arrival of a
group of migrants in another continent leads to the elimination
of a large proportion of that continent's original population.
In Season Two, millions of people from a third continent are
enslaved and shipped in to replace and augment those first
inhabitants. It doesn't get much better for several more seasons.
Zoom in on those early episodes, as I will now do, and it's a
lot more complicated, of course – but hardly less tragic, and
often farcical.

Columbus first. He was more than a migrant, a nauti-
cal nomad perhaps, who'd wandered the seas ever since
he left Genoa at the age of fourteen, sailing to the eastern
Mediterranean, to the islands off the west coast of Africa and
out into the North Atlantic as far as Iceland. He was plucky and
stubborn, and a talented navigator. He wished more than anything to be rich and famous, and in that he would be successful.
Little is known of his domestic life, except that he married a
Portuguese woman of Italian extraction who lived on an island
near Madeira, and had a long-term mistress in Cordoba. There
are no records of Columbus owning a house, or of being sedentary for any significant period of time.

When he wasn't at sea, Columbus was travelling by land,
trying to raise funds for his proposed transatlantic adventure
from the Spanish monarchs (who had no capital city and
moved around as terrestrial nomads within their own kingdoms*) or from the Portuguese king in Lisbon. When they
didn't show enough interest, he sent his brother northwards to
try to get backing from France and England. Eventually, the

---

* Isabella and Ferdinand spent much of their lives on the move, travelling in luxury
with a vast retinue, as a means of unifying their territory and ensuring alternative
centres of power could not emerge.

Spanish monarchs – concerned particularly about the spread of Portuguese influence in the Atlantic, and the opening of an African sea route to Asia – gave modest support to Columbus' project, as did, less modestly, the bankers of Seville.

Columbus was convinced that the ancient Greeks and Romans were wrong, and that the circumference of the world was much smaller than they had calculated, so it would therefore be a relatively simple matter to sail westwards from Europe to Asia. The opening of a new trade route, not the settlement of new lands, was the principal purpose of his journey. Columbus wasn't entirely clear about his destination. He had read Marco Polo's *Travels* and talked a lot about going to India and the Indies, placenames which in the fifteenth century had a far broader and vaguer meaning than today, and were often used to describe large parts of what we think of as Asia.

Columbus also spoke of travelling to China and carried a letter from the Spanish monarchs to the Great Khan, the title held by Mongol rulers in the time of Marco Polo, and two other pro forma letters with a blank space in which Columbus could write the name of the recipient. He hoped to find Japan as well, unvisited by Europeans but referred to by Marco Polo as a place where 'gold is abundant beyond all measure'. The monarchs gave Columbus an embarrassment of grand titles: Viceroy, Governor and Admiral – presumably to impress the Asian potentates he was expected to meet. And he took with him a translator who spoke Hebrew, Aramaic and some Arabic, none of which would have been much use even if they were going to visit the Great Khan.

Bizarrely, it's not known where Columbus landed first. For all his great feats as a navigator, proper records or detailed descriptions were simply not kept. It was probably an island in the Bahamas now known as San Salvador. We know from contemporary accounts, all written by Columbus or based on summaries of his logbook, that he and his crew first stepped

ashore on an island which was 'fairly large and very flat', where
he raised the royal standard in front of 'some naked people'
living there. He informed them, in a language that they obviously did not understand, that he had 'taken possession of the
island' in the name of King Ferdinand and Queen Isabella. He
gave the locals some red caps and glass beads, and they gave
him parrots and spears and cotton as return gifts.

Columbus depicted the islanders as both intelligent and
obedient, and wrote that they would make 'good servants' and
easily convert to Christianity. He kidnapped seven of them,
commenting how easy it would be to subdue the entire island
with just fifty men 'and make them do whatever we would
wish'. The three small ships continued, passing several more
islands. He noted how green and fertile they were, and he had
already begun to think about colonisation. 'Generally,' said
Columbus, 'it was my wish to pass no island without taking
possession of it; though having annexed one it might be said
that we had annexed all.'

It's hard not to snigger at Columbus' geographical impre-
cision when reading his logbook. He declared, as he passed
through the Bahamas, that he was keen to press on to Asia
'and see if I can strike the island of Japan', and from there continue to China where, as he wrote to the Spanish monarchs,
he intended 'to deliver your Highnesses' letters to the Grand
Khan'. He was only twelve thousand kilometres off course.
Eventually, after some more island-hopping, Columbus arrived
at what he decided, because of its 'size and riches ... must be
Japan'. In fact, it was Cuba. He had 'never seen a more beautiful country'. And on Cuba, the Europeans found, for the first
time, people who ate maize, gathered tobacco leaves and slept
in hammocks (before long, versions of three words in the local
language – maize, tobacco and hammock – entered the vocab-
ulary of many Europeans).

By now, Columbus and his crew were becoming increasingly

interested in gold, and this began to delay their progress and distract them from their original purpose. Columbus saw that many of the islanders – he was soon referring to them as Indians – had gold studs in their noses. When he asked where the gold came from, they pointed in the direction of other islands – which was probably a clever move on their part, whether it was true or not. And so when the Cubans were asked about the source of their gold, and they pointed in the direction of the next large island, back towards Europe, that's where the ships went. That island – Hispaniola, which is nowadays divided between Haiti and the Dominican Republic – would play a pivotal role in the early days of Spanish colonisation in the Americas.*

The early relationship with the Taino people of Hispaniola is portrayed by Columbus as tender, almost idyllic. The crew helped a Taino canoeist who was struggling in bad weather, taking him to the shore and showering him with presents. A chieftain carried high on a litter by four men soon appeared. Columbus and he exchanged gifts and words, helped by the captives from the first island who were now able to speak a little Spanish. The chieftain gave Columbus a belt and two pieces of worked gold. Columbus reciprocated with a cushion, amber beads, slippers and a gold coin. And they all ate a meal together.

Columbus was impressed by the chieftain's gentle dignity – even more so when disaster struck. On Christmas Day 1492, the largest of the Spanish ships was accidentally damaged beyond repair. Columbus recalled, in a letter to Queen Isabella and King Ferdinand, how the chieftain showed 'great sorrow at our disaster' and took immediate action to aid the Europeans by helping them unload the wrecked ship. The 'Indians' of Hispaniola, he gushed,

* Columbus called the island Isla Española because its fields and trees and its fish reminded him so much of Spain, and the name was soon Latinised as Hispaniola.

are so affectionate and have so little greed and in all ways are so amenable that I assure your Highnesses that there is in my opinion no better people and no better land in the world.

The loss of the ship meant some of the Europeans would have to remain on the island. Wood from the wreck was dragged to shore and used to build a small fort, which Columbus called Navidad, or Christmas, after the day of the shipwreck. Navidad became the first European settlement in the Americas since that of the Vikings in Newfoundland almost five centuries earlier. It would provide a temporary home for the thirty-nine Europeans who were chosen to stay behind. Building a settlement had not been part of the plan, and was a consequence of misfortune, but Columbus now saw it as an opportunity. For the Taino people had gold, which they happily exchanged for trifles – shoelaces, or broken glass and crockery. And Columbus was planning to return with more ships and more men.

Columbus did return, almost two years later, with a much larger fleet: seventeen ships, more than twelve hundred men, including labourers and miners, some 'footloose aristocrats' keen to make their fortune, twenty armoured knights with their horses, at least eight priests, some pigs, goats and sheep, as well as wheat and barley seeds, and lots of 'little trees and fruit bushes'. They were planning to stay; the migration of Europeans to the Americas had begun. Columbus set out his reasons in a letter written on that first voyage back to Europe:

Hispaniola is a wonder. The mountains and hills, the plains and meadow lands are both fertile and beautiful. They are most suitable for planting crops and for raising cattle of all kinds, and there are good sites for building towns and villages. The harbours are incredibly fine and there are many great rivers with broad channels and the majority contain gold.

Columbus' First Voyage

From
the Canary Islands

To
the Azores

Atlantic Ocean

FLORIDA

BAHAMAS

CUBA

JAMAICA

◦ San Salvador

HAITI

Navidad

HISPANIOLA

DOMINICAN
REPUBLIC

PUERTO
RICO

GUADELOUPE

DOMINICA

Caribbean Sea

◄ N

300 km

150 miles

0

0

Columbus' purpose had moved from trade, exploration and meeting foreign rulers to settlement and exploitation, with gold, cotton, mastic and slaves the key commodities he planned to send to Europe. Columbus still hoped to do some gentle exploring, and he did so on the way to Hispaniola. He landed first at some smaller southern islands where they found evidence of cannibalism, stories of which soon got back to Europe.* Then Puerto Rico, the 'best of all the islands' according to Columbus' on-board doctor, where the locals fled when they saw the Europeans. When he reached Hispaniola, though, Columbus soon learnt that the settlement of Navidad no longer existed, and every one of his former companions was dead. The idyll was over.

It wasn't clear how the Europeans had died. Several conflicting stories were circulating – largely from followers of the chieftain who had welcomed Columbus on that first trip. They said that the Europeans had fought among themselves, or that locals had taken revenge after some Taino women had been kidnapped, or that they had fallen sick, or that a rival group of Taino had killed them. The mood changed. A chieftain called Caonabo was captured and was said to have confessed. Caonabo was sent to Spain for trial, but drowned when the ship sank. He couldn't swim to safety because he was in chains. Another chieftain, whose followers were accused of stealing from Europeans, had one of his ears cut off in a public ceremony. There were small-scale skirmishes between Europeans and Taino in several parts of Hispaniola, often over women whom the migrants tried to seize. The conflict led to the disruption of the harvest, causing famine and death among many Taino. It was all turning very sour.

----

* A doctor who travelled with Columbus wrote a letter to the city council of Seville, describing the discovery of a human neck in a cooking pot on Guadeloupe and, in vivid and shocking detail, the cannibalistic rituals of the Carib people on the islands south of Hispaniola. The words Caribbean and cannibal both derive from Carib.

Columbus was, by most accounts, a disastrous administrator – and happily disappeared to 'discover' new islands, including Jamaica. The migrants were quarrelling among themselves about many matters, including whether it was acceptable to enslave 'Indians', and about gold, of course, as it became clear there was far less of it on Hispaniola than Columbus had promised. There was now a stream of ships going to and from Spain so news got back to the Spanish monarchs about how much had gone wrong, alongside the suggestion that newly mined royal gold had been embezzled. An inspector was sent out to investigate, and as a result Columbus headed back to Spain, leaving his brother in command – only returning two years later when he had got the renewed support of the King and Queen, and his Genoese bankers.

On Hispaniola the situation became even worse. There was a widespread Taino rebellion, sometimes encouraged by aggrieved Spaniards. Relations had broken down between the Europeans – Spanish and Genoese – whom Columbus had left in charge. One of them, an Andalusian magistrate named Francisco Roldan, had rebelled against Columbus' brother and taken control of the west of the island, whose 'women were more beautiful and more accommodating than elsewhere'. Roldan held the family of a Taino chieftain hostage and demanded gold as a ransom. Europeans began to kill Europeans, and several Spaniards were executed on the orders of Columbus. Soon another inspector arrived from Spain, and Columbus was placed in chains and shipped back to Europe, where he was set free and exonerated. He made only one more journey to the Americas, in 1502, when, stripped of all political responsibility, he travelled along the coastline of Panama and briefly back to Hispaniola, still believing, against all the evidence, that he was in Asia.

The Taino of Hispaniola continued to suffer at the hands of a growing number of Spanish migrants. They were soon expected to pay tribute to their new rulers in gold – which they had previously found in rocks in the rivers, and for which they now had to dig. Their birth rate fell as men and women were separated. Many Taino women were taken by Spaniards as concubines, and many men forced to work as miners. Those who refused to become Christians could be enslaved. Any sign of rebellion was crushed.

There's an extraordinary account by Bartolomé de Las Casas,* a Spanish priest who originally went to Hispaniola as a colonist in 1502 and witnessed many killings. He described in gruesome detail the punishments given to those Taino who were suspected of resisting Spanish rule. Local leaders were tied to a griddle made of wood and grilled to death over a slow fire, or hung from gibbets with straw tied to them and then set alight. Less important Taino were killed more quickly. The Spaniards, said Las Casas,

> laid wagers on whether they could manage to slice a man in two at a stroke, or cut an individual's head from his body, or disembowel him with a single blow of their axes. They grabbed suckling infants by the feet and, ripping them from their mothers' breasts, dashed them headlong against the rocks.

The Spanish, he says, came to 'an unofficial agreement among themselves that for every European killed one hundred Indians would be executed'.

Las Casas claimed that the 'Indian' population of Hispaniola had shrunk from three million in 1492 to just three hundred by the time he was writing half a century later. Las Casas was and remains a controversial figure, and undoubtedly overstated the original population (though it was then, as now, the most populous island in the Caribbean). But it is clear that a combination

---

* Attentive readers will remember Las Casas as the man who thought the people of Hispaniola belonged to one of the Lost Tribes of Israel.

of murder, famine and disease led to the almost total extinction of the language and culture of the Taino people of Hispaniola in the decades after Columbus landed there. So dramatic was the fall in population that the colonists brought in people to work as labourers from other islands, particularly the Bahamas where, according to Las Casas, 'the native population was wiped out by forcible expatriation'. But most of them died on Hispaniola and a new group of forced migrants were shipped across the Atlantic in large numbers: black slaves from Africa, setting a pattern which would be repeated in many parts of the Americas.

Cuba, Jamaica and Puerto Rico – also largely inhabited by Taino until the arrival of the Europeans – were all devastated in similar fashion. And so too, from 1519, were populations on the Central American mainland. Smallpox, brought over by Spanish migrants, was probably the biggest killer. The Aztec Empire in Mexico was defeated militarily by a small number of Europeans and some local allies, but it was disease that caused a dramatic population collapse. And then, a decade later, the Inca Empire in Peru disintegrated as the Spanish arrived with their superior military technology and their deadly diseases. Spain had gained its own American empire and was, for now, in total control.*

Overall, it's a pretty grotesque tale – a well-documented example of what we might in modern times call genocide, committed by a relatively small group of migrants over a period of about fifty years. They came largely for economic reasons, often from more impoverished parts of Spain, seeking

---

* On the mainland, local leaders were more likely to be co-opted into the new ruling elites, and so the destruction of local cultures and languages was not quite as extensive as in the Caribbean. There was also some intermarriage. Isabel Moctezuma (born Techuipo) was the daughter of one Aztec emperor and the wife of two more, who was then married, sequentially, to no fewer than three Spanish conquistadors. She also had a child out of wedlock with Hernán Cortés, who had led the conquest of the Aztec Empire. Several of her descendants married into European aristocratic families. There's a similar story with the Inca princess Quispe Sisa, later renamed Ines, who had a child with the conquistador Francisco Pizarro.

gold and other riches, though some among them sought power, or to spread the word of God in its Roman Catholic incarnation. And among those early settlers were some who were clumsily well-intentioned, including Columbus himself on that first journey to Hispaniola. Las Casas was not alone in criticising the cruelty of his fellow Spaniards. It is also worth noting that the migrants came from a brutal society, in which the Inquisition was happily torturing and burning those whose Catholic credentials were in doubt, and that some of the more sadistic methods of colonisation used in Hispaniola had been previously employed in the conquest of the Canary Islands.

But it's still hard not to flinch, even half a millennium later, at these tales of systematic murder, torture and rape. For some of the Spanish migrants, the native people of the Americas did not have souls, were less than human. Comparisons were made between them and monkeys. The Spanish also used the fact that some native Americans practised cannibalism or human sacrifice as an excuse to enslave or murder them, even though the first victims of the Spanish – the Taino – practised neither. The settlers, thanks to the support of the pope, could claim that the Spanish had a God-given right to rule over the Americas (with one medium-sized portion, known as Brazil, set aside for their Portuguese neighbours).

For some more recent defenders of the Spanish Empire, this version of the tale of Spanish migration to the Americas is the beginning of the *Leyenda Negra*, or the Black Legend, which they see as a multi-century international conspiracy to defame Spain and its achievements. According to this legend, the other nations of Europe – particularly the Protestant ones – ganged up on Spain in order to undermine its glory and its empire, to seize its territory, to demonise the Spanish people and to disparage Catholicism. For instance, there's a seventeenth-century English translation of Las Casas' *Destruction of the Indies* which has a new title, 'Popery Truly Display'd in its Bloody Colours', and continues with another explanatory sentence that was not in the original:

> A faithful Narrative of the Horrid and Unexampled Massacres, Butcheries, and all manner of Cruelties that Hell and Malice could invent, committed by the Popish Spanish Party on the Inhabitants of West-India.

It's true that the Dutch and the English showed great interest in the writings of Las Casas, which were translated and sold widely across Europe. Spain's imperial rivals were very happy to portray the Spanish as merciless butchers, both as a way of damaging the reputation of Spain but also because it might deflect attention from their own brutal treatment of native populations in the Americas and elsewhere.

The Spanish set an appallingly low benchmark for the treatment of indigenous people. And it seems safe to say that the Spanish in early sixteenth-century America must rank pretty high in any list of the most disagreeable migrants of all time. But from the perspective of the wider story I'm seeking to tell here, the Spanish normalised a kind of conquering migrant behaviour that would be repeated, with national variations, by the English, the French, the Portuguese, the Dutch and the Belgians – and, on a far smaller scale, the Danes. The age of European colonialism had begun, in ways that still shape our world.

Until this time, Europeans had very little contact with what would become known, often inaccurately, as primitive or savage people. During the Middle Ages, Europeans were used to dealing with Arabs or Mongols who were, in economic and military terms, often their equals or superiors. Not so in the Caribbean. There they encountered people who did not use the wheel, or iron, or domestic animals, who had very different ideas of God, of the position of women in society, of land ownership and of clothing – who lived in a manner that was deeply unfamiliar to them.

Columbus and others had been expecting to find the monsters spoken of in so many medieval travel texts: dog-headed humans, men with a single eye at the centre of their forehead, or an island entirely populated by women. And, of course, they found none. But they were bemused by the people they did find, who were so recognisable yet seemed so different – and they often treated them as if they were monsters, or members of another species.

In the writings of those, like Las Casas, who did recognise the native people of America as fellow humans, and who were openly critical of Spanish cruelty, it's possible to see another notion beginning to form: what became known as the idea of the 'noble savage', a romanticisation of indigenous people that lingers to this day. Las Casas says that the Taino of Hispaniola

> own next to nothing, and have no urge to acquire material possessions, and as a result they are neither ambitious nor greedy, and are totally uninterested in worldly power . . . They are innocent and pure in mind and have a lively intelligence.

It's a broadly positive view, certainly when contrasted with those of his more sadistic contemporaries, but it's also inaccurate and rather patronising, with Las Casas providing perhaps an early example of the 'white saviour' complex. For him, the Taino are empty vessels; undifferentiated, unsophisticated, unworldly people. And so it should be no surprise that Las Casas concludes his long list of Taino attributes by declaring that these 'make them particularly receptive to learning and understanding the truths of our Catholic faith'.

What's missing in this, of course, are the voices of the Taino themselves, and of members of the other communities that were torn apart by the arrival of Europeans on their shores. The fact that those voices are lost for ever should not absolve us of a responsibility to try to imagine their lives and reassemble parts of their history. Archaeology, genetics, comparative linguistics and a careful reading of European sources can give us clues as to the lives they led before 1492. And we do know a little of their deep history.

The Taino of Hispaniola were originally migrants, like all of us, from Africa, and migrants again in more recent times. Though the Taino, like the ancient Athenians, insisted that they were nothing of the sort and had always been there, and told the Spanish that they had emerged from two caves on the island. In fact, we now know the Taino shared an ancient genetic heritage with their new European rulers in two ways – both from Neanderthals, and from those more modern humans who left Africa for the Middle East about a hundred thousand years ago. While the early ancestors of Columbus and his crew turned left towards Europe, the early ancestors of the Taino turned right. Eventually they crossed from the Russian Far East to Alaska. And by doing so they, not Columbus – nor the Vikings – 'discovered' America. Then they headed south. It all gets more complicated after that, as the islands of the Caribbean were gradually settled, not by the most direct, most obvious route from Florida and what is now the United States, but from Central and South America – from where the sea currents are more friendly to would-be migrants.

Humans first settled Hispaniola by 5000 BCE. There's some archaeological evidence that these first settlers came from Central America, though later migrants came from South America, island hopping northwards from Trinidad. During the millennium that preceded the Spanish conquest there was a great mingling of the people of the Caribbean, with complex and multi-directional patterns of migration, particularly between the large northern islands: Cuba, Hispaniola, Jamaica, Puerto Rico and the Bahamas, most of whose inhabitants spoke mutually intelligible versions of the language known in more recent times as Taino. Sea travel was very important. There was much regular trade between the islands – with, for instance, cotton and salted fish from the Bahamas being exported to Hispaniola. And the Spanish were amazed to see Taino canoes, made out of a single tree trunk, carrying one hundred and fifty people.

The Taino are so named because they pointed at themselves saying the word 'Taino' to the Spanish. The word actually meant 'good' and seems to have been the Taino way of distinguishing themselves from their Carib enemies on the southern islands. For those very first Europeans travellers the Caribs were fierce bloodthirsty cannibals, in contrast with the gentle peace-loving Taino. It's a binary classification that has lingered, and still turns up in history textbooks and in literature. James Michener's 1989 door-stopper of a novel, *Caribbean*, begins with a pre-Columbus encounter between stereotypical goodies and baddies, between angelic island-dweller ('they lived in harmony with their small universe') and demonic Carib invaders ('a fierce terrible people'). 'In the short run,' Michener intones, 'brutality always wins', and so the Caribs are victorious and carry out a mass slaughter.

There are many obvious objections to be made to this kind of account, particularly on behalf of the Caribs – but also for the Taino. They're infantilised and turned into a single standardised unit by this simplistic version of their history, which sometimes veers close to suggesting that their supposed gentleness made them complicit in their own eradication by the Spanish. And it's an approach that underplays their resistance to Spanish rule and fails to acknowledge the smaller ways, cultural and genetic, in which the Taino live on. DNA tests show that many people living in the northern Caribbean, and from its large diaspora, are partly descended from the Taino – though the fact that most of that descent is matrilineal is a reminder of the ugly reality of those times: Taino men were likely to be killed or enslaved, while Taino women would often be raped and become concubines.

Those who resisted Spanish rule in Hispaniola have not been entirely forgotten. They appear first as half-drawn, marginal characters in European accounts, and then reappear much later, long after decolonialisation, in Haiti and the Dominican Republic, as ancient heroes after whom streets are named and statues erected, who are acclaimed on postage stamps and who are treated with sentimental pride. Take Caonabo, for instance, the chieftain accused of killing those first European migrants, and who drowned in chains while being taken to Spain. From European accounts we know that Caonabo was a migrant too – from the Bahamas – who ruled much of central Hispaniola. An image of him appeared, for a while, on the Dominican Republic's one-cent coin, and there's an enormous statue of him sculpted as a muscle-bound near-naked breaker-of-chains in a city park close to his adopted Hispaniola home.

Then there's his wife, the poet Anacaona,* from one of the island's princely families, who fought on after her husband's death and was hanged by the Spanish in 1504. Her life (and death) is the subject of one of the great salsa songs of the 1970s, 'Anacaona' by the Puerto Rican singer Cheo Feliciano, in which she appears as 'an Indian of the captive race' and a *buena negrona* – the archetype of the strong, good, black woman, with the 'soul of a dove', but who dies angry and does not forgive. There has been a flurry of recent English- and Spanish-language books about Anacaona, sometimes portrayed on the cover as a Disney princess, a proto-Pocahontas who usually fails, entirely plausibly, to understand why these pale-faced, covered-up foreigners are

---

* About whom Tennyson wrote what is surely one of his worst poems, in which she is described as 'Naked, and dark limb'd, and gay'. The refrain is no better: 'Who was so happy as Anacaona / The beauty of Espagnola, / The golden flower of Hayti?'

so obsessed by something so mundane as gold – and who dies a martyr to the Taino nation. Her great-nephew Enriquillo is another star of postage stamps and public statuary. He led and survived the final Taino revolt in the hills of Hispaniola in the 1530s and is sometimes portrayed as the last of his tribe. And that was, more or less, where the history of the Taino ended. Twentieth-century historians and school textbooks repeatedly refer to their extinction.

But there's a final twist to this Taino tale, a resurrection of sorts in which modern migrants play a central role. For there has been a resurgence of interest in the fate of the Taino in recent decades, largely on the part of individuals who identify as Taino – and who have attempted to revive the music, cuisine, religious rituals, and even to reconstruct the Taino language. They argue that their traditions and culture were never eliminated and that the Taino were not wiped out. For one activist, speaking in 2008, all the talk of extinction was nonsense, a crime against her community: 'The true genocide is to say that we do not exist, that we are extinct; do they not see that I am here? That I have not died!'

Taino activism is usually dated back to the late 1970s, when individuals of Puerto Rican heritage, living on the island or elsewhere in the United States, formed cultural and political groups aimed at challenging the extinction story and rebuilding the identity of their community. The response from the other islands of the north Caribbean has been more muted, and modern Taino activism has remained a predominantly Puerto Rican phenomenon. The reasons are complex. In part it's because in the other formerly Taino islands of the region there has been an emphasis on post-colonial nation-building, centred on the notion of pride in a mixed heritage – European, African and indigenous – rather than on the cultures of particular communities or on indigenous pre-colonial identities. Puerto Rico, on the other hand, is the only large Caribbean island not to have become independent and has drifted away in its own post-colonial vacuum.

For Puerto Rico is formally part of the USA (as a territory but not a state), and the rise of Taino activism has to be seen in that context. More specifically, Taino activism has also been driven, to a large extent, by first- and second-generation Puerto Rican migrants to other parts of the United States, particularly New York. The Asociación Indigena de Puerto Rico formed in Manhattan in the 1980s, but soon split into rival groups. Some sought to build a broader organisation appealing to Taino from other countries; others placed greater emphasis on music, or language, or on building closer links with nascent Taino organisations in Puerto Rico, or with Native Americans in the rest of the USA. There was no obvious objective to unite their members beyond denying the extinction of the Taino.

There is an important Native American context to the Taino revival. Recently, one of the early Taino activists remembered how when the Taino movement was beginning other Native Americans would say 'here come those effing Puerto Ricans pretending to be Indians'; more recently, he jested, they just say 'here come those freaking Tainos', and for him that represented progress. But there's a serious point here, too, because the Taino are not formally recognised by the US government's Bureau of Indian Affairs and are therefore not one of the 574 'tribes' who have varying degrees of autonomy and control over their ancestral lands. And they're unlikely ever to meet the official criteria for recognition, which, critically, depend on continuity of existence of a tribe as some kind of political body since the pre-European period. For some activists this lack of official recognition is a double injustice, given that the Taino suffered first and hardest at the hands of European migrants. Others see it as a strength of the Taino movement that it has grown without government recognition or support.

There are also vociferous critics of the movement, often from within the migrant community. There's one particularly adamant and forthright New York-based academic of Puerto Rican origin, who describes some of the 'Neo-Taino' leaders as 'extremists' and 'ethnic hustlers' who are attempting to get official recognition in order to 'grab land' and get compensation for colonial atrocities, as well as introduce 'bogus indigenous history' into school curricula in Puerto Rico and the diaspora. He asserts that the Taino extinction was simply 'a fact' because the pure bloodlines and the language died out.

In September 2018, a Taino symposium was held at the National Museum of the American Indian in New York. It took place inside the old Custom House, a fine early twentieth-century neoclassical edifice with beaux-arts trimmings, including stone busts representing the 'eight races of mankind', which was constructed on the site of Fort Amsterdam, the first European building in Manhattan, on territory that once belonged to the Lenape Indians – who were thanked and remembered in several of the speeches at the symposium. The organisers saw their event as the culmination of forty years of activism, and as a celebration of their attempts to inform the world that the Taino still existed.

It was a lively and well-attended occasion, with Taino music and prayers, and lots of talking – in Spanish and English, with a few Taino words thrown in. There was little sign of the rancour or rivalries of the recent past, referred to in passing by several participants. There were occasional notes of caution – one speaker, a teacher, prefaced her comments by saying she realised this was a touchy issue for many in the audience, and then said she didn't encourage her Puerto Rican students to say 'I am a Taino', both because it suggested they thought of themselves as pure-blooded, but also because it might imply that they were disowning their African heritage. 'We're a mix,' she declared, and said that's what she taught her students. The audience responded politely – and everyone else continued happily describing themselves as Taino.

For outsiders, the rise of Taino activism and the nuances of the great Taino extinction debate can seem quite obscure – either a straggling thread of the Colombus story or an argument between different groups of Puerto Rican migrants living in the United States. But they touch on wider issues, serving as a reminder that many migrants feel a desire both to assimilate to a new culture and rebuild and even reinvent their old one – often at the same time. And that those who have emerged as the greatest defenders of the indigenous status of the Taino are those who have left their ancestral homelands, who – living now in New York or New Jersey – can therefore no longer meaningfully call themselves indigenous. The story of the Taino is a reminder, too, of the importance that many people still place on bloodlines, as if cultural continuity was critically dependent on who had sex with whom in the forgotten past.

But, more important in the modern context, the Taino movement can also be seen as a case study in contemporary identity politics, in which power over who gets to choose that identity is no longer the prerogative of scientists and academics and the government. That power is shifting, not always comfortably, into the hands of the individuals and groups concerned. That can be both liberating and burdensome – liberating because it gives us all agency over how we are described, burdensome because it makes many of us feel we have to choose our sides, to define ourselves with a simple adjective. Ultimately, though, if individuals want to identify themselves primarily as Taino or American Indian or Latino or Black – or Yaghan or Genoese or English or European for that matter – there's usually little point in trying to persuade them to do otherwise, even if there sometimes seems to be a tenuous case for that particular identity.

There are alternatives: allowing ourselves the freedom to have multiple identities, to change our minds about who we are and acknowledge that our self-identities depend on the circumstances, or on whom we are talking to. My concern is that these categories, these self-identities, sometimes reduce our ability to imagine the lives of those who are not like us, to feel empathy for those who seem different. By focusing on our deep history, on our common descent, on our history as migrants – ancient and modern – we might begin to place a greater emphasis on our shared heritage and identity as human beings above all others.

A Sixth Intermission

Like billions of other people around the world, I spent many months of the early 2020s in lockdown. My incarceration was perfectly comfortable, but somehow inappropriate for someone writing about migration. For I was back living in the place I was born, not just the city of my birth but in the very house in which I first saw the light of day. There, my eighty-seven-year-old mother and I ate and talked and ordered supermarket deliveries and remembered old times and watched bad TV and read plague novels – and recovered rapidly from an early infection by the virus, possibly picked up by me while on the Columbus trail in Genoa.

For my daily government-prescribed outdoor exercise, I spent a lot of time in two nearby cemeteries, searching for gravestones that told a story. Brompton Cemetery is enormous, and full of fine funerary architecture and nineteenth-century neoclassical arcades. There is an eclectic, cosmopolitan mix of corpses residing here – of all religions and none – and a large number of Russians, Italians, Poles and Iranians. And amidst them all I found the grave of a visiting Sioux chieftain called Long Wolf, who came to London as part of Buffalo Bill's Wild West show in the 1890s and died of pneumonia. He was once a warrior who'd fought Custer at Little Bighorn, and then became a fairground attraction and actor who – in feathers and moccasins, whooping and scalping – was part of the vaudeville version of 'Cowboys and Indians' re-enacted for Queen Victoria and the wider British public. His bones have now gone from Brompton Cemetery, disinterred in the 1990s and sent back to his homeland for reburial. The gravestone, with its carving of a running wolf, remains.

The tiny Moravian burial ground, hidden behind a high wall, is far more exclusive – set aside for members of a Protestant missionary sect founded in the sixteenth century in what is now the Czech Republic. I knew the cemetery from my childhood as the place where a pet lion cub called Christian,* owned by two local residents, used to play, and where I played too, but not at the same time. The burial ground is an unusual sight in Britain because the gravestones all look identical and are laid flat on the grass – as if to say we are all the same in death. There's one unexpected exception, the only non-Moravian buried there: a slightly raised gravestone, in the south-west corner, with this simple inscription:

NUNAK
AN ESKIMO
BOY
1770–1788

Nunak had been brought by Moravian missionaries from his home in northern Canada to London, where he died of

---

* Christian was born in a British zoo in 1969 and then sold to two Australians who lived in Chelsea. When Christian was older, the Australians sent him to live in Kenya, where he was released into the wild. A year later, the Australians travelled to Kenya to see Christian, who recognised them, nuzzling them affectionately. The film of this reunion became one the most successful of early YouTube videos, with more than fifteen million views.

smallpox. He was buried separately because he had not been baptised.* We know nothing more of his short life.

He was just one of hundreds of early American travellers to Britain, most of them treated as specimens to be studied, or as curiosities to be displayed in public and shown to the king, or to be trained as interpreters in preparation for future conquests. Many died in Britain, one in four according to a recent study, including the best-known of them all, Pocahontas, who was buried in the Kentish port of Gravesend in 1619 – and who will reappear in this story. We don't even have the names of the first recorded Americans in Britain – three men from Newfoundland who were 'clothed in the skins of beasts, and ate raw flesh, and spoke such speech that no man could understand'. They were presented to Henry VII at the start of the sixteenth century. We don't know if they ever went home, but they do seem to have spent at least two years in Britain – long enough, perhaps, for them, unlike Long Wolf or Nunak or Pocahontas, to be described as migrants.

We could copy the strangled logic of those who still refer to Columbus' 'discovery' of America to make the playful claim that these three unnamed men from Newfoundland 'discovered' England. And by the same logic, it could be argued that those Taino who accompanied Columbus on his first eastwards trip across the Atlantic 'discovered' Europe. There were at least seven Taino on board the *Niña* as it headed back to Spain, to be used as evidence by Columbus that he had found new lands. All but two of them died before they could return to the Caribbean, killed by their exposure to European diseases. Their original names are unknown, though one of them, who was introduced to Queen Isabella in Barcelona, was baptised as

---

* There is a gravestone for another 'Eskimo' in the Moravian cemetery. A girl, unnamed but buried with all the others, and therefore presumably baptised.

Diego Colón, with Columbus as his godfather and the supplier, in its Spanish version, of his new surname.

Very little is known about Diego Colón, but there has been an attempt to resurrect his story. José Barreiro, a US-based historian and member of the Taino Nation of the Antilles, reimagined the life of Colón for his 1993 novel *Taino*. Barreiro gives him a Taino name, Guaikan, and introduces him as a plucky twelve-year-old living on that first Bahamian island visited by Columbus and his crew, whom the youngster describes as 'bearded men covered with cloth'. Guaikan is 'drunk with the pull of adventure' and chooses to leave home. He's a stowaway, travelling to Hispaniola and then Europe – becoming Columbus' favoured translator. He is unimpressed by the pomp and finery of the Spanish court and decides that of all the great European technological innovations the wheelbarrow, 'a marvel of a tool', is the most useful.

Guaikan returns to the Caribbean, witnessing the spread of European diseases through Taino lands and the execution of Anacaona. He marries her cousin and survives the last Taino revolt against the Spanish in the 1530s. By this time Guaikan has been befriended by Bartolomé de Las Casas and has time to write his memoirs in a Dominican monastery. *Taino* is not great literature, but it's a good lockdown read – as well as being a genuine attempt to capture the thoughts and life story of someone who witnessed extraordinary events and who would otherwise be voiceless. It also provides an unsettling reminder of the shadow of contagion that hangs over the early contact between Europe and the America. The Spanish brought smallpox (and other diseases) with them to the Americas and received syphilis as a less-lethal return gift.

Lockdown and quarantine, of course, are intended to stop disease by stopping the movement of human beings. And that's because there has always been an intimate, complex relationship between human mobility and contagious disease. That's often been used as an excuse, in the past and now, for blaming migrants – and their recent descendants – for pandemics, often with no evidence. In ancient times, before trains and planes, contagion spread more slowly around the world, carried by people on the move or the animals – often rats and fleas – that travelled with them. But it's probable that those individuals were rarely migrants. The precise chains of infection are seldom clear, but the evidence suggests that soldiers, merchants and those actually seeking to flee the disease were more likely to be responsible. Now it's probably business travellers and holidaymakers who are the main carriers.

But migrants and their recent descendants tend to suffer disproportionately during pandemics as societies turn in on themselves, settle old scores and seek someone to blame. That has been true since the earliest pandemic for which we have a historical account: the Athenian plague of 430 BCE, described in detail by Thucydides, in which a third of the inhabitants of the city-state, including its ruler Pericles, were killed. Resident foreigners – or *metics* – were targeted in the aftermath of the plague, their rights restricted, and some of them enslaved. During the Black Death in Europe, thousands of Jews were killed, many of them accused of poisoning wells. The worst of dozens of massacres took place in Strasbourg, where more than two hundred Jews were burnt to death, and the rest of the community dispossessed and driven into exile.

Then there are the many name games, in which it becomes easy, almost natural, to demonise foreigners with a simple adjective. And so for Italians and Germans syphilis became the 'French disease', but the 'Neapolitan disease' according to the French, and the 'Polish disease' for Russians, and so on. The same has been true of flu and modern viruses. The Spanish flu did not start in Spain, but has been mistakenly associated with that country ever since. Other major twentieth-century flu epidemics were named after Hong Kong and Russia. In the early days of the spread of HIV, Aids was portrayed as an American disease in the Soviet media, and sometimes as a Haitian disease by American journalists.

These games continue, notably with Donald Trump's attempts to relabel Covid-19 as the Wuhan or Chinese virus. But there was worse. Migrants once again became scapegoats.* In many countries there were attacks, verbal and physical, on migrants who looked, just possibly, as if they might be Chinese, though they usually weren't. There's the sorry story of Am-Shalem Singson from the north-east Indian state of Manipur, a member of the Jewish Bnei Manashe community, said to be one of the Lost Tribes, who migrated to Israel in 2017. He was hospitalised with severe chest and lung injuries after two Israeli men screaming 'Chinese' and 'Corona' assaulted him. In Dublin, a woman of Chinese origin was thrown into a canal – and the video of the incident went viral on social media; while a Korean student in New York was punched in the face, her jaw dislocated as her attacker screamed 'Where is your corona mask, you Asian bitch?' There were dozens of similar cases, from every continent.

For rich migrants, as always, life was easier, if heavily disrupted. It meant long separations for families spread out across the globe, and individuals forced to remain wherever they were when lockdown was imposed. I too was separated from my children, in India, for many months. Some, like me, spent more unbroken time in the country of their birth than at any time since childhood – though there can't have been many who found themselves back in the house in which they were born. Lockdown had finally given me a reason to stay at home.

---

* When I was in Genoa, before the disease had spread widely in Italy, Chinese shops had closed because locals were boycotting them. A few weeks later, the governor of the Italian region of Veneto declared that his country would deal with the spread of Covid much better than China, because of Italy's 'culturally strong attention to hygiene, washing hands, taking showers, whereas we have all seen the Chinese eating mice alive'.

CHAPTER SEVEN

Virginia, Slavery and the *Mayflower*

Try this. Tell a friend the story of Joseph Kearney. For he was an Irishman, a middle-aged shoemaker in the tiny village of Moneygall in County Offaly, born and brought up there in the late eighteenth century. And like hundreds of thousands of other people from Ireland, Kearney migrated to America during the Great Famine, settling in the Midwestern state of Ohio. Once there he sent back home for his family – his wife and three children – and they all came to Ohio and became citizens of the USA in the days when it was easier to do such things. Joseph Kearney died an American. Now tell your friend that a descendant of Joseph Kearney of the Irish village of Moneygall became president of the United States, and then ask your friend to guess the name of the president. Most people get it wrong, again and again. They try Clinton, or the Bushes, or Reagan, or Kennedy or Biden or even Donald Trump. The answer is Barack Obama – who was the great-great-great-great-grandson of Joseph Kearney, the shoemaker from Moneygall.

Those who do get the answer right may remember Obama's

visit to Moneygall in 2011. Amid sleet and sunshine, America's first black president flew in by helicopter as part of a state visit to Ireland, aimed at shoring up support among Irish Americans back home in the run-up to the 2012 presidential election. It was described as a homecoming for a son of the soil, and the president responded with a joke about having mislaid the apostrophe in the surname O'Bama. He met some distant cousins, visited Joseph Kearney's old house and drank Guinness in the local pub. Michelle Obama, who also has Irish heritage via a slave-owner called Henry Shields, learned to pull a pint of Guinness – and was teased by her husband for spilling some of the precious drink. The presidential visit left a deep and long-lasting impression – in the form of lots of American flags on Main Street, an Obama Café, and a nearby motorway service station called the Barack Obama Plaza, which is also very popular with hen and stag parties. And two of those distant Irish cousins were invited to Washington for Obama's second inauguration.

Obama himself has complex and eloquent views on race, and of his own racial heritage. And he wouldn't be surprised or offended, I think, that many people wouldn't choose him as an obvious descendant of an Irish shoemaker. Obama considers himself black, but has always been keen to embrace his mixed heritage – and that was how he presented himself to the American electorate during the most famous speech of his first electoral campaign:

I am the son of a black man from Kenya, and a white woman from Kansas ... I am married to a black American who carries within her the blood of slaves and of slave-owners, an inheritance we pass on to our two precious daughters. I have brothers, sisters, nieces, nephews, uncles and cousins of every hue and every race scattered across three continents.

Barack Obama's identity served as a battleground of America's racial politics. He faced accusations from the right that he was a foreigner or a Muslim, or both (and was even declared to be the Antichrist), while to a variety of genealogical pedants and amateur logicians, Obama was quite simply not black, by the fact of being half white. Which meant, therefore, that he could only be considered biracial, or of mixed race – and his own views had no relevance in the matter. To old-fashioned white racists, though, he was undeniably black (though they would often use another word) under the 'one-drop rule', only removed from the legal codes of several states during the 1960s, and according to which anyone with any black ancestry whatsoever was black.

There were challenges from elsewhere to Obama's identity, and his right to self-identify as black – particularly when he was first nominated as a presidential candidate. Some black Americans were not won over by what they saw as a blackness that was only skin deep. 'Is he really black?' they asked, rhetorically. Obama grew up, they pointed out, in a white cultural and social environment. And he wasn't descended from slaves, unlike most black people in America. The writer Debra Dickerson declared simply 'Obama isn't black' and explained that '"black" in our political and social reality, means those descended from West African slaves.' She was particularly unimpressed by all the white people swooning over Obama: 'You're not embracing a black man, a descendant of slaves. You're replacing the black man with an immigrant of recent African descent of whom you can approve without feeling either guilty or frightened.'

The debate about Obama's identity swirled on through his presidency, and was a reminder of a deeper, wider malaise in

American life. It's hard not to see this debate as a symbol of unfinished business, of the extent to which race and slavery, and the many migrations of the past, continue to play a central role in American politics and society. Those migrations are at the heart of many familiar stories that are told about the USA and its origins. And I cannot claim, as I have about other times and places, particularly in Europe and Asia, that migration tales have been ignored. It's different in the USA: migration is centre stage.

However, those American stories are often told in a contextual vacuum, as modern mythology – not necessarily false, but constructed for unhistorical purposes – to build an idea of a nation, or to assert the rights of specific communities. They are told in a way that provides support and succour for a particular version of the past and the present, and for the beneficiaries of that version. And so the stories of specific groups of migrants, forced and unforced, intercontinental and within America, have met a multitude of fates – disregarded or neglected at one extreme, romanticised and turned into legend at the other.

Ever since Europeans and Africans, usually under dramatically different circumstances, first settled in North America there's been an obsession with racial categories and hierarchies. And from this obsession two very different encapsulating migration narratives have emerged – one called Freedom, and the other called Slavery. These narratives are too often considered in isolation, as if they were unconnected stories, or perhaps as if they were twins of different colours, an embarrassment separated at birth. But, in practice, the stories of these two migrations are deeply entangled, coiling round each other like a double helix. Together they provide the rich raw material of the great American paradox: that the land of the free was also a land of enslavement. And the context of this enduring paradox are stories of injustice and hope, of dreams and nightmares, of independence and captivity, full of nuance and detail, and which need to be told and retold together – alongside those of Native Americans, many of whom themselves became unwilling migrants, often driven into reservations far from their ancestral homelands.

There are many examples of this perpetual entanglement. It is too frequently forgotten or ignored that many of America's Founding Fathers were slave-owners; that a significant number of cowboys were black, as were, earlier, a small number of slave-owners; that some Native Americans were enslaved, and some also owned slaves – and that there has been widespread miscegenation in North America ever since those first Atlantic migrations. One of the more amusing outcomes of modern DNA testing is the dismay of white supremacists who have discovered they have black African ancestry – on live TV, on one occasion. Perhaps even more striking in its symbolism is another piece of Obama trivia: the recent finding by genealogical researchers that Barack Obama was descended from a slave after all – though not via his Kenyan father but through his 'white' mother. And Obama's other line of descent from Africa came from John Punch, a man who is often – not entirely accurately – described as North America's first slave.

More on John Punch shortly. But before that some brief prehistory of slavery and the Atlantic migrations to what became the United States – including the unlikely tale of Little Stephen, and the unforgotten life and early death of Pocahontas.

Slavery was practised by some Native American groups, before and after the arrival of Europeans, though their slaves tended to be captured in war, were not defined by their skin colour and were rarely bought and sold as if they were commodities – though they might sometimes be ransomed. Early Spanish settlers in Florida and the Mexican borderlands enslaved some Native Americans, as they had in the Caribbean – and they also began to bring enslaved Africans with them, usually referred to in documents and memoirs simply as negroes. However, one of those slaves from Africa, known by his captors as Estevanico, or Little Stephen, has emerged from the footnotes of history to become something of a legend, a modern hero, his story retold and reimagined and embellished by a wide variety of writers.

It's not known where Estevanico was born, and at what point in his life he was enslaved. Confusingly he's described in the Spanish sources as an 'Arab Negro' from Azemmour in Morocco, leading to some discord about his identity, as he has been claimed in recent times as either a Moroccan or as a black African – and sometimes both. In 1528 Estevanico – and his owner – landed in what is now the USA as part of a large and particularly clueless Spanish expedition that planned to conquer and colonise Florida. The expedition was a disaster. Its leaders were distracted – again – by a futile search for gold. Desertions, shipwrecks and deaths in warfare, by drowning and by starvation all followed. A small group of Europeans became cannibals – until only one of them was left. Hundreds of would-be settlers died in Florida, or as they made their way on rafts along the coastline to Texas. The Spanish authorities thought there were no survivors. But eight years later, four members of the expedition reappeared in northern Mexico.

Estevanico and three Spaniards had walked, barefoot and naked, from Texas to the Pacific coast of Mexico, helped and hindered by different groups of Native Americans. The four men were themselves enslaved at one point by Karankawa Indians, and they then escaped, surviving by posing as miracle healers, with Estevanico as their linguist and spokesman. On his arrival in Mexico, Estevanico was then sold to the Spanish viceroy in Mexico City, where he would have witnessed the repression of a rebellion by African slaves in continental America. Five putative rebels were executed. The following year Estevanico was sent on a new mission deep into what is now Arizona and New Mexico where he disappeared, presumed dead.

But there's a different, modern happy-ending version of this story — for which there's only circumstantial evidence — in which Estevanico faked his own death to escape Spanish slavery and lived out his years among the Zuni Indians. By this account, the first of many millions of migrants to cross the Atlantic and to live in what would become the United States was not a white European but a former slave from Africa. And thereby the tale of Little Stephen had been transformed, with a final twist, into an alternative foundation myth.

There are several foundation myths that are better known and that have a stronger historical underpinning — and they each have quite different migration stories at their heart. Chronologically speaking, the next in line is the city of St Augustine in Florida, which in 1565 became the first permanent European settlement in what is now the mainland USA. It began as a Spanish military outpost aimed at stopping the French from building a permanent settlement at nearby Jacksonville and soon became the capital of Spanish Florida. But the story of St Augustine, even though it has been continuously inhabited ever since, rarely features in the grand American historical narratives — presumably because it wasn't an English settlement, and because Florida only became a full state in 1845.*

The best-known foundation myth? Well, if you ask most

---

* There are several other less well-known early foundation myths. There's a case that's been made for San Juan, for instance, founded in 1521 on the island of Puerto Rico, which can claim to be the first enduring European settlement in what is now the USA. Or there's the sketchy story of the short-lived Spanish colony of San Miguel de Gualdape (in what is probably now the state of Georgia), where, in 1526, there was a rebellion by slaves brought from Africa, many of whom fled the colony and who are thought to have mixed with local Native American populations. There's also a Francophone foundation myth, relating to the currently uninhabited island of St Croix in Maine, on the border with Canada, which was briefly settled by the French in 1604, three years before Jamestown.

people about the origins of the United States they refer to events much further north, in the area still known as New England. They usually mention the *Mayflower* and the Pilgrim Fathers and Plymouth Rock, and a boatload of stalwart English men and women who wanted religious freedom – and who were willing to risk their lives for liberty. They may also tell you that the annual Thanksgiving holiday marks the first successful harvest of the *Mayflower* pilgrims in 1621 – which was celebrated by a communal meal with friendly neighbourhood Native Americans, who'd early given them a few top tips on farming in the sandy, stony soil of coastal Massachusetts.

It's a pretty story, wrapped up in ribbons, which has served well as a foundation myth. It doesn't involve much bloodshed or slavery or miscegenation – and it's easy to draw parallels between the *Mayflower* narrative and the journey of the Israelites to the Promised Land. But it's also a story that is misleading on several counts. It's historically inaccurate and simplistic,* and it romanticises the early settlers – some of whom became land-grabbing Indian-killers, intolerant witch-hangers and slave-owners. What's more, it's chronologically misleading. The *Mayflower* passengers were relative latecomers. The story, told and retold, has been allowed to eclipse what would otherwise be America's foremost foundation myth: an ocean-crossing migration that took place in 1607, thirteen years before the *Mayflower* set sail, and which resulted in the first permanent English settlement in the Americas: at Jamestown in Virginia. For Jamestown was also the first enduring European

---

* Many of the more basic accounts of the *Mayflower* leave out key parts of the story. That the leaders, for instance, though of English origin, came from Leiden in Holland, where they had been living for more than a decade, or that the majority of those on board weren't Puritans. And that the land they settled had been recently depopulated by disease introduced by previous European travellers, or that they hadn't been planning to go to New England at all, but to Virginia. It's also sometimes forgotten that the Pilgrim Fathers never used the word Thanksgiving, that the national celebration only dates back to 1863, and that some Native Americans mark Thanksgiving as a day of mourning.

settlement within the boundaries of what would become, in 1776, the United States of America.

The story of early seventeenth-century Virginia is less easily prettified than that of New England. Overall, it has an untidy, more complex narrative, lacking a central ideological or religious thread, overshadowed by conflict with indigenous people and by African slavery; it lacks any obvious heroes and does not have the reassuring symbolism of the *Mayflower* and of Thanksgiving. It has undoubtedly had less of a hold on the American imagination, particularly in the period since the defeat of the slave-owning South, including Virginia, in the Civil War.

But it can also be argued that because of its very messiness, and because of slavery (never so important in New England), the Virginia narrative is more representative of the multiple migrations, forced and unforced, that constitute the prehistory of the United States. So what happens if we experiment by replacing the second migration – to New England – with the first – to Virginia – on the centre stage of early American history? It may allow us to view both the past and the present of modern America in a slightly different light.*

The Virginia story began with failure, repeated several times. Twice in the 1580s, the English, partly to counter Spanish dominance in the Americas, tried to settle Roanoke Island. That first group of settlers lasted about a year, during which they killed Wingina, the leader of the Secota tribe whose land they were occupying, and upon whom they relied for food. The second group of settlers – about a hundred men and women – simply disappeared, their bodies never found,

---

* Virginia was also to be the birth state of four of the first five presidents, and the location of critical battles of the Revolution and the Civil War. There have been more Virginian presidents than from any other state, but none since Woodrow Wilson (1913–21), who left the state at the age of two, but whose second wife Edith could claim, as a descendant of Pocahontas, a deep Virginian ancestry.

their fate still unknown, though it's more than possible that the Secota took their revenge.

The English waited a generation before trying again – and it was almost as disastrous. They built a new settlement beside a malarial swamp in Chesapeake Bay and named it Jamestown after their king. Of the 104 settlers who landed there in May 1607, fewer than forty survived their first winter. Reinforcements came, but the death rate got worse. The third winter became known as the Starving Time and, not for the first time, Europeans living in the Americas resorted to cannibalism. The survivors briefly abandoned Jamestown, but they were intercepted by three ships carrying yet more settlers and some supplies, and they all returned to Virginia. Such were the less-than-glorious beginnings to the English colonisation of North America's Atlantic coast.*

Those first boatloads of Englishmen are often described in terms that make them seem almost comically unsuited to their new lives. They consisted largely of either impoverished gentlemen who were seeking adventure and fortune (sometimes accompanied by a servant), or of unemployed labourers and vagrants rounded up in southern England. Neither group was used to hard work and they had little experience of farming, though not everyone was unskilled – there were two bricklayers, some carpenters, a barber, two surgeons and a fisherman among the 1607 settlers. They were soon followed by the first Englishwomen – 'Mistress Forrest and Anne Burras, her maid' – and eight craftsmen from Holland, Germany and Poland joined the small and dwindling group of settlers.

These early white migrants lacked key skills, cohesion and a common purpose. There were almost no women, and therefore very little family life – in contrast to the situation more than

---

* Jamestown, named after a man who was king of both Scotland and England, could also serve as a foundation myth for the British Empire. It was the first enduring English settlement outside Europe.

a decade later in New England. There was an untidy chain of command in Jamestown. Contemporary records show how much time the settlers spent quarrelling with each other – sometimes with fatal consequences. The general chaos, alongside the shortage of food and the possibility of sex with Native American women, led to many desertions. This became another key facet of the early years in Virginia – not replicated among the early New England settlers – as some young English migrants simply fled Jamestown and went to live with nearby Native American tribes. It's not known what happened in the long term to most of these deserters, but many were welcomed into the tribes – especially if they brought their weapons with them. And most Native Americans cared little about race, so long as the new European members of the tribe were happy to integrate.

It was far less common for Native Americans to join, freely, the growing tribe of Englishmen and women – a fact recognised over a century later in the candid words of the scientist and future Founding Father, Benjamin Franklin:

When an Indian child has been brought up among us, taught our language and habituated to our customs, yet if he goes to see his relatives and makes one Indian ramble with them, there is no persuading him ever to return ... [but] when white persons, of either sex, have been taken prisoners young by the Indians, and lived a while with them, though ransomed by their friends, and treated with all imaginable tenderness to prevail with them to stay among the English, yet in a short time they become disgusted with our manner of life, and the care and pains that are necessary to support it, and take the first good opportunity of escaping again into the woods, from whence there is no redeeming them.

There are lots of examples from Jamestown of English migrants who escaped 'into the woods' and never came back – and whose stories have been forgotten. But there's just one example of the opposite, and half the modern world seems to know her, thanks in large part to the Disney Corporation.

She is, of course, Pocahontas, whose story has been told, again and again, in many ways which have served quite different purposes. In that 1995 Disney version of her life she is an undoubted radical – a nature-loving anti-racist peace-making feminist; an inspiration, according to some young female friends of mine who first watched the film as children.* But in nineteenth-century literature she was usually an ill-fated romantic heroine, an important figure in the canon of tragedy. In Native American accounts, she's often seen as a desperate survivor and sometimes even as a traitor who sold her soul to the English, while for some white Virginians she became a meek and obliging ancestral mother figure – the repository and source of another minor foundation myth. All is possible because there are so many gaps in the narrative. Her own voice has been lost. And it's hard to discern, despite her fabled wilfulness, how much real agency she had over her life.

What we do know comes principally from a former mercenary and English settler called John Smith, who was captured by Powhatan Indians. According to one of Smith's retellings of the story, he only survived because of the intercession of Pocahontas, then a child of perhaps ten or eleven, who was a daughter of the Powhatan chief. Five years later Pocahontas, by then a married (and possibly widowed) teenager, was kidnapped by the English. While in captivity she converted to Christianity, was baptised Rebecca and then married to a widowed English tobacco farmer called John Rolfe. They had

---

* Disney's cartoon version has been accused of whitewashing colonial history. And it's also full of errors. Critically, Disney got the relationship between John Smith and Pocahontas entirely wrong. There was no romance – she was a child and he was twenty-seven, and there is no evidence that he was a paedophile. There's a lot missing from the film, including her marriage, the birth of her son and her early death. And her Powhatan name, Matoaka, is unmentioned.

a child, and the three of them travelled to England, where Pocahontas met King James and Queen Anne. Pocahontas died soon after – and John Rolfe returned to Virginia alone (where he died five years later) having left their one-year-old son in England with a relative. That son, Thomas, only returned to the land of his birth as an adult, where he married a white woman, and their descendants became leading members of Virginia's slave-owning aristocracy.

It's worth lingering on one of those versions of the story of Pocahontas – the old Virginian narrative in which she appears as a semi-mythical mother figure – because it's a discomforting example of a kind of story that triumphant conqueror-migrants sometimes tell themselves. This particular example is repeated less often these days, but appears throughout the nineteenth and early twentieth century, largely in historical and gene-alogical writings about Virginia. Typical is a description of Pocahontas by one of her descendants in which, 'though a born barbarian', she is modest, virtuous, faultless and loving, and is depicted as 'shining like a star out of the dark back-ground of her original barbarism'.

In these racist narratives Pocahontas becomes a figure from a fairy tale, an emblem of an idealised emotional connection between the earliest English settlers and Native Americans. She becomes the archetype of a 'good Indian', who recognises the superiority of Christian culture and the attractiveness of Englishmen – in contrast to the rest of her tribe and most other Native Americans. And her marriage with John Rolfe* becomes a symbolic act of miscegenation – not to be repeated – which announced and justified the permanent presence of Europeans in North America. Through her son, Pocahontas was the ancestor of many 'white' Virginian families, who

---

* John Rolfe himself became the symbol of Virginian wealth, as the man who intro-duced sweet tobacco to North America.

felt able to pride themselves on being of even older stock than other similar families.* In this version of early American history, Pocahontas has become a founding mother, and an honorary white person.

Twelve years after the foundation of Jamestown, and two years after the death of Pocahontas (and a full fifteen months before the *Mayflower* dropped anchor off the coast of Massachusetts), a British ship called the *White Lion* sailed to Virginia. It stopped just short of Jamestown at a headland called Point Comfort. There the ship's Cornish captain, John Jope, unloaded the *White Lion*'s 'cargo', which he sold to Virginian settlers for supplies of food and drink. That 'cargo' consisted of about twenty Africans, men and women. They had not left their homeland willingly, and had endured a long and eventful journey, parts of which historians have been able to reconstruct in recent years.

They were not the first African migrants in North America – preceded of course almost a century earlier by Estevanico and by other African slaves who were transported to Spanish Florida. And there were already some Africans in Virginia, who'd probably come as domestic servants of English settlers. But those who arrived on the *White Lion* in 1619 came in different circumstances – and their harrowing journey is often seen as marking the true start of the North American slave trade, and of an African presence in what would become the USA. This new group of migrants were almost certainly Kimbundu

---

* Occasionally these chauvinistic narratives became entangled. In 1924, a law banning interracial marriage was reintroduced in Virginia, under the terms of which anyone who had any non-white ancestors whatsoever was thereby not white. This would have been calamitous for many thousands of descendants of Pocahontas, stalwarts of the entirely white First Families of Virginia, and so the so-called Pocahontas Clause was added to the law, specifying that those who had one-sixteenth or less Indian ancestry would, after all, be deemed legally white.

speakers from the Kingdom of Ndongo in what is now Angola, who'd been captured in warfare and then marched down to the Kwanza River, from where they were taken by boat to be sold in Luanda, the headquarters of Portugal's African slave trade. There, they would have been baptised as Christians, and we know that they were then forced onto a Portuguese ship named *São João Bautista* to be carried across the Atlantic – destined, it seemed, for the Mexican port of Veracruz and the nearby sugar plantations, until the *White Lion* interrupted their journey.

It's known from other writings of the period what conditions were like on board a Portuguese slave ship. One priest described Africans as being forced to live like 'sardines in a bottle'. They ate gruel made from manioc flour and lay head to toe on shelves built into the hold. Each of them had a piece of cloth, which they wore in the daytime and slept on at night. Conditions on the *São João Bautista* were particularly grim, for we know that as many as one hundred of the 350 Africans on board died before their first stop, in Spanish-ruled Jamaica, where 'twenty-four slave boys' were sold for food and medicine. As the ship approached the Mexican coast it was intercepted by two British privateers – pirate ships acting with government permission. One was the *White Lion*, which came away from the encounter with twenty Africans on board. For Captain Jope they were booty; stolen property, according to the Portuguese. For the Africans themselves, it was their second kidnapping and enslavement of the year.

A lot of energy had been expended by historians, amateur and professional, on deciding whether these African newcomers should be described as slaves. There's already a broader unresolved terminological argument about whether the word 'slave' should be replaced by the term 'enslaved person', on the basis that the former is dehumanising, often countered by the suggestion that the latter is a clumsy euphemism. It's a debate that often distracts from the greater responsibility on historians and others to research, and reconstruct and even reimagine, the lives of people who were enslaved.

But there's a far more specific issue in early seventeenth century Virginia. At this stage, before lifelong hereditary slavery based around regimented industrial-scale plantation agriculture had taken root in North America, there was no formal legal category into which the new African migrants fitted. Slavery, in law, did not exist, and so they were in a legal vacuum. And those who wish to argue, often for modern political reasons, that early America was not built on slavery insist on the legal nicety that slavery did not formally exist in the early days of America's English colonies.

It is true that African migrants in this period often lived and worked alongside European indentured servants – that is, poor white migrants who, for a pre-decided number of years, would be in servitude to an individual. That individual – a named master, or occasionally a mistress – was entitled, for the period of the indenture, to sell them to someone else and, in practice, treat them as lesser human beings. But even then, most of the evidence suggests that white indentured servants received better treatment than Africans, and would usually have chosen to migrate to America in the first place. We know more about them too. Their full names and nationalities were normally listed in censuses, and they would receive tools and clothes, and sometimes land, when they had completed their indentures. For the Africans, they were often described simply as 'negroes', and if a name was recorded, it was not their African name. And it's unlikely that any of them had much choice in coming to America.

It's in this context that John Punch suddenly, briefly, appears in the history books as another possible first slave. Almost nothing is known about Punch. It's not even certain where he came from, but DNA tests on some of his descendants suggest Cameroon as the most likely location. And genealogists have

argued that he met an unnamed white woman* in Virginia with
whom he had a child (from whom Barack Obama and thousands of other modern Americans were probably descended).
But the reason he matters to this telling of the story of early
America is a single reference in the legal records of Virginia
from 1640. Punch, along with two European indentured servants – a German called Victor, and a Scotsman called James
Gregory – had run away from their English master, a landowner and fellow migrant named Hugh Gwyn. The three
fugitives were tracked down and brought back to Virginia,
where a court declared that the 'three servants shall receive
the punishment of whipping and have thirty stripes apiece'.
The two Europeans, both defined in the court ruling by their
nationality, were sentenced to an additional four-year term to
their existing indentures. But the court ruled that 'the third,
being a negro named *John Punch*, shall serve his said master or
his assigns for the time of his natural Life'. This meant that
John Punch – defined only by his colour – was, in practice, a
lifelong slave.†

Such then is the sorry story of how African slavery started in
one part of what became the United States. Back in the 1640s it
was all on a minuscule scale. There were still very few Africans
in Virginia – about three hundred of them, compared to fifteen

---

* Nothing more is known about her. Her existence has been inferred from the racial
identity of their descendants. She is thought most likely to have been a European
indentured servant.
† In the decades that followed the John Punch judgement, laws were enacted in
Virginia and the other colonies that codified slavery as an institution and characterised forced migrants from Africa, and their children, as private property – with
scarcely more rights than farm animals. In 1705, a church minister in Virginia refused
to conduct the marriage of one of John Punch's great-grandchildren, who was less
than half African by descent, to a white woman. There were still some free people of
African descent, but mixed marriages were forbidden. The law could not, of course,
prevent miscegenation: indeed, raping a female slave was not a crime in many states,
but marrying her was. Anti-miscegenation laws, of various kinds, remained in force
in Virginia and fifteen other states until they were declared unconstitutional by the
US Supreme Court in 1967. Such a law remained in the Alabama constitution until
2000.

thousand white settlers. The growth in numbers just a century later was quite staggering. By 1750, the colony of Virginia alone had a population of almost a quarter of a million, of whom almost half were slaves of African origin.

The main economic reason for this growth seems almost trivial in retrospect: that so many Europeans had become addicted to nicotine, and Virginia's new white aristocracy needed many tens of thousands of migrant labourers for the tobacco plantations which serviced that addiction. The indentured labour system was dying out. Poor Europeans could only be relied on to migrate when times were bad back home, because of failed harvests or political persecution – and were free, if they could afford it, to return home when things got better. They could assert their civil rights, and they would on occasion rebel. There was no prospect of return for Africans, torn unwillingly from their distant homes and in permanent captivity. And this was true not only for Virginia, but across North America, the Caribbean and South and Central America – in colonies belonging to eight European powers.*

The story of the Americas cannot be told without the story of slavery. And don't let anyone get away with suggesting that there were no slaves in New England, or Canada, or Argentina or Chile for that matter. The numbers were far smaller in these places, for there were no great plantations, and undoubtedly some European settlers had ethical reservations about the slave trade – but Africans were brought unwillingly to almost every part of this double continent and its many islands. And North

---

* Spain, Portugal, France, Holland, Britain, Denmark, Sweden and Russia all had American colonies. Russia controlled Alaska until 1867, when it was sold to the USA – and there had earlier been a small Russian settlement in California. Denmark colonised what are now known as the US Virgin Islands. Wilmington, Delaware, was, for seventeen years in the seventeenth century, part of Sweden's overseas empire, which also included for a longer period the Caribbean island of St Barthélemy. Italy, whose countrymen played such a role in exploring the Americas, is conspicuous by its absence from this list.

America was not even the main destination: far more Africans ended up in Brazil, and in the Caribbean. Added together, this was the greatest forced migration of all time. The statistics are staggering. More than twelve million captives, kidnapped from Africa, were carried across the ocean over a period of about 350 years. At least a million newly enslaved people are thought to have died on the journey from their homes to the coast of Africa, and almost two million died as they crossed the Atlantic.

It's a migration story that is not easy to tell, both because it is so full of pain and death and absence of choice, and because of the lack of first-hand accounts from the migrants themselves. There's also been a tendency to dress it all up, even in modern times, with contemporary euphemisms: the 'Middle Passage', for instance, to describe the journey of the slaves; the 'Seasoning', to describe their first few months on American soil; and, moreover, to tell the story teleologically, as if the most important aspect of the African slave trade was its ultimate abolition.

For the sixteenth and seventeenth centuries there are no surviving accounts from Africans, though that begins to change by the eighteenth century, with a series of 'slave narratives' published as part of the abolition movement. Novelists have sometimes tried to fill the breach, but they've usually concentrated on the later period of slavery in which abolition and the possibility of freedom had become part of the story; and they have, largely, shown more interest in the continued enslavement of the descendants of migrants rather than in the migrants themselves. And so we are dependent, to a great extent, on the accounts of slavers – in journals and letters and notebooks and business documents – and on our limited ability to imagine what it might be like to live someone else's life; the life, in this case, of an enslaved African.

There was no such thing as a typical slave. They were

kidnapped from most parts of the African continent and were also shipped in huge numbers across the Indian Ocean to the Middle East and Asia, as well as the Americas. In the early years of Atlantic slavery, they were taken from coastal areas of western Africa – usually captured in warfare or ambushes carried out by members of rival tribes or ethnic groups and then sold to European traders. The Europeans often paid for the slaves with weapons, which then created a series of regional arms races funded by selling more human beings. The captives were yoked together with branches and vines, and frogmarched to the coast, or taken down river by canoe.

As the Atlantic trade in human beings grew in scale so did the area from which slaves were captured, stretching deep into the African interior, where most people had no knowledge of ships, or the ocean, or of Europeans. Many of the captives were children. In one of the earliest slave narratives, Ukawsaw Gronniosaw describes how, as a boy of around fifteen, he left his home in what is now north-eastern Nigeria in about 1720. He was driven by curiosity when he heard a travelling merchant speak of white people, and of 'houses with wings' that can 'walk upon the water'. When he reached the coast he was kidnapped, sold to a Dutch captain for two lengths of checked cloth, and put on a ship bound for Barbados.

Gronniosaw was relatively easy to enslave and made his captors a very quick profit. The early experience of his fellow eighteenth-century autobiographer Olaudah Equiano was quite different. Equiano and his sister were in their father's house in central Nigeria when raiders seized them, tying their hands and gagging them. They were forced to walk for several days, and then separated. Equiano was just eleven years old. In his memoirs he described how he was sold locally as a slave no less than five times in a few months, before reaching the coast and meeting his first Europeans. He was terrified by them. Members of the crew, with 'horrible looks, red faces and long hair', tossed him around to see if he was healthy. He saw a large copper cauldron on the deck and was convinced that he was about to be eaten.

Years later Equiano, who like Gronniosaw would live in England and marry a white woman, remembered 'the multitude of black people of every description chained together, every one of their countenances expressing dejection and sorrow'. He was sent down into the hold of the ship where he 'received such a salutation in my nostrils as I had never received in my life'. Equiano was then whipped for not eating, and would have jumped overboard to his death had nets not been placed around the boat to stop slaves from killing themselves. Later in the journey, two slaves who were chained together manage to elude the nets and plunge into the Atlantic. They died. A third African who followed them was dragged back on board and 'flogged unmercifully, for thus attempting to prefer death to slavery'.

There are dozens of slavers' accounts of the crossing. They too are rarely anything but grim. Brutality, torture and rape were commonplace – and it is possible to extract a sense of just how terrifying the crossing must have been. The African captives, especially in the early days of the Atlantic slave trade, would have had no idea of the fate that awaited them. They knew no one who had ever been to America, no knowledge even that such a place existed. Equiano's belief that the Europeans were cannibals was widespread and would have felt quite rational. And the Africans had a broad range of responses to life, if it can be called that, in their floating dungeons. Some fell into deep melancholy, others conspired to rebel or became openly defiant; a few attempted to build relationships with their captors.

Insurrection was almost impossible. The male slaves were usually shackled together at all times and kept below deck, though they might be freed and forced to dance as a form of

exercise. The women had slightly greater freedom of movement, which meant that they were available sexually to the
crew. In one of the best-documented cases, a female slave on
an early eighteenth-century crossing managed to smuggle
a hammer to the men, who used it to break their shackles.
The leader of the rebels, an impressively large and strong man
called Tomba, killed three of the crew before he was caught.
The captain decided not to kill Tomba, but one of his associ-
ates, who he thought would be less valuable in a slave auction.
Tomba and another rebel were then forced to eat the heart and
liver of the executed man. The hammer-smuggling woman,
meanwhile, 'was hoisted up by the Thumbs, whipp'd, and
slashed ... with knives, before the other slaves until she died'.
Tomba was then sold for a high price in Jamaica. We know
nothing more of him or his fellow captives.

In fact, most captains did try to keep as many slaves alive –
and compliant – as possible. Some would attempt to have a mix
of slaves on board who didn't speak the same language. Those
who they suspected of planning to rebel would be whipped,
or thumbscrews would be used on them. There was a special
metal contraption, a *speculum oris*, designed to force open the
mouths of those who refused to eat. Dead bodies were thrown
overboard to feed the sharks that followed the slave ships across
the Atlantic, and this, or the mutilation of corpses, was seen as
a deterrent to suicide. One ship's doctor recalled how during
a hunger strike the captain whipped each of the slaves, but he
said they 'looked up at him with a smile', as if to say, 'presently
we shall be no more'. Slave suicide can sometimes be seen as an
act of rebellion.

For the 85 per cent of Africans who survived the trauma
of the crossing, there was – of course – much more to come.
Equiano described how, once anchored off the coast of
Barbados, lots of smaller boats drew up. Merchants and planters
came on board to examine the slaves carefully, and they were

made to jump up and down. Equiano and his companions were full of 'dread and trembling', still believing they were about to be eaten. Some old slaves were brought from the land to pacify them, and to explain what would happen next. They were then kept in a merchant yard and sold off, in what Equiano refers to as 'parcels', to plantation owners. He and the others were distraught at being separated from the new friends they'd made. Equiano himself was unsold.

Some slaves fell ill and died soon after arrival, often succumbing to new diseases. Others sank into depression. It was the job of older slaves, already living in the Americas and often born there, to encourage the newcomers, fatten them up, oil their skins, heal their wounds, cut their hair – all so that they would get better prices at the slave auction. The slaves would be given new names, often several times. Equiano – when he eventually was sold, and sold again – was called successively Jacob, Michael and Gustavus Vasa. That last name belonged originally to the first king of Sweden, who led his country to independence from Denmark, and some slave-owners found it terrifically amusing to name their slaves after famous figures of the past, from Caesar to Hercules. Equiano described how at first he refused to answer to his new name, but was cuffed over the head many times, 'so at length I submitted'.

Most migrants endure or welcome some kind of disruption to their culture. And many poorer European migrants to the Americas undoubtedly suffered great hardships, physical and psychological, on their journeys across the Atlantic, and in attempting to establish themselves in a new continent. But most of them had choices, could build enduring family ties, could keep their languages, for instance, and were able to pass their stories down through the generations. They experienced nothing that could begin to compare with the migration trauma forced upon enslaved Africans. For not only were twelve million Africans enslaved, and transported unwillingly over the ocean, but the cultures they carried in their thoughts and behaviours were all but eradicated. Losing their names was just one part of that, though its symbolism would matter, then and now. Equiano was able to reclaim his birth name late in life, after decades of being known, and mocked, as Gustavus Vasa. For the vast majority of enslaved Africans their names, their languages, their histories, their gods, their food, their music were all taken from them.

Of course, there was resistance, cultural and political. Occasionally, there was even full-scale rebellion, and the creation of communities of self-freed slaves. In Haiti, the western half of Hispaniola, a revolution brought African slaves to power, and full independence from colonial France. But, more generally, the breaking and rebreaking of families, together with the deep mixing of peoples from different parts of Africa, meant that even when slaves or former slaves were able to assert themselves they had little ability to reclaim their older heritage. In some places, a few words or syntactic structures survived from African languages, as did ways of cooking, or playing music or praying, shadows of a lost past. But that loss was enormous, irreplaceable – and remains part of the modern story of the USA and the Americas more widely, long, long after the formal abolition of slavery.

In 1860, just before the start of the American Civil War, an ocean-going ship called the *Clotilda*, in good condition and only five years old, was set on fire by its owner. He wanted to hide the evidence of a crime he had committed, and for which, as it turned out, he would never be punished. The burnt-out shell of the *Clotilda* soon disappeared into the alligator-infested mud-swamps of the Mobile River in the state of Alabama, not far from a place that would later become known as Africatown.

The owner of the *Clotilda** was a man called Timothy Meaher. He was the son of an Irish migrant who had fled his homeland to avoid conscription by the occupying British army and settled in Maine. Meaher himself was born in Maine but as a young man he too migrated – more than two thousand kilometres – to the Deep South, to what would have felt, in many ways, like a different country. He moved like many other white Americans to Alabama, a new state recently cleared of most of its Native American population, who had been driven to the west, beyond the Mississippi. He went to the city of Mobile, close to the Gulf of Mexico, where he and his brother made a small fortune from cotton, timber and steamboats – and where they became, in the words of one of their northern relatives, 'ardent Southerners'.

The Meahers thought it most unfair that it was no longer legal to bring African slaves into the USA. Despite the abolition of the international trade in slaves, slavery itself, as an American economic and social institution, and as a lived reality for its victims, was firmly entrenched in the south of the country – and remained so until the Civil War. And there was still a large internal slave market. The big slave-owners of the Old South – in Virginia and the Carolinas – liked this situation, because it increased the value of the human beings they considered their property, while the owners of the plantations in the newer states of the Deep South resented the fact that if they wanted slave labour – and they did – they would have to buy it at inflated prices from elsewhere. And so it was that on a steamboat ride down the Mobile River Timothy Meaher boasted to a group of friends that he knew how he could get African slaves into the country unnoticed by the authorities. According to

---

* The *Clotilda* was named after a sixth-century saint, a Burgundian princess of Gothic origin who married the Frankish king Clovis I and played an important role in the spread of Christianity in western Europe. She is venerated as the patron saint of exiles and of disappointing children.

one of those friends he laid down a bet of one thousand dollars saying, 'I myself can bring a shipful of n——s right into Mobile Bay under the officers' noses.'

It's here, then, in the year before the outbreak of the Civil War, that two very different migration narratives intersect: the minor Meaher story and the painful epic tale of the last group of enslaved Africans to be transported across the Atlantic to the USA. And for once we know more about the slaves than the slavers. In later times, journalists and writers sought out the former slaves, liberated as a result of the Civil War, the last of whom died as recently as 1940. Many of them settled in an area on the outskirts of Mobile which they called Africatown, and where some of their descendants still live.

The unwilling passengers aboard the *Clotilda* came largely from the country of Benin, then known as Dahomey, and from south-west Nigeria, and they spoke a variety of languages and practised at least three different religions. They had been captured by the army of the King of Dahomey and taken to the coast and the seaport of Ouidah, where they were placed in enclosures known as barracoons until a buyer turned up. The barracoons were remembered as places of lamentation, from where individuals were exiled, in chains, from their homeland with no chance of return. Sometimes family members were also there, outside the barracoons, offering to pay a ransom or swap places with the prisoner.

The captain of the *Clotilda*, William Foster, was brought to the Ouidah barracoons, where the captives were told to form circles of ten men and ten women so they could be inspected. This was normally done by the ship's doctor, but the *Clotilda* did not have one. So Foster himself chose 110 of them, with roughly equal numbers of men and women, girls and boys, and paid about nine thousand dollars. They were given a final meal on African soil, and then at dawn they were taken to the ship. More than half a century later, one of the Africans, born Oluale Kossàla but by then known as Cudjo Lewis, remembered how they all cried 'because we didn't want to leave the rest of our people in the barracoon. We were lonesome for our homes. We didn't know what was going to become of us.'

Most slaves were branded with a hot iron, but not those on board the *Clotilda* – for reasons that aren't clear, but possibly to make it easier for them to be sold, undetected. They were stripped of what was left of their clothing, and they remained naked for the entire journey. Cudjo Lewis recalled, 'I was so ashamed. We came naked on American soil, and so people said we were naked savages ... they don't know that our clothes were snatched away from us.' The clothing cultures of the part of Africa from which the captives came were both sophisticated and distinctive – and provided part of the way individuals and communities identified themselves. To be sent naked to a land where Africans were often imagined as naked added to their sense of indignation and humiliation.

This was made still worse when they were presented on arrival in Alabama with a large pile of European-style clothing, quite different from the loose, flowing garments they were used to. The male captives had seen on the journey across the Atlantic how American men dressed, but women didn't have a clue what to do with the clothes that were assigned to them, having not yet set eyes upon an American woman. Years later, Noah Hart, an American-born slave who was tasked with looking after the newcomers, described the scene:

> the women had the dresses tied around them by the sleeves, and the skirts trailing in the sand in front and behind them. Some had petticoats tied round the neck and one arm stuck out of the placket hole. Others had them outside the dresses, and others didn't have them on at all.

For most white people in Alabama, the newcomers were just some more slaves. For the existing black population, they were quite different. Because of the abolition of the slave trade in 1808, there were hardly any first-generation Africans in the USA, and most of them were very old. Also, the Africans on the *Clotilda* were not from a part of the continent where large numbers of slaves had been transported to the USA. Many of them had ritual scarring and filed teeth that the existing black population of Alabama would not have recognised, and many of their cultural practices would have seemed strange. They were outsiders, and many of them remained so. Noah Hart said 'they were blacker and straighter and bigger than us, and somehow they seemed fiercer, though they never fooled with us nor squabbled among themselves'. Cudjo Lewis remembered that 'we wanted to talk with the other coloured folks, but they didn't understand us. Some made fun of us.'

In April 1865, as the Civil War came to an end, federal soldiers reached southern Alabama. Cudjo Lewis described a group of them coming down to the river to eat mulberries and telling him and some of the other *Clotilda* slaves, 'You're free, you don't belong to anyone no more.' They asked, 'Where should we go?' 'Wherever you want,' came the reply. The Africans were now free but stranded – and destitute. They expected Timothy Meaher to pay for their passage back to Africa,* or to give them some land on which they could live, but he did neither. Instead, gradually, by saving some of their wages from labouring, the Africans bought small tracts of lands. They built their own community, largely self-governing – appointing as their leader one of the former *Clotilda* captives, Gumpa,

---

* In fact, they almost certainly could have had a free trip as far as the independent West African country of Liberia if they had known about a 'repatriation' scheme run by the American Colonization Society. It had been sending black Americans, mainly freed slaves, to Liberia since the 1820s – and continued to do so, on a smaller scale, after the Civil War.

principally because he had belonged to a high-ranking family back in Dahomey.

Some of the Africans had paired off by now, couples who'd first met in the barracoons or on the slave ship, forming long-term relationships that also ensured the medium-term survival of some African languages and traditions. Yoruba was spoken as a mother tongue in several families, and some African personal names were passed down the generations. But integration with the older African American community began quickly – even before emancipation. Two of the young African women soon had children with black Americans. Most of the *Clotilda* captives converted to Christianity, and they built a church in Africatown – and a school and a graveyard.

Africatown remained half-forgotten, an impoverished black suburb of Mobile. Writers began to visit from the 1890s onwards, drawn by the story of the last slave ship and by romantic expectations of an African community on American soil. In the 1920s, Zora Neale Hurston – now remembered as the first major black woman novelist in the USA – made two extended visits to Africatown, spending many hours with Cudjo Lewis, who was by then the last surviving *Clotilda* captive living there. She wrote a magazine article about him, and he's described in Hurston's own autobiography. She took photographs and filmed Lewis outside his house – a short silent clip, now on YouTube, the only moving image of someone who had been brought as a slave from Africa to the USA. And she wrote up his life story, a full-length book in which she transcribed his words as he spoke them, in dialect. Partly for this reason she could find no publisher, and the manuscript disappeared into a university archive. Cudjo Lewis died in 1935.

Africatown has survived, in poverty, often against the odds and in spite of many further migrations. And there are descendants of the *Clotilda* captives still living there. It's a friendly place,

full of small wooden houses, where everyone talks kindly to
a visiting stranger, with a mingling of sadness and hope. The
population of Africatown is shrinking. Industrial pollution from
nearby factories is widely blamed for high rates of cancer among
the older generation – Africatown's four churches have seen
many funerals. There are few jobs and no shops, and rows of
empty, boarded-up homes being reclaimed by ants and creep-
ers. Africatown is, quite literally, on the road to nowhere. For
it is located in a cleft of the Mobile River and one of its many
creeks, cut off from the rest of the city by forlorn reminders of
the industrial era: little-used railway lines and derelict factories.
And Africatown itself has been split in two by a terrifying highway, perilous to pedestrians, used by oversized trucks to bypass
Mobile. The old Baptist church with a fine bronze bust of Cudjo
Lewis is on the north side of the highway, and the cemetery in
which he is buried is on the south side.

It's hardly an obvious tourist destination. And that's why the people of Africatown instantly know why outsiders come here: I did sense among them a real pride in the area's unusual history. It's something that a younger generation has grown up with, as the story of Africatown has become better known in Mobile itself and beyond. In the 1980s, an organisation was set up to represent the descendants of the *Clotilda* captives, and the annual Africatown Folk Festival began as a celebration of the community's history and culture. And there was a renewal of contacts with Africa after more than one hundred and twenty years.*

In this century, there's been a flurry of academic research, archaeological activity in and around the community grave-yard, plans for a museum and – finally – in 2018 the publication of Zora Neale Hurston's extraordinary book *Barracoon*, telling the life story, in his own words, of Cudjo Lewis. In the same year the burnt-out shell of the *Clotilda* was located buried in river mud not far from Africatown. In 2020, the US Senate passed a resolution declaring that the discovery of the ship was a 'monumental find' of 'local, national, and international importance and educational value', and should be preserved for posterity. The *Clotilda* will be raised. A heritage centre is under construction and there are plans for a tourist trail through Africatown, with cruises down the Mobile River. In this part of the Deep South, those migrants forced to cross the Atlantic in the hold of the last North American slave ship have not been forgotten, and neither has the trauma of slavery.

---

* This included the visit of a Beninois diplomat to Africatown, and a senior African American politician from Mobile to Benin. There was also an apology from the descendants of the King of Dahomey for their family's role in the slave trade.

A Seventh Intermission

I told a friend the other day that I was writing about slavery and migration in the USA. She objected. Slaves aren't migrants, she said. I was briefly silent. And then the words 'why not?' fell weakly from my lips. Because they had no say in the matter, came the reply. Migration involves choices. She spoke as someone who had chosen to move, five years earlier, from one of the great cities of Asia to Washington DC.

It was a brief exchange, over the phone, but it's one that had me returning to my definition of a migrant, slipped into the early pages of this book. It deserves greater consideration. In that definition, taken from a modern psychotherapist, a migrant is someone

> who has moved from one culture to another where the second [culture] is experienced as significantly different from the first, and for a sufficient duration that the person engages in daily activities and is challenged to undergo some adjustment to the new place.

It's undoubtedly a broad definition. And it relies on other concepts that may deserve further elucidation, such as culture and adjustment. It's inclusive — and can apply to ancient and modern migrants. It does not refer, even indirectly, to nationality or ethnicity or race or borders. It does not get dragged down into the mud and vitriol of many contemporary migration narratives — for there is no mention of immigrants, emigrants, refugees, asylum seekers, nomads, expats, illegals, guest workers and all the other possible kinds of migrants that might exist, all the separate compartments into which migrants have been subdivided. It attempts, at least, to be universal. And above all, it emphasises the experience of the migrant.

But this definition does not pretend to deal with choice, or volition. And I think my friend was saying that the experience of a slave transported across the Atlantic differs so much from her own experience, or mine, that including both transported slaves on one hand and 'people like us' on the other under the umbrella term 'migrant' has little meaning.* For slaves do not have free will, and we do. One response is to argue that we are at an extreme end of a spectrum — and African slaves heading for North America were at the other end. Large numbers of migrants have far less choice than me or her. Transported convicts sent from Britain to Australia, for instance. Indentured labourers are often deemed to have 'chosen' temporary slavery, as if that's much of a choice. When families migrate, children are usually given no say in the matter. And historically women have been less involved in family migration decisions.

---

* Of course, many slaves were not migrants: those in the USA, for instance, who were born and died on the same plantation. But they were descendants of recent migrants. The white supremacists who drew up America's immigration quotas in the 1920s — which were based on previous migrations — did not class African Americans as descendants of migrants, because so doing would have, by their own rules, allowed new migration from Africa. These rules also served to exclude African Americans, as well as Native Americans, from a largely positive migration narrative that depicted the USA as a country of European migrants.

Communities and individuals are sometimes driven to migrate by disaster or war or persecution, and their range of choices are circumscribed. As are those who are tricked or manipulated by human traffickers.

But it's also possible, as some modern historians have done, to make what amounts to a philosophical case for enslaved people having some residual free will – and that they do have choices, albeit ones which are woefully limited. To deny that can seem disrespectful to the many acts of rebellion – almost all of them unsuccessful – that did take place in barracoons and in slave ships. After all, suicide can be an act of rebellion. And it was often viewed as such by many slave-owners, who saw it as the destruction of their property. For all these reasons it is unhelpful, misleading even, to exclude the story of slavery from the history of migration on the basis that slaves cannot make choices.

Another important issue that arises from any attempt to define migration is distance. I'm arguing that one doesn't need to be part of a long-distance mass migration to be a migrant. For many who see migrants in a largely positive light, migration has often been associated with romantic, adventurous young men who leave home and travel enormous distances, often facing great perils, in order to make a new life. But it's often been women who are more likely to move – albeit shorter distances, and with less of a fuss. In many societies, sons expected to inherit their parents' land, and therefore were less likely to migrate.

The nineteenth-century geographer E. G. Ravenstein, who is often credited with having invented migration theory, declared that 'woman is a greater migrant than man', and added 'this may surprise those who associate women with domestic life, but the figures of the census clearly prove it'. He was referring to Victorian England, when women were more likely than men to migrate within the same country in order to marry, or to work – often as governesses, domestic servants and shop workers. And in the nineteenth century it might take as long to cross a large English county as it would to fly halfway around the world today.

Migration is often messy and does not lend itself to neat, simple definitions with clear boundaries. Ravenstein talked about what has become known as 'step migration', in which people from rural areas move first to towns and then cities, and might only travel abroad after that. Meanwhile, seasonal workers, like nomads, spend parts of each year in different places. Some people leave home and don't know how long they will be away. They may go away to study, or visit somewhere and get a temporary job, and then meet someone and stay longer, and have a family, and then never leave – even though they still, at least in principle, plan to return to where they once lived. It's impossible to decide at which precise moment each person became a migrant. And many of them will never use that label for themselves.

It's important not to let the discussion of migration become hamstrung by such issues. If one is attempting to develop models or algorithms to predict or explain migrant behaviour such definitions clearly matter. My project and purpose is different. I am arguing that migration, forced and unforced and everything in between, is at the heart of the human experience. And that we can hope to understand ourselves better as a species if we remember that. While we may be able to make better sense of the modern USA, for instance, if we reflect on the entangled migrations – forced and unforced – that reach back to the seventeenth century, and earlier, back indeed to those first human journeys out of Africa.

If I were a philosopher, I might go further at this point, and allow grand theories to take over from storytelling. For there is an argument, to be gently touched on here, that the Greek philosopher Heraclitus,* two and a half thousand years ago, had it right when he said that 'all is flux'; that, in fact, animals and plants – like us – are constantly on the move, in small and large ways, and always changing. We know, in more recent times, from physicists, that not even the atoms of the dullest pebble, or any inanimate object, stay still, and neither does our universe. And so, by this argument, motion, not stillness, is the universal norm – just as on a behavioural level for humans, I've sought to point out the normality of migration over sedentariness.

That's not quite all, philosophically speaking. For the issue of how we humans imagine the concept of time also intrudes into this argument. By which I mean that our traditional ideas of time seem to slip through our fingers when we try to examine in detail the boundary between the past and present – in the sense that the present is always fleeting and becomes the past before we can ever fully experience it. And that matters here, as part of this story, because there is so much talk these days, particularly when referring to historical injustices, of slavery or imperialism, about drawing a line under the past, or of wiping the slate clean and starting anew, living in the present, as if the present could be cleanly isolated from the past.

I'm not convinced that's realistic – or desirable. For our histories are a living part of us: they go far beyond what we might learn at school or from museums. They are hard to bury, for they are fundamental to who we are. They dwell everywhere: in our languages, our foundation myths, our rituals, our stories, our families, our DNA, in our attitudes towards migrants, and in our anxieties and aspirations. And they cannot fail to appear in any discussion about migration or slavery or racism

---

* Heraclitus was from Ephesus, close to the coast of what is now western Turkey, and which was then under Persian rule. Only fragments of his writings survive, quoted by later philosophers such as Plato. He is normally remembered for his general state of gloominess and for his aphorisms, including 'everything flows' and 'you can't step into the same river twice', each of which can be seen as providing a significant starting point for a worldview in which movement of all kinds is normal.

or injustice or nationalism. I'm arguing then that we return to those histories and question and challenge them, and search for the gaps, for the many histories that are untold, and see what we can do to tell them, and – as a starting point and a bare minimum – mark their absence.

History books have, on the whole, been written by the sedentary for the sedentary, and have given us a particular view of our past. A few explorers and poets and pioneers – mainly men from Europe and the Middle East – have left their accounts of migration, but the vast majority of migrants did not. And that's why it's important to mark that absence, which for this project means pointing out the existence of many millions of individual migrants who have left no trace, for whom not even a name survives – the Unknown Migrant, perhaps. And even where those names survive, there's often little else. I've been researching the very different histories of Chinese migration to South-East Asia, and the spread of the Roma, once known as Gypsies, through Europe. There are lots of names – from court cases, government records, tombstones – but I have been unable to locate a single first-hand account from any member of these communities from before the nineteenth century.

The response to North American slavery may serve as a useful model here, for historians and novelists alike. Despite the paucity of testimony from enslaved people, it's proved feasible to reclaim, in part at least, their stories. A few sparse references, carefully triangulated, made possible the resurrection of fictional and non-fiction versions of Estevanico. Old-fashioned analysis of forgotten historical sources, combined with oral history and travel to Africa enabled the Senegalese American historian Sylviane Diouf to retell the story of the slave ship *Clotilda* and its captives while, more recently, the Ghanaian American novelist Yaa Gyasi showed – in her best-selling 2016 novel *Homegoing* – how it was possible to recreate the past based on imagining the lives of the forgotten. She invented two eighteenth-century African sisters, Effia and Esi: one enslaved and transported to America, the other married to a slaver in Ghana. And she described the lives of their descendants as they played out against major political and social events on either side of the Atlantic. It's a fine piece of storytelling, as well as a forceful example of how fiction can help us to make sense of our past.

CHAPTER EIGHT

Linnaeus, Chinatown and Fu Manchu

In the early 1660s, two Frenchmen stood side by side in an Asian city, gazing at a large new white building. One of the men, a well-travelled doctor called François Bernier, who had left France more than five years earlier, admired this building greatly. Indeed, he considered it one of the finest pieces of architecture – modern or ancient – that he had ever seen. And he was about to say so, to tell his countryman that he thought this building quite astonishing, but instead he fell silent. He felt bashful. He was worried that his compatriot, a merchant just arrived from France, would judge him, would think less of him, would consider that his 'taste might have become corrupted by long residence' away from home.

It's a revealing moment, which many migrants will recognise. Bernier felt caught between two cultures. He didn't wish to be laughed at by a fellow Frenchman or to be seen as having 'gone native'. And so he said nothing. Bernier wrote of his relief when the French merchant then turned to him and declared that he had seen nothing in Europe 'so bold and majestic' as the building they were gazing at, which was, as you may have guessed, a dazzlingly white new-build known as the Taj Mahal.

There are several other accounts of India written by white male migrants during the rule of the Great Mughals. But Bernier's is unusual. He was by this time the personal physician to a senior minister at the court of the Mughal emperor that moved in a semi-nomadic fashion around northern India. He prided himself on being a philosopher and a doctor, not a merchant or missionary or mercenary or diplomat like the many other foreigners who turned up at court. Bernier was there to observe and take part, not make money or convert souls. He was interested in trying to make sense of a world that seemed to be in permanent flux, changing more rapidly than ever before. And he didn't set out to exoticise India, or to find marvels and monstrosities to titillate European audiences. He repeatedly compared places in India to those in Europe – and so the dome of the Taj Mahal is, he insisted, like the dome of the Val de Grace church in Paris, the River Yamuna is like the Loire Valley, while Benares is the 'Athens of India'. It was a genuine attempt to help Europeans imagine the Mughal Empire, even if its effect is to simplify and to categorise India on European terms.

There's another more important reason why Bernier matters to this story; why he has, under the unforgiving floodlights of posterity, an alternative claim to fame, or infamy. For he was, in a particular sense of this word, the first 'racist'. Bernier eventually left India and returned to France, for reasons that he never explained. There he published his account of the Mughal Empire, but he also wrote a short article for the *Journal de Savants*. It's entitled 'A new division of the earth, according to the species or races of men who inhabit it, sent by a famous traveller', and it attempts to separate all human beings into four races, based primarily on their geographical location and appearance. He swept up everyone from Europe through the Middle East and deep into Asia, as well as the Americas, into one race; black Africans were a second; Asians from the Far East, who he describes as 'truly white', are the third race; while the Lapps of northern Scandinavia are an unlikely fourth. Bernier's categorisations are full of unpleasant nonsense – he says that Africans do not have hair but wool on their heads, and that Lapps are 'very ugly and look much like bears' – but this is not presented as serious science and does not have the unadulterated systematic racism of many later classifications.

In retrospect, it seems obvious that Bernier was attempting to fill a growing void. The ancient European and Middle Eastern paradigms about the world had broken down, irretrievably: their logical contradictions were too profound for them to have any practical utility. The existence, for instance, of the Americas and of sophisticated societies in Asia had undermined the biblical Table of Nations, in which the world had been populated by descendants of the three sons of Noah, as well as the classical notion of a civilised centre to the world, based in and around the Mediterranean, surrounded by an inner ring of barbarians, and an outer ring of monsters.

A new framework was needed to explain and simplify a world that had become more complex and more interconnected. And one such framework, suggested first by Bernier, would ultimately lead to a hierarchical vision of humanity, with people of European origin almost always at the top, and further subdivisions in which particular groups of Europeans granted themselves an even more superior status. It's a racist, racialised view of the world whose consequences linger today. It downplays our shared history as migrants, for it is based on a world that is frozen in time, static rather than dynamic, a world in which it is normal to be sedentary, and in which everyone belongs to a racial group. It's a world view that demonises those – such as nomads or people of 'mixed race' – who do not clearly fit into a single category; it stigmatises intermarriage; and it denies, again, our common heritage.

Bernier can't be blamed for all this. His was a first ungainly attempt at such a classification, his specific categories were rejected by later racial scientists, and his stereotypes did not survive. But about seventy years after Bernier, the Swedish biologist Carl Linnaeus published his own list of races, though he didn't use that word (he preferred 'varieties'), as part of his magnum opus classifying the entire natural world: animal, vegetable and mineral. His work, revised many times, continues to influence modern science and, it must be said, modern racism.

Linnaeus' method was to classify humans – and everything else – by kingdom (animal), class (*mammalia*), order (primate), genus (*homo*) and species (*sapiens*), and he invented the Latinate name *Homo Sapiens*, meaning wise person, by which this self-satisfied species continues to describe itself (rather than, for instance, the far more plausible *Homo Migrans*, migrant person).* And Linnaeus then unwisely subdivided the genus *Homo Sapiens* into four main subgroups: (Native) American, European, Asiatic, African. He described each subgroup not only by its continent of origin but attempted to classify the members of each group physically by their hair, their skin colour, their nostril shape – and by their moral character. And so Linnaeus, the master organiser, still a hero in his homeland, wrote in his best-known book – in which animals and plants are categorised by their physical characteristics – that Asians are, by nature, haughty and covetous, while Africans are crafty and indolent, and Europeans are, well, gentle and inventive.

Linnaeus was no traveller. He never left northern Europe, and he seems to have met very few non-Europeans – and it shows. For he also colour-coded his racial categories: not

---

* Many other alternatives to *Sapiens* have been invented, including *Narrans*, or storyteller, suggested by Terry Pratchett in the *Discworld* series, and *Faber*, meaning worker and used by Max Frisch in his 1957 novel *Homo Faber*, while David Bowie in his 1971 song 'Oh! You Pretty Things' simply referred to at least some of us as *Homo Superior*.

only were Europeans white and Africans black, but Native Americans were red and East Asians were (sometimes) yellow.* He seems to have chosen red for Native Americans because he had heard that some of them painted themselves with red lines. They would later be known as 'Red Indians', an absurd double muddle, since they were neither red nor Indian – and some people genuinely began to believe that Native Americans had red skins, despite the visual evidence to the contrary. For much of the nineteenth and twentieth centuries, Red Indians and Redskins were the most common words in English for Native Americans, and that Linnaean usage splutters on today, with public pressure forcing the Washington Redskins, an American football team, to drop the second half of its name as recently as 2020.

It's a similar story with the supposed yellowness of East Asians, except Linnaeus was slightly less precise than elsewhere. In his first attempts at classifying humans, Asians in general were brown or dark, but in the definitive 1758 edition of *Systema Naturae* he was using the Latin word *luridus*. Now, *luridus* can and has been translated in a number of ways, including lurid, pallid and deathly – and bore a connotation of sickliness – but among Linnaeus' contemporaries and successors 'yellow' was the word that stuck, in several European languages. And even his greatest rival, the French biologist Buffon, usually far less rigid in how he drew the dividing lines between species, adopted the same colour-coded view of humanity, which, he declared, was 'white in Europe, black in

---

* Linnaeus' choice of colours and some of the behavioural characteristics associated with them seem to have been drawn from the ancient Greek notion of the Four Humours, namely blood, yellow bile, black bile and phlegm (sanguine, bilious, phlegmatic). Some admirers of Linnaeus feel his ideas about race have been misunderstood, partly because he never used the word; and that he argued elsewhere that skin colour was caused by climate. As a student, and presumably as a joke, Linnaeus found another, more liquid way of categorising the four continents: Asia = tea; Africa = coffee; America = chocolate; Europe = beer. He did not invent the notion that Native Americans had red skins, but he undoubtedly popularised it.

Africa, yellow in Asia, and red in America'. East Asians were now officially, if invisibly, yellow.

The principles of racial science, and the static world which it entailed, were rarely challenged in the early nineteenth century, though there were decades of arguments between racial scientists about exactly how many races there were, and what they should be called. Linnaeus' successors dropped most of the categories named after continents and replaced them – for no obvious logical reasons, and with many variations – by Caucasian, Mongoloid and Negroid. But for most of them the yellowness of East Asians in general, and the Chinese in particular, was simply taken for granted. However, it was only later in the nineteenth century, with the arrival of the first significant waves of Chinese migration to America, Europe and Australia, that East Asians became yellow in the imagination of ordinary people, that their yellowness became part of common parlance – almost always with negative connotations. Eventually the words 'yellow peril' would come to represent, in English and other European languages, a concern about East Asian migration that often transformed itself into a paranoid and bitter anxiety.

There's more to be said about Chinese migration, Sinophobia and the yellow peril. First though, the deeper historical context – particularly in relation to many millennia of East Asian migration. That includes the curiously intertwined interactions between Europeans and Chinese which go back four centuries in South-East Asia, where both groups were migrants, sometimes murderous towards each other but also competing and cooperating. But it's also important that any retelling of the East Asia migration story takes note of the pre-European period and recognises the importance of the area in and around the South China Sea, which is larger than the Mediterranean, in area and population and has greater cultural and linguistic diversity. For the South China Sea – connecting two great oceans – has provided a fulcrum for human migration and maritime travel that goes deep into the past, one that has too often been ignored or downplayed by Eurocentric historians studying the pre-modern world.

The prehistory of migration around the South China Sea is complex and significant, in ways that are only just beginning to be understood. Take the recent discoveries of human remains in caves in Indonesia and the Philippines identified as belonging to two previously unknown species of ancient humans, each much smaller than *Homo Sapiens*. Then there are, more extraordinary still, the many ancient seagoing journeys of the 'Austronesians', speakers of a range of related languages, who almost certainly originated in Taiwan, before spreading to the South China Sea and beyond. Austronesian languages are the main languages in Malaysia, Indonesia and the Philippines – but other Austronesians live in places separated by quite staggering oceanic distances: on Easter Island off the coast of Chile and Madagascar off the coast of Africa, to the Maori of New Zealand and the original inhabitants of the American state of Hawaii. As maritime migrants, they make the Vikings look risk-averse and sedentary – and it seems likely, for instance, that the Austronesian settlement of Hawaii and Easter Island took place at roughly the same time the Vikings were exploring the North Atlantic and building a temporary settlement in the Americas.

In the millennium prior to the arrival of European settlers in East Asia, the South China Sea was a whirlpool of cultural influences, in which people and ideas from both India and China played a major role. For the South China Sea was at the heart of what has become known, in recent times, as the 'Maritime Silk Road'. It stretched from coastal China, through

The South China Sea

South-East Asia and the Indian Ocean to the Persian Gulf
and Africa, and was more significant in this period than the
more-famous terrestrial Silk Road that passed through central
Asia. Historians and archaeologists are only really beginning to
reconstruct something of this forgotten past, combing through
ancient Chinese texts, deciphering Old Javanese inscriptions
and raising ancient shipwrecks to build up a picture of a region
that was, in many ways, more sophisticated and more diverse
than that of medieval Europe.

Some of the evidence for this is in plain sight. On the
simplest level, there's the use of Sanskrit and Arabic titles
for rulers – such as Rajah and Sultan, originally from India
and the Middle East. And there are all the cultural, artistic and religious reminders of the important role played by
Hinduism, Buddhism and Islam in the region, brought there
by merchants, invaders and preachers – and sometimes, but
not always, by more substantial migration. Less well known,
for instance, is the mainly Hindu Majapahit Empire, which by
the mid-fourteenth century controlled large parts of modern
Indonesia and Malaysia. Or the many communities of Chinese
settlers in the same area – at least two of which were ruled by
migrants from China in the fifteenth century.

The great Ming sea voyages of the early fifteenth century
have attracted the attention of historians largely because a huge
Chinese fleet reached the east coast of Africa more than half
a century before Vasco da Gama. They've been portrayed as a
brief Chinese opening-up to the world, a glimmer of a China
that once before in history was tempted to become a super-
power. And the voyages – seven of them, over twenty-eight
years, with as many as two hundred ships and twenty-seven
thousand people on board – were undoubtedly an impressive
show of Chinese might and wealth and shipbuilding prowess.
The accounts of these voyages also provide intriguing detail
about the mixing of cultures in Asia, and the normality of

long-distance travel through the South China Sea and the Indian Ocean.*

But in retrospect the Ming voyages seem like an anomaly. The Chinese authorities soon discarded any sense of overseas imperial ambition. A late fifteenth-century administrator openly declared:

> There exists a paramount boundary within Heaven and Earth: Chinese on this side, foreigners on the other. The only way to set the world in order is to respect this boundary.

In many ways, China turned in on itself – until, arguably, the current century – and became far more concerned with protecting its own geographical and cultural frontiers. In the aftermath of the Ming voyages, Chinese migration happened in spite of, not because of, government policy. Such migration was discouraged – sometimes actively, and at one point even made punishable by death. Yet none of this stopped huge numbers of Chinese migrants from settling in South-East Asia and – in the nineteenth century – moving to almost every corner of the wider world. They did so in a manner and style that would be seen as distinctive, a particular model of migration that involved the creation of numerous examples of what became known much later, in English, as a 'Chinatown'.

The notion of a Chinatown is a complex one, and has in many places come to symbolise little more than a tourist attraction, best known for food and Chinese New Year celebrations. But it has its roots in some of the darkest days of early European colonialism. The creation of a Chinatown as a segregated

---

* The commander of the fleet was the Chinese Muslim eunuch Zheng He, whose father and grandfather had been on pilgrimage to Mecca. The British submariner and amateur historian Gavin Menzies claimed in his 2002 best-seller *1421: The Year China Discovered the World*, that Zheng He's fleet also 'discovered' America and circumnavigated the world. In 2008, he published a similarly ahistorical sequel entitled *1434: The Year a Magnificent Chinese Fleet Sailed to Italy and Ignited the Renaissance*.

urban enclave was a way of controlling Chinese migrants, seen as potential threats to European power but also as essential to a flourishing imperial economy. In the very earliest days of the Spanish conquest of the Philippines, the Chinese were allowed to live alongside Europeans in the capital Manila. But by 1594, many of them had left, encouraged to move to a new area allotted to them on the other side of the river from the Europeans – a place called Binondo, which today proclaims itself to be the world's oldest surviving Chinatown. Less than ten years later Manila became the scene of one of the bloodiest conflicts of all time between two migrant communities.

Chinese migrants were playing a key role in a rapidly changing world economy, and Manila was at the heart of that change. Essentially, Europeans wanted luxury Chinese goods such as silk and porcelain, while the Chinese had little interest in European merchandise – but they did want gold and silver, which the Spanish were mining in the Americas. And so the Chinese merchants of Manila were the middlemen, bringing manufactured goods from China – and elsewhere in the region – to the Philippines, and selling them for gold and silver to Spanish traders who took them back to Europe. But the Chinese of Manila were not only merchants. They were also deeply embedded in most aspects of the city's economy, and as one Spanish observer noted, they also worked as tailors, shoemakers, stonemasons, market gardeners, fishmongers, butchers, bakers, doctors, and proprietors of 'eating houses' – as well as unskilled labourers.

Many of the Spanish were unhappy about the number and influence of Chinese migrants living in Manila. They considered them a threat. There was the well-remembered story of a group of Chinese workers who had been forced to become galley-slaves and then mutinied, killing the Spanish governor. Then there was a long-standing and widespread fear, based on no significant evidence, that the Chinese government was planning an invasion. And it was after a visit by some Chinese officials in 1603 that Spanish fear turned to paranoia, and following a series of smaller incidents the Spanish – aided by local Filipino troops and Japanese mercenaries – killed more than twenty thousand Chinese migrants in and around Manila.

That there were no obvious long-term consequences to the Manila massacre is striking. Privately the Spanish recognised that they had misjudged the situation and had damaged their own economic interests. One Spaniard complained that in the aftermath of the killings there was little food, and that he had 'no shoes to wear even at excessive prices'. The Spanish moved quickly to restore trade and recompense the families of those who had been killed. And soon there was a new wave of Chinese migration to Manila – and to elsewhere in South-East Asia. The Chinese government had briefly hinted at the possibility of retribution against the Spanish, an invasion of the Philippines even, but official records show that for the authorities in Beijing the victims of the massacre were ultimately unimportant people, not worth fighting for, who had abandoned their families back home in southern China.

Beijing's response should be seen in terms of wider Chinese attitudes towards migrants. China was then, as now, the most populous country in the world; and is not, and never has been, the monolithic, monocultural society of the Western imagination. This matters to this story because of the differences, in reality and in perception, between northern and southern Chinese. And these differences have shaped the patterns of migration beyond the borders of China, simply because most Chinese migrants, then and ever since, both to South-East Asia and the rest of the world, were originally from southern China.

Those Chinese migrants who lived in Binondo, that self-proclaimed first Chinatown, and who became the victims of the Manila massacre, almost all came from one small part of southern China: the coastal province of Fujian – closer to Manila than to Beijing. Later, many would migrate from Guangdong, even further to the south. And in the great imperial cities of the north, southerners were sometimes talked about as if they were not truly Chinese, and as if the sea-going merchants of the south were really all smugglers and pirates. Powerful and enduring stereotypes emerged, described with precision by the early twentieth-century writer Lu Xun:

> Northerners are sincere and honest; Southerners are skillful and quick-minded. These are their respective virtues. Yet sincerity and honesty lead to stupidity, whereas skillfulness and quick-mindedness lead to duplicity.

As well as migrating more frequently, southerners seemed also to be less distrustful of foreigners and foreign influences. The reasons for this are complex, and clearly proximity to South-East Asia and distance from the centre of Chinese power were important. But there's something deeper here. And it seems possible that Buddhism played a role in making migration culturally acceptable. Buddhism had foreign origins, after all, and placed an emphasis on travel and pilgrimage. Confucianism – always powerful in the northern imperial cities – has a more overtly sedentary culture. Confucius was widely quoted by those who opposed migration: 'While his father and mother are alive, the son should not go on distant journeys.' Northerners did migrate, but usually within the frontiers of China – and often to the south, which helped encourage further migration by those already living there.

Even among southerners there is evidence of resistance to the notion of permanent migration, of leaving one's home for ever. The Chinese word *qiao*, usually translated as the archaic English word 'sojourner', meaning temporary migrant, has been widely used to describe those who moved abroad. It's prompted a debate about the supposedly unique qualities of

Chinese migration, with the implication that the Chinese have been temperamentally less prone than other migrants to cutting off links with their ancestral homeland. It's one of those grand generalisations that is not entirely untrue, but tends to conceal more than it reveals. In fact, until the invention of passports and visas and nationality documents and residence requirements, large numbers of migrants all over the world had no definite long-term plans, and they didn't need to have them. They often saw their stays in a new country as temporary or undefined – even if, as was so often the case, they stayed for the rest of their lives. In this, the Chinese were no exception.

But many Chinese did retain, at least in principle, a special relationship with their homeland. Until the late nineteenth century, the vast majority of Chinese migrants were men, who often left wives and children behind – as well as their parents. Many of these migrants started second families with local women – this was particularly true in the Philippines – but would still return periodically to China. Even for those who didn't travel back to China, the fiction of an anticipated return was culturally significant, as was respect for the now-distant shrines of their ancestors. Conversely, many families in China attempted to keep track of those who had migrated and their descendants, and listed them inside their ancestral shrines – and genealogy has undoubtedly played a more important role in China than in many countries.

Despite discriminatory laws and further massacres, large numbers of migrants from the coast of southern China continued to move to South-East Asia. So, of course, did a smaller number of Europeans. The Europeans were there to rule, while the role of the Chinese was more complicated and varied – and, as it turned out, longer-lasting. They undoubtedly became important players, collaborators even, in the development of European colonialism in South-East Asia, but their presence had an even deeper impact on the political geography and demographics of the region, one that has endured into the post-colonial age.

Singapore is the most conspicuous example. An almost uninhabited island until 1819, it's more than two thousand kilometres from mainland China. Two centuries after its foundation almost three-quarters of all five million Singaporeans identify themselves as Chinese, and more than half speak a Chinese language at home. Most of the major cities of the region have significant Chinese minorities. In contrast, there are very few who identify themselves as European, and the descendants of colonial migrants have largely blended into the wider population.

Those Chinese who migrated to South-East Asia after the sixteenth century were often, in practice, auxiliaries to the imperial projects and global trading ambitions of six nations: Spain, Portugal, Holland, Britain, France and the USA.* At first, they travelled south as merchants and craftsmen, and this did continue, but by the eighteenth century there was a major shift toward the large-scale employment of Chinese migrants as labourers for new economic ventures such as pepper plantations and tin mines. Recruitment was usually handled by middlemen, Chinese entrepreneurs who themselves became rich and powerful figures in the diaspora, and who maintained strong business links with their homeland.

Local leaders of the Chinese migrant community emerged, often appointed by the colonial powers, and referred to as captains. These were formal positions with a written list of duties and responsibilities, allowing the colonial governments to exercise power indirectly and providing some larger communities of migrants with a limited degree of autonomy. In one such list from 1800, written for the British-ruled settlement of

---

* Britain, France and the USA were relative latecomers, fully arriving only in 1786 (Penang), 1862 (Saigon) and 1898 (the Philippines) respectively.

Penang, the captain was 'answerable' for keeping 'good order among your People'; for holding a court 'at your own house twice a week', and for trying 'all petty cases between people of your own tribe'. They also had to maintain a register of births, deaths and marriages – as well as recording the details of any passing visitors.

Penang had been founded as a British settlement in 1786, after it had been ceded by the local sultan to the East India Company. It already had a tiny Malay population; fewer than a hundred people who made a living from fishing and extracting wood oil. The British declared Penang a free port, in which customs duties would not be payable – and for this reason it immediately attracted large numbers of migrants, including sixty Chinese families in the first year. Within a decade, Penang – officially Prince of Wales Island – had a population of more than twenty thousand people, and in 1804 its British governor Sir George Leith declared, with some pride, in a short book about the new settlement

> there is not, probably, any part of the world where, in so small a space, so many different people are assembled together or so great a variety of languages spoken . . . amongst whom are counted, the British, Dutch, Portuguese, Armenians, Arabs, Parsees, Chinese, Chooliahs, Malays, Buggesses, Burmahs, Siamese, Javanese, etc.

Leith then sets out his prejudices about the different migrant groups, full of bombastic judgements in the style of Linnaeus. The Malays, he opines, are 'indolent, vindictive and treacherous', while the 'Buggesses' (from Sulawesi) are 'bold, independent and enterprising', and the 'Parsees' are 'a remarkably quiet well-behaved People'. But Leith's most detailed remarks are about the Chinese community, one of three groups – with the Malays and the Chooliahs (from southern

India) – large enough to have their own captain, and therefore a small amount of autonomy from colonial rule.

The Chinese, writes Leith, 'are in general, a quiet industrious People and have proved a most valuable acquisition to this Settlement'. He points out that the Chinese in Penang get higher wages than other migrant workers, and that they deserve this because they are 'good workmen', but also because they have greater expenses, partly caused by gambling. He notes that 'every Chinaman makes it an invariable rule to send a certain portion of his earning annually to his friends and relations in China'. And he introduces tropes that would soon become central to Western stereotypes of Chinese migrants: that they are addicted to gambling and to smoking opium.*

There are no surviving accounts, it seems, of what the Chinese migrants thought of the British, or of much else. But it's been possible, from other sources, including family records, oral history, temple inscriptions and gravestones, to piece together a little of their early migrant life. Many travelled directly from southern China, but others moved, temporarily or permanently, from older Chinese communities in the region, particularly Dutch-ruled Malacca. In Penang, the Chinese rooted themselves more deeply, and in greater numbers than other migrant groups, with the result that even now more than half of the population of modern Penang consider themselves to be Chinese Malaysians. Elsewhere in the world, descendants of Chinese migrants were more likely to merge into the wider population.

The next phase of Chinese migration reached its apogee in the second half of the nineteenth century. Huge numbers, possibly tens of millions of migrants, many of them indentured labourers, left their homes in southern China for a range of almost unbelievably diverse destinations. More than one hundred thousand

---

* Leith then complains at length about the duration of their theatrical performances, which as governor he presumably feels obliged to attend: 'To every person but themselves these Plays, after half an hour, become tiresome in the greatest degree.'

went to Peru, for instance, working on sugar plantations or in the guano industry, where they gathered bird excrement from offshore islands for use as fertiliser. A similar number of Chinese labourers went to Cuba, and there was significant migration to Panama and Mexico. By the end of the century there were Chinese communities in almost every country of the American continent. The same was true for many Indians, though they, as subjects of the British Empire, tended to go to other British colonies: Fiji, Guyana, Trinidad and Tobago, and Mauritius, for instance – each of which have to this day Indian minorities that form about 40 per cent of the population, and more than that if all those of Indian ancestry are included.*

In economic terms, indentured labourers from China and India – widely referred to as 'coolies' – filled a gap created by the abolition of slavery. Colonial administrations and landowners in the tropics wanted workers, mainly for new sugar plantations but also to build railways, roads and canals. They could no longer simply buy kidnapped Africans – and Europeans, on the whole, refused to do manual work in hot countries. So new and revamped systems of employment were used to bring large numbers of male labourers from the most populous countries in the world. Some came willingly, many were tricked by promises of great riches, others were simply kidnapped as if they were slaves.

A British official described visiting the Chinese city of Amoy, now Xiamen, in 1853 where the barracoons differed little from those of West Africa during the heyday of transatlantic slavery:

I have myself seen the arrangements for the shipment of coolies at Amoy: hundreds of them gathering together in

---

* Each of these countries have had prime ministers of Indian ancestry, though Fiji only briefly. Mahendra Chaudhury, whose grandfather came to Fiji as an indentured labourer in 1902, was in office for just over a year, before he was overthrown in a coup led by ethnic Fijians.

barracoons, stripped naked, and stamped or painted with the letter C (California), P (Peru), or S (Sandwich Islands), on their breasts, according to the destination for which they were intended.

It took four months by ship to get from China to Peru – in conditions that were brutal. Floggings were normal for minor indiscretions: six lashes for lying, twelve for gambling. One in ten of the Chinese labourers died en route, mainly from disease, but others – particularly suspected mutineers – were murdered, and a few killed themselves.

A Cuban importer of Chinese labourers provided written guidance to ship captains for the psychological management of anyone who suffered from what was referred to as 'nostalgia':

We must endeavour to awaken his ambition: the Chinese have a natural propensity that way; it will therefore be easy to succeed. You must make him understand that he is coming to a country in which he will gain money; where he may exercise economy by means of which he will be enabled to return after the expiration of his contract.

On arrival in Cuba there were more barracoons. One unnamed indentured labourer, speaking to a commission of enquiry into the treatment of 'coolies', described how they were quarantined, their pigtails were cut off and they were stripped naked 'so that our person might be examined and the price fixed. This covered us with shame.' At the end of their contracts, most of the Chinese labourers were expected to return home, but very few of them had been able to save enough money and so they stayed, often marrying mixed-race women already living there. An American ambassador to Peru, Richard Gibbs, writing in the 1870s, said that Chinese husbands were 'looked upon as quite a catch, for they made good husbands, industrious, domestic and fond of their children'. This became the pattern throughout South and Central America, for there were very few female Chinese migrants.

More generally, large numbers of Chinese men were undoubtedly forced or tricked into migration, but many others chose to leave. And it's important to recognise the diverse experiences of migrants, even if most of them, at the start, had to endure great hardships. There were many reasons to migrate, and poverty and political instability played an important role. But many others left looking for a new life or adventure, or went in search of gold. From the late 1840s, many travelled east across the Pacific, heading for *Gum Shan*, or Gold Mountain, the Chinese name for California. They would become, over the next seventy years, minor participants and often victims in what might perhaps be described as the Golden Age of American Migration.

The story of migration to the United States has been told in many different ways. Probably the most famous book on the subject, first published in 1952, is Oscar Handlin's *The Uprooted: The Epic Story of the Great Migrations That Made the American People*. It's a stirring read, a fine piece of writing by Handlin, himself the son of Eastern European Jewish migrants. He begins with these much-quoted words, 'Once I thought to write a history of the immigrants in America. Then I discovered that the immigrants *were* American history.' It's a statement that does justice to the range and importance of the subject he is dealing with, and to the centrality of migration to the American story. And it's been persuasively suggested in this century that Handlin's book helped redefine the USA in the popular imagination as a country of recent migrants. *The Uprooted* shifted emphasis away from the early settlers, mainly

Northern Europeans, who had settled there by choice in the 150 years prior to independence. For Handlin shone his unfiltered spotlight on those other Europeans, the tens of millions of half-forgotten people – often fleeing famine or persecution – who crossed the Atlantic in the nineteenth and early twentieth centuries. But that opening statement of Handlin, and his book, as well the migration narrative that it spawned, has also been criticised for what and who it doesn't include.

Native Americans are not part of Handlin's story. There is no mention of the 'Trail of Tears', the forced nineteenth-century migrations of many Native Americans into what was designated as 'Indian Territory', often thousands of kilometres from their ancestral homes. Enslaved people from Africa and their descendants are also almost absent. White women are present in the book, but largely as bystanders – wives and daughters of European men – and rarely as individuals whose views on migration might be of interest. And the long and tortuous tale of Chinese migration is barely mentioned.

Fewer than four hundred thousand Chinese migrated to the USA between 1850 and 1910. That's a tiny number compared to about twenty-five million Europeans over the same period. But for my purposes it's not the numbers that are important. It's what the story of the Chinese in America tells us about changing attitudes towards migration. For there would be a great outpouring of hysteria about Chinese migrants, and the Chinese became in the 1880s the first nationality to be excluded on a permanent basis from entering the United States. This was long before visas and passports were part of the formal requirement to enter other countries, and prefigured a world in which one's country of origin would become critical, unless you are very rich or influential, to your travel and migration opportunities.

Significant Chinese migration to California began in 1849, at the start of the gold rush, and just two years after the territory – formerly part of Mexico – was annexed by the USA. The small port of San Francisco, with a population of a few hundred, became the destination for ships bringing thousands of gold prospectors and other migrants from all over the globe. And many of those earliest migrants came from just two small areas of the southern province of Guangdong: about five hundred of them in 1849, closer to twenty thousand in 1852. Compared to those travelling from Europe or even the eastern states of the USA (there was no Panama Canal, no transcontinental railroads), the Chinese had a far easier journey – across the Pacific. They were welcomed at first, but by the mid-1850s the mood had begun to turn and there was growing opposition to Chinese migration, particularly from gold-rush latecomers of European ancestry.

An editorial in the *New York Tribune* from 1854 was an early foray in a long public campaign to keep the Chinese out of America. There's no reference yet to the 'yellow peril' but it contains extreme examples of a number of tropes that continue to be used by anti-migrant populists around the world:

> They are uncivilized, unclean, filthy beyond all conception, without any of the higher domestic or social relations; lustful and sensual in their dispositions; every female is a prostitute, and of the basest order; the first words of English they learn are terms of obscenity or profanity, and beyond this they care to learn no more. Clannish in nature, they will not associate except with their own people ... If the tide continues they may yet outnumber the whites on the Pacific, for they have no sympathy with Americans, whether in religion, habits or language.*

---

* The editorial was written by Horace Greeley, probably America's best-known nineteenth-century journalist – who supported the abolition of slavery, greater rights for workers and a number of other liberal causes, and also employed Karl Marx as the Europe correspondent of the *New York Tribune*. Despite his opposition to Chinese migration, he's widely attributed with inventing the most famous migration slogan of all time, 'Go West, young man!' Greeley stood as a presidential candidate in 1872 and lost heavily to the Republican incumbent Ulysses S. Grant. Greeley died less than four weeks later.

It's worth noting, amidst the chauvinist rhetoric, that the word 'American', by this time, signified white migrants and their descendants. A hundred years earlier it was used, in English, to describe Native Americans.

There followed a gradual whittling away of the rights of Chinese migrants – denying their children access to education, barring them from testifying in court against white people, imposing taxes on ships bringing new arrivals, turning away Chinese women on the grounds that they might be prostitutes. This did little to stop the flow of migrants. Some of the original Chinese miners moved on, as gold was found in Canada, Australia and New Zealand. But many more came, settling in San Francisco, building its first Chinatown, setting up laundries, working in factories making anything from cigars to shoes. At least ten thousand Chinese worked on the great transcontinental railroads.

And while the economy was strong, the Chinese were tolerated, encouraged even; their labour was needed, even if there was a rising tide of anti-Chinese chauvinism. Trade unions representing white workers, often migrants themselves, complained that Chinese labourers were undercutting their wages – and they were used on at least one occasion as strike breakers. The best-known trade union leader of the day, an Irish migrant called Denis Kearney, finished every speech with the words, 'The Chinese must go!' When the first railroad across the United States was complete, not only were thousands of Chinese migrants unemployed but the railway itself was an encouragement for large numbers of white migrants to head west from the Atlantic coast. Then the Great Depression, as it was once known before another came along, struck in 1870s and suddenly the Chinese were no longer needed. It's a tale that resounds in modern times.

Eventually, most Chinese migrants were banned from entering the USA. They were the first 'race' to be excluded, in a country that had always prided itself on its open borders and continued to do so. The Congressional debates over the Chinese Exclusion Act are a dismal read, a flourish of hyperbolic racism led by West Coast white politicians deploying a wide range of metaphors against 'John Chinaman', 'Mongolians' and, yes, the 'yellow race'. For that strange notion of Chinese 'yellowness' developed by eighteenth-century race 'scientists' had by this time percolated into common hate speech – in English and several other languages. Congressman Campbell Berry of California, for instance, described the Chinese as a 'horde of Oriental invaders', 'a yellow serpent twining its coils', an 'exhaustless stream of yellow plague'. He (and others) contended that the migrants were really slaves, 'the lowest and vilest of China's teeming millions, steeped in degradation and in superstition'.

The passing of the Chinese Exclusion Act in 1882 further demonised those Chinese who were already resident in the USA. They were blamed for outbreaks of leprosy and syphilis and bubonic plague. They were sometimes driven from their homes. In 1885, the entire three-hundred-strong Chinese community of Tacoma in Washington Territory was rounded up and forced on to trains leaving the city; their Chinatown was burnt to the ground. And then there were Chinese migrants who were simply murdered. In 1885, twenty-eight coal miners were killed – some of them tortured or burnt to death – in Wyoming; and two years later thirty-five gold miners were murdered in Oregon. No one was ever convicted.

There was some resistance, often led by Chinese organisations such as the Chinese Equal Rights League, founded by a Chinese American journalist called Wong Chin Foo. He travelled around the well-organised American lecture circuit telling mainly white audiences what Chinese people were really like. That they weren't slaves, or licentious or dirty, and they didn't eat rats or cats, though a few dogs were occasionally consumed back home in China. Wong even challenged Denis Kearney, the trade union leader, to a duel, and when Kearney responded with an insult, calling him an 'almond-eyed leper', Wong countered by offering Kearney his choice of weapons for the duel: 'chopsticks, Irish potatoes, or Krupp guns'. There was no duel, but in 1887 there was a widely reported public debate – with Wong generally adjudged the winner.*

When the American economy improved, California employers needed migrant labour again, and so once more the migrants came, with larger numbers this time arriving from Japan, the Philippines – which became an American colony in 1898 – and Mexico. Some Chinese migration to the USA did continue, often illegally via Canada or Mexico, or by convincing the American border authorities on the Pacific coast that they belonged to one of the few categories of Chinese (merchants, students) who might be allowed into the country. The key location from 1910 was Angel Island in San Francisco Bay, a West Coast equivalent of New York's Ellis Island, where would-be migrants were quarantined and interrogated, and where they attempted to outwit immigration officers.

In later times, Chinese Americans recalled how they were able to rely on white people thinking that the Chinese all look alike. And it was possible for some of them to get through – with false papers, and with carefully rehearsed answers to difficult questions. Illegal migration became both a business

---

* Wong was an unusual Chinese migrant in that he came from the north of the country, from Jimo in Shandong province. As a child he was adopted by American missionaries, became a Baptist and was sent to Pennsylvania for further studies. He became an American citizen in 1874 – and reverted to Confucianism. He soon became the USA's best-known Chinese American and founded a newspaper of that name – before taking on Denis Kearney. Wong died in China in 1898, at the age of about fifty-one.

and a game. Maxine Hong Kingston, in her 1977 novel *China Men*, drew on the experiences of relatives trying every imaginable means to reach Gold Mountain. For her male ancestors, the great San Francisco earthquake* of 1906 had been a godsend, because the records office was destroyed by fire:

> An authentic citizen, then, had no more papers than an alien. Any paper a China Man could not produce had been 'burned up in the Fire of 1906'. Every China Man was reborn out of that fire a citizen.

By the end of the nineteenth century, several other countries had followed the USA by placing heavy restrictions on migration from China – mainly British-ruled territories which were, at the same time, encouraging large-scale white immigration: Canada, Australia, New Zealand and South Africa. But the old economic explanations for the exclusion of the Chinese had become redundant as a deeper Sinophobia took root among Europeans and those of European origin. Increasingly, the arguments were set out in racial and civilisational terms, similar in some ways to modern Islamophobia. And they became part of a wider narrative in which white Europeans told themselves that they were about to be overwhelmed by the 'yellow race' – a term that always included the Chinese, and sometimes the Japanese.

The earliest references to the phrase 'Yellow Peril' occur in the 1890s and soon became commonplace. Kaiser Wilhelm II even claimed to have invented the phrase, as the title of a lithograph he sent to his fellow European heads of state. He

---

* The earthquake also destroyed San Francisco's old Chinatown, which was rebuilt under the direction of a second-generation Chinese American businessman called Look Tin Eli as what he called an 'ideal Oriental city', consisting of 'Veritable Fairy Palaces filled with the Choicest Treasures of the Orient'. What had once been a Chinese ghetto was transformed into a tourist attraction, overtly aimed at white tourists from America's East Coast.

undoubtedly encouraged the notion that the colonial powers of Europe should unite 'to resist', as he put it, 'the inroads of the great Yellow race', and perhaps partition and incorporate China into their international empires. China and the Chinese became the enemy, in reality and in the imagination of many Europeans.

First, that reality. In the summer of 1900, troops belonging to a German-led eight-country alliance (including Britain, Russia, the USA and Japan) occupied Beijing, looting and killing their way through the city. It was a deliberately brutal response to a crisis, known as the Boxer Rebellion, that had originally been caused by the murder of some migrants – Europeans, this time, working in China as Christian missionaries. Part of northern China was seized by Russia, while Beijing was forced to pay reparations and oversee the suicide – or execution – of some of its own government officials considered complicit in the Rebellion.

China as a real-life battlefield enemy was soon eclipsed as the eight countries of the short-lived anti-Chinese alliance quarrelled with each other in the long lead-up to the First World War. But the wider notion of the Yellow Peril as some kind of existential threat to the 'white race' had taken hold of the Western imagination. It took various forms, and frequently made an appearance in what has become known as 'invasion literature', a genre of fiction that had its glory days in the late nineteenth century.

Some of the earliest examples were set in Australia, where the titles tend to give away the storylines. *White or Yellow? A Story of the Race War of AD 1908* (published 1888) and *The Yellow Wave: A Romance of the Asiatic Invasion of Australia* (1895). And it was in this Sinophobic context that, in 1901, the Australian government felt able to introduce the 'White Australia' policy to prevent Asian and Pacific Island migration – by requiring migrants to complete a dictation exercise in a European language.* In the debate over the new policy, the prime minister Edmund Barton asserted that 'the doctrine of the equality of man was never intended to apply to the equality of the Englishman and the Chinaman'. Another MP, with no sense of irony, or much knowledge of Australian history, declared, 'Let us keep before us the noble idea of a white Australia – snow-white Australia if you will. Let it be pure and spotless.' The aboriginal population was unmentioned, as was the fact that just forty years earlier British convicts were still being transported to Australia.

There are many other examples of the Yellow Peril in invasion literature from Europe. Because Europe experienced far lower levels of Chinese migration than Australia or North America, it was harder for European writers to depict Chinese migrants as a serious threat to the livelihoods of the white working classes. Instead, the Chinese are given a more symbolic role as the imagined Other, or as if they were members of a slightly different species, and often as preposterously cruel and cunning counterparts to Europeans.

Take *La Guerre Infernale* by Pierre Giffard, published in 1908 as a series of illustrated weekly booklets aimed at teenagers. Set twenty years in the future, it's in many ways a prescient example of early science fiction. It predicted the use of tanks and submarines and dogfights and chemical weapons in warfare, though Giffard's flying bicycles were a rare miss. The book is premised on a calamitous European war – and

* It was also used to exclude some Europeans. New arrivals were required to pass the test in 'any prescribed language', a form of words that allowed the immigration authorities to exclude migrants and visitors who were considered undesirable. On arrival at Sydney Harbour in 1934, the polyglot Prague-born communist writer Egon Kisch was asked to transcribe the Lord's Prayer dictated to him in language he definitely didn't know: Scottish Gaelic. Predictably he was adjudged to have failed the test. A British subject, Mabel Freer, deemed a 'cunning and utterly immoral woman' by the Australian authorities, was asked to write down an Italian-language weather report. She too failed, simply by putting her fingers in her ears as the report was read to her.

the Chinese take advantage, invading via Russia. In Moscow, the Chinese are revealed as the masters of pointless torture, practitioners of a stomach-churningly creative sadism displayed in words and pictures on the pages of *La Guerre Infernale*. A hungry rat is sewn into a large body wound; a woman is forced to wear an extremely tight wire jacket and any protruding flesh is snipped off; teaspoons are used for gouging out eyes. The Chinese, in Giffard's version, are cruel beyond your worst nightmare.

Britain's greatest contribution to the Yellow Peril, meanwhile, was Fu Manchu, a fictional Chinese villain who was only slightly more subtle than Giffard's nameless torturers, and just as evil. With his long droopy moustache and his faux-Chinese name, he was the anti-hero of many films and books, a TV series, a comic strip and a radio programme, which were hugely successful in English-speaking countries. Fu Manchu brought a small fortune and some fame to his creator, a London-based writer called Sax Rohmer, who provided this pen-portrait near the start of the first novel, *The Mystery of Dr Fu Manchu*, published in 1913:

> Imagine a person, tall, lean and feline, high-shouldered, with a brow like Shakespeare and a face like Satan, a close-shaven skull, and long, magnetic eyes ... Invest him with all the cruel cunning of an entire Eastern race, accumulated in one giant intellect, with all the resources of science past and present ... Imagine that awful being, and you have a mental picture of Dr Fu Manchu, the yellow peril incarnate in one man.

Almost every old Chinese stereotype can be found in the stories of Fu Manchu: opium dens, all-round inscrutability, secret societies, criminal geniuses, mysterious poisons, demoniacal cruelty, hypnotic powers. But most striking of all is the supposed yellowness of Chinese people, which permeates the book in terms that are never favourable: 'yellow scum', 'yellow devil', 'wicked yellow face', 'hideous yellow man' – no less than fifty-three such references just in that first novel. It

is an overtly racialised narrative in which, Rohmer says, Fu Manchu's 'existence is a danger to the entire white race'.

The main action of the early novels and many of the films takes place in London's old Chinatown in the East

End, where Fu Manchu has his secret headquarters in an opium den next to the Thames. The East End, close to the docks and beyond the old city walls, had for centuries been home to migrants from many parts of Britain, and more famously from elsewhere in the world: French Protestants, Scandinavian seamen, Irish weavers, former African slaves, Indian sailors, East European Jews. The Chinese came first as mariners and began to settle there in the second half of the nineteenth century, but always in very small numbers, congregating eventually in the area known as Limehouse. Sax Rohmer went there originally as a journalist, trying to track down a legendary Chinese gangster who may never have existed, and spotted instead a 'tall, dignified' Chinese man, who became his inspiration for Fu Manchu, 'the Devil Doctor', 'the Yellow Satan'.

As well as being the devil incarnate, and the harbinger of a racial Armageddon, Fu Manchu can also be seen, more parochially, as a migrant with a grudge. It's hinted that he is seeking revenge for the crushing of the Boxer Rebellion. And in the first talkie film version of Fu Manchu, it's revealed that during the Rebellion his wife and child were killed by the British. But he's also depicted as a migrant who is merely a criminal, and Sax Rohmer was convinced that many East End Chinese were simply villains. 'Of course', he said,

> not the whole Chinese population of Limehouse was criminal. But it contained a large number of persons who had left their own country for the most urgent of reasons. These people knew no way of making a living other than the criminal activities that had made China too hot for them. They brought their crimes with them.

The East End of Sax Rohmer, and many other writers of the time, was in large part fantasy; and his portrayal of London's tiny Chinatown was absurd. But stories like his were widely believed, and entered deeply into the dominant culture of the time. Take, for instance, the *Girls' Own Annual* of 1909–10, whose young readers were solemnly informed about the menace of Chinese migration:

> This enormous mass of humanity shows a marked tendency to spread out in all directions and overflow into the other countries of the world. It is this readiness of the Chinese to settle in the midst of other nations, and the evils which may follow in its train, which constitute the Yellow Peril.

Then, in the summer of 1911, the *London Magazine* ran a two-part exposé of the Chinese community in the East End which described Chinese men as holding an 'inscrutable, irresistible lure' for white women, and that the 'exotic charm' of the Chinese overcame their 'instinctive repugnance to a race of alien blood and colour'.

It's rare, as usual, to hear the voices of the migrants themselves. But a real Chinese sojourner, the teacher and novelist Lao She, who wrote his first book while living in London in the 1920s, declared witheringly that those who 'lack the money for a journey to the Orient always nose around Chinatown in quest of material for novels, travelogues or news articles'. And, he continued, they never fail to exaggerate:

> If there were no more than twenty Chinese people dwelling in Chinatown, the accounts of the sensation-seekers would without fail magnify their number to five thousand. And every one of those five thousand yellow-faced demons will smoke opium, smuggle arms, commit murder – hiding the corpses under the bed – rape women – regardless of

age – and commit an endless amount of crimes, all deserving, at the very least, gradual dismemberment and death by
ten thousand slices of the sword.

The old East End Chinatown barely survived the Second
World War – partly because the area suffered such severe bomb
damage. And apart from a weather-scarred 1990s statue of a
Chinese dragon chasing its tail opposite Limehouse police station there's little sign there was ever a Chinatown here, though
Sax Rohmer fans will be pleased that the pyramid-shaped
tombstone – supposedly an entrance to Fu Manchu's lair –
still stands in a nearby churchyard.* Other groups of migrants
moved into the area – including Bangladeshis in the poorer
parts of Limehouse; bankers and city professionals in the newly
built housing developments by the river.

London's modern Chinatown, seven kilometres away near
Leicester Square, is almost entirely a post-war creation – an
economic and culinary opportunity spotted by Chinese
migrants. For just as the old Limehouse Chinatown existed
because of the docks, so the one in the West End was all about
Chinese food, which was becoming increasingly popular in
Britain. The restaurant business began to drive further migration – particularly from what was still the British territory of
Hong Kong – and not just to the big cities. By the 1970s it
was possible to find restaurants run by Chinese migrants and

---

* Fu Manchu, meanwhile, staggered on until 1980, having enjoyed a productive
1960s as an ageless James Bond-style Asian villain in five feature films, in which the
Devil Doctor was no longer tied to London's East End but had become an international nomad. He made his final mainstream outing in the extremely silly last film
of the British comedian Peter Sellers. Fu Manchu is barely remembered now, and his
descent into cultural oblivion has been unusually precipitous. If Fu Manchu is known
at all by more recent generations it's as a description of a particularly unfashionable
variety of pendulous moustache, or as the name of a minor Californian rock band. It's
perhaps a sign of the changing times that while Donald Trump thought it was funny
to refer to Covid-19 as 'Kung Flu', more than sixty years earlier one wit decided to
rename the Asian flu epidemic 'Flu Manchu'. Rohmer died from Asian flu in 1959.

serving Anglicised Cantonese food – to eat in or take away – in many smaller towns.

Other forms of migration also continued, and then increased dramatically in the 1990s as Hong Kong prepared to return to Chinese rule. By the new millennium, there was a much wider mix of Chinese migrants in the UK than ever before; the rich and the poor and the desperate, and from many more parts of China. There were a growing number of Chinese students, often financed by well-off parents, and professionals for whom working abroad was an important stepping-stone in their careers. Many would stay on. But there were also undocumented migrants, particularly women, who ended up working in brothels and massage parlours. Much of this kind of migration went largely unnoticed – except when something went catastrophically wrong. In 2000, fifty-eight Chinese migrants were found dead in Dover, in the sealed truck that had brought them to Britain. Four years later, twenty-three undocumented Chinese labourers were drowned in the tidal sands of Morecambe Bay as they were raking for cockles.

Then there were the millionaires. In 2019, the Chinese were by far the largest group of foreign nationals applying for a Tier One Visa, nicknamed the Golden Visa, which secured the right to live in the UK in return for a couple of million pounds of investment. The billionaire property developer Xu Weiping, born in China, resident in London and bearing a Seychelles passport, became a minor media celebrity. One journalist described him, largely because of his fondness for designer clothes, as 'the antithesis of the stereotypical reserved Chinese businessman', but the reason he got so much attention was that he bought up part of London's old docklands, not far from Limehouse. And lots of other less famous Chinese migrants, largely professionals working in financial services, have moved to Limehouse itself and currently make up more than one in eight of the area's residents. I've talked to some of them as they strolled beside the upmarket new housing developments that have replaced the warehouses along the river. I couldn't find one who was aware that there had ever been a Chinatown in Limehouse.

British attitudes towards Chinese migrants have been transformed since the days of Sax Rohmer and Fu Manchu. It's true that some of the Sinophobia once conjured up by the words 'Yellow Peril' has re-emerged as China plays a much larger international role, and because of the Covid crisis. But apart from isolated Covid-related racist attacks, the perceived enemy is much more likely to be the Chinese government rather than Chinese migrants.* Sometimes it goes to another extreme. In Britain, for instance, governments that have prided themselves on opposing almost all immigration have made one significant exception. It's for about five million inhabitants of Hong Kong who have had, since early 2021, the right to settle in the UK. This is partly intended as a way of putting diplomatic pressure on China – accused by Britain of not keeping to the Hong Kong handover agreement. But it is also politically possible within the UK because the Chinese – repeatedly characterised in modern times as thrifty and well-behaved and hard-working and law-abiding – have become archetypal 'good migrants'.

---

* In the years of Covid, yellowness was barely mentioned: I found just one reference, in a French regional newspaper that referred to the coronavirus as the *péril jaune*. And no one seriously contends any more that the skin of Chinese people is yellow. However, my daughter informs me that white men who are keen on East Asian women are sometimes said to have 'yellow fever', and the Urban Dictionary offers this definition: 'Yellow Fever: A term usually applied to white males who have a clear sexual preference for women of Asian descent, although it can also be used in reference to white females who prefer Asian men.'

AN EIGHTH INTERMISSION

Chance. I happen to have been born in a country whose passport allows me to travel easily – very often without a visa. It's a passport that opens doors and borders, rather than closing them, and it's relatively simple for me to get permits to work and live in lots of different countries. I even have, quite legally, two passports – so I can travel with one of them, while the other is being fingered and stickered and franked in the London consulate of the next country in which I'm planning to work. There are world-famous downsides to being British – the climate, the cuisine, the poor quality of political debate, the indignant self-righteousness – but because of my passport I can escape all that. And, if I set my mind to it, migration to almost anywhere is a possibility.

The UK has, in recent years, dropped slightly in the Passport Index, an annual list of countries ranked in order of ease of travel for their nationals. In 2022, Japan was on top for the fifth year in succession while the UK, which was in first position as recently as 2015, has tumbled out of the top ten, partly due to Brexit. I sometimes complain about that, until I'm reminded how different my life would be if my country was near the bottom of that long list. The last three names on the Passport Index are Syria, Iraq and Afghanistan – countries that

I've visited as, respectively, a language student, a tourist and a journalist, and each of which have played a significant role in my adult life. It's far more difficult for Syrian, Iraqi and Afghan friends to come to my country, for any reason. But there is also a much deeper asymmetry here. Their nationalities and passports limit their key life choices, and mine don't. There's nothing I or they have done to deserve this. It feels to me like a fundamental injustice; one that goes largely unchallenged. And there seems to be little prospect of change.

It's in this context that passports have come to symbolise, particularly if your country is near the bottom of the Passport Index, a deep, seemingly ineradicable inequality between peoples, and between nation-states. For it has become almost impossible to imagine a world where all passports are equal, or in which they are no longer needed. We all need them, or their identity card equivalent, for international travel – unless you're the Queen of England or the King of Saudi Arabia. And it's become unthinkable, these days, for anyone to suggest, seriously, that they should be abolished. That wasn't the case a hundred years ago.

In the final chapter of his autobiography, the Viennese novelist Stefan Zweig, one of the most successful and best travelled writers of his time, devoted four and a half precious pages to a tirade on a single subject: the passport. He hated them. 'Nothing,' he argued, 'more graphically illustrates the monstrous relapse the world suffered after the First World War.' He described the 'looks of amazement' on the faces of young people when he told them that before 1914 he travelled to India and America without a passport. Zweig looked back on those years with sentimentality and great nostalgia, quoting a (male) Russian exile who told him, 'A man used to have only a body and soul; now he needs a passport too, or he won't be treated as a man.'

Stefan Zweig was born into a world where passports were rarely mandatory, and usually unnecessary – and when the word did not mean quite the same as it does today. The term 'passport' was originally brought into English and many other languages from French, where a *passeport* had been a document that gave the person carrying it permission to enter or leave through a city gate. There had been repeated attempts in several places, including eighteenth-century France, to introduce passports, but they never really caught on internationally and were often seen as a symbol of despotism. Where they were in use, they looked quite different from what we now think of as a passport, and performed a different function.

These pre-war passports generally took the form of a letter of introduction, purportedly written by one government to another on behalf of the bearer, on a single sheet of paper. They didn't provide a reliable guide to the bearer's identity, since most of them did not carry photographs, though some did have detailed physical descriptions – of the shape of noses, for instance. There was little attempt at consistency between countries: no standard format for passports, nor any agreement about who could issue them. So a British traveller going across the Channel would often carry a French or Belgian passport. And because so many borders were unmarked or unpatrolled, passports could make no real impact in stopping even slightly determined travellers from moving around.

Zweig was right to think that this all changed after 1914, though it is probable that the war simply speeded up what would have happened anyway. Europe during the First World War was a more paranoid place – and governments sought, often ineffectively, to exert greater control over population movements. Passports were issued, and then inspected at borders, and sometimes internally; and these passports frequently served as internal identity documents, bearing detailed descriptions of distinguishing characteristics and, sometimes, a photograph. They became part of a new wartime surveillance infrastructure aimed at rooting out spies and saboteurs, and spotting deserters and traitors – an infrastructure that survived into peacetime, at a time when many borders were redrawn and millions of people were on the move.

After the war, many people talked, optimistically, about returning to the good old passport-less days. They did do so for a very broad range of reasons: humanitarian and economic ones, and not just the libertarian and nostalgic sentiments professed so passionately by Stefan Zweig. For some economists, for instance, the free movement of workers across borders was not only critical to rebuilding the post-war economy, it was also an ideological cornerstone of capitalism. Humanitarian organisations emphasised the importance of letting people move freely to escape civil war and persecution, and build new lives elsewhere.

The first International Conference on Passports,* held in Paris in 1920 under the auspices of the newly formed League of Nations, foresaw a time when there would be no passports, and a 'total abolition of restrictions' on movement. But not quite yet. National governments were worried about revolution and the Spanish flu being spread by migrants. And the growth of nationalism also played an important role as many countries, some of them newly formed, sought to define themselves in terms of a community of people who had similar attributes: the same language, history and culture – and the same passport.

And so, instead, the delegates at the Paris Conference set out to provide an interim solution to a pressing problem: the lack of international agreement and consistency over the function and format of passports. They announced a new standardised design for passports, a design that is immediately recognisable today: passports issued by all countries would henceforth take

---

* The full title was the Conference on Passports, Customs Formalities and Through Tickets. Twenty-two delegations, most of them European, took part, along with four non-European countries: China, Japan, Uruguay and Venezuela. The Soviet Union, the United States and Turkey were unrepresented.

the form of a booklet with a certified photograph, an issue and an expiry date, empty pages for visa stamps, lots of personal details and distinguishing characteristics, and text in at least two languages. The conference agreed on meticulous design specifications: a passport size of 15½ cm by 10½ cm, thirty-two pages bound in cardboard, with the country name at the top of the cover, its coat of arms in the middle and the word 'Passport' at the bottom. The age of passports had begun, and there would be no going back.

Stefan Zweig was wealthy and famous, and some of his nostalgia smacks of privilege and snobbishness and impatience.* For many people, pre-war pre-passport travel was never such an idyll. It was always far harder for the poor or for single women, and the Chinese, after all, had been excluded as a race from America since the 1880s. But Zweig's tirade did touch on something important about how migrants have come to be treated. He described the way in which migrants are expected to show undying gratitude to their hosts, 'to offer special thanks for every breath of air that I take in a foreign country, thus depriving its own people of its benefit'. Still more important, he set out the dehumanising, unequal way in which we have come to be defined by our passport – or more precisely how we as individuals have been reduced, at first sight, to what our passports tell people about us.

And by the end of his days, Zweig was writing from experience. He was Jewish – and after the incorporation of Austria into Hitler's Germany he knew he could not return home. In exile in Britain, he requested and was given the white passport of a stateless refugee, a document that described him 'as an alien'. 'This English document,' he said, felt like 'a favour that could be withdrawn at any time'. And when the Second World

---

* 'In the last decade,' he declared, 'knowing a girl who works in a consulate and can cut the waiting time short has been crucially more important than the friendship of someone like Toscanini or Rolland.'

War began, he was told that he now had the status of 'an enemy alien' and might be interned as a result. Zweig left Britain in search of a new home across the Atlantic. He moved to Brazil, to the city of Petrópolis in the hills above Rio – where he finished his autobiography, tidied up his affairs and wrote sad poetry, as if he were Ovid, for his sixtieth birthday. In one of his last letters he declared, 'my inner crisis consists in that I am not able to identify myself with the me of my passport, the self of exile'. On 22 February 1942 Stefan Zweig and his second wife Lotte lay down on their bed and took an overdose of sleeping pills. They never woke up.

In the aftermath of the Second World War, the notion that passports might be abolished was not quite unthinkable, but it had taken on the status of a well-respected pipe dream – something that everyone would agree to, in principle, and then ignore. Well into the 1960s there are traces of that Zweigian yearning for a passport-free existence. A series of UN conferences on passports and travel continued to refer to the issue, usually as a long-term aspiration coupled with the phrase 'not feasible at present'. And then it slowly faded into unthinkability, as those who remembered a passport-free existence passed into history. Today, there is no international movement for the abolition of passports and no serious politician who would even suggest such a policy.

But passports – and the inequalities that they symbolise – remain at the centre of the modern story of migration. Today, there are many millions of people from countries in the bottom half of the Passport Index who want a better passport – one that gives them the right to live somewhere else and to travel more freely. If you're very rich, it's pretty easy. There's a multi-billion-dollar financial sector, known as 'investment migration', to help you. There are many dozens of companies that are happy, for a substantial fee, to guide you through the labyrinthine and often grimy world of Golden Visas, and 'citizenship by investment' – and who won't ask you too many questions about where you got your money. For less than half a million dollars you can 'buy' a passport from one of a number of Caribbean countries; for slightly more money, and a more complex process, an EU country is possible. In the UK, there's a sliding scale, set out on a government website, according to which those who have more than ten million pounds to invest can be fast-tracked towards citizenship.

If you're not rich, it's much more complicated. There are a number of options, though: you might acquire a new passport through marriage, sham or not. Or because of an ancestor – real or invented. Then there's the old slow employment route to citizenship – Green Cards for the USA, and similar schemes elsewhere – especially if you have a skill that's in high demand. Or there's the fraudulent impersonation of existing passport-holders or their relatives, as practised by some Chinese migrants in the late nineteenth and early twentieth centuries. These are some of the safer options. Others are more perilous, and even less likely to result in a passport.

Most of these other options involve crossing an international border without authorisation – and then either simply disappearing from official view or asking for asylum as a refugee by claiming to have been persecuted. Those border-crossing risks are evident. Death is the biggest one. Death by drowning in the sea, or by falling from the landing gear of a plane, or from hypothermia in a refrigerated truck, or being shot while climbing a wall, or being murdered by traffickers. But there's also enslavement, rape, injury – or simply being pushed back into one's old country, minus all the money you had saved to pay for your journey. Despite all these risks, many millions take these routes each year – evidence again of the deep-seated need or desire among many human beings to live somewhere else, and of a dysfunctional system that seeks, and fails, to prevent them from doing so.

CHAPTER NINE

Zionists, Refugees and Great Aunt Polly

My grandmother's family was huge and Jewish and noisy – and every year or so they would gather for a lunch party in someone's London garden. Almost all of them were very English Jews. By which I mean that they spoke with precise Edwardian accents, their manners echoed those of the upper classes and they were physically unscathed by the wars and the killings that devastated the Jews of continental Europe in the twentieth century. But two of my grandmother's brothers married a pair of sisters, Russian migrants, whose distinctive accents would always mark their origins. And these two sisters were, in turn, as different from each other as could be imagined. Miriam, the younger, was sweet and kind and warm, with a big smile and a gentle guttural laugh. Polly, older by fourteen years, was grand and intimidating and, just possibly, a genius.* After all, she had

---

* Polly was not her real name. She was born Esther Polianowsky and became Esther Salaman, but because her husband had a younger sister called Esther a shortened version of her surname was widely used. She was also known as Big Esther, in contrast to her sister-in-law Little Esther, who was almost twice her size. And some people referred to her as Polly-Esther, which – in a family with many scientists – led to a flurry of inorganic chemistry jokes.

once worked, we were told repeatedly, as a physicist alongside Albert Einstein.

My parents had many Polly stories. Most of them were unflattering: that she was rather self-important and patronising, that she had once congratulated my father for having 'brought on' my mother, intellectually speaking, and that she only turned on her hearing aid when she was herself talking. They said that she would not waste her time with other women at family parties and would instead search out the cleverest men she could find. Secretly I was always rather excited to see Polly. She had taught me to play chess and usually remembered my name – and for a small graceless child these were important things. But it's only recently, more than a quarter of a century after she died, and more than forty years after she declined into dementia, that I learned about her remarkable early life, thanks to an autobiography that she never completed.

Polly was born on the sixth day of the new century in the city of Zhitomir – then part of the Russian Empire, and now in western Ukraine. One of her earliest memories was of anti-Jewish violence, a pogrom, in 1905, during which her family had to flee their home. Five-year-old Polly remembered crowds of people fighting on the street, and one man with his 'brain lying beside him on the ground'. After the 1905 pogrom there was much talk of migration among the Jews of Zhitomir. Her uncle was sent an open ticket to America by a friend, but he never used it, just keeping the ticket on him, as a talisman, in case things got worse. Polly's father, a success-ful timber merchant, was adamant on the subject, declaring that it was 'mainly tailors' who would leave. 'No Jew of any standing,' he said, 'would be in a hurry to leave the graves of his parents.' He had served in the army, spoke Russian and sent some of his children to Russian schools. Polly was scath-ingly dismissive about her mother tongue, Yiddish, while her admiration for the Russian language and for Russian literature knew no bounds. She had begun to show some interest in Zionism but she was, at this stage, an unlikely candidate for migration.

In January 1919, during the civil war that followed the Russian Revolution, there was another attack on the Jews of Zhitomir. Polly describes how men on horseback rode down her street, chasing and whipping two Jews, a father and son. They were then trampled beneath the horses' hooves. Another group of men robbed and killed some of her neighbours, and after that forced their way into her parents' house. And it was Polly, still a teenager, who stood up to the armed intruders, arguing with them, offering them tea, staring them down and eventually convincing them to leave. Polly's family all survived, but about four hundred Jews are thought to have been murdered in two pogroms in Zhitomir in early 1919.

Soon after, with Zhitomir still on the frontline of the civil war, and threatened by Jew-hating militias, Polly fled. She had no passport or identity papers. First, she went to Kiev, and later to the port of Odessa on the Black Sea coast. She and a group of friends had decided to migrate to Palestine. Two of them were killed near Odessa, while Polly and her boyfriend were almost burned alive by farmers who mistook them for Bolsheviks. She described how she caught typhoid, was 'plagued by lice' and endured real hunger for the first time in her life. Eventually Polly and her boyfriend found a ship full of Jews heading for Palestine. Part one of her adventure was over.

In Palestine, she learned Hebrew and worked on a farm planting eucalyptus trees. But she hadn't heard from her family since she left Russia and her priority, now she had found a place of relative safety, was to get her mother and her four younger siblings out of Zhitomir. To do this, she travelled alone, bearing a Palestinian passport, across Europe to Poland, where she witnessed another pogrom and saw Jewish men being thrown out of the window of a moving train. She reached the border with Russia and paid local farmers to sneak her family across the frontier – and she led them all to her new home in Palestine. Polly was just twenty-one.

She had decided that a farmer's life in Palestine was not for her, and that she wanted to resume her education, which had been interrupted by the Russian Revolution. And so, with an introduction to Einstein, she moved to Berlin and studied mathematics and physics. Einstein, in turn, recommended she continued her research in Cambridge, where she met my great-grandfather, a recently widowed scientist called Redcliffe Salaman, who was part of a committee which gave

scholarships to impoverished Jews. Redcliffe proposed marriage to Polly, who turned him down. She instead set her
sights on his oldest son Myer, whom she soon married. And
so she stayed, living in Cambridge and London, raising four
children and writing novels and books about memory – all
of them in English, her sixth language.* She had found her
home. Her mother and brothers remained in Palestine and
became, in 1948, citizens of Israel, while her two sisters followed her to Britain.

This then, in its barest bones, is the story of Polly. Her autobiography is a frank, moving and unexpectedly modest account
of her early life. And it's now harder to see her as a cartoonish
figure of fun, or to remember her only as an old woman holding forth at family parties. Her tale is a reminder, of course,
of the history that so many migrants carry with them, that
those histories are often ignored or misunderstood in their
new homes, and that each migrant has a different story. Polly's
words have survived, and that's rare, particularly for female
migrants. And through those words, so has Polly's small role
in two huge and contentious migration narratives, whose origins go back many centuries but which continue to define our
world, and the language we use to talk about migration: the
story of Zionism, and the story of the refugee.

Zionism first. It's a word that was coined as recently as
1890, to describe a movement and an ideology whose aim
was to create a homeland for Jews in Palestine through large-
scale migration. But the roots of Zionism are complex and
far older. After all, migrations – and homecomings – have
always been part of the stories that Jews have told about
themselves, as far back as Moses and the Promised Land, and
the Babylonian Captivity and the Lost Tribes. But there had

---

* Her first five languages were Yiddish, Ukrainian, Russian, Hebrew and German.
She also spoke good French.

been no homecoming for almost two thousand years, since the destruction of Jerusalem in 70 CE, and the expulsion and enslavement of many Jews by the Roman Empire. And Palestine had, in the centuries that followed, been transformed into both a holy land and a battlefield for two other religions. Small communities of Jews had continued to live in Palestine, but they were a tiny minority in a land that had been ruled since the sixteenth century – almost without interruption – by the Ottoman Empire.

Jews in the diaspora often talked, usually metaphorically, of a return to the Promised Land, to Palestine, but very few did anything about it. Two words: Jerusalem and Zion, originally just the name of a city and a hill within that city, would gather many layers of meaning and become almost interchangeable. For Jews and Christians, and more recently Rastafarians, they were used to describe a glorious past or a heavenly utopia of the imagined future when the Messiah would appear (for Jews) or reappear (for Christians). There was much talk of building Jerusalem elsewhere – even, as William Blake suggested, in 'England's green and pleasant land'.

It became customary for European Jews to recite the words 'Next Year in Jerusalem' during the Passover festival, but this had become a statement of yearning, not intent. Among Jews, Palestine was usually depicted as barren, and anyway belonged to others; the notion of a return was seen as an impractical if heart-warming fantasy.* When Jews did begin to talk, seriously and practically, in the late nineteenth century, about a homeland to which they would migrate, it was not taken for granted that it would be located in Palestine. And the motives for

---

* Moreover, from the seventeenth century onwards it was not Jews but millenarian Christians who were the most important proponents of Jewish migration to Palestine, and more specifically Jerusalem, since they believed this was a precondition for the second coming of Jesus. Some millenarian Christians began, from the early twentieth century, to refer to themselves as Christian Zionists – a category that includes many modern American evangelicals, among them the former Vice-President Mike Pence.

migration were often unrelated to Jewish history or to Jewish religious traditions.

Indeed, Zionism of the kind encountered by Polly in Zhitomir only really makes sense in its immediate European historical context. Undoubtedly, it was in part a protective, defensive response to the massacres of Jews in eastern Europe and to continued discrimination against them elsewhere; a recognition that in most European countries they would never be treated as equals – however much they attempted to assimilate. But Zionism was also, critically, an assertion of a dream of a separate Jewish destiny at a time of growing nationalist feeling almost everywhere in Europe.

In most of the continent this meant communities of people – speakers of the same language, or practitioners of the same religion or sharers of the same traditions – claiming, often successfully, the right to form their own sovereign homeland, a nation-state. Italy and Germany emerged as recognisable versions of their modern selves in the 1870s, while Romania and Serbia became fully independent from the Ottoman Empire in 1878, and Bulgaria in 1908. Nationalism of this kind was based around an existing territory, where people describing themselves as Romanians or Serbs or Bulgarians could convincingly, if not always accurately, claim to be a majority. Jews, however, thinly spread across many countries and empires, were not able to make such a claim about anywhere. Nationalism in Europe always, in practice, entailed some migration – into and out of that core territory. But for Zionism, migration was elevated into a precondition and a defining characteristic even if the long-term goal was to find a permanent home, for Jews to become sedentary in one place.

Modern discussion of early Zionist writing usually starts with a pamphlet anonymously published in 1882, entitled *Auto-Emancipation: An Appeal to his People by a Russian Jew* – and given to Polly when she first showed interest in Zionism as a schoolgirl.* It was in fact written by Leon Pinsker, a doctor living in Odessa, who was fond of medical metaphors. He was writing in the aftermath of pogroms in southern Russia, which had convinced him that attempts at assimilation had become pointless, and that hatred of Jews, or 'Judeophobia' as he called it, was a 'psychic aberration' that is 'hereditary and, as a disease transmitted for two thousand years, it is incurable'. But he was also keen to acknowledge the role of nationalism in his appeal for the creation of a Jewish homeland. 'We pray only,' Pinsker says,

> for a little place somewhere to lay our weary head ... Grant us but our independence, allow us to take care of ourselves, give us but a little strip of land like that of the Serbians or Romanians.

Pinsker called for an international conference of Jewish leaders to decide where in the world Jews should settle, followed by a diplomatic effort to convince the great powers to support their plans and the raising of enough money to acquire 'a tract of land sufficient for the settlement, in the course of time, of several million Jews'. Pinsker himself didn't favour Palestine for the new homeland, because recent small-scale attempts to settle there had not been very successful. Instead, he proposed that 'this tract might form a small territory in North America,

---

* Polly's first memories of Zionism are from those final years at school. It had come to describe one of a range of possible ideological choices for people like her, and didn't really imply an actual commitment to migrate to Palestine. It was as if each of her friends, at a certain point in their teenage lives, took a decision about what they would 'be': a socialist perhaps, or a Marxist, or a Tolstoyan ... or a Zionist. Polly describes herself as unpolitical. She liked a young Tolstoyan man, but was less impressed by his beliefs. She eventually fell in, half-heartedly, with some Zionists who had formed a reading group and was introduced, like most young Zionists of the time, to Pinsker, and to George Eliot's final novel *Daniel Deronda*, the story of an English Jew who decides to migrate to Palestine. Polly, however, was far more interested in the main female character, Gwendolen Harleth, who is not Jewish, and who remains in England.

or a sovereign Pashalik in Asiatic Turkey'. Personally, Pinsker favoured a North American homeland, and Jews, he argued, should 'hasten' to buy land in the USA before it became over-populated by other migrants.

At the time Pinsker was writing, the USA was already home to about a quarter of a million Jews, most of them nineteenth-century migrants from Europe. That number increased fourfold over the next twenty years. There had even been an abortive pre-Zionist attempt to carve out a separate Jewish ter-ritory when, in the 1820s, an American Jew called Mordecai Noah tried to create a place of 'refuge' for Jews by buying land on a large island in the Niagara River close to the Canadian border. He laid a foundation stone for his new colony, known as Ararat, after the mountain on which the Ark belonging to the original Noah had landed. But a group of European chief rabbis pointed out that no holy text had ever prophesied that a 'marsh in North America' would become a future homeland for the 'dispersed remnants of Israel', and not a single Jew, not even Noah, moved to Ararat.*

There would be a large number of similarly half-baked attempts to create homelands in places that weren't Palestine. The most famous and most serious of these was the Uganda plan of 1903, supported by the British, in which a rectangular area of land in East Africa, only slightly smaller than modern Israel, would be turned into an autonomous Jewish settlement. The British described the land – which was not actually in Uganda but in Kenya – as unoccupied, simply because most

---

* Mordecai Noah is often remembered as the first American Jew to achieve national prominence. He was the US consul in Tunisia, a prolific playwright, a well-known journalist and a leading advocate of the notion that American Indians were the descendants of the Lost Tribes of Israel. He was also a friend and admirer of Abbé Grégoire, the inventor of the word 'vandalism'. The foundation stone for Ararat, with its inscription in English and Hebrew, is now on display in Buffalo Museum in upstate New York. The actual site is now occupied by a Radisson Hotel and an eighteen-hole golf course.

of its existing inhabitants were nomads. The Uganda proposal split the Zionist movement, and a minority continued to search for substitutes to what they saw as the fantasy of a Jewish homeland in Palestine – in Angola, in Libya, in Paraguay and Argentina. One of the reasons that they failed was because their preferred destinations were not as appealing as several other alternatives to Palestine, which were still places of greater safety than anywhere in mainland Europe. These included Britain – where Polly and her sisters would eventually settle – several South American countries, South Africa, Australia and of course the USA. And the USA continued – even when there was an upsurge of migration to Palestine in the years before the First World War – to be the most popular destination for Jews leaving Europe.

By the end of that war, the notion of Palestine as a putative Jewish homeland, even possibly an independent Jewish state, had become less of a fantasy. The Ottoman Empire had collapsed and Palestine was now ruled by Britain. British officials were clumsily navigating their way through their commitment, known as the Balfour Declaration, to 'facilitate' the establishment in Palestine of 'a national home for the Jewish people'. For many Zionists, this implied, at least in the long run, the mass migration of Jews – at a time when Jews formed only 12 per cent of the population of Palestine. The British, and several Zionist leaders, attempted to control migration carefully, and that meant, at first, no new wave of Jewish migrants. And for that reason, some of those Jews who did migrate in the immediate post-war years, such as my great aunt, had to lie in order to get there. Indeed, the majority of those who travelled with her from Odessa claimed, contrary to the truth, that they had previously lived in Palestine.

The ship on which Polly arrived in Palestine in 1919 was not just any ship. It was the SS *Ruslan*, which has in recent times been given a prominent role, as the 'Zionist *Mayflower*', in Israel's foundation mythology and became the subject of a centenary exhibition at the Israel Museum in Jerusalem. The 644 Jewish passengers on board were the first large group of migrants to enter Palestine after the British announced their support for a Jewish homeland – and therefore the arrival of the *Ruslan* has become, in retrospect, a key moment in Israel's prehistory. For this was the start of a new wave of Jewish migration to Palestine, which became known as the 'Third Aliyah'. And that term *aliyah*, together with its ordinal number, is important to understanding the modern Israeli migration narrative, for its use is a telling example of how one migrant community has used language to create a distinctive identity that sets it apart from other groups of migrants.

The Hebrew word *aliyah* has a meandering history – and, in recent times, has tiptoed into other languages. It originally meant 'going up' or 'ascent', in the sense of going up a hill. But it's also been used for some centuries to describe the religious ritual of an individual in a synagogue 'going up' to the place where the Torah is kept, and then, by the nineteenth century, *aliyah* had also come to mean the migration of a Jew to Palestine. In the 1920s, the word had begun to carry more specifically ideological overtones, so that such a migrant was seen as performing a patriotic or sacred duty by migrating. It was used in deliberate contrast to the old generic Hebrew word for migration, *hagira*, which thereafter carried the sense that a Jew might be migrating for more selfish reasons, or used for migrants who aren't Jewish. And so *aliyah* has been transformed into a moral imperative, not a lifestyle choice – and not just an act of migration, but also a homecoming.

There's another important way in which the word *aliyah* has been repurposed in modern times, and that's by historians of Israel who've used the term to describe waves of migration rather than the actions of individuals. So, for instance, the seventy-odd years leading up to the creation of Israel in 1948 have been subdivided into five numbered periods of varying lengths – the First Aliyah from 1881 to 1903, the Second Aliyah from 1904 to 1914 and so on.* By so doing, they assert, rightly, the central role that migration played in the prehistory of Israel, but they do so in a way that has sometimes sidelined other stories, and created what has almost become a competition over which *aliyah* was most important.

There are striking similarities, in these specific respects, to the ways in which the prehistory of the United States has been told. For these are stories that matter, in both places, because they help decide who controls the broader national narrative and who defines the country's modern identity. In Israel, for instance, religiously minded Zionists are more likely to emphasise the continuity with the ancient migration-homecomings from Babylon, while left-wing Zionists will often highlight the nation-building role played by the many socialists and trade unionists, including the first three prime ministers of Israel, who came to Palestine from the Russian Empire as part of the Second Aliyah.† Others stress the national origins of particular groups of migrants – so the Fourth Aliyah from 1924 is also known as the Polish Aliyah, while the fifth wave of immigration from 1933 is sometimes referred to, not very accurately, as the German Aliyah.

The periodisation and the descriptions of each *aliyah* are

---

* The earliest example of this periodisation came just two months after the Balfour Declaration, when a Zionist writer, Isaac Nissenbaum, eagerly declared that the Jewish people were ready to start the Third Aliyah 'in order to revive their nation in its ancient land'. But he had a very different timeline in mind from that used by more modern Zionists. For Nissenbaum and other Zionists of the period, the First and Second Aliyah were not recent migrations but were instead the two ancient homecomings from Babylon, led by Ezra and Nehemiah respectively, described in the Old Testament. There were obvious objections to Nissenbaum's periodisation because it excluded, and thereby belittled, the pre-war migrations to Palestine; and so, with a bit of elegant retrofitting, the dates of the First Aliyah (shifted to 1881–1903) and the Second Aliyah (1904–14) were moved into the modern era.
† The fourth prime minister of Israel, Golda Meir, was also born in the Russian Empire, but came to Palestine via the USA as part of the Third Aliyah.

often – as many historians have pointed out – dangerously simplistic. They leave little room for nuance, and it's revealing to note what and who is excluded. The narratives of other Jewish migrants, particularly those who didn't come from Europe, are often ignored, as are the migration stories of the Arabs who were already living in Palestine – many of whom were displaced by the newcomers. It's also usually forgotten, in the nation-building narratives of the First and Second Aliyah, for instance, that a majority of those Jews who migrated to Palestine decided not to stay, and instead headed elsewhere in the world or back to their old homes.

These *aliyah* narratives also attempt, misleadingly, to ascribe to each diverse group of migrants a vague common purpose. And so the Third Aliyah is sometimes described as the 'Pioneer Aliyah', as if all of those on board the *Ruslan*, and the ships that followed, were young and keen to work in the fields and build a new nation. They weren't. One of the travellers on the *Ruslan*, Yehuda Levitov – a future kibbutz founder – wrote that he was disappointed by the age and diversity of his shipmates, complaining that many of them were 'speculators' and that only 'a handful' could be described as 'a positive element' in the growing community of Jews in Palestine. And indeed, the passengers on the *Ruslan* were not united by background or age or purpose, or indeed a commitment to Zionism. Many were simply fleeing pogroms and the civil war.

The individual motives of those who travelled to Palestine on board the *Ruslan* are largely lost to history. Even for my great aunt Polly, whose words do survive, there's a complex web of reasons for her journey, as is so often the case for individual acts of migration. She was going to Palestine partly because her Jewish friends were planning to do the same – but also because it felt like an adventure. The Zionist dream was a factor too, though it is hard to avoid the feeling that the relative proximity of southern Russia to Palestine was critical to deciding that

Palestine, not western Europe or the USA, was her destination. Palestine was just a train and boat journey away, the nearest place of safety. And she, and many of the other passengers, had very little idea what to expect when they got there.

It's important to note that Palestinian Arabs, in particular, are barely mentioned in early Zionist writings. And the myth of an almost entirely barren, unpopulated Palestine, of 'a land without a people for a people without a land', was pervasive – even if any Zionists who had travelled there knew that it wasn't true. And so, it's revealing that when Polly arrived at the port of Jaffa in December 1919, she seems surprised to see anyone but Jews:

> There were Arabs walking about: their clothes were strange, their loud voices frightened me. 'Why are they so angry?' I asked. 'They are not angry at all; they just want to sell you oranges.'

It's a rare moment of dissonance for this self-assured teenager, remembered more than half a century later. She has reached Palestine, against the odds, but in doing so she has lost her sense of purpose, of direction. It's a feeling described by many migrants – as if the journey and the getting-away were more important than the destination. For Polly had no clear plans for her new life, just the vague idea that it might involve ploughing some fields.

She provides lots of details about her early months there. She considered first joining a group of Zionists fighting against Arabs in the north but her friends persuaded her not to go. Then, while visiting a friend in Jerusalem at a time of Arab-Jewish riots, she carried a gun strapped to her stomach through British checkpoints. After that a militant Zionist politician asked her to befriend the leader of an Arab militia – what thriller writers call a honey-trap – so that he might then be murdered. She refused.* She began working on a farm, planting trees to help drain the land of its malarial swamps – but soon caught malaria. She described one particularly bad attack while on her own in the countryside with a donkey that wouldn't move. A local Arab took pity on her, showed her how to get the donkey moving again, and then accompanied her home and fetched a doctor. She doesn't quite say so, but this feels like an epiphany, as if she now knows that she is not a country girl and that Arabs are not the enemy, and that she is not really, as she puts it, 'a pioneer'. Palestine was not for her.

There's a word in Hebrew to describe Polly's actions in leaving Palestine. It's *yerida*, which means the precise opposite of *aliyah* in both its ancient and modern meanings; that is, both descent and emigration from the Promised Land. In Israel, it's a word that would take on strongly negative connotations – of disappointment with undertones of apostasy and treason. Yitzhak Rabin, the first Israeli prime minister to be born in Palestine, and whose mother arrived with Polly on the *Ruslan*, referred to such emigrants in the 1970s as 'dropout weaklings'. *Yerida* has continued into the twenty-first century, at a lower rate than *aliyah*, but enough to be a matter of embarrassment to some Zionists – though there are others who see it as a welcome sign that Israeli citizens and their skills are in demand in a globalising world.

---

* She planned to join Jewish paramilitaries led by a Russian-born one-armed former dentist called Joseph Trumpeldor, who was killed while fighting Bedouin at the Battle of Tel Hai on what is now the border between Israel and Lebanon. Trumpeldor is a national hero in modern Israel. The politician who tried to recruit Polly was another modern Israeli hero, the Odessa-born former journalist Ze'ev Jabotinsky, whose militant Zionism inspired the future prime ministers Menachem Begin and Benjamin Netanyahu. More streets, parks and squares in Israel are named after Jabotinsky than any other historical figure. Trumpeldor and Jabotinsky were co-founders of the Zion Mule Force, which supported the British army during the Gallipoli campaign in 1915, and later went on to form the Jewish Legion, which fought alongside the British against Ottoman forces in Palestine.

There's now an Israeli diaspora, that overlaps with but is also quite different from the Jewish diaspora, with significant communities in Los Angeles, New York and London, and – to the consternation of some Israelis – Berlin. The Hebrew-language song 'Berlin' by the Israeli rock group Shmemel celebrates *yerida*. It also caused some offence, with its sweeping reflection on why earlier generations of Jews had migrated to the Promised Land:

> Let's be honest.
> Grandma and Grandpa didn't come here for Zionism
> They fled because they didn't want to die . . .

It also pointed out that *yerida* has a very long tradition indeed; with a pointed reminder that, in ancient times, Jacob and his family left the Promised Land for economic reasons

> Even Jacob, our patriarch, 'descended' to Egypt
> Where rents were one-third and salaries were double.

It's certainly true that low salaries and a shortage of affordable housing are widely cited as the reason why so many young Israelis migrate. But it's always more complex than that; Israelis, like many others around the world, leave for a wide range of unsurprising and interwoven reasons including love and work and politics and adventure – or simply because they can.

Polly, like her fellow passengers on the *Ruslan*, was a refugee. Or at least that's the word the British consul-general in Odessa used in a letter certifying that, as 'Jewish refugees', they had a right to return 'to their homes in Palestine'. The term 'refugee' was in common use by then, though it hadn't quite settled down into its modern juridical meaning. It carried a general sense of seeking refuge or safety, but it was also being used to designate people who were emerging as anomalies in a world of nation-states and their sedentary citizens.

By the 1920s, a new infrastructure aimed at controlling mobility and migration had appeared – one that is broadly recognisable today – in which clearly defined borders, passports, immigration quotas, visas and work permits all played a central role. And the changing use of the word 'refugee' in the twentieth century should be seen in the context of this infrastructure. It can serve as a reminder of how, in law and in language, the sedentary world sought to categorise and classify people on the move.

The word 'refugee' was first used in English in the late seventeenth century. It had been borrowed from the French *refugié* for a very specific and language-appropriate purpose: to describe persecuted French Protestants who had fled to England and elsewhere. Gradually it came to be used for other groups, not just from France, who left their homes because of persecution and who were in search of refuge. The associations of the word were strongly sympathetic, particularly so in the First World War, when the meaning shifted again to emphasise the role of war as a causative factor. In wartime Britain, for instance, it became normal to see refugees as innocent civilians who were the unfortunate victims of German atrocities, forced to flee for their lives.

The quintessential refugees were the more than a quarter of a million Belgians who were sent to live in camps and homes across the UK, where they were looked after by hundreds of local communities and small charities, all overseen by what was called the War Refugees Committee. It's still the largest-ever influx of refugees into Britain. The story of 'poor little Belgium' or 'brave little Belgium' and its fate at the hands of

Germany became central to the British propaganda narrative, and the government discouraged any negative media coverage of the refugees. Instead, the Belgians became part of a story in which the British were life-saving heroes, and the refugees were desperate and passive and helpless and grateful. This was a narrative that ignored the stories of those who chose to remain in Belgium during the German occupation – and downplayed the larger number of Belgians who took refuge in France and the Netherlands. And it's worth noting that Belgian wartime migration, devastating as it was to many of those involved, was tiny compared to the displacement of people in Eastern Europe and the Balkans, which had far more significant long-term consequences that would even extend across the Atlantic to the USA.

Europe first, though – which in the years immediately after the First World War had several new countries and thousands of kilometres of new borders. There were also many millions of largely unwilling migrants, criss-crossing the continent, only some of whom were formally recognised as refugees. The immediate cause of all this migration was the final violent collapse in war of three empires, Russian, Ottoman and Austro-Hungarian, and their replacement by nation-states, each dominated, in theory at least, by a single community, usually speaking a common language.*

The implications of all this were chaotic and far-reaching. Nationalist politicians set about a process that came to be known, euphemistically, as the 'unmixing of peoples', as if Europe were some kind of salad whose ingredients could be separated out as easily as they been put together. In

* Two of the new countries – Yugoslavia and Czechoslovakia – which emerged from the collapse of the Ottoman and Austro-Hungarian Empires were constructed as what have been called 'halfway houses' between the old multi-ethnic imperial entities and the new nation-states. The names of both countries (Yugoslavia was, until 1929, the Kingdom of Serbs, Croats and Slovenes) reflected their multi-ethnic characters, and both would ultimately break up into smaller nation-states in the 1990s.

practice, this meant the adjusting of borders to suit 'peoples', or adjusting those peoples to suit borders, or — most commonly — doing both. It would soon become normal for the vast majority of Europeans to expect or desire to live in a country in which their own language and their own community were dominant.

For millions of individuals and families these post-war years were harrowing, precarious, pivotal times — especially if they found themselves on the 'wrong' side of a new international border. Hungarian-speakers, say, living in Romania in the early 1920s. They were faced with the binary nature of this new nationalism and had an invidious choice: should they stay or should they go? They could remain on their ancestral lands and become part of an enfeebled minority in a recently enlarged and assertive nation-state. Or they could leave, often with nothing, to become part of the majority community in a new nation-state and accept the near-certainty of never being able to return to their old homes. More than a hundred thousand Hungarian-speakers living in Romania chose to migrate across the new border before Hungary felt so overwhelmed it closed its frontiers. Many more stayed behind, and most of their descendants still live in Romania. These were the kind of decisions that migrants and countries were making throughout Europe.

Many others were given no choice. In 1923, in the aftermath of a calamitous war, Greece and Turkey agreed to an 'exchange of populations', overseen by the League of Nations. More than a million Greeks were forced to leave Turkey, some of them from places where Greek-speaking people had been settled for more than three thousand years — these were deeply rooted communities of people who had been away from their putative homeland even longer than the Jews. It was simply taken for granted by both governments and the League of Nations that they would leave — and that this migration could be dressed up as some kind of homegoing, so these migrants were therefore really being repatriated.*

The 'unmixing of peoples' in this part of the eastern Mediterranean was messy and cruel, and did not take into account the views of those who migrated. It was particularly hard for those who did not quite fit the obvious binary linguistic criteria of who was a Turk or who was a Greek. For instance, Turkish-speaking Christians of Greek ancestry living in Cappadocia in central Turkey were made to leave. As were the Greek-speaking Muslims of Crete, many of them descendants of recent converts to Islam. The Cretan novelist Pandelis Prevelakis, who was fourteen when the Muslims left, said news of the population exchange came as a 'terrible shock' to the island's communities. They were, he said, 'like a couple whose divorce is pronounced at the very moment when they have buried the hatchet'. About one thousand Cretan Muslims attempted to reconvert to Christianity at the last moment, but permission was refused by the Greek Orthodox Church and they too were forced to leave.

None of these migrants – Hungarians, Greeks or Turks – were officially considered refugees by the League of Nations, though they were informally referred to as just that, even by the governments involved. In 1921, when the League of Nations appointed the Norwegian explorer Fridtjof Nansen as the first High Commissioner for Refugees, he had been given a very specific and limited responsibility: to assist the millions of refugees from Russia, and only Russia, who had fled their homeland because of war and famine. Most of the Russian refugees recognised by the League of Nations were homeless

---

* Only those Greeks who lived in Constantinople, renamed Istanbul, or on two nearby islands were allowed to stay. About three hundred thousand Turks were forced to leave Greece; only those living in Western Thrace, close to the Turkish border, were able to stay.

migrants living on roadsides, railway stations or in camps – far from their old homes, to which they would never return.*

There were, for instance, more than a million Russian refugees in Poland – including, for a while, Polly's family; a hundred thousand more in and around Constantinople, and two hundred thousand who'd fled through the Russian Far East to the Chinese city of Harbin. Some were eventually repatriated voluntarily to what had become the Soviet Union, but most of the others sought and found new homes, helped by temporary League of Nations identity papers known as the Nansen passport. The USA was the most desired destination, but by 1924, as we will see, it had begun to close its border to many groups of migrants. France and Germany became the key destinations for refugee resettlement, often with fatal long-term consequences for the large number of Russian Jews who moved there.

The League of Nations did expand its role slightly, assisting Armenians and Assyrians who had fled from Turkey, but the organisation was unable to play a significant role in the great refugee crises of the 1930s and 40s.† And even when the role of the High Commissioner for Refugees was reinvented by the United Nations in 1950, its early work was restricted to Europe and it was saddled with a limited definition of who might deserve protection as a refugee, based around a 'well-founded fear of being persecuted' – a definition that is still used today. Migrants who leave their homes because of destitution,

---

* Sometimes these refugees weren't actually migrants, which happened when it was the border, rather than the individuals, which had moved. The American writer Daniel Mendelsohn retells an old joke about 'a man who's born in Austria, goes to school in Poland, gets married in Germany, has children in the Soviet Union, and dies in Ukraine. Through all that,' the joke goes, 'he never left his village!' This could be true of anyone born before 1918 in or near what is now the Ukrainian city of Lviv (formerly Lvov, Lwow and Lemberg), and lived until the 1990s and never left home.
† These included the European migration crises related – directly or indirectly – to the rise and fall of Nazi Germany, but also those caused by the creation of several new nation-states, among them India, Pakistan and Israel.

starvation, climate change or natural disaster are not considered to be refugees and are therefore provided less protection.

It's not always easy to get clarity about the distinction between refugees and other kinds of migrants, for many reasons. That narrow legal definition of a refugee is interpreted differently around the world – particularly that notion of 'a well-founded fear of being persecuted'. Governments in rich countries often insist that you should only be considered as a refugee in the first country to which you flee; many insist on proof of actual or potential persecution that simply isn't available; others deliberately create an unwelcoming environment for would-be refugees. It's a system that is now largely broken, and recognised as such. It's patched together by the UN and by NGOs, and the issue of refugee recognition is often played out as a cynical game between governments and migrants – sometimes with deadly consequences. And it is a system that, at its worst, favours those migrants who are willing to take extreme risks, and those who are good actors and persuasive liars.

Take HG, for example, who took many risks but wasn't persuasive enough. He appeared in the life of one of my oldest friends in 2012, when she volunteered at a refugee rights centre in Sheffield. HG was then a homeless, orphaned, twenty-one-year-old, who had fled persecution in Eritrea as a teenager. My friend described him as both endearing and pathetic, and she offered him her spare room. He stayed with her, on and off, for the next few years as he tried and failed to be recognised as a refugee at a series of immigration tribunals. I got to know HG on my visits to the UK as an outgoing, determined young man, who talked vividly about his time in a Libyan detention camp, or about how he'd travelled from Sicily to Calais by train without a ticket, or how he had stowed away in a truck that brought him to Britain. But he clammed up when I asked him about his life back home in Eritrea. It's all too painful, my friend explained, when he was out of the room.

Several years later HG admitted to my friend that he'd been lying to her, and to everybody else. He was older than he'd claimed, his parents were alive and he wasn't Eritrean at all, but Ethiopian. He apologised, and explained that the only person he knew in Britain when he arrived had told him to lie, saying that Ethiopians had no chance of being granted asylum in the UK at the time. But Eritreans did. And so HG became, over-night, an Eritrean. And he thought he could pull it off, because he'd lived in Eritrea as a child and could speak the country's main language, Tigrinya. But when questioned by the British immigration authorities he had been unable to show sufficient geographical knowledge of his home town, and could not recall the colour of Eritrean vehicle number plates.

After admitting that he'd lied, HG then submitted a new application for asylum as an Ethiopian who had been perse-cuted for his political activity. He could provide more evidence this time. But it was not convincing enough for an immigra-tion tribunal. At the time of writing, HG's been in the UK for almost a decade, is not allowed to work, is staying in a hostel for the homeless and doesn't want to talk to me – but still talks sometimes to my friend, who thinks he's depressed. She says he's accepted that he will be sent back to Ethiopia, which will be humiliating and dangerous, and she's worried for him. So am I.

There are a number of possible lessons to be drawn from HG's story – quite apart from the ineffectiveness of the asylum process. One of those is the role of empathy and sentiment in how we form our views about migration. Some of those I've told this story feel little sympathy for HG. They say that he was unwise to have left Ethiopia, was wrong to have claimed asylum so far from his homeland, was wrong to have lied, and they suspect that he is still lying, with his story of persecution in Ethiopia. And they may be right. But they haven't met HG – and that can make all the difference. I have. I like him. I feel as if he's part of my extended family. I've even lived for a few months, as a well-heeled expat, in the country he fled. All that makes me wish it was easier for him to live wherever he wants to. And I'm also reminded that many migrants in this long history, from Aeneas of Troy to Great Aunt Polly, have told lies and taken huge risks. It comes, so to speak, with the territory.

And, in that context of deep history, there is much to be said, more specifically, about Africa and migration. Not just that we are all descended from Africans, and most of us from migrants who left Africa, but also the experiences of more recent times: of the slave trade and of colonialism. It wasn't so long ago that Europeans forced millions of Africans to leave Africa and proceeded to share out most of that continent between themselves. One might imagine, even expect, that these more recent historical experiences would inculcate a sense of greater humility among Europeans. That even the most stony-faced among them might feel slightly uncomfortable when they look an African migrant in the eye, and say, as if it were a self-evidently reasonable statement, 'No, you can't come to Europe.'

A Ninth Intermission

Careful readers may have noticed that I used the word 'expat' to describe myself towards the end of the last chapter. It's a troubling, troubled word that I normally avoid. I was able to shake it off as a description when I lived for more than a decade in Delhi, since I was married to an Indian – and was therefore not really an expat. The two of us would talk, dismissively, of the 'expat crowd', who spent most of their time together, who didn't speak any Indian languages and whose employers disbursed huge sums of money keeping them in the manner to which they were rapidly becoming accustomed. 'Expat' became our shorthand for well-off, self-important Westerners living in poor countries.

And then, reader, I became one. I hopped around the globe on my own, working for several months at a time in a series of countries in Africa and Asia with which I did not have strong existing ties. I tried and failed to learn new languages. My friends were fellow foreigners. My employer provided me with health insurance for 'expatriates', the services of a specialist 'expatriate tax adviser'. When I went to Tanzania in 2013 I was provided with a fifty-six-page document full of advice for expats – about how to hire a maid and a gardener, that 'rail services are poor and not recommended for expatriate use', and that *'O'Willie's Irish Pub* is extremely popular with the expatriate community'. I had a privileged existence – free housing, flights, an iPhone, a laptop and several other minor perks. It had become harder for me to deny that I was an expat.

I also came to realise that others used the word with pride and boastfulness. As if they had gained access to an exclusive club; as if they were better than others – back home, and around them. In Addis Ababa in 2018, I briefly joined an international association for expatriates called InterNations, whose emails continued to follow me around the world. InterNations declares that 'there's something unique about expats – a strength and a spirit that drives us to move towards the unknown and embrace it', and goes on to refer to them as pioneers and explorers, as if they were moving to uninhabited land rather than some of the biggest cities in the world. It all felt a little colonial. And a bit desperate, as if expats were terrified that they might be mistaken for some more prosaic kind of migrant – a migrant worker, perhaps.

If you ever want to deflate an expat, ask them the question 'What is the difference between an expat and a migrant worker?' It's quite funny really – and telling. Your respondent will generally splutter out a series of linguistic contortions in order to avoid the most obvious response – which is that they are the same, except expats are richer and whiter. It's possible, of course, to come up with more detailed, technical answers, which might emphasise differences in the nature and length of the work assignment, or the identity and location of the employer, or the professional skills of the employee.* And these are all relevant, no doubt, to our understanding of expats, but none of them really justify us seeing them as anything other than a particular variety of migrant worker.

---

* In recent years, 'expatriate studies' has become a serious subject of research for HR professionals and management specialists. One weighty academic 'handbook' on the subject even complains 'about the increasing proliferation of terms and sloppy application of concepts in the field of expatriate studies', and goes on to talk about AEs (assigned expatriates), SIEs (self-initiated expatriates), flexpatriates, glopatriates and so on.

Like so many words used to describe migrants, 'expatriate'
has had a twisted, meandering existence that helps explain some
of its modern ambiguities. Its first appearance in English was in
the eighteenth century in the form of the verb 'to expatriate'. It
was borrowed from French and its meaning, to banish or exile
someone, would have been obvious to anyone who'd studied
any Latin. It was soon being used reflexively, as in 'to expatriate
oneself', which edges it closer to one of its modern meanings[*]
by emphasising the free choice in leaving one's homeland. But
expatriate doesn't become a noun until the late nineteenth century, when it began to be used to describe a particular group
of migrants – wealthy, white Americans who had moved to
France, and who became famous for their louche lifestyle.

Many of them were novelists and poets, and as a result their
world was immortalised in lyrical detail, memorably – in relation to expatriates specifically – by Ernest Hemingway in *The
Sun Also Rises*. The main character, a Paris-based American
journalist called Jake Barnes, who bears a strong similarity to
Hemingway, is accused by a newly arrived fellow American of
a sizeable number of expatriate vices:

> You've lost touch with the soil. You get precious. Fake
> European standards have ruined you. You drink yourself to
> death. You become obsessed by sex. You spend all your time
> talking, not working. You are an expatriate, see? You hang
> around cafés.

Hemingway's self-mocking tirade provided readers of the
1920s with a new image of rich Americans abroad – a stereotype which even now may have some basis in the truth.

---

[*] In the 1850s the American essayist Ralph Waldo Emerson describes how, two
decades earlier, the German-born British astronomer William Herschel 'expatriated
himself for years at the Cape of Good Hope' so that he could get better sightings of
the southern skies.

Particularly the notion that these migrant workers don't always do a great deal of useful work. It's a meaning that survived, too, as a secondary usage of 'expat', notably in English tabloid newspapers – where it's used to describe British people, a few of them criminals, who moved to the Costa del Sol to retire or to escape justice.

But that more humdrum primary meaning, widely used in the modern corporate world, seems instead to have emerged from the dying embers of the British Empire, and then become widely employed in the global oil industry. And it was used by British civil servants trying to justify paying expatriates so much more than local staff. 'At first sight,' argued one of them with respect to Nigeria in the 1940s,

> it may appear unjust that an expatriate officer is paid more than an inhabitant of the Colony who is ostensibly carrying out exactly similar duties, but in fact on closer examination it will be found that the expatriate is not as well off as his local confreres ... [since] it will be necessary for the expatriate to keep another home elsewhere and educate his children out of the Colony.

Similar arguments are still being used to justify staggering salaries paid to expatriates in poor countries. But more than that, such arguments create a class apart. They serve to maintain the fiction that expats are somehow so special and so different that we should not refer to them as migrant workers.*

---

* There's a long tradition of young white men of modest abilities and expectations who can very quickly become minor potentates by migrating to the colonies. It's a tradition well represented in fiction by Kipling's short story 'The Man who Would be King' and in real life by numerous white mercenaries. These include George Thomas from Tipperary in Ireland, who became the Raja of Hansi in northern India, and the English adventurer James Brooke, who founded a dynasty that ruled Sarawak on the island of Borneo for more than a century. Brooke himself handed power to his nephew and returned to England in his old age where, according to a modern biographer, he was 'carnally involved with the rough trade of Totnes'.

It's possible to perform this kind of etymological exercise on many other terms associated with migration, in English and other languages. *Emigré*, for instance, which was widely deployed for and by Russian migrants in France in the inter-war era, but rarely encountered these days. Or 'alien', which only gained its extra-terrestrial meaning in recent times, but is still used in legal documents to describe those who come from foreign lands. Or those mirror twins, emigrant and immigrant, hero and villain respectively in the modern Western imagination, even when they're used to describe exactly the same person. Or the often-toxic argument within the UN between those who think refugees are migrants and those who do not. The list is almost endless. In many cases, the effect is to segregate one group of people from the rest, to argue that the members of that group – like expats – are so special that they should not be contaminated by association with migrants of other kinds.

And this, in turn, represents a shrinking of the common ground, a reduction in the number and type of people whom we can refer to, uncontentiously, as migrants. Not only does this transform the debate into one about the language we use, rather than about the migrants themselves and the choices they face, but it also means we are left with a smaller rump of undisputed migrants who now appear, to the sedentary world, as either unwanted or undeserving or both. And who often become the enemy, or scapegoats – easy to blame for almost anything.

This is undoubtedly a failure of empathy, an inability to imagine the lives of those who are not like us. This failure is occasionally corrected when a dead child, who looks pale-skinned and is wearing Western clothes, is washed up on a beach; or when a group of frozen migrants are found entwined and dead in a refrigerated truck. In those brief moments, the world seems to care. And then it doesn't – as migrants become, once again, people who are not like 'us'.

But it is also more than a failure of empathy. It's all part of what might be called, tendentiously, the tyranny of sedentarism. A world in which it is normal to stay where you are. In which migration is an aberrant activity. A world in which migration is only meant to happen in certain special circumstances – when one's life is in danger, or when one possesses skills that are required in some other part of the globe. Otherwise, one should remain at home, or at least in the country to which your birth assigned you. While those migratory urges, any cravings for somewhere else, can be treated with such harmless proxies as foreign holidays and pilgrimages.

An unreal, parallel world has been created in which migration is an anomaly, in which we are encouraged to forget the guiding role migration has played in human history. Instead, home is sanctified and sentimentalised, while foreignness is feared. We are urged to deny our migratory past, as if, like the people of ancient Athens, we believe that our ancestors were born from the soil of the land we now occupy.

CHAPTER TEN

Liberty, Harlem and the Rainbow Tribe

Green-eyed, strikingly tall, perfectly poised and with a BMI of more than sixty, she's arguably America's best-known migrant – instantly recognisable, even from her silhouette. She became a film star of sorts, with cameo appearances in many dozens of films – from Charlie Chaplin's *The Immigrant* to *Planet of the Apes, The Godfather* and *Superman*. More significantly, she became the symbol of her new nation, whose people would always treat her as their own, often forgetting that she was conceived in France and inspired by a Roman goddess. She had, in fact, been brought by ship across the Atlantic from the northern French city of Rouen in 1885 – landing, like so many migrants of the time, in New York Harbour. And once there she was placed on a pedestal and has not moved since. She's a little worse for wear these days, suffering the depredations of age and, for reasons entirely beyond her control, is not the beacon that she once was to her fellow migrants. Because those migrants no longer come by ship to Ellis Island, and they are anyway less welcome these days.

In the old days, European migrants to the USA knew they

were near when they spied the Statue of Liberty, just seven hundred yards from Ellis Island.* Many would have heard that the statue was there to welcome immigrants. A 'world-wide welcome' according to Emma Lazarus, whose poem 'The New Colossus' was inscribed inside the base of the statue – a poem in which Liberty herself addressed the Old World, the 'ancient lands' across the Atlantic, with words that seemed to promise that anyone could take part in the American Dream:

> Give me your tired, your poor,
> Your huddled masses yearning to breathe free,
> The wretched refuse of your teeming shore.

But it wasn't quite like that when they got to Ellis Island – if they got there at all. For by the early 1920s, the USA was closing its doors to most migrants. This led to a fundamental change in both the way the USA saw itself and was seen by the rest of the world, and it also played a central role in redefining, more generally, the possibilities of migration. And it contributed directly to the invention and expansion of a migration bureaucracy – a world of quotas and visas, consular officials, interviews, sponsorship letters, health certificates and bank statements.

The American decision about its borders was, in part, a response to the huge numbers of people who wished to migrate, but it was also because some Americans had become far more discriminating about which kinds of migrants should be allowed in. They had become distinctly less keen on the poor, on those 'huddled masses', particularly if they came from southern and eastern Europe, or if they were Jewish.

America had, of course, closed its borders a lot earlier to

---

* Ellis Island, like Plymouth Rock, Roanoke and Jamestown, is a contender for a prime place in the foundation mythology of modern America. St Augustine and Angel Island are much lower down this particular pecking order.

certain groups of people. The Chinese had been excluded since 1882, as had some other Asian migrants. So too – since the Immigration Act of 1891 – were a memorably diverse list of 'undesirables':

> idiots, insane persons, paupers or persons likely to become public charges, persons suffering from a loathsome or a dangerous disease, persons who have been convicted of a felony or other infamous crime or misdemeanor involving moral turpitude, polygamists.

This particular list was gradually extended to include, from 1903, epileptics, professional beggars, anarchists and prostitutes. Imbeciles, feeble-minded persons, unaccompanied children and those who had not paid for their own ticket were added four years later, while alcoholics and illiterates were banned from 1917.

It was the job of federal officers at Americans ports and borders to spot these excluded groups – and then deport them at the expense of the steamship company that had brought them over. At Ellis Island officers walked up and down the queues of newcomers, chalking symbols on their backs. The letter 'L' stood for lameness, 'E' for eye problems;* 'X' was used for those who might be feeble-minded. The inspectors were taught to recognise 'idiots' and 'imbeciles' from the shape of their skulls: a 'low receding forehead', for instance, or excessively deep eye sockets. Between 1 and 2 per cent of migrants who reached Ellis Island each year were deported. But not nearly enough for the large number of

---

* By 1905, all migrants who reached Ellis Island were inspected for trachoma by a doctor who would use a hook to flip back an eyelid to look for sign of the disease – which would lead to automatic deportation. Between 1904 and 1914 almost twenty-five thousand would-be migrants were deported with suspected trachoma, accounting for nearly two-thirds of all deportations related to 'loathsome' or contagious diseases.

prominent Americans who demanded much tighter restrictions on migration.

The anti-immigration lobby had been growing stronger for some time – particularly among Americans of English ancestry. A decade after Lazarus' paean to the impoverished migrant, Thomas Bailey Aldrich wrote his 'Unguarded Gates', a similarly florid poem that also imagines the Statue of Liberty as a sentient being. But Aldrich had a very different message. He represented America as an 'enchanted land', whose existence was menaced by migrants in the same way that 'the thronging Goth and Vandal trampled Rome'. Liberty – a 'white goddess' – was under threat from modern barbarians, from those who speak 'strange tongues':

> Wide open and unguarded stand our gates
> And through them presses a wild motley throng
> Men from the Volga and the Tartar steppes
> Featureless figures of the Huang-Ho
> Malayan, Scythian, Teuton, Kelt and Slav
> Flying the Old World's poverty and scorn.

By the early twentieth century Aldrich's racialised, racist view of the world was commonplace among 'Old Stock' Americans, citizens whose northern European ancestors had arrived before independence. Among them was a New Yorker called Madison Grant – a well-connected, self-taught naturalist who founded the Bronx Zoo, and who then transformed himself into the leading ideologist of what became known as scientific racism. His 1916 book, *The Passing of the Great Race*, was enormously influential (Hitler would later describe it as 'my Bible') and in the 1920s Grant himself played a major role in the campaign to close America's borders to most foreign migrants.

He had a particular distaste for the notion of America as a

'melting pot' of people of different origins, which had been popularised in the pre-war years of mass migration.* Grant used the older racial classifications based on skin colour that date back to Linnaeus and Bernier, but his innovation was to divide Europeans into three further subspecies or sub-races: the sluggish, artistic Mediterraneans; the submissive, subdued Alpines; and the virile, noble Nordics, who were entirely admirable (when pure) – and to which he, Grant, belonged.

Grant's Nordic race consisted of northern Europeans, particularly those who were tall, blond and blue-eyed, and who, he argued, had been responsible for much of the early colonisation of North America. He even referred to himself and other descendants of 'Nordic' migrants as Native Americans – in comparison with those who had migrated more recently. And the Nordics were, of course, the 'Great Race' of his book title, threatened by the other European sub-races, or the 'mongrel race' created by miscegenation.

> The danger is from within and not from without. Neither the black, nor the brown, nor the yellow, nor the red will conquer the white in battle. But if the valuable elements in the Nordic race mix with inferior strains or die out through race suicide, then the citadel of civilization will fall for mere lack of defenders.

The Mediterranean and Alpine sub-races, argued Grant, should be stopped from migrating to America.

---

* The term 'melting pot' was popularised by the successful play of the same name set in New York and written by the London-born Jew Israel Zangwill, and first performed in Washington in 1908. The main character is a Jewish migrant called David Quixano, who fled the Kishinev pogrom of 1903. He declares that 'America is God's Crucible, the great Melting Pot where all the races of Europe are melting and re-forming'. And, indeed, he falls for a fellow European migrant, Vera – a Russian Christian, whose father, it turns out, was the leader of the pogrom. True love eventually prevails.

At first, little notice was taken of Grant's book, but an existing anti-migrant narrative was soon strengthened both by the chaotic aftermath of the First World War in Europe and an America that was becoming increasingly isolationist. Grant was an extremely effective lobbyist, and his key political ally was Albert Johnson, a former journalist who chaired the House of Representatives' Committee on Immigration and Naturalization. Johnson – spurred on by Grant – was responsible for a Congressional report in 1920 that shocked many of his fellow politicians into action. The report contained a general warning, amid many mixed metaphors, about an 'avalanche of new arrivals' at Ellis Island, a 'flood of immigration' caused by 'unsettled conditions in Europe', declaring that there might be as many as eight million migrants preparing to come to America. He went on to argue for a suspension of almost all migration.

Johnson's report includes an appendix with comments from US government officers who had recently visited Europe. It makes uncomfortable reading. A despatch from an official in the Netherlands referred to the large numbers of Eastern European Jews in Rotterdam who were ready to cross the Atlantic, and described them as of the 'usual ghetto type ... [who] are filthy, un-American and often dangerous in their habits'. From Poland came the view that more than 90 per cent of would-be migrants were Jewish – often refugees from Russia and 'of the very lowest classes'; 'thoroughly undesirable' and 'mentally deficient'. Peasants planning to migrate from southern Italy are described as 'unassimilable' and having 'a low order of intelligence', while the rest of the country is 'so honeycombed with socialistic ideas and activities' that the writer suggests that all immigration from Italy to the USA should be suspended. The Swiss and the Germans were let off more lightly, while the British and the Scandinavians go unmentioned. But the overall message was clear: most of those who wanted to migrate to the USA should be stopped, at any cost.

And so in 1921, under the terms of the Emergency Quota
Act, devised by Grant and introduced by Congressman
Johnson, the American government for the first time set a limit
to the number of migrants who could enter the country each
year. It was a complex formula, based on old censuses, a way
of avoiding the diplomatic consequences of naming specific
countries in the legislation. What it meant in practice was that
most nationalities were given what was in effect a monthly
quota. Anyone who arrived in America once that quota had
been filled was automatically deported – though there was a
short list of exceptions, including priests, dancers, nurses and
domestic servants. The new system was deliberately biased
against southern and eastern Europeans – and led, for instance,
to an immediate 80 per cent fall in the number of migrants
from both Italy and Greece, and similar reductions for eastern
Europeans. Great Aunt Polly and her family, if they had chosen
the USA rather than Palestine, would almost certainly have
been turned away.

The new legislation also turned the process of reaching Ellis
Island into a farce, which became known as 'the Midnight
Races'. Just before the start of a new month, steamships carrying migrants gathered in Lower New York Bay. Each would
then race to cross an imaginary line drawn between Brooklyn
and Staten Island. And by being first across the line just after
midnight they ensured that their passengers would be included
in the new month's quota.

But it all went ridiculously wrong on the night of 30 August
1923, when one ship was adjudged to have crossed the line
five minutes too early and three more, in hot pursuit, followed before midnight. The 1,896 passengers were disbarred
from being part of the new month's quota – which meant the
steamships received automatic fines of two hundred dollars
per passenger, and almost all those on board faced immediate
deportation. It was front-page news in the American press,

and there was considerable embarrassment all round. The mistake was blamed on an inaccurate ship's chronograph. The steamships paid their fines, and the government was eventually persuaded to consider the passengers as part of the new month's quota and, in this case, there was no mass deportation.

In 1924, new tighter rules – suggested again by Madison Grant – were introduced. The annual quotas were even smaller, down again by 50 per cent, and they were even more biased in favour of northern Europeans. Grant declared the new legislation 'an amazing triumph ... we have closed the doors just in time to prevent our Nordic population being overrun by the lower races'. But the new law also changed the process by which most migration happened in the USA. The key role once played by Ellis Island was brought to an end – as was the chaos of the Midnight Races – by permanently increasing the power of America's consular officials abroad.

Decisions about who should be allowed to settle in the USA were no longer taken on Ellis Island or other entry points but in embassy buildings far from the prying eyes of the New York media, or the many immigrant aid societies that often took up the cases of migrants who were about to be deported. Would-be migrants now needed an immigrant visa issued in their home country; they were expected to supply photographs, certified copies of birth certificates and the names of relatives or friends in the USA. They were asked to declare whether they had ever been in a prison or an almshouse, or whether either of their parents had ever been treated in an institution for the insane; and the long list of mental and physical health conditions that would have disqualified them at Ellis Island was used to deny them an immigrant visa while they were still in their country of origin. It had become very hard for most people to migrate to the USA. Their American Dream was over. In 1914, more than 1,200,000 people migrated; twenty years later the figure was just under thirty thousand.

The growth of a new external bureaucracy to deal with migration, which soon became normal for many richer nations, was just the first of several cascading consequences of America's decision to close its borders to most newcomers. A second was that the measures achieved, at least temporarily, what many of its proponents hoped: it helped to ensure the continued political and economic domination of the USA by people of northern European heritage – by excluding large numbers of southern and eastern Europeans. That exclusion also made it harder for refugees and persecuted groups to escape by migrating. And among those would-be migrants were many European Jews who later perished at the hands of the Nazis.*

Third, the new measures also helped to create a competitive and heavily racialised pecking order of nationalities and ethnic backgrounds – a pecking order that discouraged solidarity among those who were excluded. Take the case of Bhagat Singh Thind, an Indian migrant who claimed that he was a member of the Aryan race because he came from a high caste and was therefore legally white (the US Supreme Court disagreed). Or the New York-based Yiddish-language newspaper editor William Edlin, who argued that Jews are Caucasians, in contrast to 'the Chinese, Hindus, and other races [that] do not have those things that we call civilization'. Meanwhile, some Italians jockeyed for position among their own compatriots – with a few northerners arguing that they were whiter and more literate and civilised than southern Italians – and therefore more suitable for admission to the USA.† And the notion that Italians were not quite white was widespread in inter-war

---

* The most famous example was the SS *St Louis*, which left Germany in May 1939 with more than nine hundred Jewish refugees. The ship was not allowed to land and returned to Europe, where 254 of the refugees are thought to have died in the Holocaust.
† Grant and his allies even gave a special dispensation to long-dead northern Italians whom they admired – Columbus, Leonardo da Vinci and Dante – declaring them (along with Alexander the Great and Jesus Christ) to have 'Nordic characteristics'.

America. There's a government report about Californian factories in the 1930s that is friendly towards racial mixing but refers to the way 'white women worked with Mexican and Italian women, but refused to work with Negroes'. Italians and other southern Europeans had become what the historian John Higham calls 'in-between' people, that is those who were not quite white, or not white enough.

Fourth, there was, as so often happens when governments attempt to introduce restrictions on one type of migration, a dramatic growth in other types of migration: external and internal, authorised and unauthorised. This meant, for instance, that those Europeans who were determined enough and willing to break the rules could find other ways of getting into the USA – largely via Canada or Mexico.

The USA's northern and southern land borders, more than ten thousand kilometres long, proved almost impossible to guard. In the 1920s, the US Border Patrol had a staff of about 750 officers and could not begin to keep up with a rapidly developing human trafficking infrastructure. A *New York Times* report from 1927, entitled 'Alien gate-crashers still pour in over our frontiers', claimed that more than one hundred thousand migrants crossed illegally into the USA every year. The report described how 'Poles, Russians and other northern races ... take the Canadian route', particularly near the Great Lakes, with some migrants smuggling themselves onto the commuter ferry across the Detroit River. Others were taken across on a small boat and were given 'an American suit of clothes and hair-cut to match', so they would blend in on the other side. Each migrant was charged up to a hundred dollars for the crossing, but 'endless blackmail' on the short journey meant many of them paid much more.

The southern route then – as now – was more popular and it was easier for would-be migrants to get into Mexico, or to a Caribbean island, in the first place. Large numbers of

Europeans, particularly Greeks and Italians, as well as some Syrians, according to the *New York Times*, chose this route, travelling onwards either by boat from Cuba to Florida, or overland through Mexico. The report said the seaborne migrants were sometimes abandoned by traffickers on small islands and brought to the mainland by sponge fishermen. Land migrants were taken over the US–Mexico border by traffickers known as 'horsepackers', after the teams of pack horses carrying 'whisky, narcotics or aliens' they led through remote fords on the Rio Grande into Texas. There was little chance of being spotted by the Border Patrol.

But the continuing migration of Europeans, authorised or unauthorised, was dwarfed by larger movements of population within North America. In part, these movements were a knock-on effect of the labour shortages caused by new anti-immigration measures. And so, unwittingly, the anti-migrant laws devised by white (and Nordic) supremacists like Madison Grant and Albert Johnson set off new waves of non-European immigration. In the 1920s, about 450,000 Mexicans crossed the international border for agricultural work, largely in the fruit farms and canneries of Texas, New Mexico and California. But most significant of all, even though no international border was crossed, was what has become known as the Great Migration, in which several million Black Americans left the old slave-holding regions of the South for the big cities of the north – and a few of them would travel even further afield.*

It's hard to overstate the scale and importance of the Great Migration in reshaping the United States. It was a vast, leaderless

---

* It's often forgotten that, during this period, white migration to the north was, in numerical terms, significantly larger – though Black migration from several of the states of the Deep South was more extensive. Whites were also much more likely to return to the South. White migration was less visible, though there were parts of several major cities which were predominantly settled by southern whites. Chicago's Uptown, for instance, had a high population of southern whites, and was often stereotyped as a 'hillbilly' ghetto.

movement that in the words of its best-known historian, Isabel Wilkerson, would 'recast the social and political order of every city it touched'. It helped create a new vision of what it might be like to be a Black person in America. And it also gave many Black Americans another migration narrative, not forced transportation on a slave ship but a story of choice and risk and freedom. For Alain Locke, the Black American philosopher, writing in 1925 in the midst of the Great Migration, it was a 'deliberate flight not only from the countryside to the city but from medieval America to modern'. It was a flight from discrimination and lynching and poverty, and more widely the unresolved legacies of slavery and the Civil War.

That flight began in earnest in 1916, spurred on by a first, brief, wartime collapse of European immigration to the USA. Northern factories needed workers. They sent recruiters to the South, often disguised as insurance sellers or salesmen, who would, according to one contemporary account, sidle up to gatherings of Black people and whisper, 'Anyone want to go to Chicago, see me.' Some southern white racists were delighted to see them leave, but others saw the danger to their economy of losing cheap labour. Recruitment agencies were told to pay huge licence fees; would-be migrants were threatened and their train tickets torn up. But it was too late: word had got about, recruiters were no longer needed – and the flow of young Black men and women northwards was unstoppable, with opportunities for them in the big cities expanding as the doors to European immigration closed.

Take Chicago. By 1930, more than 70 per cent of the city's Black population of about 230,000 were migrants from the southern USA – many of them encouraged to come there by the country's most popular Black-run newspaper, the weekly *Chicago Defender*. It wasn't easy for the newcomers, and they faced race riots, discrimination and ghettoisation in the South Side of the city, but for most of them it was far better than what they had left behind. The views of a sample of early Black migrants have survived in a government-sponsored survey from the early 1920s: some described the noise and loneliness of the new city, and others talked about how much more they could earn in Chicago, but many also felt an unexpected freedom, of the kind described by this interviewee:

> When I got here, and got on the street car, and saw colored people sitting by white people ... I just held my breath, for I thought any minute they would start something. Then I saw nobody noticed it, and I just thought this was a real place for colored people.

Some members of the city's small long-standing Black community were embarrassed by the newcomers, and often treated them as if they came from another world – which in some ways they did. The *Chicago Defender* gave advice to the new migrants about how to 'fit in', with lists of 'do's and don'ts' – mainly don'ts – instantly recognisable, in form if not content, to most migrant communities:

> Don't sit around in the yard and on the porch barefoot
> and unkempt
> Don't wear handkerchiefs on your head
> Don't use vile language in public places
> Don't appear on the street with old dust caps, dirty aprons
> and ragged clothes

Despite the condescension towards the migrants often shown by older Black communities, it was the newcomers who played the leading role in what would later be described as a cultural renaissance. In Chicago, the new stars included the jazz musicians Louis Armstrong and King Oliver, and – a little later – the author Richard Wright and the poet Gwendolyn

Brooks. In New York, the renaissance took the form of a movement, centred around Harlem, previously the home of new European migrants who had since moved further into the city, or out of New York altogether. By the 1920s, central Harlem was predominantly Black and gaining an international reputation as a place of culture and entertainment. In 1925 the historian James Weldon Johnson, himself an early migrant from Florida and of Bahamian heritage, declared Harlem to be

> the great Mecca for the sight-seer, the pleasure-seeker, the curious, the adventurous, the enterprising, the ambitious and the talented of the whole Negro world; for the lure of it has reached down to every island of the Carib Sea and has penetrated even to Africa.

Most of the key figures of the Harlem Renaissance migrated from the southern states, but Johnson was right to ascribe a cosmopolitan character to the movement. The poet Langston Hughes and novelist Nella Larsen came from the Midwest, while the Black nationalist Marcus Garvey and the writer Claude McKay were Jamaican. And one of the by-products of the Harlem Renaissance was a growing interest in a more distant past, in an older homeland and an earlier migration.

Countee Cullen, in his 1922 poem 'Heritage', asked repeatedly 'What is Africa to me?', and was only able to give the partial answer, involving jungles and snakes and heathen gods, of someone who was ' . . . three centuries removed / From the scenes his fathers loved'. Langston Hughes imagined an ageless 'Negro' man speaking of ancient rivers, including the Congo, the Nile and then the Mississippi, all of them 'older than the flow of human blood in human veins'.

Marcus Garvey preached a return to Africa, founding the Black Star Line part of whose purpose was to take the descendants of slaves back 'home'. The West African state of Liberia, created by Black American descendants of slaves in the early nineteenth century, was to be one of the first destinations – but the shipping line soon collapsed, Garvey went to jail, Liberia closed its borders to Garvey's followers and there was no reverse migration. Alongside the obsession with the idea of Africa, usually as a lost Eden, was a striking unwillingness to actually go there. For most participants in the Harlem Renaissance, including Garvey, Africa remained a place of the imagination.

In the inter-war period, Langston Hughes was the major exception, travelling by passenger ship to West Africa and visiting its ports during the daytime, which meant that he never actually spent a night on African soil. In his autobiography, he recalled his excitement at seeing the land of his ancestors for the first time: 'My Africa, Motherland of the Negro peoples! And me a Negro! Africa!', he told himself. But he was in for a disappointment. In Africa, despite all his protestations ('I am a Negro, too!'), he was told, quite firmly, 'You – white man!' For Hughes, who would always be seen as a Black man in the USA, was of mixed heritage – African, Jewish, French, Scottish and Native American – and was too light-skinned to pass as an African in Africa.

However, large numbers of Black Americans, many of them originally part of the Great Migration, did cross the Atlantic – but to Europe. The most popular destination was France. About two hundred thousand Black Americans had served there during the First World War, and word soon got around that France was less bigoted than the USA. A small number of soldiers stayed on.* In 1922, one ex-soldier called Albert Curtis

---

* There were Black Americans living in France before the First World War, including the painter Henry Ossawa Tanner, who studied in France in the 1890s and spent most of the rest of his life there, dying in Paris in 1937. America's first Black fighter pilot, Eugene Bullard, who was also a boxer and a jazz drummer, arrived in Paris as a teenager in 1913 and only went back to the USA because of the German invasion of France in 1940.

Langston Hughes in the 1940s

wrote to the *Chicago Defender*, which he'd once sold on the streets of Chicago, explaining that he had chosen to settle in France because there was no colour prejudice. This wasn't exactly true, as other accounts from the period show, but it's undeniable that many Black Americans found life in France liberating and wanted to remain there. By the mid-1920s, there were several thousand Black Americans living in Paris, some of them there temporarily – including the ubiquitous Langston Hughes, who spent most of 1924 in the city working as a doorman and a dishwasher. There were many others who were long-term residents – including the entertainer Josephine Baker, who would later become a hero of the wartime Resistance, the nightclub owner Ada 'Bricktop' Smith and the musician Henry Crowder.

Paris – with its reputation as a place of easy exile, of tolerance and of sexual and cultural adventure – was more welcoming to foreigners than most cities, and it had become established as a home for many displaced writers, artists and performers,

Joyce, Picasso, Stravinsky and Hemingway among them. And the white Parisian elite, French and foreign, developed a welcoming, though often patronising and exoticising, interest in people of African ancestry.

This was the age of *négrophilie*, or 'negrophilia', once a pejorative word in French, but by the 1920s it had become a largely positive term. It was used first to denote an admiration for 'primitive' African art and culture, but was soon extended to 'negroes' in general, even when their ancestors had left Africa a long time ago. Black Americans in 1920s Paris were often treated as if they'd come straight from the jungle. So when the nineteen-year-old Josephine Baker moved from Harlem to Paris in 1925, she was soon performing a bare-breasted '*danse sauvage*' on stage wearing nothing more than a few pink flamingo feathers, which were then swapped for a string of priapic rubber bananas. The dance critic André Levinson described Baker as having the 'splendour of an ancient animal' and 'the grin of a benevolent cannibal'. When the white Anglo-American heiress Nancy Cunard was overheard telling her long-term boyfriend, the jazz pianist Henry Crowder (from Gainesville, Georgia), to 'be more African', he replied, 'But I ain't African. I'm American!'

Baker and Crowder are chiefly remembered, respectively, as a sex symbol and as half of the most famous mixed-race couple of the time. They were, like others of their generation of Black American migrants to France, transformed into exotic and erotic fantasies for white people. For most of them – particularly those who liked to stand out or play to a crowd – this was a life that was far preferable to the one they had left behind. As a child, Josephine Baker had witnessed race riots in East St Louis, during which she'd fled across the Missouri River. She recalled how everyone ran across a bridge to escape the rednecks, the white people killing and beating them. I never forget my people scream-ing, a friend of my father's face shot off, a pregnant woman cut open. I see them running to get to the bridge. I have been running ever since.

She said she felt 'liberated' in Paris, and 'more French than the French'. She became a superstar in her adopted homeland and remembered with pride how the French 'all went to the beaches to get dark like Josephine Baker'. These views were echoed by Crowder, who had witnessed race riots in Atlanta and Washington DC, and faced prejudice in England, and declared that in his experience 'to be colored in France is never a mark of inferiority'.

Escaping from the racial prejudice of the USA was not the only advantage of migrating to France. There were few social or family pressures about how to behave, in public or in private, at a time when even alcohol was illegal in their homeland. Baker's friend Ada Smith, born in West Virginia and known to everyone as Bricktop because of her red hair, made and lost a fortune through her nightclubs, and was happy in later years to remember the sexual freedom that life in Paris made possible: 'I had a lot of men – a whole passel of men – and I did it up and down alleys, in taxi cabs, in the bed, out of the bed, all around the bed ... I slept with white men and black men.' She, too, noticed 'very little racial dis-crimination', but that had changed when she visited France after the Second World War, when she said that 'Parisians had started picking up some distinctly American attitudes towards Negroes'.

The Nazi occupation of Paris scattered the already shrinking Black American migrant community – they were too visible to remain. I can find evidence of only one Black American, a translator in his seventies married to a

Frenchwoman, who managed to stay in the city. Bricktop left for the USA a month after the war started, and later moved to Mexico City and then Rome. Henry Crowder spent two years in Nazi prisoner-of-war camps in Belgium and Germany before returning to America, while Josephine Baker initially went to a rented chateau in the Dordogne, using her celebrity to shield her from persecution and working secretly for the French Resistance. Eventually, she too left France, heading to Marrakesh with three monkeys, two mice, a hamster and a dog called Bonzo. And in 1942, her death at the age of thirty-six in a Moroccan hospital was reported around the world. Langston Hughes wrote her obituary in the *Chicago Defender*, declaring that she was 'as much a victim of Hitler as the soldiers who fall today in Africa fighting his armies. The Aryans drove Josephine away from her beloved Paris.'

In fact, Josephine Baker was very much alive – and would become the protagonist in an eccentric migration experiment of the 1950s. She'd been quite ill in Marrakesh, but later told an American journalist that she was much 'too busy to die'. And she soon set about reinventing herself. There were to be no more bananas. She worked for the Red Cross, raised money for the Resistance, sang the Marseillaise to the troops, and as the war neared its end moved back to her adopted homeland, buying the Dordogne chateau she had once rented. Already a French citizen, she was made a captain in the French Air Force and proudly wore her uniform in public. In the 1950s she began to speak up on civil rights issues in America,* deliberately

---

* She was pilloried for doing so. 'When one talks of the equality of races or human beings,' she said in 1952, 'one is immediately branded a liberal, anti-American, or a Communist.'

challenging rules on racial segregation when she travelled back to the country of her birth.

At home in France, Josephine Baker was devising a new project – a novelty at the time, though aspects of it have been repeated by other entertainers, among them Mia Farrow, Michael Jackson, Madonna and Angelina Jolie. Baker decided to create, with her fourth husband, a French bandleader called Jo Bouillon, a multi-racial family which she called her 'Rainbow Tribe'. 'Jo and I plan,' she explained, in what was to be the first of many iterations of her idea,

> to adopt four little children: red, yellow, white and black. Four little children raised in the country, in my beautiful Dordogne. They will serve as an example of true Democracy, and be living proof that if people are left in peace, nature takes care of the rest.

She soon dropped the Linnaean colour scheme and switched, temporarily, to a more country-specific wish-list: five two-year-old orphan boys – one from Japan, an 'Israelite', 'a dark-skinned black' from South Africa, 'a Nordic' and an 'Indian' from Peru. Her aim, she later explained was 'to prove that all people are equal'.

Baker began to collect her family in 1954: while on tour in Japan, she visited a Tokyo orphanage and chose a small boy of Korean ancestry, and then she saw another boy she couldn't resist, Japanese 'with solemn eyes' and, as if she were on a shopping trip and couldn't decide, she took them both back to France with her. They were the first of twelve, most of them boys, all of them toddlers – from Algeria, Morocco, Ivory Coast, Venezuela, Colombia, Finland and France. She struggled to find a Jewish boy. She was performing in Tel Aviv in the winter of 1954 and tried to adopt an orphan. The Israeli government released a press statement explaining that while 'Miss Baker's humanitarian impulse is appreciated, the Ministry could not permit a Jewish child to be taken away from Israel at a time when every effort is being made to bring Jewish children into the country'. She didn't give up. And Josephine Baker found, in a French orphanage, 'a dark-skinned baby with a stubborn set to his chin' whom she and Jo Bouillon decided would be Jewish, and whom they gave the name Moïse.*

The twelve children were raised in the Dordogne in the vast Chateau de Milandes, with the help of Baker's mother, brother and sister, who came from St Louis to help care for them. It was important to Baker that her adopted children were, discreetly, on public display. And so the grounds of the

---

* There was a longer-term plan, too. As teenagers most of the adopted children were sent back, for a while, sometimes unwillingly, to the lands of their birth, to learn more about the culture that they were supposed to represent. Moïse, born in France, was sent to an Israeli kibbutz.

chateau were turned into a kind of theme park, including a J-shaped swimming pool and a waxworks museum dedicated to the life of Josephine Baker which were open to fee-paying visitors who might catch sight of the Rainbow Tribe.

It all turned a little sour in the 1960s. Jo Bouillon left to live in Argentina, there were teenage rebellions, the money ran out and Josephine Baker was unable to cope. She was forced to sell up: some of the children departed – for boarding school, or to stay with friends, or with Jo Bouillon. Grace Kelly, another entertainer-migrant from the USA, by then Princess Grace of Monaco, rescued Josephine and her dwindling 'tribe' of children and lodged them in a large house overlooking the Mediterranean. Josephine Baker returned to the stage to pay her debts and she died in her beloved Paris in 1975 – not long after her final performance.

The Chateau de Milandes is now a museum, a memorial to the life of a migrant, a 'plain ghetto girl' from the Midwest who moved to New York during the Great Migration, took part in the Harlem Renaissance and then crossed the Atlantic to the Old World, where she became, arguably, and against all odds, the best-known international celebrity of her time. Other Black Americans would follow in her footsteps in the post-war era: the writers James Baldwin and Richard Wright, and the musicians Memphis Slim and Nina Simone all left the land of their birth, the land in which their ancestors had been enslaved, and each of them went to live, and die, in France.

Josephine Baker's Rainbow Tribe experiment is also com-memorated at the chateau, and remembered by her many children spread around the world: some are happy to talk in public about their mother and their unusual upbringing, others less so. It's an experiment that has not aged terribly well, with hindsight. Perhaps it's best seen as a well-meaning but naive attempt to create a multi-racial utopia. It involved uprooting small children from around the globe, a forced migration of sorts, and bringing them together as if they were part of some circus act. But it did represent a very visual and touching challenge to widely held ideas about race and nationality – and to ideas about where each of us belong.

A FINAL INTERMISSION

It's hard to be sure how many nomads there are left in this world. We were all nomads once, of course, before agriculture domesticated us, and we became tied to particular pieces of territory. And so the share of the world's human population which might be considered nomadic has declined over the last twelve thousand years, from 100 per cent to considerably less than 1 per cent. But it's not always easy to count nomads, since they're not usually interested in answering the questions of census-takers sent by governments. Nor is it easy to define them.

Ask most people and they'll come up with a negative definition – that a nomad is someone who has no permanent residence. They're really describing what's left of the human race after subtracting the vast majority of 'normal people' who have a fixed place that they call home. That leaves an assortment of hunter-gatherers, pastoralists and members of travelling communities, many of whom move around according to the seasons, and who are often treated with a mixture of pity and ignorance and distrust by the sedentary world. But there's also a twist here, for the word 'nomad' has taken on new life and new meanings. It has become a catch-all term, romanticised by many of those who choose, like me, to spend much of their lives on the move, or would like to do so.

These nomadic newcomers come in several varieties (though they do largely consist of white people from rich countries). There are 'digital nomads', for instance, who are able to work wherever they want because of the internet. And the American seasonal workers whose homes are campervans – and who were the stars of the 2021 Oscar-winning film *Nomadland*. Some Australians refer to 'grey nomads', older people who follow the sun, moving to warmer climates in the summer – also known as 'snowbirds' in America. And I shouldn't exclude, even if I'd like to, those wandering glitzy creatures who seem to exist only in lifestyle magazines, where they are labelled 'glomads' – the gl- prefix can stand for either global or glamour. Then there are royal families, moving between their palaces, who have long had nomadic tendencies of the grandest kind, mirrored in modern times by many of the world's multi-billionaires. And so the word 'nomad' has been stretched to include some of the poorest people in the world, homeless and drifting, and some of the very richest, who flit between their mansions in private jets. New nomads have property.

Old-style nomads owned almost nothing. And prehistorically, we humans did not have property – at least not in the sense that we use the word now. We may have had a few belongings, objects that we could carry, and we probably had proprietorial feelings towards territory that we knew well, especially when a new group of humans turned up. But it's only when we first become sedentary, with the arrival of agriculture, that property became central to our lives and to our identity. It's a moment that Rousseau imagined, with melodramatic regret, as a turning point in our common history:

> The first person who, having enclosed a plot of land, took it into his head to say 'This is mine' and found people simple enough to believe him, was the true founder of civil society. What crimes, wars, murders, miseries and horrors the

human race would have been spared, if someone had pulled up the stakes or filled in the ditch and cried out: 'Beware of listening to this imposter. You are lost if you forget that the fruits of the earth belong to everyone and that the earth itself belongs to no one!'

We do not know precisely how the earth first came to be divided up as the property of humans, and we never will, but Rousseau was surely right to see it as a species-defining development. Yet its modern implications are rarely discussed and we seldom seek a justification for the way the world has been parcelled up into units of property. And there are important questions that are often left unaddressed. Ones that are essential to the lives of traditional nomads, and the answers to which may even tell us something about ourselves. How would you explain to nomads why land that they once used for hunting and gathering and scavenging and grazing is no longer theirs to use? Or why, all of a sudden, can nomads no longer move freely across an area of land because sedentary people have created a border across the middle of it?

And there's an even bigger question, which sweeps up all the others. It's the kind of question that some people will just ignore or swat aside, but it also makes many others deeply uncomfortable or defensive ('thinking like that's a recipe for chaos', one friend told me) because it scrutinises so much that is taken for granted by sedentary people. The question: why does anyone, philosophically speaking, have more of a right to be at a particular place on this earth than anyone else? It's a question that encounters several levels of hostility. For not only might it imply a migration free-for-all, but it also challenges the sovereignty of a nation-state over its territory. And, by suggesting that anyone might have the right to be anywhere at all, it questions the notion of land ownership. After all, there is very little that isn't owned by a nation, or a company, or a family or an individual. And so the assertion that 'no one has more of a right to be at a particular place on this earth than anyone else' might provide a justification for me, or a total stranger, to camp on your golf course, or village green, or move onto your land, into your home.

To some people this can feel like an unimportant, impractical question, simply because there are systems of law and tradition developed over many generations that establish both territorial borders and property rights, and very few people in the world see any realistic possibility of their wholesale abolition. When pressed, there are many ways in which humans have explained or justified the origins of land ownership. The Athenians, after all, claimed to have always been in Athens, were born from its soil – so it clearly belonged to them from the start. Many monarchs have claimed God-given ownership of particular territories. While Catholic popes, as the representatives of God on earth, felt able to assign whole continents to particular kings, as Alexander VI did in 1493 when he divided the 'newly discovered' Americas between Spain and Portugal.

There have been more subtle attempts to explain the origins of land ownership. These include the idea that the first person to work a particular piece of land owns it – and therefore has the right to sell or give or bequeath it to whoever they wish. And, so the theory goes, all ownership originates in this way, so that one could, in principle, trace back the ownership of anywhere in the world to such an event. It's a useful fiction, which may even be true in a small number of cases. But such chains of ownership are almost always broken, and that land was simply taken at some point from earlier owners: as the result of some kind of power struggle such as a war, or a simple land grab, or confiscated under laws that the original occupants never recognised – as is often the case with indigenous people and nomads faced with legal systems created by new settlers. Or there are those famous 'negotiated' deals – the Dutch giving Native Americans sixty guilders' worth of trinkets in exchange for the island of Manhattan – possibly the most one-sided transaction in history.

But it wasn't only greed that motivated these new owners. Large numbers of nomads lost their lands in the process of being 'civilised' by sedentary people. Most sedentarists believed, and many still do, with what seems like absolute certainty, that their way of life is superior to that of nomads. And they considered that nomads were savages who need to be saved from either the devil or poverty or both. They therefore believed they were doing nomads a favour by rounding them up, taking them from their land and employing them in menial jobs. In return they expected these former nomads to be grateful for the benefits of civilisation, such as some money to pay the rent for their new homes and to buy food. Some nomads were considered unsavable, because they showed little interest in these 'benefits'. So instead their children were taken away and put into schools where they would learn how to be 'normal'.

It's often hard for people from a sedentary background to imagine the lives of nomads. There's a brief sentence, a much-quoted question, in a book written in the 1960s by the Canadian anthropologist Richard Lee, which served as my entry point. Lee quoted an unnamed !Kung nomad from southern Africa who was asked why he had not become a farmer. He replied, 'Why should we plant when there are so many mongongo nuts in the world?' Now, there's a philosophy of life buried in that sentence, as well as a statement of fact. For the !Kung, mongongo nuts were a nourishing and plentiful source of food, supplemented by more than one hundred other edible plants, as well as the animals that they occasionally hunted. This meant each adult could spend considerably less than twenty hours a week collecting food, giving them much more free time than most sedentary people. The !Kung were not very interested in the accumulation of wealth, or in building permanent homes: they preferred to have a good time and tell stories. And that 'mongongo nut' response represents what was, for many nomads, a life of luxury – and a life less stressful and less materialistic than that enjoyed or endured by most sedentary people.*

Most migrants aren't nomads, of course. But the experiences of nomads, ancient and modern, traditional and digital, might offer us a few clues as to how to deal with some of the wider issues connected with mobility and migration. For it's just possible that the emergence of new types of self-identifying nomads – drawn from settled populations – might lead to greater understanding of others who are on the move, such as migrants with lower-status passports and meagre bank accounts. It may even help us reconsider our answers to those questions raised earlier in this intermission – about borders and land, and our right to live where we want. It might normalise the idea that, in principle at least, anyone might live any-where – and not be limited to the country of their birth. And we might begin to ask instead, not why do people move, but rather why do people stay still?

---

* The !Kung (now usually referred as the Ju/'hoansi) belong to the group of southern African hunter-gatherers still widely known as Bushmen or San, and traditionally lived in the area near the modern borders of Namibia and Botswana. More than half a century after Richard Lee's research, the lives of the !Kung have changed: they have permanent villages and a few schools, as well as Western clothes, Christianity, mobile phones, gonorrhoea, alcohol and HIV/Aids. They are no longer nomadic, and many of them face a lifetime of poverty. They fight to retain aspects of their former life-style, including the custody of their ancestral lands. The mongongo nut plays a much smaller role in their lives.

CHAPTER ELEVEN

Guest Workers, *Braceros* and Wetbacks

In September 1964, a shy, gaunt Portuguese carpenter called Armando Rodrigues de Sá clambered aboard a special train from Lisbon to Cologne. The thirty-eight-year-old would later remember little about his three-day journey to Germany, except that he had felt very nervous, was troubled by doubts about leaving behind his village and his family, and that he had a constant headache. When he arrived at Cologne's Deutz station, he was amazed to hear his name, and his alone, being announced on loudspeakers. He couldn't imagine why. He had done nothing wrong. Rodrigues de Sá later described how he felt terrified and was overtaken by paranoia, believing – for no particular reason – that the Portuguese secret police were after him.

A few minutes later, Rodrigues de Sá was in the spotlight – a symbolic hero. He was standing in the station forecourt astride a new motorcycle, a bouquet of carnations lying across the handlebars. There were more than a thousand people watching him, including dozens of journalists and the Portuguese ambassador. A man in a suit and tie made a speech in German,

and formally presented him with the motorcycle, the flowers
and a certificate of honour. A band played the West German
and Portuguese national anthems. There was a crowd of jos-
tling photographers and images of Rodrigues de Sá, rigid as a
waxwork, a frightened man in a fedora trying and failing to
smile, were published in the following day's newspapers. The
reason? He had been chosen at random from this latest train-
load of migrants as West Germany's one millionth *Gastarbeiter*,
or guest worker. And he and his fellow foreigners were being
thanked for their role in what had become known as Germany's
economic 'miracle'.

The ceremonial presentation of a motorcycle to the bemused
Armando Rodrigues de Sá, and the extensive media coverage it received, was part of a larger narrative, and important
for wider reasons. It and similar ceremonies later in the 1960s
helped advertise a new non-aggressive German self-confidence
less than two decades after the end of the war. And the invention of the 'guest worker' model for international migration
became a matter of national pride. This narrative presented
West Germany as an unlikely success story – a paradise of
cooperation – in contrast to America at the time of the Civil
Rights movement, or to the bitter political arguments about
race and empire and migration and decolonisation that were a
feature of French and British politics at the same time.

The truth, of course, is more complex. First, that term 'guest
worker' deserves some gentle deconstruction. Look at it again.
It's a fine example of an oxymoron. For there's a contradiction
at its heart, given that it's hardly normal to put one's guests to
work. And it is also a carefully designed euphemism. It had
been coined as a replacement for *Fremdarbeiter*, literally 'foreign worker', which had been tarnished by association with
the Nazis. And indeed the use of the word 'guest' might even
be seen as a promise that the workers would be treated more
hospitably than in the past. But it also signified the temporary

nature of the migration. Guest workers, you see, were expected to go home. They were only there as workers, to perform a specific economic function.

There's also the context of the Second World War and its tumultuous aftermath, which was, at the time the guest worker programme began, still a recent memory. Germany's wartime economy had been dependent on migrant workers, most of whom had been brought to the country under conditions of extreme duress. Among them were some Jews and Roma – also transported in special trains – who were then taken to concentration camps to be murdered, though the able-bodied among them were often set to work first. And then there were the *Fremdarbeiter*, chosen from other nationalities – many of them Poles. There was no mass extermination programme for the Poles, but they suffered appallingly as they became, in practice, slaves. They were rounded up in Poland and brought to Germany. They were supposed to live in barracks, they could not attend German church services, they received lower wages, they were banned from using facilities such as express trains or swimming pools, they had to wear the letter P on their clothing and Polish men could be publicly executed for having sex with a German woman. There was a clear pecking order among nationalities – and Poles, in general, had a harder time than migrant workers coming from France, Italy or Scandinavia.

It's hard to overstate the chaos in much of east and central Europe at the end of the war, in large part because of the extraordinary numbers of people on the move. Among them were millions of migrant workers, concentration camp survivors and prisoners of war trying to make their way home. Heading in the opposite direction were former German soldiers, no longer heroes and despised almost everywhere they went. Many took shelter in bombed train stations and ruined buildings. The German journalist Ursula von Kardorff described the misery at Halle railway station four months after the end of the war:

Terrible images. Rubble, amongst which wander creatures that seem no longer to be of this world. Homecomers in ragged, wadded uniforms covered with boils, creeping along on makeshift crutches. Living corpses.

Also heading west was an even larger number of ethnic Germans from Eastern Europe, as many as twelve million people, perhaps the biggest European migration of all time. In the wake of the German defeat they had been forced out of their old homes in Poland, the Soviet Union, Hungary, Czechoslovakia, Romania and Yugoslavia. They had no choice but to migrate, often on foot, pulling and pushing wooden handcarts to an occupied, partitioned and shrunken fatherland – which many of them had never even visited. They were not, by and large, welcomed. They were described as gypsies and Polacks and mongrels, caricatured for their love of garlic and paprika. In the northern city of Bremen they were met by posters screaming 'We can't take any more people! A stop to immigration!' They were seen as a burden, an emblem of Germany's humiliation. Historians now argue that their arrival was actually beneficial to the West German economy, a flexible, ambitious, hard-working labour force who helped drive a new industrial revolution, which would, by the mid-1950s, require many more migrant workers.

Given this recent migration trauma, it's perhaps unsurprising that Germany took a top-down, government-led approach. It chose to 'import' workers in a controlled, regularised way, through formal labour recruitment agreements with other countries, in contrast to France and Britain, which both also relied on migrants coming from their former or current colonies. In 1955, the first agreement was signed with Italy. There was some mild opposition from trade unions, but the notion of allowing Italians to work in Germany did not prove controversial. Italians, after all, had migrated to Germany since medieval times, just as Germans had migrated southwards in the medieval and Roman periods. And Italians hadn't felt the need, as had so many Poles, to Germanicise their names. Indeed, the West German Foreign Minister at the time of the 1955 agreement bore the splendidly hybrid name of Heinrich von Brentano, his ancestors having left Italy several centuries earlier.

To implement the agreement West Germany set up recruitment offices in Verona and Naples to bring as many as one hundred thousand Italians to construction sites, factories and farms in Germany, for up to a year at a time. Almost all the early recruits were men, who were discouraged from bringing family members. It was a model that was soon deemed a success, and in the early 1960s – as the economy boomed and the Cold War prevented labour recruitment in the Soviet bloc – Germany reached similar agreements with Spain, Greece, Turkey, Portugal and Yugoslavia.

Armando Rodrigues de Sá's initial experience was fairly typical. He had made the first contact – in his case with the German labour recruitment office in Lisbon. He had to provide a detailed employment record, and was sent for blood and urine tests, and a chest X-ray. Eventually, after his files had been sent to Germany, he was paired up with a new employer, a cement factory in a small town in the south of the country. The factory paid for his travel on the guest workers' train and organised his housing. He stayed, like most guest workers, in a large hostel near the factory. There was one toilet and two kitchens – and he shared his room with seven other men. On Sundays, Rodrigues de Sá met other Portuguese men at a café, but according to his wife he lived frugally, didn't go to the cinema and sent most of his earnings – and his motorcycle – back home. He felt homesick, was only really there for the money, and never quite adapted to life away from Portugal.*

---

* An industrial accident brought a premature end to his role as West Germany's best-known guest worker, and Armando Rodrigues de Sá returned to his family and his village. He died of stomach cancer at the age of just fifty-three. His motorcycle – purchased from his widow – is now on display in the House of History museum in Bonn.

Many other guest workers were far happier in Germany and stayed on, some of them permanently. The original idea of rotating workers was a mirage. It suited no one. Employers wanted workers whom they knew, who had learned some German, who were experienced. Employees wanted security and continuity – as well as the high wages that working in Germany gave them. Some found new jobs for themselves, or fell in love, or just preferred to be in a new country. And while the economy was strong and needed still more workers, there was little resistance to their remaining.

In practice, guest workers from most European countries began to show less interest in coming to Germany as their own economies grew, while Italians were soon able to move freely under the rules of what would eventually become the European Union. But not Turks. Before long, Turkey had become West Germany's largest single source of foreign labour, so much so that the entire guest worker programme would in later times be associated with Turkish migrants.

As with other migrant workers, the Turks travelled by train, a three-day journey from Istanbul through the Balkans to Munich – though those who came from rural Anatolia travelled a lot further. Each worker was allowed to bring one kilo of cheese and olives on the train, as well as ten cartons of cigarettes. The rest of their food, pork-free but not always halal, was provided by the German organisers. The passengers were given a Turkish-language pamphlet called *Hallo Mustafa* (there were similar Greek, Italian and Spanish publications welcoming, respectively, Spiros, Mario and José), which advised them, with helpful cartoons, on the importance of good timekeeping in German workplaces. The pamphlet refers to Turks as 'hot-blooded', and the imaginary Mustafa is told that 'it is not always advisable to demand an egg when you can, through the same means, have the entire hen tomorrow'. He is advised that it's best 'to rein in one's temperament and feelings'. Those first

Turkish workers faced barely any Islamophobia, just plenty of ignorance piled high with stereotypes, which barely distinguished them from other migrants.*

The West German guest worker scheme ended with the world economic downturn and the oil crisis of 1973, as if it were a tap that could be turned off. But no one by then really thought of guest workers either as just guests or just workers. It had become unsustainable to maintain the notion that migrants could be defined solely in terms of their short-term economic value to a society. The Swiss playwright Max Frisch summed up the moral vacuum at the heart of such programmes: 'We called for workers, and human beings came instead.' Millions of humans came. It's more than sixty years since the appearance of the first Turkish guest workers, and it's estimated that there are now at least seven million Germans who have recent Turkish heritage.

There were attempts in the 1970s and 80s to persuade some migrants to leave, or even to force them to do so, which were largely ineffective. By this time many guest workers, particularly those from Turkey, had secured the right to remain in Germany permanently – and to be joined by family members. Attempts to restrict migration were, as is so often the case, counterproductive – in part because of how they affected the attitudes of actual and potential migrants. The fact that migration became harder in the 1970s meant that fewer migrants were willing to return to their original homelands, even temporarily, and they often rushed to persuade uncertain family members to join them, so as not to lose their entitlement to come at a later date. Their right to remain in Germany felt, to

---

* Devotees of deep history may see a certain irony here, for there's little that's new about migration from Turkey. Neanderthals and modern humans almost certainly first entered Europe through Turkey, while migrants – real or imagined – from Troy and Phocaea, in what is now Turkey, played a central role in this story of migration and, of course the foundation mythology of Rome and Marseille, as well as what is sometimes referred to as Western civilisation.

many of them, like an economic asset, something of real value, which they would not easily give up – even if they would otherwise have been tempted to return. And migrants were no longer so dependent on factory employment, and had moved out of the dormitories. Some had created their own businesses – restaurants for instance, which would in turn become employers of migrants. Their lives were now in Germany.

Prejudice against migrants also increased with the economic downturn – as it did in other countries, such as Austria and Switzerland, which had adopted the guest worker model. This often had the effect of encouraging migrant communities to organise themselves more effectively, and to develop support networks in the form of trade unions or social and cultural associations. It also made migrants from a particular country more likely to want to live close to each other. It wasn't until the 1980s that there was significant anti-Turkish or anti-Muslim resentment in Germany, along with more general anti-migrant feeling, and sometimes violence, towards those who had come from even further away: Vietnam and Ethiopia, for instance. Even then it was usually on a smaller scale than anti-migrant prejudice and violence seen elsewhere, such as in France or Britain (or the USA) from the 1950s onwards.

In France and Britain, post-war migration became entangled with the slow, bloody collapse of both countries' empires. Large numbers of migrants came to live in France and Britain, quite legally, from their former and current colonies – principally from the West Indies and South Asia for Britain, and from North Africa for France. Germany had no empire and could at least pretend to draw a line under its past, and with the aid of a few euphemisms, some good intentions and a booming economy, muddled its way through the 1950s and 60s without race riots, and without migrants being murdered on the streets of its capital.

New mythologies of migration were articulated in post-war France and Britain – largely by members of the sedentary white majority population – which would be enormously influential and transform the way migration was imagined. These mythologies helped produce what might best be called 'migration amnesia', an infectious, multi-symptom condition that spread through much of the West. An amnesia which may also help provide a partial explanation of why our common history as migrants has been so neglected, why this book and others like it need to be written. And the Second World War became the starting point, a sort of watershed from which this amnesia set in. In the sense that migration before and after the war would be envisaged quite differently, and many migration-related continuities between the pre-war and post-war eras would simply be disregarded or denied.

Try this crude experiment. Imagine a migrant. Conjure one up right now in your mind's eye. Go on. Are they white? Are they European? Probably not. Migrants tend to be imagined, in modern times, as poor, darker-skinned people from developing countries, searching for work or safety or both.* I doubt that would have been the case with a similar experiment between the wars. For many people, particularly Westerners, white Europeans heading to the Americas or Australasia would have been the archetypal migrant of the inter-war period (and before). And, critically, since the war, white people have, by and large, no longer imagined themselves as actual or possible migrants. They may instead use the words emigrant or expat – and, in English at least, tend to use the word 'immigrant' to categorise those migrants who are also people of colour.

What does this tell us? It's obviously a reminder of how

---

* There's a minor exception to this among the many Westerners on whom I've tried this highly unscientific experiment. Some British people's first reaction is to think of migrants as Eastern European – often Polish or Romanian and, most recently, Ukrainian.

racialised modern debates about migration have become. But it also reflects the emergence of a dominant and often misleading narrative relating to modern migration, which has only very recently begun to be unravelled. It's a narrative that includes the notion, in defiance of clear evidence to the contrary, that Britain and France were white and monocultural before the 1950s. And, in its most tendentious form, that the ancestors of the white inhabitants of both France and Britain, like those ancient Athenians, had lived there since the beginning of history – a triple glorification of sedentarism, racial purity and the nation-state. On a more detailed level, it's a narrative that usually omits the important role played in Europe during the two world wars by people from Asia, Africa and the Caribbean – as part of the armed forces, or in support roles. But in the retelling of European history before the 1950s, there was little space for people of colour. They were airbrushed out and are only now being gradually reinstated.

As for narratives about the post-war period, the amnesia took another form, almost its mirror image, in which white migration – inward or outward – was largely ignored, or treated as if it were a different phenomenon altogether, deserving of a special category of its own. In fact, for most of the 1950s, fewer people entered Britain each year than departed – and among those who left permanently were the so-called 'Ten Pound Poms': more than a quarter of a million poor white British people whose journeys to Australia and New Zealand were subsidised by their new countries.* And for that period, by far

---

* 'Pom', as an Australian moniker for a person from Britain, has a disputed etymology. But the best-attested version – dating it to the early twentieth century – suggests it comes, circuitously, from the word 'immigrant'. An immigrant became, for one Melbourne joker, 'Jimmy Grant', which soon morphed into 'pomegranate', which became 'Pom'. Two future Australian prime ministers, Tony Abbott and Julia Gillard, were beneficiaries of what was officially known as the Assisted Passage Migration Scheme, according to which adults paid just ten pounds to go to Australia (or New Zealand), and children travelled free. So were the Gibb brothers, Barry, Maurice and Robin – better known as the Bee Gees.

the largest numbers of new migrants to the UK came not from the Caribbean or South Asia but from the Republic of Ireland. In France, probably the most significant post-war French mass migration was the movement of more than a million *pieds noirs*, white settlers and their descendants, from Algeria to mainland France in the 1960s. And Italian, Spanish and Portuguese migrants to France were more populous in the 1950s and 60s than Muslim North Africans.

What was also lost is the sense of continuity with the past, and of both the normality and interconnectedness of migration. And sometimes it's important to search for them. Take the *Windrush*, for example – probably the most famous British ship of modern times, remembered for bringing more than four hundred black Jamaicans to the UK in 1948.* The Windrush generation became the collective name given to those early migrants from the West Indies, while the Windrush scandal of 2018, caused by attempts to deport some of those early migrants, forced the resignation of a senior government minister. But despite the renown of the *Windrush*, and its symbolic role in the creation of a more multicultural Britain, it has a largely forgotten migration backstory.

The ship once had another name. It was launched as the *Monte Rosa*, a German ocean liner built in Hamburg, which led a double life for much of the 1930s. In the summer, it was a European cruise ship, while in the winter it was used for transporting migrants, carrying tens of thousands of Germans across the Atlantic to new lives in South America. After the USA closed its borders to most Germans in the mid-1920s, Brazil, Argentina and Uruguay had all become popular destinations;

---

* In fact, the *Windrush* was not the first shipload of West Indian migrants to Britain after the war. Nor did it mark the start of a significant wave of West Indian migration: that would only happen in the mid-1950s. And a large number of the Windrush Jamaicans – possibly as many as two-thirds – were ex-servicemen who had been to Britain before.

many Germans left, as they had for centuries, simply to make new lives for themselves, while others were fleeing Nazi persecution. During the war the future *Windrush* was used to carry Norwegian Jews to Hamburg from where they were taken by train to Auschwitz to be murdered. At the end of the war, the *Monte Rosa* was seized by the British as enemy property and its name changed to the *Empire Windrush*, after a minor tributary of the Thames. It was put to use as an intercontinental troop carrier, and then to bring British families back from newly independent India – some of whom had been living there for several generations.

In the summer of 1948, the *Windrush* made the Caribbean journey for which it is best remembered – the story of which conceals another neglected tale of migration. For the *Windrush* didn't only go to Jamaica, but also to Mexico to collect sixty-six extraordinarily well-travelled Polish refugees. They'd been on the move for eight years, forced eastwards from their homeland by the Soviet army, taken to Siberian labour camps, then transported to India, from where they were shipped halfway round the world to a former internment camp for Japanese Americans in California. They were then given temporary asylum over the border in Mexico. After the war most of them didn't want to return to Poland, now under communist rule, and many went to the USA or stayed in Mexico, but sixty-six of them applied to settle in the UK. And the *Windrush* had been sent to pick them up, their fares paid by the British government.

The ship had also been instructed to pick up some British troops in Jamaica – and it's only because of that that the better-known *Windrush* story happened. There weren't nearly enough passengers to fill the ship, so its enterprising owners decided to advertise cut-price tickets to Britain in the Jamaican newspaper, the *Daily Gleaner*. And several hundred even more enterprising Jamaicans bought those tickets and sailed away to

Passenger Opportunity

To United Kingdom

Troopship "EMPIRE WINDRUSH" sailing
about 23rd MAY.
Fares:— Cabin Class £48
            Troopdeck £28
Royal Mail Lines, Limited—8 Port Royal St.

Tilbury Docks, just outside London.* There they were met by a
Pathé film crew who showed no interest in the Windrush Poles
but ensured the enduring fame of the Windrush Jamaicans via a
two-minute news story in which several explained that they'd
come to Britain in search of work. One of the passengers, the
calypso performer known as Lord Kitchener, was filmed sing-
ing 'London is the Place for Me' and referring to Britain as the
'mother country'.

Those words, 'mother country' are important, and are central to understanding the Jamaican experience of migration to
Britain. In interviews with post-war migrants from Jamaica and
the rest of the Caribbean they are used again and again. The
migrants were coming to a country they thought they knew.
They spoke English. They could sing British nursery rhymes.
They had learnt all about British history and geography and

---

* This was not the *Windrush*'s first voyage up the Thames Estuary. It was used as a
cruise ship from Germany to the Mediterranean, Scandinavia and the UK, and made
at least twenty trips to London. A 1936 poster using an image of a Beefeater guarding
the Tower of London advertised a special six-day trip for Germans to visit London
on the *Monte Rosa*, costing sixty-five Reichsmark. After the Caribbean journey for
which the *Windrush* is now remembered, it became a troop carrier for British ser-
vicemen and women in Korea. It was heading back to the UK in March 1954, with
fifteen hundred people on board, when the engine room caught fire off the coast of
Algeria. Everyone was evacuated except for four crew members killed by the fire, and
the *Windrush* sank to the bottom of the Mediterranean.

literature from the colonial education system, and practically nothing about slavery, or Africa, or Jamaica for that matter – and certainly not earlier inhabitants of the island such as the Taino. Many bore Christian names like Winston, or Nelson or Gladstone as a tribute to British heroes. And they had the right to live and work in Britain. They considered themselves British and, according to the laws of the British Empire, they were.

Many of them described a sense of surprise and disappointment when they arrived. Britain was darker, colder and shabbier than they had expected. There were bomb sites everywhere. And rationing. But worst of all was the everyday racism they encountered. Their education and work experience were rarely recognised by employers, some of whom would not take on black people at all – though the need for labour was so great that finding some kind of job was not difficult.

The biggest problem was housing. Many British houseowners would not rent rooms to black people. And they were quite open about it, writing 'no coloureds' on rental advertisements for rooms. And so instead many newcomers had no choice but to live in run-down areas with slum landlords who exploited them. Those who struck up relationships with white women would remember many decades later how they faced racist taunts on the streets, spitting and sometimes bodily violence.

It might seem surprising, then, given this kind of reaction to the arrival of a relatively small number of West Indian migrants, that British politicians took so long to restrict migration from non-white countries. And the explanation lies in the way in which migration policy was interwoven with British nostalgia for the recent past, and an imperial mindset that would outlive Britain's crumbling empire. For although many politicians made it clear that they didn't want migrants from the Caribbean to come to Britain, the actual limitations placed on such migration were almost non-existent. There were two main reasons for this.

The first was very practical, and usually unspoken – though evident in internal government documents of the time. Successive administrations did not want to introduce generalised immigration restrictions because they did not want to make it harder for white people of British ancestry – and there were millions of them throughout the Empire and Commonwealth – to come to Britain. They feared that if they overtly discriminated in law between white and non-white migrants they would anger current and former non-white colonies, who were at the time being courted by the Soviet Union. And indeed, when migration restrictions were eventually introduced in 1962, there was no mention of skin colour, and instead convoluted legal formulations and schemes were concocted that appeared colour-blind, but which in practice discriminated against non-white migrants.

The second reason was much more high-flown. It was based upon an idea of empire and of free movement within that empire which echoed the distant past – and which was particularly popular among those with a classical education. This is how it was set out by a government minister called Henry Hopkinson in a parliamentary debate about Jamaican migration in 1954:

> As the law stands, any British subject from the colonies is free to enter this country at any time as long as he can produce satisfactory evidence of his British status ... We still take pride in the fact that a man can say *civis Britannicus sum* whatever his colour may be, and we take pride in the fact that he wants and can come to the Mother country.

Those three Latin words, *civis Britannicus sum*, meaning 'I am a British citizen', were intended to evoke the Roman Empire. Hopkinson was showing off to his fellow MPs by updating Cicero, perhaps the greatest of Roman orators, whose *civis*

Romanus sum represented an imperial guarantee of the rights of any Roman citizen anywhere in the empire. They were the words repeated in Jerusalem by St Paul, who had never been anywhere near Rome, as a way of getting a fair trial in the imperial capital.*

But the sun was setting on the British Empire. The disastrously mismanaged departures from India and Palestine, each of which created enduring migration crises of their own, had already happened by the time the Windrush Jamaicans turned up in London. In 1954, when Hopkinson made his speech, Britain was fighting brutal wars in Kenya and Malaya in which imperial troops used summary execution and torture to subdue people who were demanding independence and who were, by Hopkinson's definition and by imperial law, British citizens. Two years later, Britain (and France) would be humiliated by Egypt during the Suez Crisis.

The decline of the British Empire meant, at the same time, a decline in a particularly privileged kind of migration. Fewer British men (they were almost all male) were required to run that empire – as administrators, or working for private companies. For an adventurous, confident young man growing up in Britain, there were suddenly a lot fewer career choices that would involve moving thousands of miles away from home to one of those places where he would be very powerful at an early stage in his career. And instead a flow of other groups

---

* Hopkinson was also echoing the nineteenth-century prime minister Lord Palmerston, who used the original Ciceronian phrase to explain why his government had sent a squadron of gunboats to Greece after some Athenians ransacked the house of a British citizen living there. John F. Kennedy, visiting Berlin in 1963, also quoted Cicero, before coming up with his own version, which denoted international rather than national solidarity: *Ich bin ein Berliner.* That too was echoed in the aftermath of the 2015 attack on the Parisian magazine *Charlie Hebdo,* which spawned the ubiquitous hashtag *Je suis Charlie.* Another classical phrase, this time from Virgil's *Aeneid,* was used by the British politician Enoch Powell in 1968 in what became known as his 'Rivers of Blood' speech – in which he quoted Virgil's description of the 'River Tiber, foaming with blood' as a warning against allowing more migrants into the UK.

of adventurous, confident young men, who were far less privileged than their British counterparts, began to go in the opposite direction. This was what the Jamaican poet Louise Bennett referred to as 'colonisation in reverse', or as the Sri Lankan political theorist A. Sivanandan put it, 'we are here because you were there'. For there was a certain symmetry to these flows of populations, staggered by time, that made it far harder for Britain to justify the exclusion of migrants from what was once the empire.

For France, the flows of population associated with the post-war years and the end of empire were even more complex – and continued, as in Britain, to play a pivotal role in the country's cantankerous debates and disputes about its modern identity. There was plenty of labour migration to France from Italy, Spain and Portugal, largely forgotten now, which proved relatively uncontroversial and became even less so once there was free movement under the aegis of the future European Union. But the reverse was true for North Africa, and particularly Algeria, where millions of migrants were caught up in a particularly bloody and unforgiving war of independence.

Algeria is a special case. Decolonisation there was different from anywhere else, largely because Algeria's modern history and legal status were quite distinct from France's other major colonies, even its neighbours Tunisia and Morocco – both of which were officially protectorates, with local rulers still in place. Algeria, however, had been fully annexed and widely settled by white colonists from the 1830s onwards, and was considered an integral and inseparable part of France.* Those who migrated between Algeria and mainland France prior to independence in 1962 were, in legal terms, internal migrants moving between different parts of the same country.

---

* Algeria had been French for longer than Nice, which only became part of France in 1860. Algeria also constituted, until 1962, about 80 per cent of France's total land area, largely because of the size of its almost empty southern territories in the Sahara.

So when Algeria became independent, France was, in effect, partitioned. The poorer, larger Muslim-majority southern part of the country broke away, after years of violent struggle, to form its own nation-state. And this had immense implications for no less than four large groups of migrants (and several smaller ones), who were in the early 1960s making the short trip across the Mediterranean to what was left of France: first, white settlers of European origin known as *pieds noirs*; second, members of Algeria's large Jewish communities; third, those Algerian Muslims known as *harkis* who had collaborated with the French; and lastly, Algerian Muslims who were migrating in search of work and other opportunities.

That last group – the focus of this part of the story – migrated far more gradually than the first three,* and with less drama and news coverage, but their experience was similarly overshadowed by the war of independence. They're normally classified as labour migrants and were overwhelmingly young and male. They are equivalent in many ways to the Turks of Germany or the West Indians of the UK. But because of Algeria's pre-independence status they had a longer, deeper history of settlement, and it was only from 1962 that they had to cross an international border in order to migrate. By the late 1930s, for instance, there were already more than half a million Algerians who had experience of living in mainland France – many of whom had stayed a year or two, working

---

* The first three groups consisted of migrants most of whom felt they had no choice but to leave. Some *pieds noirs* families had been in Algeria for more than a century. But during the 1960s almost all of them left, 'repatriated' to France, a country many had never lived in. Algeria's large Jewish community, about 140,000 strong, had an even more tenuous link to Europe – though some remembered their migrant pasts as the descendants of Jews expelled from Spain in the fifteenth century. The vast majority of them were also 'repatriated' to France. About sixty thousand *harkis* were killed as collaborators in 1962; around eighty-five thousand made it to France, where they were treated not as citizens but as unwelcome refugees. They were widely seen as an embarrassment, a reminder of France's humiliation in Algeria. Some were placed in forest camps, isolated from the general population; many lived in *bidonvilles* or shanty towns, often hiding their *harki* identity from other North African migrants.

for dramatically higher wages than they would have got in Algeria, and then returned home. And after the war, the numbers of migrants increased again, as workers were needed to rebuild a shattered economy.

There had been some opposition to the migration of Algerian Muslims in the immediate post-war era, but not really from mainland France. It came instead largely from *pieds noirs*, who complained that the migrants' departure disrupted the labour market, driving wages up – and that those migrants who then returned to Algeria were much more confident about asserting their political and social rights. In the mid-1950s, there was another rapid increase in migration from Algeria – ironically driven, in part, by the need for workers to replace large numbers of white French soldiers conscripted to fight in Algeria, as well as by young Algerian men who were keen to avoid being caught up in the war.

But as the situation in Algeria deteriorated, the conflict spilled over into mainland France, bringing down a series of governments and the collapse of the Fourth Republic. Anti-Algerian racism increased, as did the ghettoisation of the new migrants in the suburbs of many French cities, which became, in turn, easy recruiting grounds for Algerian nationalist groups. There were a series of attacks on the French police, and the mass detention of large numbers of Algerian migrants. In October 1961, the Parisian police broke up a pro-independence rally with quite spectacular brutality, tying up some protestors and throwing them into the Seine to drown. At least forty migrants were killed, and possibly as many as three hundred – the police covering up their action so effectively that a detailed account of what became known as the Paris Massacre was not revealed for another thirty years.

Less than six months later, Algeria was a new nation-state – and there was a general expectation in both countries that many migrants in France would return to their newly independent homeland. They didn't. Indeed, more kept coming, in still larger numbers. Algeria needed the remittances they sent home, and migration provided a sort of social safety valve for adventurous young men – and, increasingly, young women. France, meanwhile, needed workers, and wanted to remain on good terms with Algeria for very practical reasons: they wished to control the oil industry, and to make sure Algeria didn't become too friendly with the Soviet Union. Migration continued to suit both countries, with the Algerian government identifying potential migrants and negotiating annual quotas with France.

But the long war of independence had left its scars, and there was a deep distrust of Algerian migrants. It was particularly evident among the *pieds noirs*, and the two million white Frenchmen who had served in the armed forces during the Algerian war. Algerian Muslim migrants were repeatedly described as 'unassimilable'. A series of opinion polls from the 1970s and 80s gave significantly higher negative ratings to Algerians than to any other group of migrants. While the arrival of more women migrants opened up a new battleground: female clothing. The French colonial obsession with removing the headscarves worn by many Algerian women was imported to France – and, unlike much of the rest of Europe, the headscarf (and then the burkini*) would become a contentious issue during the migrant culture wars of the early twenty-first century.

Labour migration to France, as elsewhere in Europe, slowed dramatically in the 1970s, partly because of the economic downturn caused by the oil crisis. But it was the killing

---

* In 2015, several French towns, including Nice and Cannes, banned the burkini, a female swimsuit designed to cover most of the body and therefore in keeping with conservative Muslim tradition. The main reason given for the ban was that the burkini was a symbol of Islamic extremism. It proved hard in practice to distinguish, in legal terms, a burkini from a wetsuit – and the burkini became popular with skin cancer survivors, as well as with those who burn easily in the sun.

of Algerian migrants by French racists in 1973 that led to the formal ending, after seventy years, of authorised labour migration. It was a unilateral decision made by the Algerian government, which was taking control of the country's oil industry and was now far more confident about the economic future. Some migration from Algeria continued, but usually by the back door, or through family reunification – wives and children joining the more than three-quarters of a million Algerians already living in France.

These tales of migration and imperial collapse continued to play a major role in French politics well into the new millennium (as they did in Britain). It's an entanglement that often went unacknowledged, and there are those who would prefer to treat modern migration from former colonies as if it were unconnected with colonialism, as if it were possible simply to draw a line under the recent past.

The historian Benjamin Stora, an Algerian Jew whose family fled to France when he was a child, speaks of 'a state of amnesia' that prevailed for thirty years after the war of independence, as if the horrors, the torture, the rapacity of this particular colonial endgame had traumatised both France and Algeria into silence and forgetfulness. And then it all burst forth in the 1990s, with outpourings of anger and pain – and not just from those who had been colonised. Stora, writing in 1991, described what this trauma meant for those in France who regretted the loss of the empire:

The former colonised person, by his intrusion into the metropolis, is perceived as colonising the territory of 'civilised' people ... the Algerians are objects of repulsion whose presence reminded them of the last war that the French had fought (and lost), the cause of a deep national wound that has never been closed.

That 'national wound' represented by the loss of empire, and the survival of imperial mindsets in both France and Britain, have helped frame wider attitudes toward migrants which are deeply ahistorical. The migratory histories of the majority white populations of both countries are largely forgotten. And when they are recalled they are often memorialised as special cases, as migrations with a difference, as attempts to deliver civilisation to barbarous people, while the notion that France and Britain might have a lot to learn from their migrant populations is often treated as an affront. And migrants themselves are, almost universally, judged before they get an opportunity to open their mouths. For even among those who have been welcoming, there's a tendency to patronise – to behave as if migrants are sorry creatures, lost souls in a sedentary world, searching for a permanent home, when the opposite might sometimes be just as true. For there are many of us who yearn to be on the move.

In terms of their post-war economic role, the closest American equivalent to the labour migrants of Europe were Mexicans, who travelled northwards in their hundreds of thousands, often without authorisation. But in fundamental ways that story is also quite different – in large part because of the role played by the US–Mexico border, a three-thousand-kilometre line drawn across the continent in the nineteenth century, jagged in the west as it crosses the desert, meandering in the east as it follows the Rio Grande. And it's a border whose geography and history (and prehistory) have made it a source of embroilment and high emotion to this day.

The first humans to cross what is now the US–Mexico border did so more than ten thousand years ago. They were travelling – unlike so many of their modern counterparts – from north to south. Indeed, the ancestors of all the early settlers of central and southern America – the Yaghan, the Taino, the Maya and the Inca included – made that journey. The ancestors of the Aztec, too, who like so many others around the world had migration at the heart of their foundation myth. They believed they had been ordered by their supreme god to travel to what would later become known as Mexico City from their old homeland in the north, a place called Aztlan – often identified in modern times with the south-western quarter of the United States that stretches from Texas to California, from the Caribbean to the Pacific.

It's often forgotten in the contemporary arguments over Mexican migration that until the middle of the nineteenth century Mexico extended deep into what is now the USA – and included both Texas and California. For that reason, the first major increase in America's Mexican population was not caused by migrants, but by conquest. For in 1848, following a disastrous war, Mexico was forced to hand over half its territory to the USA. And one of the immediate consequences was that more than a hundred thousand Mexicans became residents of a new country – without moving.

Many of these brand-new Americans were members of indigenous communities, and for the nomadic Apache, in particular, the appearance of a new border would prove disastrous. The two governments signed a treaty, which referred to the Apache as 'savage Indians', and gave either country the right to pursue them across the border. In 1886, Geronimo, the last of the Apache leaders, was captured by US troops inside Mexico and brought back to the USA; he spent the rest of his life as a prisoner, available on request as an attraction for touring Wild West shows. The frontier region had, from the American point of view, been subdued. But there was no wall, not even a fence. The border was porous, and largely unmarked and unguarded. And Mexicans could move pretty freely to the north.

There were, by the 1920s, some checkpoints. Particularly where new towns had sprung up on the Mexican side, partly to cater to Americans heading south for alcohol and brothels at the time of prohibition. And there were a few border patrol officers too, who were more mobile, and attempted to identify and turn back unauthorised migrants from Europe and Asia trying to avoid the heavily inspected seaports of the USA. But most Mexicans were allowed in. This was because they were (and often still are) treated as a reserve labour force, cheap and always available – to be used when needed, and sent home when not.

At this stage Mexicans were not seen as posing a demographic threat, partly because of the way they were imagined racially. As the historian Rachel St John points out, American employers and politicians argued that

> Mexicans' innate submissiveness, willingness to work for low wages, and clannishness made them ideal laborers who would stick to themselves and return to Mexico once their work was done. The proximity of the border and ease with which Mexicans could return to Mexico contributed to characterizations of Mexicans as unthreatening 'birds of passage'.

Mexicans were also seen by employers as having 'a natural aptitude' for what became known as 'stoop labour' – that is, any work that involving bending over, or crouching. One farmers' spokesman explained that he'd seen Mexicans 'work stooping over for hours at a stretch, without straightening up. An Anglo simply couldn't take it ... Mexicans are generally a good deal shorter than the Anglos – they're built closer to the ground.' The main objection to Mexican migrants was that they might be carrying diseases. And so those who crossed the border were expected to undergo intrusive health checks – including the disinfection of groups of naked Mexican men in special holding pens.

But with the Great Depression of the 1930s, Mexican labour was no longer needed. Hundreds of thousands of Mexicans living in the USA were deported. There were raids, for instance, on public parks where Mexicans and Mexican Americans gathered in Los Angeles. Those who could not prove American citizenship were often sent straight to the border. Some who were unwilling to leave 'voluntarily' were 'persuaded' to do so after being told that only if they left of their own accord would they ever be allowed in again. Convoys of vehicles known as 'caravans of sorrow' headed south, others were put on special deportee trains or buses and dumped just inside Mexico.

And then in the 1940s everything changed again. The moment the USA entered the Second World War there was a desperate need for labour to fuel a rapidly growing wartime economy. Workers were needed to replace men who had gone off to fight, or who had left the fields to work in factories, or had been placed in internment camps because they had Japanese ancestry. And soon Mexicans were more than welcome – with public ceremonies to greet the arrival of large groups of manual labourers known as *braceros*.* A migrant labour agreement had been negotiated between the Mexican and US governments – prefiguring in many ways Germany's post-war guest worker programme – which was aimed at managing the flow of workers into the USA. The *bracero* programme brought in young male workers, selected by the Mexican authorities, on short-term contracts to work on farms or the railways. It came into effect just in time for three thousand Mexicans to take part in the Californian sugar-beet harvest of 1942. 'Mexicans,'

---

* *Bracero* comes from the Spanish *brazo*, meaning arm – and *braceros* are literally people who work with their arms.

declared the grateful *New York Times* headline, 'help save beet crop'.

Over the next twenty years, more than 4.5 million work contracts would be issued, and, if you believed official accounts, the *bracero* programme was a great success. It gave both governments a much-publicised example of neighbourly cooperation, as well as providing them with closer control over migration. The short duration of the *bracero* contracts helped appease those in the USA who were generally opposed to migration of any kind – as did the absence of any provision for the migration of women and children. The limited nature of the programme also reassured labour unions that the presence of *braceros* wouldn't be used to depress wages, and it provided big employers with a regular supply of workers who were forbidden by the terms of their contracts from going on strike. And in principle, at least, it brought considerable advantages to the *braceros* themselves. They could enter the USA legally; they had the protection of both governments; their pay scales were guaranteed, and their transport, housing and food were all taken care of – and some of them happily returned on *bracero* contracts every year.

But for many it wasn't really like that. The *braceros* found the compulsory health inspections humiliating. One of them, Benny Carranza, remembered how they were told to open their mouths to have their teeth examined – 'like a horse; we felt degraded'. And the mass fumigations of the 1920s continued, as another *bracero* remembered,

> they'd send us in groups of two hundred, as naked as we came into the world, into a big room about sixty feet square. Then men would come in masks, with tanks on their backs, and they'd fumigate us from top to bottom.

Some *braceros* weren't paid what they were promised in their contracts, or were assaulted or poorly fed by employers. They were often lodged in dormitories far away from the nearest towns, or any kind of entertainment or female company. A large number of *braceros*, more than 10 per cent in some places, 'skipped' – that is, they simply left their jobs and stayed on in the USA.

On a wider level, it's hard not to see the *bracero* programme as a failure, even in terms of the goals that were set for it. It was never large or flexible enough to deal with the demand for Mexican labour from American employers, nor with the desire of so many young Mexicans to migrate to the north. And, over the same period, unauthorised migration spiralled. For this was also the era of the 'wetback', the dismissive name given in America to 'illegal' migrants who had swum across the Rio Grande. Many millions crossed the border without authorisation during the twenty-two-year existence of the *bracero* programme (and most of them didn't even need to get wet).

A US government report from 1954 described the mass migration, in terms normally used to describe a natural disaster:

> The influx of aliens illegally entered from Mexico appears like an incoming tide, with mounting waves of people entering the country and being sent back, and returning again but in ever greater volume, and always reaching further inland with each incoming wave.

And so, periodically, Mexicans were forced back over the border. In 1954, under a programme officially called Operation Wetback, one million Mexicans and Mexican Americans were deported – the largest such operation in American history. Many deportees were dropped on the Mexican side of the border, from where many simply made their way back into the USA. Others were deliberately taken much further into the interior. Ten of thousands of deportees were shipped from

Texas to a Mexican seaport.* None of this stopped the flow of migrants.

It's now seems entirely plausible that the *bracero* programme actually had the effect of increasing rather than decreasing unauthorised migration. One reason for this was that the official accounts of its success made migration to the USA feel like a normal, desirable, realistic life choice for millions of young Mexicans. But the programme was also heavily restricted. Women couldn't take part. The programme mainly recruited men from the rural interior of Mexico, and this was widely resented, especially among people living near the border, who had the contacts and knowledge that made it relatively easy for them to cross into the USA. Some keen, articulate would-be *braceros* later described how the recruiting officers were only looking for docile farmhands, and so they would reject anyone who had soft hands, or 'looked intelligent', or wore shoes. A few played along by wearing sandals, pretending to be stupid, roughing up their hands by rubbing them on stones. Others simply made their own way across, or with the assistance of traffickers known as coyotes – and usually found it easy to get work on the other side.

Another reason was poor management and supervision. This meant that some migrants took the decision not to work as *braceros*. Take the case of Carlos Morales, a *bracero* who wasn't paid his full wages and decided that he preferred being a wetback.

> As a wetback, alone, safely across the border, I may find a farmer who needs one man. He will pay me honestly, I think. But as a *bracero*, I am only a number on a paycheck . . . and I am treated like a number . . . not like a man.

---

* There was some criticism in the USA and Mexico about the overcrowded 'hell ships', and conditions on board were compared to slave ships. In 1956, four deportees were either drowned or eaten by sharks during an attempted escape – and the sea deportations ended soon after.

Migrants like Morales got the support of some American employers, particularly those running small farms, who did not like the bureaucracy of the official programme and sometimes even threatened patrol officers attempting to raid their farms looking for workers who had crossed the border without authorisation. And because the *bracero* programme excluded women altogether, as well as any kind of family reunification involving parents and children, many of the most vulnerable would-be migrants had to use unauthorised and often dangerous means of crossing the border.

There had been some kind of fencing along parts of the border since the 1930s, though back then it existed principally to stop cattle from wandering or being smuggled between the two countries. There were border patrols, too – often using traditional stalking methods. One officer, remembering the 1930s, described how he would look for human footprints: 'A Mexican always walks heavy on the outside of his feet ... Indians will do that too. Whites and blacks ordinarily put their feet down flat.' It's hard to believe that many Mexican migrants were caught this way.

Chain-link fences recycled from a dismantled Japanese American internment camp were introduced along six miles of the California border in 1945. But migrants soon learned how easy it was to cut holes in these fences, or dig beneath them, and simply throw mattresses or old coats over any barbed wire. When these fences were then raised and lengthened and strengthened, migrants just moved further along the border, though this made crossing more dangerous. In 1952, for instance, the desiccated corpses of five Mexican men were found in the California desert; beside them was a 'water bag, two cans of sardines and two loaves of bread'. They were never identified.

By the 1950s, new tactics were emerging. Migrants began to make use of sophisticated fake documents provided by traffickers – who would also sometimes get them to carry drugs into the USA. The US Border Patrol, frustrated by the numbers of deported migrants who returned immediately, came up with a series of low-tech responses largely aimed at discomforting the Mexicans. They began strip-searching and detaining many more migrants in holding centres, rather than dumping them over the nearest border. Or they dropped them off at a completely different part of the border from where they'd been picked up, to stop them using their local networks to get back in immediately. In one part of Texas, the Border Patrol shaved the heads of repeat offenders, even giving some of them 'Apache' haircuts. A former officer remembered how 'one old boy had a big bushy moustache . . . [we] shaved off half of it'. The border guards saw it more as an opportunity to embarrass and emasculate male Mexican migrants than as a serious attempt to make them more readily identifiable if they tried to return.

The Border Patrol also attempted to shift wider public attitudes towards migration. It began to portray unauthorised migrants as criminals and discouraged the use of 'wetback' because, as a senior patrol officer argued, it creates 'a picture in the minds of the public and the courts of a poor emaciated Mexican worker entering the United States illegally to feed a starving family at home'. In fact, he insisted, detained migrants 'consist in the main part of criminals, often vicious in type, and of hardened and defiant repeaters'. He called for the words 'deportable alien' or 'criminal alien' to replace 'wetback'. It was a language and a narrative echoed half a century later by a presidential candidate called Donald Trump, who said of migrants crossing the Mexican border, 'they're bringing drugs, they're bringing crime, they're rapists'.*

---

* 'And some, I assume, are good people,' he added. Later in the same speech, he said, 'I will build a great, great wall on our southern border. And I will have Mexico pay for that wall.'

The *bracero* programme ended in the 1960s, replaced by an annual cap on migration from Mexico. Large numbers of Mexicans would continue to try to cross the border without authorisation, as would migrants from the rest of the Americas – and many of them succeeded. US attitudes towards migration across the Mexican border have swung wildly in the decades since, largely depending on the state of the American economy at the time. In the 1980s, for instance, President Reagan granted an amnesty to almost all undocumented migrants who had been in the country for at least four years, a measure that affected more than two and half million people, many of them Mexicans. More recent presidents have attempted to be tougher, with little long-term effect on the flow of people over the border despite increasing threats to the life and liberty of would-be migrants.

Successive administrations believed that they could use fear, coupled with more enforcement officers and modern technology – including drones, remote sensors, 'smart' walls and facial recognition software – to ensure that very few migrants could cross the border. That hasn't happened. In 2021, a group of several thousand Haitians found a very low-tech solution. They waded across the Rio Grande using a rope strung across the river to guide them, watched by TV crews. Other migrants have simply swum around the fence that stretches into the Pacific and which separates the beaches of Tijuana from those of San Diego. Elsewhere along the border, elaborate tunnels have been found, complete with lifts and ventilation systems, while in one place migrants used portable leaf blowers to cover their tracks in the sand. As one governor of Arizona put it, 'show me a fifty-foot wall, and I'll show you a fifty-one-foot ladder'. The ingenuity and resolve of migrants in response to technological advances and the full force of the law has been remarkable, and chastening to those in power. And not just in America.

It's worth reflecting on that modern failure to control movements across borders in the context of the deep history of migration. For what is so often shocking to the sedentary world – among them people who are broadly supportive of migrants – is just how determined, or perhaps foolhardy, many migrants appear to be. That they are willing to take such seemingly suicidal courses of action. And that deterrence doesn't appear to work. The sedentary world expects would-be migrants to be put off by the fear of detention, and even more so by the fear of death. Some are, undoubtedly; but many aren't.

In fact, a significant number of migrants have always taken what appear to many modern humans to be unfathomable risks. In the ancient past, migrants paddled their canoes deep into the ocean, not knowing whether they would ever find land – or crossed unexplored wildernesses patrolled by carnivorous animals in order to see what was on the other side. That willingness to take risks, to disappear into the unknown, is a huge part of the human story. Some of their modern equivalents might attempt to cross the English Channel on a plank of wood or reach a new continent by stowing themselves away in the landing gear of an aeroplane, or hiding in a refrigerated, unventilated container. We've tended to explain this behaviour in terms of desperation, and of the search for safety and a new home. And despair and the search for a home – as a response to poverty, or starvation, or natural disaster, or persecution, or climate change – often play their part. But they also provide a far from sufficient explanation.

It is striking, for instance, how many former wetbacks and *braceros* interviewed in later life use the word 'adventure' to describe why they were so keen to cross the border. They no longer felt the need to pretend that it was simply desperation that made them migrate. For many of them, despite (and sometimes because of) the risk, migration was very exciting. It could feel like a game, outsmarting border guards, marshalling limited resources, hiding one's identity. Then impressing one's peers by being able to send money back home, while still young, to support parents and siblings. And perhaps returning at some point, wearing fashionable clothes, driving a new car filled with foreign gifts for everyone. It was a dream for many, and it came true for some.

For many young Mexicans, and for huge numbers of migrants around the world, the idea of migrating also represented the possibility of independence – of escaping family control in a conservative culture, of not becoming like one's parents, of meeting new people quite different from oneself, of finding a spouse from beyond one's home town. Risks would have to be taken if one wanted to achieve any of that. And remember, for one moment, the kind of absurdly risky behaviours we expect of the young at other times: when fighting for their countries, for instance. Why would they not put up with similar risks for their own benefit rather than that of their particular nation-state?

Some of those possible benefits are practical ones: the prospect of a decent job, better health care, a room of one's own, a longer life, a good education for one's children and, of course, freedom from persecution. But there are, and always have been since the most ancient of times, a tangled mixture of less tangible reasons why humans migrate. Too often in this sedentary world of borders and nation-states, we forget that history. We forget that we humans also migrate because we are bored, or curious, or adventurous, or enjoy a challenge or because we wish to fulfil a dream. And we have, over the millennia, migrated almost everywhere, and continue to do so, despite every attempt to stop us. Our migration history is one of the things that differentiates us most starkly from our closest cousins, our fellow apes. Can we begin to commemorate that? And can we recognise that our history as migrants and the descendants of migrants is something that we all have in common?

Note from the Author

This book has been on a long, shape-shifting journey. Its first words – prompted by the plight of Bangladeshi migrants in India – were written in Delhi in the early years of this millennium. Several dozen paragraphs and a rough outline were then carted around the world in the hard drives of a succession of ill-treated laptops. A plaintive first chapter was composed in Dar es Salaam – and completely rewritten as an angry polemic in Abuja. Then, while living in Kabul, surrounded by people who wished to migrate but couldn't do so legally, I lost heart and stopped writing.

There were two reasons I gave up. First, because the public debate about migrants, particularly in the West, had become so unpleasantly vitriolic, so deeply partisan, so shockingly chauvinistic that I felt that no one would listen. Second, I had plunged, in my reading, deep into the academic domain that has become known as migration studies, which is preoccupied with migration as a contemporary phenomenon and often typecasts, for well-meaning reasons, the migrant as a 'special case', as an anomaly in the modern world. And this made me feel that I was on my own, a lonely outlier. I had been searching – and failing – to find others who argued that migration is at the centre, not the periphery, of the human story – now, and in the past. Perhaps, I told myself, I was wrong.

The book was resurrected and recast in 2018, largely as a result of a conversation with a friend in a London pub, who was about to start a novel that dealt, philosophically speaking, with similarly broad and ambitious themes. A chance re-reading of the *Aeneid* (the Robert Fagles translation), picked up dog-eared and ouzo-splashed from a hotel bar on the Greek island of Mathraki, gave me my entry point – a migration story for all ages. I visited the Neanderthal Museum outside Düsseldorf, and began to see a different approach to writing this book, one that was less aggressive, more thoughtful – and one that drew from deep history in a way that could re-establish migration not sedentariness as a constant.

More than that, I had begun to realise I was not alone, and that there were many others who are also discontented with the myth of sedentarism – though they would use different words to describe that discontent. For a growing number of writers, from an unexpectedly broad range of disciplines, seemed to be approaching similar issues in the same spirit as me, even if their detailed approach was often very different. The geographer Tim Cresswell's distinction between a sedentarist and a nomadic metaphysics is a good example of this, as is the philosopher Donatella di Cesare's notion of the 'resident foreigner', and her observation that 'the state . . . is the obstacle that prevents us even thinking about migration'.

Both Cresswell (*On the Move*, Routledge, 2006) and di Cesare (*Resident Foreigners*, Polity, 2021) have had a strong influence on this book. So too have a series of writers who elegantly straddle the worlds of archaeology, anthropology and political science – including James C. Scott (*Against the Grain*, Yale, 2017) and, most recently, David Graeber and David Wengrow (*The Dawn of Everything*, Allen Lane, 2021) – whose works have demythologised and given nuance to our understanding of pre-literate societies, and reminded us of the complexity and variety of the ways humans have organised themselves. Sedentary people living in nation-states was never the inevitable outcome of human evolution, nor is it an accurate description of the modern world.

Reading Robert Garland's *Wandering Greeks* (Princeton, 2014) provided a different kind of breakthrough. Garland, a historian, placed the issue of migration at the heart of the story of ancient Greece – an example that those working in many other fields of history would do well to consider. While Isabel Wilkerson's *The Warmth of Other Suns* (Knopf Doubleday, 2010) played a similar role for me at the other end of the timescale covered in this book, as a superb study of twentieth-century black migration within the USA – and one which focuses on the voices of migrants themselves. Other noticeably well-thumbed books include Sonia Shah's *The Next Great Migration* (Bloomsbury, 2020), Robert Winder's *Bloody Foreigners* (Abacus, 2005) and Reece Jones's *Violent Borders* (Verso, 2016).

I also wish, briefly, to apologise and explain myself to those who were hoping for something else from this book. It does not aim to be a comprehensive history of migration, and there are many important migration stories that I ignore or mention only in passing. Instead, it is – at its most ambitious – a deliberate attempt to reset the dominant historical narrative about migrants, and to provide suggestions as to how that might be done. Nor does this book address directly contemporary issues of migration; indeed it stops quite deliberately in the 1970s, as a way of encouraging us to look at our deep history as migrants, as *Homo Migrans*. Nor does it seek to measure the economic advantages and disadvantages of migration – though I do find it disappointing that so many modern analyses of immigration fail to include the cost of the upbringing and education of future migrants, which are usually borne by poorer countries. And nor, finally, does *Migrants* attempt to provide more than a tangential study of how humanity slipped into sedentarism, or how the idea of 'home' became so important. That's another book, perhaps.

I've relied on several readers. The most assiduous has – as always – been my mother, Jane Miller, a defiant sedentarist who has lived in the same house since before I was born, and has been editing me since the age of three. This book, quite obviously, would not exist without her. Less obviously, it would also not exist without the inexhaustible encouragement, friendship and editorial skills of Janice Pariat, whose effulgent new novel, *Everything the Light Touches*, was published a few months before this. Special thanks also to Daniel Lak, Rana Dasgupta, Kristin Wagner, Alice Alunni, Saskya Jain, Andrew Whitehead, Roxy Miller, Zubin Miller, Penny Richards, Mischa Snaije and Benedict Leigh, each of whom read some or all of the manuscript and helped – in my view at least – to make this a better book. Thanks also to my father, Karl Miller, a migrant from Scotland who also became an arch-sedentarist, and who liked to promulgate the slogan 'East, West? Home's best.' He died several years ago now, but his deep imprint on my thinking and my writing remains. The second half of the book was written in his study, surrounded by his books and his pictures and his ancient typewriters – and, at times, it was as if he was there too.

Then there are those who have supported and suffered this book in other ways, which they may well have forgotten by now, or never known about in the first place. These include Catherine Heaney, Catherine Goodman, Stephen Sackur, Andy Bell, Giulia Negrini, Anita Roy, Urmila Jagannathan, Chloe Saint Laurent, Chloe Paidoussis, Mary Fitzgerald, Rahul Noble Singh, Jenine Abboushi, the Dalrymple family, Anthony Sattin, Neal Ascherson, John Sutherland, Catrin Ormestad, Maurice Aeek, Neil Curry, Kate Miller, Kaia Bell, Rashmee Roshan Lall, Michael Macy, Eloise Carbert, Raz Weiner,

Jennifer Cohen, Maeve Wiley, Mary Kay Magistad, Ferzina Banaji, James Stout, Felix Tusa, Hiang Kee, Fanny Durville, Iman Simon, Niranjani Iyer, Aanchal Kapoor, Martine Taube, Robert Darke, Charlotte Owen, Fiona Green, Clemency Fraser, Elise Ketelaars, Dan Franklin, Bea Hemming, Michael Dwyer, Rachel Dwyer, Salim Murad, Nancy Abdelmalak, Michele Weldon, Martin Hayes, Hugh Thomson, Tira Shubart, Pascale Harter, Peter Sunde, Alexandra Elbakyan, Aaron Swartz, Chas Hamilton, Martin Plaut, Keith Somerville, Elizabeth Wright, Shireen Vakil Miller, Georgia Miller, Ardashir Vakil, Daniel Miller, Sue Preston, Kieran Day, Sherina Feliciano-Santos, Mark Hauser, Hari Menon, Jonathan Crush, Natalia Leigh, Christina Noble, Annette Ekin, Tom Allard, Lucy Peck, Chris Cramer, Caroline Howie, Thalia Polak, Louisa Polak, Jenny Manson, Saul Wordsworth, Laura Payne, Tara Lal, Aradhana Seth, Tom Miller, Christian the Lion and Fergus the Cat.

There are three wider categories of people to whom I have debt of gratitude: librarians, swimmers and colleagues. In that first category I am particularly grateful to those who helped me at the British Library, the Bibliothèque Nationale de France and Totnes public library. Then there are my warm-water sea-swimming companions in Greece, Italy, Turkey, Oman and Mexico – who've endured or encouraged my migration monologues whenever we've been on dry land – and my BBC Media Action colleagues based in India, Tanzania, Nigeria, Afghanistan, Cambodia, Ethiopia, Lebanon, Tunisia and Indonesia, whose views and experiences of migration have helped shape some of the discussions within this book.

Thanks to the publishing professionals who shepherded this book towards publication – these include my agent Eleanor Birne, and her colleagues Margaret Halton, John Ash and Patrick Walsh at Pew Literary. And, of course, Richard Beswick, Zoe Gullen, Linda Silverman, Marie Hrynczak, Bekki Guyatt and the rest of the Little, Brown team.

It has been a tradition of mine to blame my children, Zubin and Roxy, for any errors in my writings, since the days when we shared one computer. That is no longer credible, so it's time to admit that the mistakes are all mine. But I have, in the continuance of another tradition, inserted a very minor error as a small joke. If you are the first to spot it, tell me: you will be rewarded appropriately, as will anyone who can tell me why this book ends with the word 'breathe'.

References

Prologue

2 *He is Aeneas of Troy:* My account of Aeneas as a migrant is based on Virgil's *Aeneid* – written more than a millennium after the events it purports to describe. Shadi Bartsch's English-language version of the *Aeneid* (Random House, 2021) is highly recommended. In the opening lines of her translation, Aeneas is a refugee: 'My song is of war and a man: a refugee by fate.' Elsewhere, he is typically described as an exile or a fugitive.

5 *a broad definition:* Greg Madison, *The End of Belonging: Untold Stories of Leaving Home and the Psychology of Global Relocation* (Createspace, 2009), p. 27n.

7 *'We called for workers':* My translation of *Wir haben Arbeitskräfte gerufen, und es sind Menschen gekommen.* From Max Frisch's introduction to Alexander Seiler's *Siamo Italiani – die Italiener: Gespräche mit italienischer Gastarbeitern* (EVZ-Verlag, 1965), p. 7.

7 *Migration, some are now arguing:* See, for instance, Gaia Vince, *Nomad Century: How to Survive the Climate Upheaval* (Allen Lane, 2022).

8 *Canadian city of Kingston:* Robert MacNaughton et al., 'First steps on land: Arthropod trackways in Cambrian-Ordovician eolian sandstone, southeastern Ontario, Canada', *Geology*, 30:5 (2002), pp. 391–4.

9 *animals known as cynodonts:* Kennth D. Angielczyk and Christian F. Kammerer, 'Non-mammalian synapsids: The deep roots of the mammalian family tree', in Frank E. Zachos and Robert J. Asher (eds), *Mammalian Evolution, Diversity and Systematics* (De Gruyter, 2018), pp. 162–3.

10n *The cynodonts' world:* On Pangaean distribution, see ibid., p. 203. For rat–human ancestry, see Guillaume Bourque, Pavel A. Pevzner and Glenn Tesler, 'Reconstructing the genomic architecture of ancestral mammals: Lessons from human, mouse, and rat genomes', *Genome Research*, 14:4 (2004), p. 513.

10n *daily micro-migrations:* Barbara Fruth, Nikki Tagg and Fiona Stewart, 'Sleep and nesting behavior in primates: A review', *American Journal of Physical Anthropology*, 166:3 (2018), p. 501.

10n *the lemurs of Madagascar:* Jason Ali and Matthew Huber, 'Mammalian biodiversity on Madagascar controlled by ocean currents', *Nature*, 463 (2010), pp. 653–5.

12 *forty thousand years ago:* Tom Higham et al., 'The timing and spatiotemporal patterning of Neanderthal disappearance', *Nature*, 512 (2014), pp. 306–9.

Chapter One

13 *This part of the Neander valley:* Frederic Rich, 'The Neander Valley: The place we learned we were not alone', *SiteLINES: A Journal of Place*, 11:2 (2016), pp. 5–7.

14 *those of modern humans:* Rebecca Wragg Sykes, *Kindred: Neanderthal Life, Love, Death and Art* (Bloomsbury Sigma, 2020), p. 21.

14 *named Homo Neanderthalensis:* By Professor William King. See *Report of the 33rd Meeting of the British Association for the Advancement of Science* (John Murray, 1864), Notices and Abstracts, pp. 81–2.

14n *Homo Stupidus:* James Walker, David Clinnick and Mark White, 'We are not alone: William King and the naming of the Neanderthals', *American Archaeologist*, 123:4 (2021), p. 9.

14n *Professor August Mayer:* Wragg Sykes, 2020, p. 25.

15n *The valley was named after:* Helmut Ackermann, *Joachim Neander: Sein Leben, Seine Lieder, Sein Tal* (Grupello, 2005), p. 10.

19 *Neanderthals and Sapiens had sex:* David Reich, *Who We Are and How We Got Here* (OUP, 2018), p. 40.

19n *A number of other hominids:* João Teixeira et al., 'Widespread Denisovan ancestry in Island Southeast Asia but no evidence of substantial super-archaic hominin admixture', *Nature Ecology & Evolution*, 5:5 (2021), p. 616.

21 *a third of the world's population was nomadic:* James C. Scott, *Against the Grain* (Yale, 2017), p. 14.

22 *southernmost tip of South America:* For the earliest evidence of human settlement on Tierra del Fuego see Luis Alberto Borrero, 'Taphonomy of the Tres Arroyos 1 Rockshelter, Tierra del Fuego, Chile', *Quaternary International*, 109–10 (2003), pp. 87–93. On genetic isolation see Constanza de la Fuente et al., 'Genomic insights into the origin and diversification of late maritime hunter-gatherers from the Chilean Patagonia', *Proceedings of the National Academy of Sciences of the USA*, 115:17 (2018).

22 *earliest humans in North America:* For a summary of recent research on early human migration to the Americas see Ben A. Potter et al., 'Current evidence allows multiple models for the peopling of the Americas', *Science Advances*, 4:8 (2018). For the Kelp Highway Hypothesis, see Jon M. Erlandson et al., 'The Kelp Highway Hypothesis: Marine ecology, the Coastal Migration Theory, and the peopling of the Americas', *Journal of Island and Coastal Archaeology*, 2:2 (2007), pp. 161–74.

24 *Magellan of Portugal:* Anne Chapman, *European Encounters with the Yamana*

People of Cape Horn, Before and After Darwin (CUP, 2010), p. 193. The Yaghan are also often referred to as Yahgan or as Yamana – the last of these is the name by which they usually describe themselves. However Yamana is also used to denote all humanity, while Yahgan or Yaghan originally referred to people who live on either side of a particular stretch of water known in English as the Murray Narrows.

24 *the Elizabethides:* Ibid., p. 18.

24 *seventeen sailors from a Dutch fleet:* Ibid., p. 26.

25 *Captain FitzRoy took hostages:* Ibid., pp. 122, 145.

25 *sent to boarding school:* Ibid., p. 155.

25 *only surviving portraits:* Ibid., pp. 165–6.

25 *Darwin later described the teenage Jemmy:* Entry for 5 March 1834, in Nora Barlow (ed.), *Charles Darwin's Diary of the Voyage of HMS* Beagle (CUP, 1933), p. 215.

25n *FitzRoy was of royal blood:* Peter Nichols, *Evolution's Captain: The Story of the Kidnapping That Led to Charles Darwin's Voyage Aboard the* Beagle (HarperCollins, 2004), pp. 15, 21. Devotees of the British shipping forecast may know that in 2002, the Finisterre shipping area in the Atlantic Ocean was renamed FitzRoy in honour of his role in British meteorology.

25n *Button was bought:* Chapman, 2010, pp. 127–41.

26 *These poor wretches:* Charles Darwin, *Journal of Researches into the Natural History and Geology of the Countries Visited during the Voyage of the HMS* Beagle *round the World* (Appleton, 1871), pp. 213, 215–16.

27 *'We could not recognise poor Jemmy':* Charles Darwin's Diary, 1933, p. 215.

27n *Darwin's low opinion:* Chapman, 2010, pp. 181–2.

28 *Yaghan-researching journalist:* Jack Hitt, 'Say no more', *New York Times*, 29 February 2004. According to Hitt, Cristina Calderón asked 'impossible sums of money' for an interview. Instead, he spoke to her sister-in-law.

29 *cult movie, Life in a Day:* Documentary film directed by Kevin Macdonald, Scott Free Productions, 2011. The explanation of *mamihlapinatapai* is at 51′40″.

29 *the concept of mamihlapinatapai:* For the history and mythology that surrounds this word, see Anna Bitong, 'Mamihlapinatapai: A lost language's untranslatable legacy', BBC.com, 3 April 2018.

An Early Intermission

32 *a string of markers in our genome:* The distribution of the gene was discussed as long ago as 1996 in F. M. Chang et al., 'The world-wide distribution of allele frequencies at the human dopamine D4 receptor locus', *Human Genetics*, 98:1 (1996), pp. 91–101.

33 *growing evidence of a correlation:* The migration context is considered in depth in Luke Matthews and Paul Butler, 'Novelty-seeking DRD4 polymorphisms are associated with human migration distance out-of-Africa after controlling for neutral population gene structure', *American Journal of Physical Anthropology*, 145:3 (2011), pp. 382–9. See also J. L. Royo et al., 'A common copy-number variant within SIRPB1 correlates with

human Out-of-Africa migration after genetic drift correction', *PLOS One*, 13:3 (2018).

Chapter Two

36 *About twelve thousand years ago:* Scott, 2017, p. 5.

36 *first non-migrants lived in places of abundance:* Ibid., pp. 65, 72.

36 *border of two climatic zones:* Ibid., p. 52.

36n *such as Göbekli Tepe:* E. B. Banning, 'So fair a house: Göbekli Tepe and the identification of temples in the pre-pottery Neolithic of the Near East', *Current Anthropology*, 52:5 (2011), pp. 619–60.

36n *villages in Palestine:* Ofer Bar-Yosef, 'The Natufian culture in the Levant, threshold to the origins of agriculture', *Evolutionary Anthropology*, 6:5 (1998), pp. 159–77. Some of the earliest villages were not in Mesopotamia but in Israel/Palestine. These were part of what is referred to as the 'Natufian culture', which flourished at least twelve thousand years ago. Most Natufians remained hunter-gatherers, but they also cultivated grain and baked bread. Hunter-gatherers had used some agricultural techniques for millennia – harvesting wild grains, burning the undergrowth, killing only male animals – but year-round agriculture was only possible for people who lived in one location.

37 *single-room circular huts:* Kent Flannery, 'The origins of the village revisited: From nuclear to extended households', *American Antiquity*, 67:3 (2002), pp. 417–33. On agriculture and inequality, see Kent Flannery and Joyce Marcus, *The Creation of Inequality: How Our Prehistoric Ancestors Set the Stage for Monarchy, Slavery, and Empire* (Harvard, 2012).

37 *earliest significant evidence of human inequality:* There's been much recent discussion about this following the publication of David Graeber and David Wengrow, *The Dawn of Everything: A New History of Everything* (Allen Lane, 2021). They argue persuasively that greater inequality was not an immediate or inevitable outcome of the agricultural revolution. But it did, one can still argue, make it more likely.

38 *first city-states emerged:* Marc Van De Mieroop, *A History of the Ancient Near East* (Wiley Blackwell, 2016), p. 24.

38 *personal property in land:* Jane R. McIntosh, *Mesopotamia and the Rise of Civilization: History, Documents, and Key Questions* (ABC-CLIO, 2017), pp. 67–70.

40 *what we would now refer to as racism:* I have come across one description of a specific member of a nomadic group being a 'monkey from the mountains', and having the 'mind of a dog'. See Anne Porter, *Mobile Pastoralism and the Formation of Near Eastern Civilizations* (CUP, 2012), p. 295.

40 *'Pure are the cities':* Translation from Jeremy Black et al., *The Electronic Text Corpus of Sumerian Literature (ETCSL)*, Oxford 1998–2006, https://etcsl. orinst.ox.ac.uk/cgi-bin/etcsl.cgi?text=t.1.1.1.

40 *the Marriage of Martu:* Ibid., lines 126–41. Discussion in Porter, 2012, pp. 290–4.

41 *world's first great work of literature:* Many overlapping versions of *Gilgamesh*

have survived in varying degrees of completeness. I've used the accessible but scholarly edition (with lacunae) compiled and translated by Andrew George as *The Epic of Gilgamesh* (Penguin, 2003).

42 *'Enkidu was erect'*: Gilgamesh, 2003, lines 193–4.

43–4 *'fugitive and a vagabond'*: Genesis 5:12. All quotations are, unless indicated, taken from the King James version of the Bible

44 *'be fruitful, multiply'*: Genesis 9:1.

44 *Table of Nations*: Genesis 10.

44n *Mrs Noah and her three daughters-in-law*: R.H. Charles, *The Book of Jubilees or the Little Genesis* (Adam and Charles Black, 1902), pp. 42, 60–1.

46 *'Get thee out of thy country'*: Genesis 12:1.

46 *'I will make of thee a great nation'*: Genesis 12:2.

46 *having made a fortune*: According to Genesis 13:2, Abraham became 'very rich in cattle, in silver, and in gold'.

47 *descendants of Abraham happily settled in Egypt*: Genesis 47:27, 'Israel dwelt in the land of Egypt, in the country of Goshen; and they had possessions therein, and grew, and multiplied exceedingly.'

48 *four generations earlier*: According to Exodus 12:40, they had actually been in Egypt for 430 years. But generations in the early parts of the Bible last a lot longer than they do today.

48 *'more and mightier than we'*: Exodus 1:9.

48 *'a stranger in a strange land'*: Exodus 2:22.

48n *He said this while*: Christiana van Houten, *The Alien in Israelite Law: A Study of the Changing Legal Status of Strangers in Ancient Israel* (Bloomsbury, 1991), pp. 15–20.

49 *married a non-Israelite*: Numbers 12:1. Moses' siblings Aaron and Miriam refer to their sister-in-law as Cushite (Ethiopian in the Vulgate and King James versions), which could bear the sense of being dark skinned. Because of her unfriendly and arguably racist attitude toward Moses' wife, God gives Miriam leprosy.

49 *'keep alive for yourselves'*: Numbers 31:18. Though the Midianites magically reappear for Gideon to destroy them all over again in Judges 7.

49 *adult male migrants*: Numbers 14:30. They were Moses, Joshua and Caleb.

50 *'ye were strangers'*: Exodus 22:21, 23:9; Leviticus 19:34; Deuteronomy 10:19. And Moses also declares (Leviticus 19:10, 23:22) that farmers should not cut their crops to the very edges of the field, nor should they gather gleanings nor fallen grapes. Instead, he says 'thou shalt leave them for the poor and the stranger'.

51 *exiled Jewish king, Jeconiah*: Edwin Yamauchi, 'The Eastern Jewish Diaspora under the Babylonians', in Mark W. Chavalas and K. Lawson Younger, *Mesopotamia and the Bible: Comparative Explorations* (Sheffield Academic Press, 2003), pp. 359–61. The King James Bible has several different versions and spellings of Jeconiah, including Jehoiachin, which is more widely used by modern archaeologists and historians, and is closer to the name the Babylonians used for him. For discussion of the ration tablets and other foreigners in Babylon, see Tero Alstola, *Judeans in Babylonia: A Study of Deportees in the Sixth and Fifth Centuries BCE* (Brill, 2019), pp. 65–9.

51 *the most populous city:* Ian Morris, *The Measure of Civilization: How Social Development Decides the Fate of Nations* (Princeton, 2013), pp. 147, 155.

52 *mingling of 'the holy seed':* Ezra 9:2.

52 *'put away' or expel all the foreign wives:* Ezra 10:19.

52n *the 42,360 Jews:* Ezra 2:64–7.

52n *Esther, the great-granddaughter:* Esther 2:5–17.

53n *there's a cuneiform tablet:* K. Lawson Younger, 'Recent Study on Sargon II, King of Assyria: Implications of Biblical Studies', in Chavalas and Younger, 2003, p. 291.

54 *Bartolomé de Las Casas:* Tudor Parfitt, *The Lost Tribes of Israel: The History of a Myth* (Weidenfeld & Nicolson, 2002), pp. 34–5,

55 *Juan de Torquemada decided:* Ibid., p. 26.

55 *'Their eye is little and black':* William Penn, *Select Works of William Penn*, vol. 3 (London, 1825), pp. 227–32.

55 *Newark Holy Stones:* J. Huston McCulloch 'The Newark, Ohio Decalogue Stone and Keystone' (1999), accessible at https://www.asc.ohio-state.edu/mcculloch.2/arch/decalog.html.

56 *the British were also a Lost Tribe:* Parfitt, 2002, pp. 52–65.

56 *two million members:* Ibid., p. 52.

56 *'Dan' or almost-Dan in their name:* See Philip Neal, *America & Britain: Two Nations that Changed the World* (York Publishing Company, 2014), pp. 78–80.

58 *The Babylonish EU:* See https://www.britishisrael.co.uk/showart.php?id=113.

58 *in the Nordic countries:* For Nordic Israelism, see Mikkel Stjernholm Kragh, 'Witnesses to the Israelite origin of the Nordic, Germanic, and Anglo-Saxon Peoples' (2008), accessible at http://www.nordiskisrael.dk/artikler/WitnessestoIsraeliteOriginofPeoples.html.

58 *Germans were descended from the Assyrians:* Herbert W. Armstrong, *The United States and Britain in Prophecy* (Everest House, 1980), pp. 178, 183.

A Second Intermission

60 *undermine many of our ethnic and racial certainties:* See Bessie L. Lawton, Anita Foeman and Nicholas Surdel, 'Bridging discussions of human history: Ancestry DNA and new roles for Africana studies', *Genealogy*, 2:1 (2018), and Keith Hunley et al., 'Colonialism, ethnogenesis, and biogeographic ancestry in the US Southwest', *American Journal of Physical Anthropology*, 176:4 (2021).

62 *wonderfully unforgettable name of Israel Israel:* Arthur Ellis Franklin, *Records of the Franklin Family and Collaterals* (Routledge, 1915), p. 111.

62 *three of them married their own first cousins:* Ibid., p. 108.

63n *This is something borne out by genetic studies:* See Dr Gil Atzmon, quoted in Nicholas Wade, 'Studies show Jews' genetic similarity', *New York Times*, 9 June 2010.

Chapter Three

64 *Dido:* Dido was also known as Elissa, the name commonly used in modern Tunis. Her tyrannical brother was called Pygmalion, one of two important figures in classical history with that name. They are sometimes confused. The other Pygmalion fell in love with his own sculptures, and is best remembered now through George Bernard Shaw's play *Pygmalion*, which became the musical *My Fair Lady*. It's been suggested that Shaw named his heroine Eliza because he got his Pygmalions mixed up. If so, he's in good company – Goethe did the same in his *Italian Journey*. Virgil, meanwhile, in his version of the Dido story, gets confused about where she comes from. In the *Aeneid*, he refers to both Tyre and Sidon, still the two biggest cities of southern Lebanon, as her original home. For Shaw, see Derek McGovern, *Eliza Undermined: The Romanticisation of Shaw's Pygmalion*, doctoral thesis, Massey University, 2011, p. 33. In his translation of Goethe's *Italian Journey*, W. H. Auden surreptitiously corrected Goethe's text, substituting Galatea for Elise. For Tyrian Dido see the *Aeneid* Book 1, 446, for Sidonian Dido see Book 9, 266.

65 *The skeleton of the Young Man of Byrsa:* Jean-Paul Morel, 'Les fouilles de Byrsa (secteur B) à Carthage: un bilan', *Comptes rendus des séances de l'Académie des Inscriptions et Belles-Lettres*, 155:1 (2011), 330–1.

65 *A forensic reconstruction:* See 'Documentaire: le jeune homme de Byrsa', 2013, on YouTube https://www.youtube.com/watch?v=hL3HNg6KMpY

65 *DNA was extracted from the bone fragments:* Lisa Matisoo-Smith et al., 'A European mitochondrial haplotype identified in ancient Phoenician remains from Carthage, North Africa', *PLOS One*, 11:5 (2016).

67 *stray reference in Aristotle's* Politics: Aristotle, *Politics* (Penguin, 1992), p. 159, 2.1273b

68 *the Greeks built no less than 270 independent settlements:* At least 279 such settlements according to Robert Garland, *Wandering Greeks: The Ancient Greek Diaspora from the Age of Homer to the Death of Alexander the Great* (Princeton, 2014), p. 35. For a list of settlements see Mogens Herman Hansen and Thomas Heine Nielsen, *An Inventory of Archaic and Classical Poleis* (OUP, 2004), pp. 1390–6.

69 *It is clear that the city-state:* I've joined together two translations from Garland, 2014, p. 26, and altered the first one so that *polis* is translated as city-state throughout. Original from Aristotle, *Politics*, 1.1253a.

69 *When Zeus the Thunderer:* Homer, *Iliad*, 24.531–33.

69 *'no life is worse for mortals than roaming':* Homer, *Odyssey*, 15.343.

70 *'the greatest misfortune':* Euripides, *Phoenician Women*, 1.389. Garland, 2014, translation, p. 21. The speaker is Polyneices, talking to Jocasta, who was both his mother and his paternal grandmother – which some might consider a greater misfortune. Polyneices' father was, of course, Oedipus.

70 *he was accused:* Particularly by Plutarch in his essay 'The Malice of Herodotus', *On Writing History from Herodotus to Herodian: Lucian Dionysius & Plutarch* (Penguin, 2017), pp. 296–326.

70 *notion of 'the Greeks':* The word 'Greece' comes to us from Latin and was

used to describe Greek migrants in Italy. *Hellas* is the Greek word, while many west Asian and south Asian languages use varieties of the word Ionian, so that in Sanskrit, Greece is *yavana* and in Arabic it is *yunan* and in Hebrew it is *yawan*. That Hebrew version is reflected in the name of Noah's grandson Javan, who is mentioned in the Table of Nations in the Old Testament, and who became the legendary founder of the Greeks in some Jewish and Christian traditions.

71 *apoikia, meaning 'home away from home':* Garland, 2014, pp. 35, 241–3. See also Robin Osborne, 'Early Greek Colonization? The Nature of Greek Settlement in the West', in Nick Fisher and Hans van Wees (eds), *Archaic Greece: New Approaches and New Evidence* (Duckworth, 1998), pp. 268–9.

72 *Greek poet Pindar, 'born of the earth':* Garland, 2014, p. 32, and see further discussion in Jonathan M. Hall, *Ethnic Identity in Greek Antiquity* (CUP, 2000), p. 54.

72 *'We Athenians, the most ancient people':* Herodotus, *Histories* 7.161. For this translation and wider discussion, see Benjamin Isaac, *The Invention of Racism in Classical Antiquity* (Princeton, 2006), pp. 114–15.

72n *According to Apollodorus:* See his *Biblioteca*, 3.14.6. Euripides, *Ion*, 542. Thucydides, *History of the Peloponnesian War*, 1.2.1.

73 *a large community of foreign migrants:* Garland, 2014, pp. 155–64. For further discussion on the number of *metics* in Athens see James Watson, 'The origin of metic status at Athens', *Cambridge Classical Journal*, 56 (2010), pp. 259–78.

73 *'He behaved as resident foreigners should behave':* Euripides, *The Suppliants*, 891–3. Translation from Garland, 2014, p. 163.

74 *Miletus, on what is now the coast of Turkey:* Garland, 2014, p. 30. Pliny in his *Natural History* (V.112) says 'Miletus is the mother of over ninety cities'.

74 *Greek is still spoken:* See Neal Ascherson, *Black Sea* (Jonathan Cape, 1995), pp. 187–96; on the Pontic Greek language see Nataliya Hrystiv, 'Translating from Mariupolitan Greek, a Severely Endangered Language, into Ukrainian: Historiographic and Sociological Perspectives', in Michał Borodo et al., *Moving Texts, Migrating People and Minority Languages* (Springer, 2017), pp. 33–4.

74 *The Marseille story:* Emile Temime, *Histoire de Marseille* (Editions Jeanne Lafitte, 2006), pp. 7–15. Thucydides, in the *History of the Peloponnesian War*, makes one of the earliest references (1.13.6) to the Phocaean origins of Marseille. The marriage story is told by the third-century CE writer Athenaeus of Naucratis in *The Deipnosophists*, 13.36, which he took from the now missing *Constitution of the Massiliotes* by Aristotle.

74n *the 'Spartan bastards':* see Aristotle, *Politics*, 1306b 20–31.

75 *the earliest known reference to Britain:* Pytheas' book has not survived. However, it is described and quoted from by several later writers, including in Strabo's *Geography*, where Pytheas is described as 'a man upon whom no reliance can be placed' (1.4.2) and 'a charlatan' (3.2.12).

75 *Greek sources about female migrants:* Garland, 2014, pp. 10, 44–5.

76 *relations were said to have been good:* Kathryn Lomas, 'The Polis in Italy: Ethnicity, Colonization, and Citizenship in the Western Mediterranean', in Roger Brock and Stephen Hodkinson, *Alternatives to Athens: Varieties*

of *Political Organization and Community in Ancient Greece* (OUP, 2000), pp. 177–8.

76 *existing inhabitants were driven out:* Thucydides, *History*, 6.3.2.

76 *'where they gather together':* Athenaeus, *Deipnosophists*, 14.31, who referred to Posidonia as Paestum.

76 *informal code of practice:* Garland, 2014, pp. 38–47.

76 *The word asylum was closely associated:* Ibid., pp. 114–30.

77 *madness in the case of one Spartan king:* Herodotus, *Histories*, 6.75.3.

77 *'outrage without limit':* Diodorus Siculus, *Bibliotheca Historica*, 17.13.6.

78 *genial and sophisticated contempt:* Peter Green, *Alexander of Macedon: A Historical Biography* (University of California, 2013), p. 6.

79 *to settle cities and transplant populations:* Diodorus Siculus, *Bibliotheca*, 18.4.4. Translation (with my punctuation) from M. M. Austin, *The Hellenistic World from Alexander to the Roman Conquest: A Selection of Ancient Sources in Translation* (CUP, 2006), p. 56. There's some doubt about whether these were actually Alexander's plans. It's possible that they were drawn up after his death, by one of his successors, see Austin, 2006, p. 55.

81 *compared their nomadic neighbours to real animals:* Mu-Chou Poo, *Enemies of Civilization: Attitudes towards Foreigners in Ancient Mesopotamia, Egypt and China* (State University of New York, 2005), pp. 46, 65–6.

81 *'wolves, to whom no indulgence should be given':* Ibid., p. 65.

81 *'are like the deer, wild birds and the beasts':* Ibid., p. 66. For translation and context see John Knoblock and Jeffrey Riegel (trans.) *The Annals of Lü Buwei* (Stanford, 2000), p. 512.

81 *some writers of this period:* Poo, 2005, pp. 123–4.

81 *one Chinese writer:* The fourth-century BCE Confucian philosopher Mengzi or Mencius. See James Legge, *The Life and Works of Mencius* (Trübner & Co., 1875), p. 368. There is a mysterious absence, almost total, in these ancient accounts, of foreigners who live in Chinese territory. There is one that has been tracked down, from the second century BCE, a prince from a nomadic group, who surrendered to the Chinese at the age of fourteen and became a fully assimilated and successful member of the ruling elite. Except, we are told without further explanation, that 'he did not forget that he was a foreigner': Poo, 2005, p. 129.

82 *Officers are appointed:* J. W. McCrindle (trans.), *Ancient India as Described by Megasthenes and Arrian* (Trübner & Co., 1877), p. 44. The quote is from Diodorus Siculus, *Bibliotheca*, 2.42.3–4.

82 *'of good family, loyal':* Kautilya, *Arthashastra*, 1.12. For translations see R. Shamasastry, *Kautilya's Arthasastra* (Mysore Press, 1951), p. 20.

82 *find out the causes of emigration: Arthashastra*, 2.35 Translation from Shamasastry, 1951, p. 159.

83 *'When the householder notices his wrinkles': Manusmriti*, 6.2 Translation from Ganganatha Jha, *Manu-Smriti: The Laws of Manu with the Bhasya of Medhatithi* (University of Calcutta, 1922), p. 189.

83 *spend a lot of time praying:* Jha, 1922, pp. 190–210.

84 *several scholars noted the similarities:* The eighteenth-century British Orientalist William Jones is usually given credit for first making this observation. For

earlier observers see Edwin Bryant, *The Quest for the Origins of Vedic Culture: The Indo-Aryan Migration Debate* (OUP, 2001), p. 16, and for a broader counter-view see Lyle Campbell and William J Poser, *Language Classification: History and Method* (CUP, 2008), pp. 32–4.

84 *called the Indo-Europeans:* Bryant, 2001, p. 20.

84 *migrants or invaders from the west:* Ibid., pp. 20, 27, 30–5.

84 *homelands were suggested for the Aryans* Ibid., pp. 37–43.

84 *Houston Stewart Chamberlain:* Carl Müller Frøland, *Understanding Nazi Ideology: The Genesis and Impact of a Political Faith* (McFarland, 2020), pp. 68–70, 130. Houston Stewart Chamberlain married Wagner's daughter. On Chamberlain and the intemperate modern arguments about the relationship between European Aryanism and Nazism see Karla Poewe and Irving Hexham, 'Surprising Aryan meditations between German Indology and Nazis: Research and the Adluri/Grünendahl debate', *International Journal of Hindu Studies*, 19:3 (2015), 266–8.

85 *more temperate modern supporters:* Bryant, 2001, p. 306.

85 *Megasthenes had asserted:* Diodorus Siculus, *Bibliotheca*, 2.38.3.

86 *P. N. Oak, an amateur Indian historian:* P. N. Oak, *Some Missing Chapters of World History* (Hindi Sahitya Sadan, 2003).

86n *the uncertain existence of horses:* Bryant, 2001, pp. 169–75.

87 *growing scientific consensus:* See, for instance, Vigheesh Narasimhan et al., 'The formation of human populations in South and Central Asia', *Science*, 365:6457 (2019). The article was co-authored by 117 scientists, historians, archaeologists and anthropologists from India and around the world.

87 *Tony Joseph was accused:* See VijayVan's comments on the review of *Early Indians* at https://www.brownpundits.com/2018/12/29/tony-josephs-early-indians/. See also A. L. Chavda, 'Propagandizing the Aryan Invasion Debate: A Rebuttal to Tony Joseph', Indiafacts.org, 22 June 2017, and comments by Suyash Pandey about Joseph's book posted on Amazon.in on 13 September 2019.

A Third Intermission

90n *named after Persian emperors:* There were seven emperors called Bahram, three called Ardashir, and just one Anoshirvan – which was an alternative name for Khusrow I.

91 *local king held out a jug of milk:* The story is retold, for instance, in Boman Desai's novel *The Memory of Elephants* (University of Chicago, 2001), pp. 22–3.

91 *five anti-Parsi riots:* Namely the 'Bombay Dog' riots of 1832; the Muslim-Parsi riots of 1851, 1857 and 1874; and the anti-Parsi Prince of Wales riots of 1921. See Mitra Sharafi, *Law and Identity in Colonial South Asia: Parsi Legal Culture 1772–1947* (CUP, 2014), p. 29.

91 *Qissa-i Sanjan:* S. H. Hodivala, *Studies in Parsi History* (published by the author, 1920), pp. 102–3. Hodivala's book has a full translation of the *Qissa-i Sanjan* (which he transcribes as Kissah-I-Sanjan).

Chapter Four

94 *'dancing in the dark'*: Ovid, *Black Sea Letters*, IV.2.33–4. All translations from the *Black Sea Letters* and *Tristia* are taken from Peter Green, *Ovid: The Poems of Exile* (University of California, 2005).

94 *'a more remote and nastier spot'*: *Black Sea Letters*, I.3.83.

94 *unsolved mystery*: Green, 2005, pp. xxiv–xxvi. There are some who believe Ovid was never exiled, and that his time in Tomis – described in such detail in *Tristia* – was a literary fiction. See Bram van der Velden, 'J. J. Hartman on Ovid's (non-)exile', *Mnemosyne*, 73 (2020), pp. 336–42.

94n *of Aromanian heritage*: Mike Dickson, 'Wimbledon champion Simona Halep opens up on Covid, breast surgery and her spectacular demolition of Serena in the 2019 final …', *Daily Mail*, 23 June 2021. For Hagi's Aromanian ancestry see Jonathan Wilson, 'Why Gheorghe Hagi is a footballing icon', fourfourtwo.com, 24 July 2017. The town of Ovidiu is just north of Constanta, and was named in modern times after the lake-island of Ovidiu on which, according to local tradition, Ovid was buried. For other 'tombs of Ovid', see J. B. Trapp, 'Ovid's tomb: The growth of a legend from Eusebius to Laurence Sterne, Chateaubriand and George Richmond', *Journal of the Warburg and Courtauld Institutes*, 36:1 (1973), pp. 35–76.

95 *perpetual snow*: Ovid, *Tristia*, III.10.13–16.

95 *treeless, birdless landscape*: *Tristia*, III.10.75; *Black Sea Letters*, III.1.21.

95 *barbarian inhabitants Tristia*, V.10.24.

95 *frozen wine*: Ibid., III.10.23–4.

95 *poems in the local language*: *Black Sea Letters*, IV.13.17–20.

95 *exempting him from local taxes*: Ibid., IV.9.111–12.

95 *'tactless talent'*: Ibid., IV.14.19.

95 *I've done nothing wrong*: Ibid., IV.14.23–4.

95n *Ovid's sentence was formally and unanimously revoked*: See Jon Henley, 'Ovid's exile to the remotest margins of the Roman empire revoked', *Guardian*, 16 December 2017.

96 *'Ovid writes for millions of us'*: Jan Morris, 'Far away and long ago . . .', *Guardian*, 18 June 2005.

96 *'capital of the world'*: Ovid, *Amores*, 1.15.26, or *Metamorphosis*, 14.435. Rome was probably by this time the most populous city in world, with a population of about one million (Morris, 2013, p. 147). Several decades after Ovid referred to Rome as the capital of the world, the Spanish-born Roman poet Lucan was probably the first to use the phrase *caput mundi* – which became in more recent times the best-known Latin version of 'capital of the world', rather than the *caput rerum* or *caput orbis* used by Ovid and others. Lucan, *Pharsalia*, 2.136 and 2.655. For Lucan, Livy and Ovid as sources of the phrase see Charles Tesoriero (ed.), *Lucan* (OUP, 2010), p. 32, and https://www.rerumromanarum. com/2018/10/why-rome-is-called-caput-mundi.html

96 *the city's inhabitants*: Margaret Antonio et al., 'Ancient Rome: A genetic crossroads of Europe and the Mediterranean', *Science,* 366:3466 (2019), pp. 708–14.

96 *'what people is so remote'*: Martial, *Liber Spectaculorum*, 3.1–2.

96n *Unlike the Athenians:* Seneca, *Of Consolation to Helvia*, 7.5. Seneca – born in Cordoba – was writing to his mother Helvia from Corsica where he had been exiled by Emperor Claudius for adultery with the Emperor's niece Julia Livilla. He later killed himself on the orders of Emperor Nero.

97 *the only Trojan destined to survive:* Homer, *Iliad*, 20.349.

97n *'the Trojan king, as will his descendants':* Ibid., 20.355

98 *claimed direct descent from Aeneas:* The family was called the gens Julia. See Livy, *History of Rome*, I.3

98 *given a magical shield:* Virgil, *Aeneid*, VIII.625.

98 *'as various in their dress and weapons':* Ibid., VIII.723.

98 *'miscellaneous rabble':* Three different translations of the same passage by Livy, *History of Rome*, I.8, by, respectively, Benjamin Oliver Foster (1919), Aubrey de Sélincourt (1960) and William Mesfan Roberts (1912). The translation 'wanting nothing but a fresh start' is also from de Sélincourt.

99 *story of Romulus and the Sabine women:* See the discussion in Mary Beard, *SPQR: A History of Ancient Rome* (Profile, 2016), pp. 60–4, and Robert Brown, 'Livy's Sabine women and the ideal of Concordia', *Transactions of the American Philological Association*, 125 (1995), pp. 292–7. On *raptio* see William Smith, *Latin–English Dictionary* (John Murray, 1947), p. 615.

99 *pre-Tomis* Ars Amatoria: Ovid, *Art of Love*, 1.101–134.

100 *a lengthy war:* Livy, *History of Rome*, I.8–13.

100n *uniting and blending the two peoples:* Plutarch, *Romulus*, 14.6. Translation: Bernadotte Perrin, *Plutarch's Lives*, vol. 1 (Heinemann, 1914), p. 131. Recording of 'The Sobbin' Women' available at https://www.youtube.com/watch?v=846by3LOKlA. Lyrics by Johnny Mercer and Gene de Paul.

101 *Livy describes them as 'savage Gauls':* Ibid., V.36–43. Quotations from Aubrey de Sélincourt (trans.), *The Early History of Rome* (Penguin, 1980).

102 *There's a brief, revealing conversation:* Acts 23.28.

102 *'I appeal unto Caesar':* Acts 25.12.

102 *a friendly centurion called Julius:* Acts 27.1–3.

103 *he was executed on the orders of Emperor Nero:* In the *Apocrypha*, Acts of Paul, 14.5, or see General Audience of Pope Benedict XVI, 4 February 2009, available at https://www.vatican.va/content/benedict-xvi/en/audiences/2009/documents/hf_ben-xvi_aud_20090204

104 *Rome had been brought to the provinces:* There's a continuing debate about the extent of Romanisation in the Empire, and the degree to which local practices and traditions endured. See David Mattingly 'Being Roman: Expressing identity in a provincial setting', *Journal of Roman Archaeology*, 17 (2004), pp. 5–25.

104 *the town of Italica:* Appian, *Iberian Wars*, VII.38. Italica was probably the second Roman settlement outside Italy, after Taracco, modern Tarragona, also in Spain.

104 *the first Roman emperor who didn't come from Italy:* Or, strictly speaking, the Roman province of Italia, which covered most of modern Italy, and parts of Slovenia and Croatia.

104 *adopted as the successor:* Beard, 2016, pp. 419–20.

104 *model himself on Alexander:* Julian Bennett, *Trajan Optimus Princeps: A Life and Times,* (Routledge, 1997), p. 192.

105 *the Roman Empire was its largest:* Rein Taagepera, 'Size and duration of empires: Growth-decline curves, 600 BC to 600 AD', *Social Science History,* 3:4 (1979), pp. 115–38.

105 *rationale for Hadrian's Wall:* Beard, 2016, pp. 484–5.

105 *excavations at Vindolanda:* Philip Parker, *The Empire Stops Here* (Jonathan Cape, 2009), pp. 36–7.

106 *One letter-writer:* Vindolanda Tablet 164. See https:// romaninscriptionsofbritain.org/inscriptions/TabVindol164

106 *'some socks and two pairs of underpants':* Vindolanda Tablet 346. See https:// romaninscriptionsofbritain.org/inscriptions/TabVindol346

106 *a tombstone was unearthed:* See https://romaninscriptionsofbritain.org/ inscriptions/1065

107 *Julia was born:* Anthony Birley, *Septimius Severus: The African Emperor* (Routledge, 1988), p. 72.

107 *reference to his non-Roman accent:* Historia Augusta: Severus, 19.9; Birley, 1988, p. 35.

107 *a very wide range of ethnic backgrounds:* Beard, 2016, pp. 521–2.

107 *skin pigmentation is barely mentioned:* See Mary Beard, *It's a Don's Life* (Profile, 2009), pp. 80–2, for a broader discussion of race and colour in ancient Rome.

108 *One modern historian believes:* Beard, 2016, p. 527.

108 *why Caracalla took this step:* Ibid., pp. 528–9.

108n *One much later writer:* Birley, 1988, pp. 36, 131.

109 *a man called Gaiseric:* There are no contemporary references to the birthplace of Gaiseric, but the Vandals were thought – at the time of his birth – to have been in the Upper Tisza Valley in what became known as Transcarpathia, and are now the borderlands of Hungary, Romania and Ukraine. See Andy Merrills and Richard Miles, *The Vandals* (Wiley, 2014), pp.30–4.

109 *the remains of the churches:* Merrills and Miles, 2014, pp. 241–8. Lilian Ennabli, *Carthage Chrétienne* (Tunisian Culture Ministry, 2000).

109 *It's Greek originally:* Guy Halsall, *Barbarian Migrations and the Roman West 376–568* (CUP, 2007), pp. 45–7.

110 *the Gauls were war-mad:* Strabo, *Geography,* 4.4.2.

110 *the Irish were promiscuous* Ibid., 4.5.4.

110 *the Ethiopians were crafty* Halsall, 2007, p. 52.

110 *'here I'm the barbarian':* Ovid, *Tristia,* V.10.37.

110 *friendly towards barbarians:* Harold Mattingly, *Tacitus on Britain and Germany* (Penguin, 1948), p. 24.

110–11 *'satisfied with one wife each':* Tacitus, *Germania,* 18. For Tacitus, the British were also barbarians, 'Who the first inhabitants of Britain were, whether natives or immigrants, remains obscure; one must remember we are dealing with barbarians.' *Agricola,* 18.

110n *The Roman orator and philosopher:* Cicero, *Republic,* 1.58, and see Carlos Lévy, 'Cicero, Law, and the Barbarians', in Katell Berthelot et al., *Legal*

Engagement: The Reception of Roman Law and Tribunals by Jews and Other Inhabitants of the Empire (L'Ecole française de Rome, 2021), pp. 29–46.

111 *influence on Nazi ideas:* See Christopher Krebs, *A Most Dangerous Book: Tacitus's Germania from the Roman Empire to the Third Reich* (Norton, 2011).

111 *the English, the Goths and the Vandals:* Tacitus, *Germania*, 40, 43 and 2 respectively.

111 *'astonishingly wild and horribly poor':* Ibid., 46

111 *'the faces and features of men':* Ibid.

112 *A modern German historian:* Alexander Demandt, *Der Fall Roms: die Auflösung des römischen Reiches im Urteil der Nachwelt* (Beck, 1984), p. 695. List available at https://courses.washington.edu/rome250/gallery/ROME%20 250/210%20Reasons.htm

113 *the contemporary Roman writer:* Ammianus, *The Roman History of Ammianus Marcellinus*, 31.4–13.

114 *strongest and more eloquent criticism:* Ibid., 31.2.

114n *Mary Beard, the modern historian:* Mary Beard, 'Ancient Rome and today's migrant crisis', *Wall Street Journal*, 16 October 2015.

115n *Historians now tend:* For further discussion of the historiography of these terms see Chapter One of Walter Goffart's *Barbarian Tides: The Migration Age and the Later Roman Empire* (University of Pennsylvania, 2009), while the political scientist Jakub Grygiel, in his *Return of the Barbarians: Confronting Non-State Actors from Ancient Rome to the Present* (CUP, 2018), sets out what he sees as the similarities between Rome and today in terms of the threat posed by 'barbarians'.

117 *widow of the emperor:* Merrills and Miles, 2014, p. 116.

117 *specific acts of vandalism:* Ibid., p. 117. They also took objects stolen by the Romans during the destruction of the 2nd Temple in Jerusalem in 70 CE.

117 *striking continuity with the Roman period:* Walter Pohl, 'The Vandals: Fragments of a Narrative', in Andy Merrills (ed.), *Vandals, Romans and Berbers: New Perspectives on Late Antique North Africa* (Routledge, 2004), pp. 42–6.

118 *a revolutionary French priest:* Merrills and Miles, 2014, pp. 12–14.

118n *modern experts on the Vandals:* Ibid., pp. 11, 185–92.

119 *ruined arcades of a forgotten church:* Ibid., pp. 156–7.

119 *one of the great battles of ancient times:* Peter Heather, *The Fall of the Roman Empire: A New History of Rome and the Barbarians* (OUP, 2006), pp. 402–6. Heather argues that the defeat of the Byzantine armada at Cap Bon 'doomed one half of the Roman world to extinction'.

Chapter Five

126 *He was Abd al-Rahman:* The most detailed version of the life of Abd al-Rahman is by the seventeenth-century North African historian Ahmad Ibn Maqqari. See Pascual de Gayangos, *The History of the Mohammedan Dynasties in Spain by Ahmed ibn Mohammed al-Makkari*, vol. 2, book 5 (W. H. Allen, 1840), pp. 59–72. He is also sometimes referred to as 'the Entrant', an alternative translation for the Arabic *dākhil*, and as 'the Falcon' – a nickname bestowed on him by his Abbasid enemies.

126 *its tolerance and learning:* See the discussion in Robert Irwin, 'The contested legacy of Muslim Spain', *New York Review of Books*, 12 March 2019.

126n *Andalusia is Vandalusia:* For an extended discussion see Alejandro García-Sanjuán, 'al-Andalus, etymology and name', *Encyclopedia of Islam* (Brill, 2017), pp. 18–25.

127 *A palm tree stands:* de Gayangos, 1840, Vol 2, Book 7, p. 77. Translation from D. Fairchild Ruggles, *Gardens, Landscape, and Vision in the Palaces of Islamic Spain* (Pennsylvania State University, 1999), p. 42.

127 *Some etymologists argue:* Tim Mackintosh-Smith, *Arabs: A 3,000–year History of Peoples, Tribes and Empires* (Yale, 2019), pp. 38–40, 44.

127 *a record of the word Arab being used:* Daniel Luckenbill (trans.), *Ancient Records of Assyria and Babylonia*, vol. 1 (Chicago, 1926), p. 223. For discussion, see Mackintosh-Smith, 2019, pp. 30–1.

128 *a culture of wandering:* Mackintosh-Smith, 2019, p. 77.

128 *the so-called 'brigand poets':* Ibid., p. 99.

128 *'nose-rein of a camel':* Charles Horne and George Sale (trans.), *The Sacred Books and Early Literature of the East*, vol. 5 (Parke Austin and Lipscombe, 1917), p. 23.

128 *'worn out my mounts':* Mackintosh-Smith, 2019, p. 98.

128 *An unnamed Arab:* Ibid., p. 38.

128n *Imrul Qays died near Ankara:* Ibrahim Mumayiz, 'Imru' al-Qays and Byzantium', *Journal of Arabic Literature*, 36:2 (2005), pp. 135–51.

129 *one of the most populous cities in the world:* Tertius Chandler and Gerald Fox, *3000 Years of Urban Growth* (Academic Press, 1976), p. 308. Chandler and Fox estimate the population of Cordoba in the year 1000 to be 450,000. However, recent studies suggest that Kaifeng in China was by then the most populous city in the world, with Cordoba the largest in Europe. Morris, 2013, pp. 147–50, 156–8.

129 *stories from the life of the Prophet:* The most easily accessible early sources are Ibn Ishaq's *Sirat Rasul Allah*, translated by Alfred Guillaume as *The Life of Muhammad* (OUP, 1955), and Ma'mar ibn Rashid's *Kitab al-Maghazi*, translated by Sean Anthony as *The Expedition: An Early Biography of Muhammad* (NYU, 2014).

130 *That first longer migration:* See Guillaume, 1955, p. 146, in which Ibn Ishaq refers to the journey to Ethiopia as the 'first hijra'.

130n *According to some accounts:* See Mackintosh-Smith, 2019, p. 126, who makes the comparison with boarding schools.

131 *probably larger than Rome's:* Taagepera, 1979, p. 125, and Rein Taagepera, 'Expansion and contraction patterns of large polities', *International Studies Quarterly*, 41 (1997), p. 481.

132 *Cornelius, a Roman centurion:* Acts 10.1–33. For the Ethiopian eunuch see Acts 9.38. It's possible that the Ethiopian was a Jew prior to converting to Christianity.

133 *two dozen non-Arabs:* Including in Wikipedia: see https://en.wikipedia.org/wiki/List_of_non-Arab_Sahabah

133 *thirty-three thousand descendants:* By the tenth-century Arab historian Mas'udi. See Paul Lunde and Caroline Stone (trans.) *The Meadows of Gold* (Routledge, 1989), p. 202.

134 *pre-Islamic aristocracy:* Brian Catlos, *A New History of Islamic Spain* (Hurst, 2018), pp. 35–6.

134n *There was also some intermarriage:* Évariste Lévi-Provençal, 'Du nouveau sur le royaume de Pampelune au IXe siècle', *Bulletin hispanique* (1953), pp. 18–21.

135 *future Christian saint:* Catlos, 2018, pp. 155–6.

135 *future Pope Sylvester:* Ibid., p. 170.

135 *Eastern European slaves:* Ibid., pp. 86, 148–9.

135 *a Viking raid on Seville:* Philip Parker, *The Northmen's Fury: A History of the Viking World* (Vintage, 2014), pp. 81–2.

135 *worked as cheesemakers:* Hugh Kennedy, *Muslim Spain and Portugal: A Political History of al-Andalus* (Routledge, 1996), p. 46. Some recent historians have argued that the Viking cheesemakers never existed and are a misreading of the ninth-century Arab legal scholar Ibn Habib. See Ann Christys, *Vikings in the South: Voyages to Iberia and the Mediterranean* (Bloomsbury, 2015), pp. 20–1.

136 *slightly apologetic Anglophone historians:* The pushback against the stereotypical view of Vikings among English-language writers goes back to the 1960s. See, for instance, Peter Sawyer, *The Age of the Vikings* (Edward Arnold, 1962), pp. 8–9. However, some continue to cleave to those older stereotypes. See Melanie McDonagh, 'Sorry – the Vikings really were that bad', *Spectator*, 10 August 2013.

136n *The Viking Age:* See Clare Downham, 'Viking ethnicities: A historiographic overview', *History Compass*, 10:1 (2012), pp. 1–12; and on those horned helmets see Roderick Dale 'From Barbarian to Brand: The Vikings as a Marketing Tool', in Tom Birkett and Roderick Dale (eds), *The Vikings Reimagined: Reception, Recovery, Engagement* (De Gruyter, 2019), pp. 215–16, 225–7.

138 *The archaeological evidence:* Birgitta Wallace, 'The Norse in Newfoundland: L'Anse aux meadows and Vinland', *Newfoundland Studies*, 19:1 (2003), pp. 5–43. For a more recent dating see Margot Kuitems et al., 'Evidence for European presence in the Americas in AD 1021', *Nature,* 601 (2022).

139 *'people would be much more tempted to go there':* In Chapter 1 of the *Graenlendinga Saga* and Chapter 2 of *Eirik's Saga.* See Magnus Magnusson and Hermann Palsson (trans.), The *Vinland Sagas: the Norse Discovery of America* (Penguin, 1965), pp. 50, 78.

139 *'great talk of discovering new countries':* Ibid., p. 54.

139 *'white sandy beaches':* Ibid., p. 59.

139 *'it is beautiful':* Ibid., p. 60.

139 *'could never live there in safety':* Ibid., p. 100.

140 *earlier human settlers:* See Jens Fog Jensen, 'Greenlandic Dorset', in T. Max Friesen and Owen K. Mason (eds), *The Oxford Handbook of the Prehistoric Arctic* (OUP, 2016), pp. 737–57.

140 *The last Scandinavians had died out:* Eleanor Barraclough, *Beyond the Northlands: Viking Voyages and the Old Norse Sagas* (OUP, 2016), p. 153. Jared Diamond attempted to solve the mystery in *Collapse: How Societies Choose to Fail or Survive* (Allen Lane, 2005), pp. 266–76.

140 *a few Greenlanders had survived:* Parker, 2014, pp. 194–7.

140n *several hundred half-American Icelanders:* Egill Bjarnason, *How Iceland Changed the World: The Big History of a Small Island* (Penguin, 2021), p. 150.

140n *largest foreign-born population coming from Poland:* From Statistics Iceland website, https://px.hagstofa.is/pxen/pxweb/en/Ibuar/Ibuar__ mannfjoldi__3_bakgrunnur__Faedingarland/MAN12103.px/table/ tableViewLayout1/?rxid=5b891d9a-d61e-4ed1-9758-f994efa05835

141 *DNA studies of maternal ancestry:* Sunna Ebenesersdóttir et al., 'Ancient genomes from Iceland reveal the making of a human population', *Science*, 360 (2018), pp. 1028–32.

141 *main form of portable wealth:* Cat Jarman, *River Kings: The Vikings from Scandinavia to the Silk Roads* (William Collins, 2021), p. 61.

141 *principal source at that time:* Ibid., pp. 174–6.

142 *family of Rurik:* Samuel Hazzard Cross and Olgerd P. Sherbowitz-Wetzor (trans.), *The Russian Primary Chronicle: Laurentian Text* (Medieval Academy of America, 1953), pp. 59–60.

142 *source of the word Russia:* Jarman, 2021, pp. 196–9, 224–6.

142 *'I have never seen bodies more perfect':* Ibn Fadlān, *Ibn Fadlān and the Land of Darkness: Arab Travellers in the Far North* (Penguin, 2012), p. 45.

142 *'filthiest of God's creatures':* Ibid., p. 46.

142 *sex with slave girls:* Ibid., p. 47.

142 *cruel Viking death ritual:* Ibid., pp. 51–3.

143 *'treat their slaves well':* Ibid., p. 126.

143 *'little trust in one another':* Ibid., p. 127.

143 *'their clothing is always clean'* Ibid., p. 126.

143 *'Halfdan was here':* Jarman, 2021, pp. 270–1.

144 *Ormika and Ulfhvatr:* Raymond Page, *Chronicles of the Vikings* (University of Toronto, 1995), p. 12.

144 *who partitioned the country:* Dorothy Whitelock, *English Historical Documents c. 500–1042* (Routledge, 1979), p. 417.

145 *softening of English attitudes towards the Vikings:* See for instance National Curriculum guidance to teaching history for seven- to eleven-year-olds: 'How have recent excavations changed our view of the Vikings?' https://www.keystagehistory.co.uk/keystage-2/ recent-excavations-changed-view-vikings-key-question-4-2/

145 *The actual excavations in York:* David Palliser, *Medieval York 600–1540* (OUP, 2014), pp. 66–9, and Dawn Hadley, *The Vikings in England: Settlement, Society and Culture* (Manchester University Press, 2006), p. 149.

145n *'396 years from when his race':* Dorothy Whitelock (trans.), *The Anglo-Saxon Chronicle* (Eyre and Spottiswoode, 1961), p. 4.

145n *descended from Woden:* Simon Keynes and Michael Lapidge (trans.), *Alfred the Great: Asser's Life of King Alfred and other Contemporary Sources* (Penguin, 1983), p. 57.

146 *most action-packed of all Icelandic sagas:* Snorri Sturluson, *King Harald's Saga: Harald Hardradi of Norway* (Penguin, 2005).

146n *a letter written in 1027:* Timothy Bolton, *The Empire of Cnut the Great: Conquest and the Consolidation of Power in Northern Europe in the Early Eleventh Century* (Brill, 2008), p. 246.

147 *thoroughly Scandinavian Gytha Thorkelsdóttir:* For the 'multicultural' context of Harold's upbringing see Emma Mason, *The House of Godwine: The History of a Dynasty* (Hambledon Continuum, 2004), p. 35.

147 *attempted to invade England:* In 1069 in support of Edward Atheling, and in 1075 in support of the Revolt of the Earls. In both cases Sweyn's forces took control of York. Richard Huscroft, *The Norman Conquest: A New Introduction* (Routledge, 2009), pp. 14–19.

147 *a Viking raider called Rollo:* Elisabeth van Houts (trans. and ed.), *The Normans in Europe* (Manchester University Press, 2000), pp. 14–15.

149 *aristocratic diaspora:* Robert Bartlett, *The Making of Europe: Conquest, Colonialization and Cultural Change 950–1350* (Penguin, 1994), p. 24.

150 *'an untamed race':* van Houts, 2000, pp. 77–8.

150n *It was Virgil who claimed Antenor founded Padua:* Aeneid, 1.242.

151 *twentieth-century researcher:* Maria Klippel, *Die Darstellung der Fränkischen Trojanersage in Geschichtsschreibung und Dichtung vom Mittelalter bis zur Renaissance in Frankreich* (Marburg, 1936).

151 *all claimed Trojan ancestry:* Jacques Poucet, *Le mythe de l'origine troyenne au Moyen âge et à la Renaissance : un exemple d'idéologie politique,* Folia Electronica Classica, 2003, available at http://bcs.fltr.ucl.ac.be/fe/05/anthenor2.html

151 *the site of the Trojan War:* Franz Babinger, *Mehmed the Conqueror and His Time* (Princeton, 1978), pp. 209–10.

151 *the avenger of Troy:* Philip Hardie, *The Last Trojan Hero: A Cultural History of Virgil's Aeneid* (IB Tauris, 2014), p. 125. The phrase 'avenging the blood of Hector' is used in a letter purportedly written by the Sultan to the Pope, but which is now thought to be a contemporary French forgery. See Steven Runciman, 'Teucri and Turci', in Sami Hanna (ed.), *Medieval and Middle Eastern Studies in Honor of Aziz Suryal Atiya* (Leiden, 1972), p. 345.

151 *a Trojan called Corso:* 'Chronique de Giovanni Della Grossa', in Agostino Giustiniani, *Histoire de la Corse,* vol. 1 (Bastia, 1888), pp. 99–101, available at https://gallica.bnf.fr/ark:/12148/bpt6k480065p/f145.image

152 *named after Brutus:* Nennius, *The Historia Brittonum* (J. and A. Arch, 1819), pp. 5–6.

152 *'the best of islands'* Geoffrey of Monmouth (trans. Neil Wright), *The History of the Kings of Britain* (Boydell, 2007), p. 6.

152 *'except for a few giants':* Ibid., p. 26.

152n *a notorious seventh-century remark:* Stephen Barney et al., *The Etymologies of Isidore of Seville* (CUP, 2006), p. 198.

153 *The story of Brutus also appears:* Edmund Spenser, *The Fairie Queene,* Book 2, Canto Ten.

153 *contribution from Milton:* John Milton, *The History of Britain* (R. Wilks, 1818), p. 10.

153 *Pope contemplated writing a Brutiad:* Felicity Rosslyn, *Alexander Pope: A Literary Life* (Palgrave Macmillan, 1990), pp. 138–9. The lesser-known Brutiad writers were Hildebrand Jacob (*Brutus the Trojan: Founder of the British Empire* (London, 1735)) and John Ogilvie (*Britannia: A National Epic Poem* (Aberdeen, 1801)).

153 *Blake, who famously wondered:* Jason Whittaker, *William Blake and the Myths of Britain* (Macmillan, 1999), pp. 20–2.

154 *'came ashore at Totnes':* Geoffrey of Monmouth, 2007, p. 26.

154 *Now here I sit, and here I rest:* It dates to at least the nineteenth century. See Sabine Baring-Gould, *A Book of the West: Being an Introduction to Devon and Cornwall,* vol. 1, (Methuen, 1899), p. 314.

154n *lynched in the early days of the Turkish republic:* Norman Stone, 'My dream for Turkey, by Boris's great-grandfather', *Spectator,* 26 April 2008.

156 *The Totnes passport:* See Adam Lusher, 'How the independent city state of Totnes will start the reformation of Brexit Britain', *Independent,* 28 July 2018.

A Fifth Intermission

160 *sells Mein Kampf from its website:* See http://www.leaguestgeorge.org/forsale.htm.

160 *Greek-Egyptian geographer Ptolemy:* G. J. Toomer (translator), *Ptolemy's Almagest* (Duckworth, 1984), p. 88.

160 *the French region of Brittany:* Geoffrey of Monmouth, 2007, p. 115, where he uses the phrase '*in minorem Britanniam*', meaning 'in Brittany'.

160n *Elsewhere Ptolemy:* Versions of the toponyms Hibernia and Albion, both originally Greek words, are used, in that order, in Ptolemy's *Geography* as chapter titles. See Edward Stevenson (translator), *Claudius Ptolemy: The Geography* (Dover, 1991), pp. 48–9 – and Stevenson's introduction for the complications surrounding the Greek, Latin and Arabic manuscripts of the *Geography.*

161 *criticism from Northern Ireland:* See Martha Kelner, 'Olympic officials would resist DUP demand for Team GB to be Team UK', *Guardian,* 9 June 2017.

161 *'Atlantic archipelago':* Suggested by the New Zealand historian J. G. A. Pocock in 'British history: A plea for a new subject', *Journal of Modern History,* 47:4 (1975), 606. Other suggestions include Islands of the North Atlantic (or IONA) and the West European Isles.

Chapter Six

163 *the house is a fake:* William Curtis, *The Relics of Columbus* (Lowdermilk, 1893), pp. 27–8.

165 *another Trojan migrant:* Steven Epstein, *Genoa and the Genoese 958–1528* (University of North Carolina, 1996), pp. 164–5, 173.

165 *before its main local rivals:* Ibid., p. 30.

165 *highly suspect Holy Grail:* Ibid., p. 31.

165 *Lord of Giblet:* Ibid., p. 51, and Steven Runciman, *The Crusades,* vol. 2 (CUP, 1959), p. 69. Giblet or Gibellet is a mangled version of Jbail, a city north of Beirut better known internationally by its Greek name, Byblos.

165 *In Antioch, for instance:* Epstein, 1996, p. 32.

165n *improbable backstory:* Martin Conway, 'The Sacro Catino at Genoa', *Antiquaries Journal,* 4:1 (1924), pp. 11–18. For a wonderfully detailed nineteenth-century version of the story from Lucifer to Napoleon see

William Bell, 'On the legend of the Holy or San Graal: Its connection with the Order of the Knights Templars, and the Masonic traditions; as also with the Sacro Catino at Genoa', *Freemasons' Quarterly Review*, 30 September 1853, pp. 402–27. On its chemical composition see Marco Verità et al., 'The Sacro Catino in Genoa', *Journal of Glass Studies*, 60 (2018), pp. 115–28.

166 *a great city along the sea-coast:* H. A. R. Gibb (trans.), *The Travels of Ibn Battuta*, vol. 2 (CUP, 1962, p. 470. Kaffa, now Feodosia, was once a Greek settlement – the Milesian colony of Theodosia.

166 *Kaffa was at war:* Mark Wheeler, 'Biological warfare at the 1346 Siege of Caffa', *Emerging Infectious Diseases*, 8:9 (2002), pp. 971–5.

166 *half of the population would die:* John Aberth, *From the Brink of Apocalypse: Confronting Famine, War, Plague and Death in the Later Middle Ages* (Routledge, 2010), p. 80. For recent discussion of the figures see Carl Zimmer, 'Did the "Black Death" really kill half of Europe? New research says no', *New York Times*, 10 February 2022.

166 *'as large as Seville':* Malcolm Letts (trans.), *Pero Tafur: Travel and Adventures 1435–1439* (Routledge, 1926), p. 132.

167 *the sellers make the slaves:* Ibid., p. 133.

167n *The island of Chios:* Thanks to my late stepfather-in-law Tony Mango – himself of Chiot extraction – for suggesting this to me.

168 *And so many are the Genoese:* Epstein, 1996, p. 166.

168 *when Jews were massacred or expelled:* For instance, from Gascony in the late thirteenth century. Simon Schama, *The Story of the Jews: Finding the Words 1000 BCE–1492 CE* (Bodley Head, 2013), pp. 324–5.

168n *The same poet:* Epstein, 1996, p. 169.

169 *Marco Polo encountered:* Henry Yule (trans.), *The Book of Ser Marco Polo*, vol. 1 (John Murray, 1871), p. 70. There's a minority of historians who believe that Marco Polo never actually made it to China. See Frances Wood, *Did Marco Polo go to China?* (Routledge, 1996).

169 *Andrew of Perugia:* Christopher Dawson (ed.), *Mission to Asia: Narratives and Letters of the Franciscan Missionaries in Mongolia and China in the Thirteenth and Fourteenth Centuries* (Harper, 1966), p. 236.

169 *the Vivaldi brothers:* Epstein, 1996, p. 181.

169 *searching for the Vivaldis:* Francis Rogers, 'The Vivaldi Expedition', *Annual Report of the Dante Society, with Accompanying Papers* (1955), p. 34.

169 *Genoese traveller to the Malian empire:* Epstein, 1996, p. 286.

169 *special privileges in the city:* Sandra Origone, 'Colonies and Colonization', in Carrie E. Beneš (ed.), *A Companion to Medieval Genoa* (Brill, 2018), pp. 513–14.

170 *three-quarters of the nobility:* Felipe Fernandez-Armesto, *Columbus* (OUP, 1992), p. 14.

171 *150,000 Jews are thought to have fled:* See Norman Roth, *Conversos, Inquisition and the Expulsion of the Jews from Spain* (University of Wisconsin, 2002), pp. 374–5. Felipe Fernandez-Armesto, *1492: The Year Our World Began* (Bloomsbury, 2009), p. 99, suggests 100,000 as a more likely figure.

171 *Jewish refugees in Portugal:* Schama, 2013, pp. 416–17.

171 *African island of São Tomé:* Ibid., pp. 414–15.

172 *trying to raise funds:* Fernandez-Armesto, 1992, pp. 54–65.

173 *modest support to Columbus' project:* Ibid., p. 63. The King and Queen actually put up no money of their own. The much-repeated tale of Isabella pawning her jewels is untrue.

173 *Greeks and Romans were wrong:* Except for the second century CE geographer Marinus of Tyre, who Columbus believed, erroneously, had got it right. Ibid., pp. 36–7.

173 *far broader and vaguer meaning:* Sam Miller, *A Strange Kind of Paradise: India through Foreign Eyes* (Penguin, 2015), pp. 103–13.

173 *letters with a blank space:* David Abulafia, *The Discovery of Mankind: Atlantic Encounters in the Age of Columbus* (Yale, 2008), p. 28.

173 *'gold is abundant beyond all measure':* Ibid., p. 26.

173 *Hebrew, Aramaic and some Arabic:* Clements Markham (trans.), *The Journal of Christopher Columbus (during his first voyage 1492–93)* (Hakluyt, 1893), p. 66.

174 *'fairly large and very flat':* Christopher Columbus, *Four Voyages* (Penguin, 1969), p. 57.

174 *'some naked people':* Ibid., p. 53.

174 *'taken possession of the island':* Ibid.

174 *He gave the locals:* Ibid., p. 55.

174 *they would make 'good servants':* Ibid., p. 56.

174 *'do what whatever we would wish':* Ibid., p. 59.

174 *'to pass no island':* Ibid., p. 60.

174 *'strike the island of Japan':* Ibid., p. 57. Like Marco Polo, Columbus used the word 'Chipangu' for Japan.

174 *'letters to the Grand Khan':* Ibid., p. 72.

174 *'a more beautiful country':* Ibid., p. 75.

174 *maize, tobacco and hammock:* Ibid., pp. 79–80. The words 'barbecue', 'canoe', 'hurricane' and 'potato' are also all thought to have come from Taino.

175 *gold studs in their noses:* Ibid., p. 57.

175 *the direction of other islands:* Ibid., p. 80.

175 *The crew helped a Taino canoeist:* Ibid., p. 86.

175 *'great sorrow at our disaster':* Ibid., p. 92.

175n *Columbus called the island:* Ibid., pp. 85–6.

176 *thirty-nine Europeans:* Ibid., p. 95.

176 *'footloose aristocrats':* Hugh Thomas, *Rivers of Gold: The Rise of the Spanish Empire from Columbus to Magellan* (Random House, 2003), p. 127.

176 *'little trees and fruit bushes':* Ibid., p. 130.

176 *Hispaniola is a wonder:* Columbus, 1969, p. 117.

178 *gold, cotton, mastic and slaves:* Ibid., p. 122.

178 *evidence of cannibalism:* Ibid., pp. 133–7.

178 *Several conflicting stories:* Ibid., pp. 147–8.

178 *Caonabo was captured:* Bartolomé de Las Casas, *A Short Account of the Destruction of the Indies* (Penguin, 1992), p. 21.

178 *one of his ears cut off:* Columbus, 1969, p. 167.

179 *gold had been embezzled:* Fernandez-Armesto, 1992, pp. 110–11.

179 *'women were more beautiful':* Columbus, 1969, p. 233.

179 *that he was in Asia:* Ibid., p. 294.

179 *tribute to their new rulers:* Ibid., p. 190.

180 *Their birth rate:* Abulafia, 2008, p. 208.

180 *leaders were tied to a griddle:* de Las Casas, 1992, p. 15.

180 *slice a man in two:* Ibid.

180 *'an unofficial agreement':* Ibid., p. 17.

180 *population of Hispaniola had shrunk:* Ibid., p. 11.

181 *'native population was wiped out':* Ibid.

181 *disease that caused a dramatic population collapse:* Massimo Livi-Bacci, 'The depopulation of Hispanic America after the Conquest', *Population and Development Review*, 32:2 (2006), pp. 224–7.

181n *There was also some intermarriage:* Hugh Thomas, *The Golden Age: The Spanish Empire of Charles V* (Allen Lane, 2010), pp. 132, 269.

182 *Comparisons were made:* Ibid., p. 497.

182 *the Leyenda Negra:* See, for example, Sam Jones, 'Spain fights to dispel legend of Inquisition and imperial atrocities', *Guardian*, 29 April 2018.

184 *expecting to find the monsters:* See Markham, 1893, p. 68. For Columbus' expectation of finding one-eyed or dog-nosed men see Abulafia, 2008, pp. 20–1.

184 *own next to nothing:* de Las Casas, 1992, p. 10.

184 *'make them particularly receptive':* Ibid.

185 *Humans first settled Hispaniola:* William Keegan and Corinne Hofman, *The Caribbean before Columbus* (OUP, 2017), p. 147.

185 *some archaeological evidence:* Ibid., p. 27.

185 *later migrants came from South America:* Daniel Fernandes et al., 'A genetic history of the pre-contact Caribbean.' *Nature*, 590:7844 (2021), pp. 103–10.

185 *great mingling of the people:* Keegan and Hofman, 2017, p. 135.

186 *cotton and salted fish:* Ibid., p. 183.

186 *amazed to see Taino canoes:* Columbus, 1969, p. 84.

186 *The Taino are so named:* Keegan and Hofman, 2017, p. 13.

186 *angelic island-dwellers:* The angels in Michener's account are referred to as Arawaks, a word used – often as island-Arawaks – as an alternative to Taino. Michener's story is set on the island of Dominica, eight hundred kilometres south-east of Hispaniola and the modern Dominican Republic.

186 *'they lived in harmony':* James Michener, *Caribbean: A Novel* (Random House, 1989), p. 9.

186 *'a fierce terrible people':* Ibid., p. 10.

186 *'brutality always wins':* Ibid., p. 18.

186 *DNA tests show:* Daniel Fernandes et al., 2021, and Hannes Schroeder et al., 'Origins and genetic legacies of the Caribbean Taino', *Proceedings of the National Academy of Sciences,* 115:10 (2018), pp. 2341–6.

188 *'an Indian of the captive race':* Lyrics available at https://www.lyrics.com/lyric/23237433/. Thanks to Giulia Negrini for help with the translation.

188n *About whom Tennyson wrote:* Hallam Tennyson (ed.), *The Works of Tennyson* (Macmillan, 1925), pp. xx–xxi. The poem is missing from most editions of Tennyson's poems, and the poet himself left it out of his published works. His son Hallam included the poem in an introduction to his father's work published in 1925.

189 *'The true genocide is to say'*: Quoted in Sherina Feliciano-Santos, *An Inconceivable Indigeneity: The Historical, Cultural, and Interactional Dimensions of Puerto Rican Taíno Activism*, PhD dissertation (University of Michigan, 2011), p. 30.

190 *Asociación Indigena de Puerto Rico*: Ibid., p. 39.

190 *'those effing Puerto Ricans'*: Jorge Estevez speaking at Session 1, Taino Symposium, 8 September 2018, New York, https://www.youtube.com/watch?v=_GJvoODyGBw (9' 56").

191 *'extremists' and 'ethnic hustlers'*: Gabriel Haslip-Viera, 'The Taíno Question: Haslip-Viera Responds to Levins Morales', *National Institute for Latino Policy's Network on Latino Issues*, 2 March 2015.

191 *'We're a mix'*: Carlalynne Yarey Meléndez speaking at Session 2, Taino Symposium, 8 September 2018, New York, https://www.youtube.com/watch?v=NK4AgvbmmHE (13' 13").

A Sixth Intermission

194 *a visiting Sioux chieftain*: See https://www.royalparks.org.uk/parks/brompton-cemetery/explore-brompton-cemetery/famous-graves-and-burials/chief-long-wolf

195 *pet lion cub*: Mark Duell and Richard Eden, 'What happened to the lion from Harrods?', *Daily Mail*, 26 January 2022.

195 *Nunak had been brought*: George Bryan, *Chelsea in the Olden & Present Times* (published by the author, 1869), p. 48.

196 *the first recorded Americans in Britain*: Coll Thrush, 'The iceberg and the cathedral: Encounter, entanglement, and Isuma in Inuit London', *Journal of British Studies*, 53:1 (2014), p. 64. My translation from sixteenth-century English.

196 *seven Taino on board*: Jace Weaver, *The Red Atlantic: American Indigenes and the Making of the Modern World 1000–1927* (University of North Carolina, 2014), pp. 44–7.

196n *There is a gravestone*: Kenn Harper, 'The lonely grave of an Inuit child', *Nunatsiaq News*, 15 November 2019.

197 *'bearded men covered with cloth'*: José Barreiro, *Taino* (Fulcrum, 1993), p. 48.

197 *'drunk with the pull of adventure'*: Ibid., p. 57.

197 *'a marvel of a tool'*: Ibid., p. 129.

197 *syphilis as a less-lethal return gift*: Mary Dobson, *Murderous Contagion: A Human History of Disease* (Quercus, 2015), pp. 60, 282–3.

198 *the Athenian plague*: Thucydides, *History*, 2.48.1–2.52.4. See also Javier Martinez, 'Political consequences of the Plague of Athens', *Graeco-Latina Brunensia*, 22:1 (2017), pp. 135–46.

198 *two hundred Jews were burnt to death*: Jacob Rader Marcus and Marc Saperstein, *The Jews in Christian Europe: A Source Book: 315–1791* (University of Pittsburgh, 2015), pp. 155–7.

199 *sorry story of Am-Shalem Singson*: 'Indian immigrant beaten in Tiberias in apparent coronavirus-linked hate crime', *The Times of Israel*, 16 March 2020.

199 *thrown into a canal:* Jack Beresford, 'Chinese woman filmed being pushed into Dublin river by vile teenage thugs', *Irish Post*, 16 June 2020.

199 *punched in the face:* Kim Bo-gyung, 'Korean punched in the face in NY for not wearing mask', *Korea Herald*, 13 March 2020.

199n *the governor of the Italian region:* See *La Stampa*, 28 February 2020, https://www.lastampa.it/politica/2020/02/28/video/coronavirus_zaia_la_cina_ha_pagato_un_grande_conto_perche_loro_mangiano_i_topi_vivi_-152245/. The governor, Luca Zaia, later apologised for these comments.

Chapter Seven

201 *a slave-owner called Henry Shields:* Rachel L. Swarns, *American Tapestry: The Story of the Black, White, and Multiracial Ancestors of Michelle Obama* (Amistad, 2012), pp. 297–303.

201 *considers himself black:* Barack Obama, *Dreams from My Father* (Canongate, 2007), p. 115, where he writes, 'Whatever my father might say, I knew it was too late to ever truly claim Africa as my home. And if I had come to understand myself as a black American, and was understood as such, that understanding remained unanchored to place.'

201 *I am the son of a black man:* 'Transcript: Barack Obama's speech on race', *New York Times*, 18 March 2008.

202 *declared to be the Antichrist:* See https://www.politifact.com/factchecks/2008/apr/02/chain-email/complete-distortion-of-the-bible/

202 *'one-drop rule':* Kevin Brown, 'The Rise And Fall Of The One-Drop Rule: How the Importance of Color Came to Eclipse Race', in Kimberly Jade Norwood (ed.), *Color Matters: Skin Tone Bias and the Myth of a Post-Racial America* (Routledge, 2014), pp. 72–3.

202 *'Obama isn't black':* Debra Dickerson, 'Colorblind: Barack Obama would be the great black hope in the next presidential race – if he were actually black', Salon.com, 22 January 2007.

204 *a significant number of cowboys were black:* Bruce Glasrud and Michael Searles, *Black Cowboys in the American West: On the Range, on the Stage, behind the Badge* (University of Oklahoma, 2016), pp. 9–10.

204 *small number of slave-owners:* Larry Koger, *Black Slaveowners: Free Black Slave Masters in South Carolina 1790–1860* (McFarland, 1985), pp. 1–2.

204 *and some also owned slaves:* Barbara Krauthamer, *Black Slaves, Indian Masters: Slavery, Emancipation, and Citizenship in the Native American South* (University of North Carolina, 2015), pp. 2–5.

204 *dismay of white supremacists:* See https://www.youtube.com/watch?v=p-XDKiO-i4Q, and Aaron Panofsky and Joan Donovan, 'Genetic ancestry testing among white nationalists: From identity repair to citizen science', *Social Studies of Science*, 49:5 (2019), pp. 653–81.

204 *Slavery was practised:* See Leland Donald, *Aboriginal Slavery on Northwest Coast of North America* (University of California, 1997), p. 17.

205 *his story retold and reimagined:* Dennis Herrick, *Esteban: The African Slave who Explored America* (University of Mexico, 2008), pp. 10, 17.

205 *as an 'Arab Negro':* Alvar Nuñez Cabeza de Vaca (trans. Fanny Bandelier), *Chronicle of the Narvaez Expedition* (Penguin, 2002), p. 108.

205 *conquer and colonise Florida:* Ibid., p. 5.

205 *Europeans became cannibals:* Ibid., p. 47.

205 *linguist and spokesman:* Ibid., p. 87.

205 *a rebellion by African slaves:* Herrick, 2008, pp. 153–4.

206 *happy-ending version:* Ibid., pp. 181–90.

206n *other less well-known early foundation myths:* On San Miguel de Gualdupe see Ciara Torres-Spelliscy, 'Everyone is talking about 1619. But that's not actually when slavery in America started', *Washington Post*, 23 August 2019, and David Weber, *The Spanish Frontier in North America* (Yale, 1992). On St Croix see David Fischer, *Champlain's Dream* (Simon & Schuster, 2008), pp. 170–3.

207n *basic accounts of the Mayflower:* See Nathaniel Philbrick, *Mayflower: A Story of Courage, Community, and War* (Viking, 2006), p. 29 (on passenger numbers), p. 48 (on disease), pp. 353–6 (on Thanksgiving).

208 *tried to settle Roanoke Island:* James Horn, *A Land as God Made It: Jamestown and the Birth of America* (Basic Books, 2005), pp. 31–2.

209 *fewer than forty survived:* Ibid., p. 57.

209 *resorted to cannibalism:* Ibid., p. 176.

209 *labourers and vagrants:* Alan Taylor, *American Colonies: The Settling of North America* (Penguin, 2001), p. 131.

209 *two surgeons and a fisherman:* Joseph Kelly, *Marooned: Jamestown, Shipwreck and a New History of America's Origin* (Bloomsbury, 2019), p. 35.

209 *the first Englishwomen:* Ibid., p. 135.

210 *Contemporary records show:* See John Smith, *The Generall Historie of Virginia, New England & the Summer Isles*, vol. 1 (MacLehose, 1907), pp. 88–9.

210 *many were welcomed:* Kelly, 2019, p. 341.

210 *When an Indian child:* Letter to Peter Collinson, 9 May 1753, in Benjamin Franklin, *The Complete Works of Benjamin Franklin*, vol. 2 (Putnam's, 1887), p. 294.

211 *She is, of course, Pocahontas:* See Neil Rennie, *Pocahontas, Little Wanton: Myth, Life and Afterlife* (Quaritch, 2007).

211 *In Native American accounts:* Rebecca Jager, *Malinche, Pocahontas, and Sacagawea Indian Women as Cultural Intermediaries and National Symbols* (University of Oklahoma, 2015), pp. 234–7.

211n *Disney's cartoon version:* See Alex von Tunzelmann 'Poverty, alcoholism and suicide – but at least the natives can paint with all the colours of the wind', *Guardian*, 10 September 2008.

212 *That son, Thomas:* Rennie, 2007, p. 94.

212 *'though a born barbarian':* Wyndham Robertson, *Pocahontas and her Descendants* (Randolph and English, 1887), p. 16.

212n *John Rolfe himself:* Iain Gately, *Tobacco: A Cultural History of How an Exotic Plant Seduced Civilization* (Simon & Schuster, 2001), pp. 70–4.

213 *the White Lion sailed to Virginia:* Engel Sluiter, 'New light on the "20. and Odd Negroes" arriving in Virginia, August 1619', *The William and Mary Quarterly*, 54:2 (1997), pp. 395–8.

213 *almost certainly Kimbundu:* John Thornton, 'The African experience of the "20. and Odd Negroes" arriving in Virginia in 1619', *The William and Mary Quarterly*, 55:3 (1998), pp. 421–4.

213n *Occasionally these chauvinistic narratives:* Kevin Maillard, 'The Pocahontas exception: The exemption of American Indian ancestry from racial purity law', *Michigan Journal of Race & Law*, 12:107 (2007).

214 *'sardines in a bottle':* Linda Heywood and John Thornton, 'In search of the 1619 African arrivals', *The Virginia Magazine of History and Biography*, 127:3 (2019), p. 208.

214 *'twenty-four slave boys':* Sluiter, 1997, p. 397.

214 *unresolved terminological argument:* See, for instance, Katy Waldman, 'Slave or enslaved person? It's not just an academic debate for historians of American slavery', Slate.com, 19 May 2015.

215 *no formal legal category:* See William Cummings, 'Virginia Gov. Ralph Northam slammed for referring to "first indentured servants from Africa" instead of slaves', *USA Today*, 11 February 2019.

215 *DNA tests on some of his descendants:* Sheryl Gay Stolberg, 'Obama has ties to slavery not by his father but his mother, research suggests', *New York Times*, 30 July 2012. For the detailed research see Anastasia Harman et al., 'Documenting President Barack Obama's maternal African-American ancestry: Tracing his mother's Bunch ancestry to the first slave in America', Ancestry.com, 16 July 2012, available at https://archive.org/details/25004473

216 *'three servants shall receive':* Henry McIlwaine (ed.), *Minutes of the Council and General Court of Colonial Virginia* (Virginia State Library, 1924), p. 466.

216 *very few Africans:* Philip Alexander Bruce, *Economic History of Virginia in the Seventeenth Century*, vol. 2 (Macmillan, 1907), p. 74.

216n *one of John Punch's great-grandchildren:* Henry McIlwaine (ed.), *Executive Journals of the Council of Colonial Virginia*, vol. 3, pp. 28, 31.

216n *in the Alabama constitution:* Peggy Pascoe, *What Comes Naturally: Miscegenation Law and the Making of Race in America* (OUP, 2009), p. 309.

217 *the colony of Virginia:* Taylor, 2001, p. 154. Geographically, Virginia had shrunk in this period, with new colonies – the Carolinas and Georgia – taking some of its territory.

217 *addicted to nicotine:* Ibid., p. 134.

218 *twelve million captives:* Marcus Rediker, *The Slave Ship: A Human History* (John Murray, 2007), p. 5.

219 *'houses with wings':* Ukawsaw Gronniosaw, *A Narrative of the Most Remarkable Particulars in the Life of James Albert Ukawsaw Gronniosaw an African Prince, as Related by Himself* (W. Gye, 1772), p. 5.

219 *'horrible looks, red faces':* Olaudah Equiano, *The Interesting Narrative and Other Writings* (Penguin, 2003), p. 55. Some scholars believe Equiano invented the early part of his story, and was actually born in America. For further discussion see Paul Lovejoy, 'Autobiography and memory: Gustavus Vassa, alias Olaudah Equiano, the African', *Slavery and Abolition*, 27:3 (2006), pp. 317–47.

220 *'the multitude of black people':* Equiano, 2003, p. 55.

220 *'received such a salutation'*: Ibid., p. 56.

220 *'flogged unmercifully'*: Ibid., p. 57.

221 *best-documented cases*: Rediker, 2007, pp. 15–16.

221 *a mix of slaves on board*: Ibid., p. 212.

221 *One ship's doctor*: W. O. Blake, *The History of Slavery and the Slave Trade, Ancient and Modern* (H. Miller, 1861), p. 130.

222 *'dread and trembling'*: Equiano, 2003, p. 60.

222 *'so at length I submitted'*: Ibid., p. 64.

224 *to avoid conscription*: Joseph Casimir O'Meagher, *Some Historical Notes on the O'Meaghers of Ikerrin* (n.p., 1890), p. 175.

224 *'ardent Southerners'*: Ibid., p. 177.

224n *The Clotilda was named*: See the website entitled *CatholicSaints.Info: notes about your extended family in heaven* at https://catholicsaints.info/saint-clotilde/

225 *a shipful of n—s*: Sylviane Diouf, *Dreams of Africa in Alabama: The Slave Ship Clotilda and the Story of the Last Africans brought to America* (OUP, 2007), p. 21.

225 *The unwilling passengers*: Ibid., pp. 30–54.

225 *The captain of the Clotilda*: Ibid., pp. 56–7.

226 *'we didn't want to leave'*: Ibid., p. 58.

226 *'I was so ashamed'*: Ibid., p. 61.

226 *the women had the dresses* Ibid., p. 85.

227 *ritual scarring and filed teeth* Ibid., p. 111.

227 *'they were blacker'*: Ibid., p. 106.

227 *'we wanted to talk'*: Ibid.

227 *Cudjo Lewis described a group*: Zora Neale Hurston, *Barracoon: The Story of the Last Slave* (Harper Collins, 2018), p. 63.

227 *appointing as their leader*: Ibid., p. 66.

227n *In fact, they almost certainly*: Diouf, 2007, p. 139.

228 *Yoruba was spoken*: Ibid., p. 190.

228 *Two of the young African women*: Ibid., pp. 112–14.

228 *Writers began to visit*: Ibid., pp. 245–7.

228 *now on YouTube*: See https://www.youtube.com/watch?v=DK7Pt9UQQoE

229 *high rates of cancer*: Kevin Lee, 'America's cancerous legacy for the descendants of the kidnapped Africans who arrived on the last slave ship', *The Daily Beast*, 3 February 2021.

230 *an organisation was set up*: Diouf, 2007, p. 235.

230 *burnt-out shell*: See the book written by the man who rediscovered the *Clotilda*: Ben Raines, *The Last Slave Ship: The True Story of How Clotilda Was Found, Her Descendants, and an Extraordinary Reckoning* (Simon & Schuster, 2022).

230 *the US Senate passed*: Senate Resolution 315, 116th Congress. Passed unanimously, 27 February 2020, https://www.congress.gov/bill/116th-congress/senate-resolution/315

230n *the visit of a Beninois diplomat*: Ben Raines, '"Forgive us, because we sold them," says African ambassador on possible slave ship find', al.com, 07 March 2019.

A Seventh Intermission

232n *The white supremacists:* See Chapter Nine. In fact, very small-scale migration from some parts of Africa was possible. Under the 1924 Immigration Act, a large number of mainly non-European countries and territories were given a quota of one hundred migrants per year who could enter the USA. Some of these were in Africa, including the French and British mandates of Togoland and Cameroons. *Supplement to the Messages and Papers of the Presidents: Covering the Term of Warren G. Harding, March 4, 1921, to August 2, 1923, and the First Term of Calvin Coolidge, August 3, 1923, to March 4, 1925* (Bureau of National Literature, 1925), pp. 9427–8.

233 *as some modern historians:* See Terri L. Snyder, *The Power to Die: Slavery and Suicide in British North America* (Chicago University Press, 2015) and Richard Bell, *We Shall Be No More: Suicide and Self-Government in the Newly United States* (Harvard, 2012).

233 *'woman is a greater migrant':* E. G. Ravenstein, 'The laws of migration', *Journal of the Statistical Society of London*, 48:2 (1885), p. 196.

234 *'step migration':* Ibid., pp. 198–9.

235 *'all is flux':* Quoted by, among others, Socrates in Plato's *Cratylus*, 401b, 402a.

235n *Heraclitus was from Ephesus:* For a fine guide to all things Heraclitean see Charles Kahn, *The Art and Thought of Heraclitus* (CUP, 1979).

Chapter Eight

238 *'taste might have become corrupted':* François Bernier, *Travels in the Mogul Empire* (OUP, 1916), p. 295.

239 *dome of the Taj Mahal:* Ibid., p. 297.

239 *the River Yamuna:* Ibid., p. 241.

239 *the 'Athens of India':* Ibid., p. 334.

239 *help Europeans imagine the Mughal Empire:* See in particular Peter Burke, 'The Philosopher as Traveller: Bernier's Orient', in Jaś Elsner and Joan-Pau Rubiés, *Voyages and Visions, Towards a Cultural History of Travel* (Reaktion, 1999), pp. 124–37.

239 *'A new division of the earth':* François Bernier, *Journal de Sçavans*, 24 April 1684, pp. 133–40, https://gallica.bnf.fr/ark:/12148/bpt6k56535g. English translation available in *Memoirs Read Before the Anthropological Society of London, 1863–4*, vol. 1 (Trübner, 1865), pp. 360–4.

240 *'truly white':* Bernier, 1684, p. 136.

240 *'very ugly and look much like bears':* Ibid., p. 136.

241 *(he preferred 'varieties'):* Nicholas Hudson, 'From "Nation" to "race": The origin of racial classification in eighteenth-century thought', *Eighteenth-Century Studies*, 29:3 (1996), pp. 253–4.

241 *Linnaeus' method was to classify:* Charles Linne, *A General System of Nature*, vol. 1 (London, 1806), p. 3.

241 *four main subgroups:* Ibid., p. 9. He included a fifth variety: Wild Man, described as 'four-footed; mute, hairy'.

241 *Asians are, by nature, haughty:* Linne, 1806, p. 9.

241 *colour-coded his racial categories:* for Linnaeus' annotated version of these colour-codings, see Staffan Müller-Wille, 'Linnaeus and the Four Corners of the World', in Kimberley Coles et al. (eds), *The Cultural Politics of Blood* (Palgrave Macmillan, 2014), p. 202.

241n *Many other alternatives:* Terry Pratchett et al., *The Globe: The Science of Discworld II* (Ebury, 2013), on the final page of which humans are referred to as *Pan Narrans*, or storytelling apes. Max Frisch, *Homo Faber* (Penguin, 2006). David Bowie on the 1971 album *Hunky Dory*. For further alternatives to *Sapiens* see Luigi Romeo, *Ecce Homo: A Lexicon of Man* (John Benjamins, 1979).

242 *Native Americans had red skins:* See Nancy Shoemaker, 'How Indians got to be red', *American Historical Review*, 102:3 (1997), pp. 625–44, for the complex story of how Native Americans came to be identified with the colour red – an identification that pre-dated Linnaeus.

242 *Washington Redskins:* See Emma Bowman, 'For many Native Americans, the Washington Commanders' new name offers some closure', NPR.org, 06 February 2022. Since early 2022 the team has been officially known as the Washington Commanders.

242 *the Latin word luridus:* Christina Skott, 'Human taxonomies, Carl Linnaeus, Swedish travel in Asia and the classification of man', *Itinerario*, 43:2 (2019), pp. 219, 224–5.

242–3 *'white in Europe, black in Africa':* Georg-Louis de Buffon, *Histoire Naturelle, Générale et Particulière*, vol. 8 (Paris, 1769), p. 93, available at https://archive.org/details/cihm_42934/page/n5/mode/2up

242n *presumably as a joke:* Müller-Wille in Coles et al., 2014, p. 199.

244 *larger than the Mediterranean:* The Mediterranean is about 2.5 million km² and the South China Sea is approximately 3.5 million km². In terms of diversity, the South China Sea is home to a larger number of language groups and a wider range of belief systems than the Mediterranean. For other comparisons between the two seas, see Heather Sutherland, 'Southeast Asian history and the Mediterranean analogy', *Journal of Southeast Asian Studies*, 34:1 (2003).

244 *discoveries of human remains:* They've been given – like the Neanderthals before them – tentative Linnaean classifications, *Homo Floresiensis* and *Homo Luzonensis*, after the islands on which they were found. There's little doubt that their ancestors, like those of all humans, also came originally from Africa, and though it's not yet clear when and how they reached South-East Asia – it almost certainly involved travel by boat. See David Abulafia, *The Boundless Sea: A Human History of the Oceans* (Penguin, 2019), p. 7, and Florent Détroit et al., 'A new species of *Homo* from the Late Pleistocene of the Philippines', *Nature*, 568 (2019), pp. 181–6.

244 *ancient seagoing journeys:* Abulafia, 2019, pp. 3–5.

244 *originated in Taiwan:* Ibid., p. 11.

244 *Austronesian settlement of Hawaii:* Ibid., p. 24.

244 *'Maritime Silk Road':* Kwa Chong Guan, 'The Maritime Silk Road: History of an Idea', Nalanda-Sriwijaya Centre, Working Paper No. 23, October 2016.

246 *Historians and archaeologists:* Abulafia, 2019, pp. 11–13.

246 *migrants from China:* Louise Levathes, *When China Ruled the Seas: The Treasure Fleet of the Dragon Throne 1405–1433* (Simon & Schuster, 1994), pp. 98–9.

246 *Ming sea voyages:* Jun J. Nohara, 'Sea power as a dominant paradigm: the rise of China's new strategic identity', *Journal of Contemporary East Asia Studies*, 6:2 (2017), pp. 12–14.

246 *two hundred ships:* Sally K. Church, 'Zheng He: An investigation into the plausibility of 450-ft treasure ships', *Monumenta Serica*, 53:1 (2005), pp. 6, 16.

247 *There exists a paramount boundary:* Timothy Brook, *Great State: China and the World* (Profile, 2019), epigraph.

247 *made punishable by death:* Lynn Pan, *Sons of the Yellow Emperor: The Story of the Overseas Chinese* (Mandarin, 1990), p. 8.

248 *a place called Binondo:* Edgar Wickberg, 'The Chinese mestizo in Philippine history', *Journal of Southeast Asian History*, 5:1 (1964), pp. 69–70.

248 *Manila was at the heart:* Pan, 1990, p. 25.

248 *one Spanish observer:* Bishop Fray Domingo in a letter dated 24 June 1590 to the Spanish King, translated in full in Emma Blair and James Robertson, *The Philippine Islands 1493–1898*, vol. 7 (Arthur H. Clark Company, 1903), pp. 225–31. The bishop tells the story of a Spanish bookbinder who came to Manila from Mexico to set up a new business. He took on a Chinese assistant – who watched him 'secretly' and was soon skilled enough to be able to put his former employer out of work. The Chinese bookbinder, the bishop declared, was as good as any to be found in Seville.

248 *well-remembered story:* José Eugenio Barao, 'The massacre of 1603: Chinese perception of the Spaniards in the Philippines', *Itinerario*, 23:1 (1998), p. 3. The killing of the Spanish governor took place in 1593.

249 *planning an invasion:* Ibid., p. 7.

249 *killed more than twenty thousand Chinese:* Ibid., p. 1.

249 *'no shoes to wear':* The colonial official was Antonio De Morga. Blair and Robertson, 1904, vol. 16, p. 42.

249 *official records show:* Barao, 1998, p. 11.

249 *the coastal province:* Pan, 1990, pp. 12–15.

250 *Northerners are sincere and honest:* Quoted in Lung-Chang Young, 'Regional stereotypes in China', *Chinese Studies in History*, 21:4 (1988), p. 34.

250 *'While his father and mother are alive':* Confucius, *Analects*, 4:19. See Burton Watson (trans.), *The Analects of Confucius* (Columbia, 2007), p. 34. The rest of the saying contains a minor loophole for would-be migrants: 'If he travels, he must have a fixed destination.'

250 *Chinese word qiao:* See, for instance, Wang Gungwu, 'Sojourning: The Chinese Experience in Southeast Asia', in Anthony Reid (ed.), *Sojourners and Settlers: Histories of Southeast Asia and the Chinese* (University of Hawaii, 2001), pp. 1–14.

251 *second families with local women:* Steven Miles, *Chinese Diasporas: A Social History of Global Migration* (CUP, 2020), pp. 44–8.

251 *many families in China:* Ibid., pp. 38–41.

251 *further massacres:* There were two more massacres of Chinese migrants in Manila in the seventeenth century, and one in Dutch-ruled Jakarta, then known as Batavia, in 1740.

252 *almost uninhabited island:* Thomas Newbold, *Political and Statistical Account of the British Settlements in the Straits of Malacca*, vol. 1 (John Murray, 1839), p. 279.

252 *identify themselves as Chinese: Singapore Census of Population 2020, Statistical Release 1: Demographic Characteristics, Education, Language and Religion*, https://www.singstat.gov.sg/publications/reference/cop2020/cop2020-sr1/census20_stat_release1. See 'Basic Demographic Characteristics', Table 1 for ethnic identity, and 'Language Most/Second Most Frequently Spoken at Home', Table 41 for language issues.

252 *Chinese migrants as labourers:* Miles, 2020, pp. 64–8.

252 *referred to as captains:* Ibid., p. 43, and Choon San Wong, *A Gallery of Chinese Kapitans*, (Singapore Ministry of Culture, 1963).

252 *One such list:* J. W. Norton Kyshe, 'A judicial history of the Straits settlements 1786–1890', *Malaya Law Review*, 11:1 (1969), pp. 57–9.

253 *a tiny Malay population:* Norman Macalister, *Historical Memoir relative to Prince of Wales Island in the Straits of Malacca* (London, 1805), p. 23.

253 *George Leith declared:* George Leith, *A Short Account of the Settlement, Produce and Commerce of Prince of Wales Island* (London, 1804), pp. 24–9.

254 *half of the population:* In the 2010 census, 54 per cent of the population of Penang island described themselves as Chinese, while the whole province, which includes a large area on the mainland, was 36 per cent Chinese. See http://www.statistics.gov.my/portal/download_Population/files/population/03ringkasan_kawasan_PBT_Jadual1.pdf

254 *tens of millions of migrants:* Miles, 2020, p. 93.

254n *Leith then complains:* Leith, 1804, p. 49.

255 *went to Peru:* Isabelle Lausent-Herrera, 'Tusans (*Tusheng*) and the Changing Chinese Community in Peru', in Walton Look Lai and Tan Chee-Beng (eds), *The Chinese in Latin America and the Caribbean* (Brill, 2010), p. 143.

255 *I have myself seen:* Letter from John Bowring to the British Foreign Secretary, the Earl of Malmesbury, 3 August 1852, reproduced in *The Anti-Slavery Reporter*, 1 February 1855. The Sandwich Islands is the old Anglophone name for Hawaii.

256 *Floggings were normal:* Don Aldus, *Coolie Traffic and Kidnapping* (McCorquodale & Co., 1876), p. 51.

256 *One in ten of the Chinese:* Arnold Meagher, *The Coolie Trade: The Traffic in Chinese Laborers to Latin America, 1847–1874* (Xlibris, 2008), p. 170.

256 *We must endeavour:* Ibid., p. 165.

256 *'our person might be examined':* Ibid., p. 215.

256 *quite a catch:* Ibid., p. 236.

257 *a history of the immigrants:* Oscar Handlin, *The Uprooted: The Epic Story of the Great Migrations That Made the American People* (Little Brown, 1979), p. 3.

258 *has also been criticised:* John Bukowczyk, 'Oscar Handlin's America', *Journal of American Ethnic History*, 32:3 (2013), pp. 7, 13.

258 *four hundred thousand Chinese:* See US government census website, https://

www2.census.gov/library/publications/1949/compendia/hist_stats_1789-1945/hist_stats_1789-1945-chB.pdf, pp. 35–6.

259 *port of San Francisco:* There were 459 inhabitants of San Francisco in 1847. John Hittell, *A History of the City of San Francisco* (Bancroft, 1878), p. 117.

259 *province of Guangdong:* Philip Kuhn, *Chinese Among Others: Emigration in Modern Times,* (Rowman and Littlefield, 2009), p. 202.

259 *five hundred of them:* Ibid., pp. 141–2.

259 *They were welcomed at first:* In 1850 the mayor of San Francisco invited three hundred 'China Boys' to take part in public ceremonies marking the death of President Zachary Taylor. See Frank Soule et al., *The Annals of San Francisco* (Appleton, 1855), pp. 287–8.

259 *They are uncivilized: New York Tribune,* 29 September 1854.

259n *'Go West, young man!':* Thomas Vinciguerra, 'Greeley only wished he had said it', *New York Times,* 13 February 1994, letters column.

260 *rights of Chinese migrants:* See, for example, People vs Hall, 1854, in which a murder conviction against a white man was reversed because three of the witnesses were Chinese. *California Supreme Court Historical Society Newsletter,* spring/summer 2017, available at https://www.cschs.org/wp-content/uploads/2015/01/2017-Newsletter-Spring-People-v.-Hall.pdf, and Kuhn, 2009, p. 206.

260 *the Chinese were tolerated:* In the 1860s several countries negotiated treaties with the Qing rulers of China that encouraged migration from China. Miles, 2020, p. 137.

260 *'The Chinese must go!':* Beth Lew-Williams, *The Chinese Must Go: Violence, Exclusion, and the Making of the Alien in America* (Harvard, 2018), p. 42.

261 *'horde of Oriental invaders': Congressional Record – House,* 18 March 1882, https://www.govinfo.gov/content/pkg/GPO-CRECB-1882-pt3-v13/pdf/GPO-CRECB-1882-pt3-v13-2.pdf, pp. 2032–5.

261 *blamed for outbreaks of leprosy:* Joan Trauner, 'The Chinese as medical scapegoats in San Francisco, 1870–1905', *California History,* 57/1 (1978), pp. 70–87.

261 *Chinese community of Tacoma:* Lew-Williams, 2018, pp. 1, 102.

261 *tortured or burnt to death:* Ibid., p. 91.

261 *murdered in Oregon:* Ibid., p. 250.

261 *American lecture circuit:* Scott Seligmann, *The First Chinese American: The Remarkable Life of Wong Chin Foo* (HKU Press, 2013), pp. 63–6, 134.

262 *'almond-eyed leper':* Ibid., p. 116.

262 *'Irish potatoes, or Krupp guns':* Ibid.

262 *widely reported public debate:* Ibid., pp. 150–1.

262 *one of the few categories:* Craig Robertson, *The Passport in America: The History of a Document* (OUP, 2010), p. 172.

262 *thinking that the Chinese all look alike:* Ibid., p. 173; Pan, 1990, p. 109.

263 *An authentic citizen:* Maxine Hong Kingston, *China Men* (Picador, 1981), p. 149.

263 *restrictions on migration from China:* Miles, 2020, pp. 137–41.

263 *phrase 'Yellow Peril':* Michael Keevak, *Becoming Yellow: A Short History of Racial Thinking* (Princeton, 2011), pp. 125–8.

263n *San Francisco's old Chinatown:* Look Tin Eli, 'Our New Oriental

City – Veritable Fairy Palaces Filled with the Choicest Treasures of the Orient', in Hamilton Wright, *San Francisco: the Metropolis of the West* (Western Press Association, 1910), pp. 90–3.

264 *'the great Yellow race':* Keevak, 2011, p. 127.

264 *looting and killing:* Paul Cohen, *History in Three Keys: The Boxers as Event, Experience and Myth* (Columbia, 1997), pp. 180–5.

264 *examples were set in Australia:* See Catriona Ross, 'Prolonged symptoms of cultural anxiety: The Persistence of Narratives of Asian invasion within multicultural Australia', *Journal of the Association for the Study of Australian Literature*, 5 (2006). The books cited are William Lane, *White or Yellow? A Story of the Race War of AD 1908*, serialised in *Boomerang* magazine, 1888, and Kenneth Mackay, *The Yellow Wave: A Romance of the Asiatic Invasion of Australia* (Richard Bentley, 1895).

264 *complete a dictation exercise:* Clause 3a of the Australian Immigration Restriction Act 1901, https://www.legislation.gov.au/Details/C1901A00017

265 *'the doctrine of the equality of man':* Timothy Kendall, *Within China's Orbit? China through the Eyes of the Australian Parliament*, official publication of the Australian Parliament, 2008, p. 17.

265 *'noble idea of a white Australia':* Ibid., p. 1. Words spoken in 1901 by James Black Ronald, Labor MP for South Melbourne.

265n *It was also used:* Kel Robertson, 'Dictating to one of "us": The migration of Mrs Freer', *Macquarie Law Journal*, 5 (2005), pp. 241–75.

266 *hugely successful in English-speaking countries:* Sascha Auerbach, *Race, Law, and 'The Chinese Puzzle' in Imperial Britain* (Palgrave Macmillan, 2009), pp. 77, 90. The US President Calvin Coolidge was a big fan, and used to send out a White House messenger with the task of getting an advance copy of the latest Fu Manchu story. See William Chenery, *So It Seemed* (Harcourt Brace, 1952), pp. 225–6

266 *Imagine a person:* Sax Rohmer, *The Mystery of Dr Fu-Manchu* (Methuen, 1929), p. 21.

267 *'danger to the entire white race':* Ibid., p. 118.

268 *always in very small numbers:* In 1911 there were just 101 Chinese people living in Limehouse, and 337 ten years later. The equivalent figures for London were 247 and 711, and for the UK 1,120 and 2,419. See John Seed, 'Limehouse blues: Looking for "Chinatown" in the London Docks, 1900–40', *History Workshop Journal*, 63 (2006), pp. 63–5.

268 *a legendary Chinese gangster:* Christopher Frayling, *The Yellow Peril, Dr Fu Manchu & The Rise of Chinaphobia* (Thames & Hudson, 2014), pp. 66–7.

268 *first talkie film version of Fu Manchu: The Mysterious Dr Fu Manchu*, 1929.

268 *not the whole Chinese population:* Cay van Ash and Elizabeth Sax Rohmer, *Master of Villainy: A Biography of Sax Rohmer* (Tom Stacey, 1972), p. 73. These words were not in fact Sax Rohmer's, but what his wife thought her late husband would have said.

269 *other writers of the time:* Thomas Burke's 1916 short-story collection *Limehouse Nights*, largely set in the Chinese community of the East End, was also very popular, inspiring a series of films including D. W. Griffith's *Broken Blossoms*.

269 *This enormous mass of humanity:* Frayling, 2014, p. 208.

269 *'inscrutable, irresistible lure':* Auerbach, 2009, p. 66.

269 *'lack the money':* Lao She, *Mr Ma and Son* (Penguin, 2013), p. 15.

270n *Fu Manchu, meanwhile:* For Fu Manchu in the 1960s, the James Bond connection and Peter Sellers's final film see Frayling, 2014, pp. 42–5, 332–3. For the earliest recorded reference to 'Flu Manchu' see Ardie Rettop's letter to the *Daily News of New York*, 27 August 1957 ('Hysteria is mounting about this Asiatic flu from far-off places. If that's the way it is to be, let's go all the way and call it Flu Manchu.')

271 *wider mix of Chinese migrants:* Caroline Knowles, *Young Chinese Migrants in London*, Runnymede Trust, 2015, pp. 3–5, available at https://www.runnymedetrust.org/uploads/publications/pdfs/Young_Chinese.pdf

271 *largest group of foreign nationals* Ollie Williams, 'China's richest start leaving as the trade war escalates', Forbes.com, 28 May 2019.

271 *'reserved Chinese businessman':* Louise Dransfield, 'Meeting Mr X', *Building* magazine, 21 April 2017.

271 *one in eight of the area's residents:* Knowles, 2013, p. 7.

272n *In the years of Covid:* For *péril jaune* see *Le Courrier Picard*, 26 January 2020, and for yellow fever see Urban Dictionary, https://www.urbandictionary.com/define.php?term=yellow+fever

An Eighth Intermission

273 *the Passport Index:* The Henley Passport Index rankings since 2006 are available at https://www.henleyglobal.com/passport-index/ranking

274 *a tirade on a single subject:* Stefan Zweig, *The World of Yesterday: Memoirs of a European* (Pushkin Press, 2009), pp. 435–9.

275 *There had been repeated attempts:* John Torpey, *The Invention of the Passport: Surveillance, Citizenship and the State* (CUP, 2018), pp. 23, 26–63.

275 *These pre-war passports:* Martin Lloyd, *The Passport: The History of Man's Most Travelled Document* (Queen Anne's Fan, 2008), p. 5.

276 *many people talked, optimistically:* Ibid., p. 98.

276 *'total abolition of restrictions':* Introductory statement of the 'Resolution Adopted by the Paris Conference on Passports, Customs Facilities and Through Tickets', on 21 October 1920. Available at c.641 m.320 1925 VIII in the UN archives.

276 *standardised design for passports:* Ibid., Annex 1.

277 *'to offer special thanks':* Zweig, 2009, pp. 438–9.

277 *'This English document':* Ibid., p. 435.

277n *'In the last decade':* Ibid., p. 438.

278 *'my inner crisis':* see George Prochnik, 'A touch of eternity', *Lancet*, 2:11 (2015), pp. 698–70, quoting Zweig's letter to Jules Romains.

278 *'not feasible at present':* 'Recommendation on International Travel and Tourism', United Nations Conference on International Travel and Tourism, Rome 21 August to 5 September 1963, United Nations, 2.A.1, p. 6.

278 *known as 'investment migration':* See, for instance, the Investment Migration Council at https://investmentmigration.org/

279 *set out on a government website:* See https://www.gov.uk/tier-1-investor. Since February 2022, new 'Tier 1' applications have not been allowed.

Chapter Nine

281 *her earliest memories:* Esther Salaman, *The Autobiography of Esther Polianowsky Salaman* (privately published, 2012), p. 5.

281 *'No Jew of any standing':* Ibid., p. 23.

282 *about four hundred Jews:* Jeffrey Veidlinger, *In the Midst of Civilized Europe: The Pogroms of 1918–1921 and the Onset of the Holocaust* (Picador, 2021), pp. 57, 72.

282 *'plagued by lice':* Salaman, 2012, p. 121.

284 *coined as recently as 1890:* Jess Olson, 'The late Zionism of Nathan Birnbaum: The Herzl Controversy reconsidered', *Association for Jewish Studies Review*, 31:2 (2007), p. 243n6.

285 *'Next Year in Jerusalem':* Anita Shapira, *Israel: A History* (Brandeis, 2012), p. 15.

285n *former Vice-President Mike Pence:* Dan Hummel, 'What you need to know about Mike Pence's speech to Christians United for Israel', *Washington Post*, 17 July 2017.

287 *'psychic aberration':* Leon Pinsker (trans. D. S. Blondheim), 'Auto-Emancipation', *Essential Texts of Zionism* (Federation of American Zionists, 1916), available at https://www.jewishvirtuallibrary.org/quot-auto-emancipation-quot-leon-pinsker

287n *Polly's first memories of Zionism:* Salaman, 2012, pp. 54, 66.

288 *a quarter of a million Jews:* Arnold Dashefsky and Ira M. Sheskin (eds), *American Jewish Year Book 2019* (Springer, 2020), p. 144.

288 *abortive pre-Zionist attempt:* Adam Rovner, *In the Shadow of Zion: Promised Lands before Israel* (NYU, 2014), pp. 15–43.

288 *'marsh in North America':* Letter from the Chief Rabbi of Cologne, *Journal des Débats Politiques et Littéraires*, 18 November 1825.

288 *not actually in Uganda:* Rovner, 2014, p. 52.

288n *Mordecai Noah is often:* See Jonathan Sarna, *Jacksonian Jew: The Two Worlds of Mordecai Noah* (Holmes & Meier, 1981). For the foundation stone see Brian Hayden, 'Artifact Spotlight: The Ararat Stone', Buffalo History Museum website, 4 April 2022.

289 *split the Zionist movement:* Rovner, 2014, pp. 57–9.

289 *the most popular destination:* More than 2.5 million Russian Jews had migrated to the United States by 1914. Benny Morris, *Righteous Victims: A History of the Zionist–Arab Conflict 1881–2001*, (Vintage, 2001), p. 17.

289 *only 12 per cent of the population:* Shapira, 2012, p. 61.

289 *'Zionist Mayflower':* The *Ruslan* is also often referred to as the Israeli or Jewish *Mayflower*. Gur Alroey, 'Migrating over troubled water: the voyage to Palestine in the first decade of the British Mandate, 1919–1929', *Jewish Culture and History*, 22:3 (2021), pp. 17–18. The comparison seems only to date back to 1991, and Dan Tsalka's novel *A Thousand Hearts*, in which the Ruslan is referred to as 'this pitiable *Mayflower*'.

290 *centenary exhibition:* See the exhibition at https://www.imj.org.il/en/exhibitions/cultural-pioneers-aboard-ruslan, which includes a video presentation by the curator Talia Amar – with documentation about the 644 passengers and their official status as people returning to Palestine.

290 *Hebrew word aliyah:* Hizky Shoham, '"Great history" to "small history": The genesis of the Zionist periodization', *Israel Studies*, 18:1 (2013), pp. 33–4.

291n *The earliest example:* Ibid., pp. 36–7.

292 *historians have pointed out:* Shapira, 2012, pp. 103–4.

292 *majority of those Jews:* Ibid., p. 33.

292 *many of them were 'speculators':* Shoham, 2013, p. 38.

293 *'a land without a people':* Morris, 2001, p. 42. The Christian proto-Zionist British social reformer Lord Shaftesbury seems to have actually come up with the phrase: see Adam M. Garfinkle, 'On the origin, meaning, use and abuse of a phrase', *Middle Eastern Studies*, 27:4 (1991), p. 543.

293 *There were Arabs:* Salaman, 2012, p. 121.

294 *'dropout weaklings':* The Hebrew phrase was *nefolet shel nemushot*, which is also sometimes translated as 'fall-out of weaklings'. Hila Amit, 'Israel, Zionism and emigration anxiety: The case of Israeli academia', *Settler Colonial Studies*, 9:1 (2019), p. 10.

294n *named after Jabotinsky:* Ofer Petersburg, 'Jabotinsky most popular street name in Israel', ynetnews.com, 28 November 2007. See also Oren Kessler, 'The long shadow of Joseph Trumpeldor', *Mosaic* magazine, 2 March 2020, https://mosaicmagazine.com/observation/israel-zionism/2020/03/the-long-shadow-of-joseph-trumpeldor/

295 *Hebrew-language song 'Berlin':* Available on YouTube at https://www.youtube.com/watch?v=j0uosb26w9c. Thanks to Raz Weiner for the translation. For a wider discussion of *yerida* songs see Jasmin Habib and Amir Locker-Biletzki, '*Ḥama venehederet* (hot and wonderful): Home, belonging, and the image of the Yored in Israeli pop music', *Shofar: An Interdisciplinary Journal of Jewish Studies,* 36:1 (2018), pp. 1–28.

295 *the British consul-general:* Letter of Certification from John Lowdon, Acting British Consul-General in Odessa, 27 November 1919, reprinted in *Jewish News*, 10 January 2020, https://www.jewishnews.co.uk/exhibit-opens-on-israeli-mayflower/

296 *borrowed from the French:* The first usage in English, spelled 'refugies', was – according to the *Oxford English Dictionary* – in 1685, and two years later as 'refugees'. In fact, the word *refugié* was rarely used in French at this time: see David Agnew, *Protestant Exiles from France* (privately published, 1856), p. 159.

296 *more than a quarter of a million Belgians:* Christophe Declercq, 'The odd case of the welcome refugee in wartime Britain: Uneasy numbers, disappearing acts and forgetfulness regarding Belgian refugees in the First World War', *Close Encounters in War Journal*, 1:2 (2020), p. 3.

297 *British propaganda narrative:* Ibid., pp. 5–9.

297 *'unmixing of peoples':* The phrase is said to have been first used by the British Foreign Secretary Lord Curzon. For further discussion see Sadia Abbas, 'Unmixing', *Political Concepts: A Critical Lexicon*, issue 5, 2019, available at https://www.politicalconcepts.org/unmixing-sadia-abbas/

298 *to return to their old homes:* Under Article 64 of the Treaty of Trianon they had six months to make the decision – to stay in Romania or go to Hungary. And according to Article 66, husbands made the choice for their wives, and fathers for their children under eighteen.

298 *a hundred thousand Hungarian-speakers:* Michael Marrus, *The Unwanted: European Refugees in the Twentieth Century* (OUP, 1985), p. 72.

298 *More than a million Greeks:* Peter Gatrell, *The Making of the Modern Refugee* (OUP, 2013), p. 64.

299 *'buried the hatchet':* Bruce Clark, *Twice a Stranger: The Mass Expulsions that Forged Modern Greece, and Turkey* (Harvard, 2006), p. 31.

299 *appointed the Norwegian explorer Fridtjof Nansen:* Gatrell, 2013, p. 55. Nansen's full title was High Commissioner on Behalf of the League in Connection with the Problem of Russian Refugees in Europe. There wasn't yet a detailed legal definition of the word 'refugee', but Nansen's mandate referred to Russians who had lost their old nationality, and didn't have a new one – who were, for all practical purposes, stateless, in a world of nation-states.

299n *Only those Greeks:* Clark, 2006, p. xii.

300 *in and around Constantinople:* Marrus, 1985, p. 59, and for the lower Constantinople-specific figures see Pınar Üre, 'Remnants of empires: Russian refugees and citizenship regime in Turkey, 1923–1938', *Middle Eastern Studies*, 56:2 (2019), p. 1.

300 *to the Chinese city of Harbin:* Gatrell, 2013, p. 56.

300 *assisting Armenians and Assyrians:* Marrus, 1985, p. 96.

300 *restricted to Europe:* The UN refugee definition was not given a global scope until 1967. See Anne Hammerstad, *The Rise and Decline of a Global Security Actor: UNHCR, Refugee Protection, and Security* (OUP, 2014), p. 80.

300n *Sometimes these refugees:* Daniel Mendelsohn, *The Lost: A Search for Six of Six Million* (Harper 2007), pp. 42–3.

A Ninth Intermission

304 *fifty-six-page document:* This took the form of a Country Profile supplied to the BBC by an organisation called Employment Conditions Abroad Limited. Copy in the author's possession.

305 *'there's something unique about expats':* See https://www.internations.org/about-internations/albatross/

305n *'expatriate studies' has become:* Yvonne McNulty and Jan Selmer, *Research Handbook of Expatriates* (Edward Elgar, 2017), pp. 21–2.

306n *In the 1850s:* Ralph Waldo Emerson, *Emerson: The Essential Writings* (Random House, 2009), p. 511.

307 *it may appear unjust:* Walter Harragin, *Report of the Commission on the Civil Services of British West Africa* (HMSO, 1947), p. 10.

307n *'carnally involved with the rough trade of Totnes':* Nigel Barley, *White Rajah: A Biography of Sir James Brooke* (Abacus, 2003), p. 208.

Chapter Ten

310 *BMI of more than sixty:* The statue weighs 141,521kg, and is 46.94m high. The formula for Body Mass Index = kg/m^2, so Liberty's BMI is approximately 64. Measurements available at https://home.nps.gov/stli/learn/historyculture/statue-statistics.htm

310 *French city of Rouen:* Yasmin Sabina Khan, *Enlightening the World: The Creation of the Statue of Liberty* (Cornell, 2010), p. 173.

311 *Give me your tired:* Ibid., p. 6.

312 *idiots, insane persons:* Vincent Cannato, *American Passage: The History of Ellis Island* (HarperCollins, 2009), p. 52.

312 *Imbeciles, feeble-minded persons:* Ibid., p. 128.

312 *alcoholics and illiterates:* Ibid., p. 242.

312 *'L' stood for lameness:* Ibid., p. 7.

312 *'low receding forehead:* Ibid., p. 252.

312n *By 1905, all migrants:* Ibid., p. 158.

313 *an 'enchanted land':* Thomas Bailey Aldrich, *Unguarded Gates and Other Poems* (Houghton Mifflin, 1895), p. 15.

313 *Grant – a well-connected:* Jonathan Peter Spiro, *Defending the Master Race: Conservation, Eugenics, and the Legacy of Madison Grant* (University of Vermont, 2009), p. xiii. Grant was friends with three presidents: Taft and both the Roosevelts, and was an acquaintance of President Harding.

313 *Hitler would later describe:* Ibid., p. 357.

313 *a particular distaste* Madison Grant, *The Passing of the Great Race* (Scribner's, 1936), p. 263.

314 *his innovation:* Ibid., pp. 20–1, 226–9.

314 *as Native Americans:* Ibid., p. 5.

314 *The danger is from within:* Ibid., p. xxxi (introduction to the fourth edition).

314n *The term 'melting pot':* Israel Zangwill, *The Melting-Pot* (Macmillan, 1909), p. 53.

315 *Congressional report in 1920: House Reports, 66th Congress,* December 1920 to March 1921, vol. 1, pp. 2–3.

315 *eight million migrants:* Ibid., p. 6.

315 *uncomfortable reading:* Ibid., pp. 9–10.

316 *a monthly quota:* Cannato, 2009, pp. 333–4. The monthly quota was actually a maximum of 20 per cent of the yearly quota per month, starting in July (which was when the old US fiscal year started).

316 *list of exceptions: Congressional Record, 67th Congress,* 19 May 1921, section 2d.

316 *80 per cent fall:* Spiro, 2009, pp. 209–10.

316 *'the Midnight Races':* Robertson, 2010, pp. 204–5.

316 *all went ridiculously wrong: New York Times,* 2 September 1923.

317 *'an amazing triumph':* Spiro, 2009, p. 233.

317 *twenty years later the figure:* See US government census website, https://www2.census.gov/library/publications/1949/compendia/hist_stats_1789-1945/hist_stats_1789-1945-chB.pdf, p. 33.

318 *Bhagat Singh Thind:* Anu Kumar, 'Bhagat Singh Thind: The soldier whose fight for US citizenship reverberated for decades', Scroll.in, 23 November

2021, https://scroll.in/global/1011124/bhagat-singh-thind-the-soldier-whose-fight-for-us-citizenship-reverberated-for-decades. Thind was eventually granted citizenship in 1936 because he had served in the US armed forces during the First World War.

318 *'the Chinese, Hindus and other races':* Hearings before the Committee on *Immigration and Naturalization: House of Representatives*, vol. 1 (Government Printing Office, 1924), p. 373.

318 *Italians were not quite white:* Robert Orsi, 'The religious boundaries of an inbetween people: Street feste and the problem of the dark-skinned other in Italian Harlem, 1920–1990', *American Quarterly*, 44:3 (1992).

318n *The most famous example:* Sarah Ogilvie and Scott Miller, *Refuge Denied: The St Louis Passengers and the Holocaust* (University of Wisconsin, 2006), p. 174.

318n *Grant and his allies:* Spiro, 2009, pp. 149–50.

319 *white women worked:* Isabel Wilkerson, *The Warmth of Other Suns: The Epic Story of America's Great Migration* (Knopf Doubleday, 2010), p. 234.

319 *'in-between' people:* John Higham, *Strangers in the Land: Patterns of American Nativism 1860–1925* (Rutgers, 1955), p. 169. See also James R. Barrett and David Roediger, 'Inbetween peoples: Race, nationality and the "new immigrant" working class', *Journal of American Ethnic History*, 16:3 (1997).

319 *about 750 officers:* Timothy Henderson, *Beyond Borders: A History of Mexican Migration to the United States* (Wiley-Blackwell, 2011), p. 42.

319 *'Alien gate-crashers':* 'Alien "gate crashers" still pour in over our frontiers; bootleggers reap rich harvest in smuggling foreigners here from Canada and Mexico', *New York Times*, 19 June 1927.

320 *about 450,000 Mexicans:* See the US government's historical statistics website, https://www2.census.gov/library/publications/1949/compendia/hist_stats_1789-1945/hist_stats_1789-1945-chB.pdf, p. 35.

320 *several million Black Americans:* A total of about 1.6 million moved in the 1910s, 20s and 30s. A further five million moved from the 1940s to the 70s. James Gregory, 'The Second Great Migration: A Historical Overview', in Kenneth Kusmer and Joe Trotter (eds), *African American Urban History since World War II* (University of Chicago, 2009), p. 21.

320n *It's often forgotten:* James Gregory, *The Southern Diaspora: How the Great Migrations of Black and White Southerners transformed America* (University of North Carolina, 2005), pp. 15–16, 160.

321 *'the social and political order':* Wilkerson, 2010, p. 9.

321 *a 'deliberate flight':* Alain Locke, *The Works of Alain Locke*, vol. 1, (OUP, 2012), p. 444.

321 *'Anyone want to go to Chicago':* Emmett Scott, *Negro Migration during the War* (Arno Press, 1969), p. 37.

321 *would-be migrants:* Ibid., pp. 73–9, and Wilkerson, 2010, p. 163.

321 *more than 70 per cent:* Gregory, 2009, p. 22.

321 *weekly Chicago Defender:* Ethan Michaeli, *The Defender: How the Legendary Black Newspaper Changed America* (Houghton Mifflin Harcourt, 2016), pp. 65–76.

322 *When I got here:* Wilkerson, 2010, p. 349.

322 *Don't sit around:* Ibid., p. 291.

323   *was predominantly Black:* See https://www.gothamgazette.com/index.php/demographcis/4077-harlems-shifting-population

323   *the great Mecca:* James Weldon Johnson, 'The making of Harlem', *The Survey Graphic,* 53:11 (1925), p. 635.

323   *Langston Hughes imagined:* 'The Negro Speaks of Rivers', available at https://poets.org/poem/negro-speaks-rivers

324   *Liberia closed its borders:* Colin Grant, *Negro with a Hat: The Rise and Fall of Marcus Garvey* (Jonathan Cape, 2008), p. 386.

324   *'My Africa, Motherland':* Langston Hughes, *The Collected Works, Volume 13, Autobiography: The Big Sea* (University of Missouri, 2002), pp. 36–7, 96.

324   *About two hundred thousand Black Americans:* Tyler Stovall, *Paris Noir: African Americans in the City of Light* (Houghton Mifflin, 1996), p. 5.

324n *There were Black Americans:* See Naurice Frank Woods, *Henry Ossawa Tanner: Art, Faith, Race, and Legacy* (Routledge, 2018) and Craig Lloyd, *Eugene Bullard: Black Expatriate in Jazz-age Paris* (University of Georgia, 2006).

325   *there was no colour prejudice:* Ibid., p. 36.

325   *a doorman and a dishwasher:* Hughes, 2002, p. 132.

326   *a largely positive term:* Carole Sweeney, *From Fetish to Subject: Race, Modernism, and Primitivism, 1919–1935* (Praeger, 2004), pp. 2–4.

326   *'splendour of an ancient animal':* Jean-Claude Baker and Chris Chase, *Josephine: The Hungry Heart* (Cooper Square, 1993), p. 7.

326   *'be more African':* Anne Chisholm, *Nancy Cunard* (Sidgwick & Jackson, 1979), p. 134.

327   *ran across a bridge:* Ean Wood, *The Josephine Baker Story* (Sanctuary, 2000), pp. 30–1.

327   *'more French than the French':* Matthew Pratt Guterl, *Josephine Baker and the Rainbow Tribe* (Belknap Press, 2014), p. 143.

327   *'to be colored':* Anthony Barnett, *Listening for Henry Crowder: A Monograph on His Almost Lost Music* (Allardyce Barnett, 2007), p. 65.

327   *'I had a lot of men':* Bricktop with James Haskins, *Bricktop* (Scribner, 1983), p. 131.

327   *'very little racial discrimination':* Ibid., p. 127.

327   *'Parisians had started':* Ibid., p. 238.

327   *only one Black American:* Stovall, 1996, p. 124.

328   *heading to Marrakesh:* Wood, 2000, p. 226.

328   *'a victim of Hitler':* Langston Hughes, *Langston Hughes and the 'Chicago Defender': Essays on Race, Politics, and Culture, 1942–62* (University of Illinois, 1995), p. 195.

328   *'too busy to die':* Guterl, 2014, p. 14.

328n *She was pilloried:* Ibid., p. 69.

329   *'Jo and I plan':* Josephine Baker and Jo Bouillon, *Josephine* (Harper & Row, 1977), p. 190.

329   *country-specific wish-list:* Guterl, 2014, p. 88.

329   *'with solemn eyes':* Ibid., p. 93.

330   *'Miss Baker's humanitarian impulse':* 'Adoption of Israeli child by Josephine Baker rejected', Jewish Telegraph Agency, 30 December 1954.

330   *'a dark-skinned baby':* Guterl, 2014, pp. 97–8.

330n *There was a longer-term plan:* Ibid., pp. 173–5.

331 *'plain ghetto girl':* Ishmael Reed, 'Remembering Josephine', *New York Times*, 12 December 1976.

A Final Intermission

334 *The first person:* Jean-Jacques Rousseau, *Œuvres Complètes de J. J. Rousseau*, vol. 1 (Hachette, 1865), p. 105. My translation.

337 *'so many mongongo nuts':* Richard Lee, 'What Hunters Do for a Living, or, How to Make Out on Scarce Resources', in Richard Lee and Irven DeVore (eds), *Man the Hunter* (Aldine de Gruyter, 1968), p. 33.

338n *The !Kung:* Richard Lee, *The Dobe Ju/'hoansi* (Wadsworth, 2013), pp. 175, 183–210.

Chapter Eleven

339 *his three-day journey:* Alexandra Ventura Corceiro and Klaus Schmidt, 'Der millionste Gastarbeiter, das Moped und die bundesdeutsche Einwanderungsgesellschaft: Biografie Armando Rodrigues de Sá', 2004, available at https://iberer.angekommen.com/Mio/bio3.pdf.

340 *extensive media coverage:* Rita Chin, *The Guest Worker Question in Postwar Germany* (CUP, 2007), pp. 1–6.

340 *replacement for Fremdarbeiter:* Ibid., pp. 8–10, 52–3, and interview with Ulrich Herbert, 'Wer sprach vom "Fremdarbeiter"', *Frankfurter Allgemeine Zeitung*, 04 July 2005.

342 *publicly executed for having sex:* Ulrich Herbert, *Hitler's Foreign Workers: Enforced Foreign Labor in Germany Under the Third Reich* (CUP, 1997), pp. 69–79.

342 *Terrible images:* Harold Jähner, *Aftermath* (W. H. Allen, 2021), p. 42.

343 *'We can't take any more people!':* Ibid., p. 67.

343 *first agreement was signed:* In fact there was an earlier 1952 recruitment programme with Italy involving the province of Baden-Württemburg. See Deniz Göktürk, David Gramling and Anton Kaes, *Germany in Transit: Nation and Migration 1955–2005* (University of California, 2007), pp. 23, 27–8.

344 *Verona and Naples:* Ibid., pp. 29–30.

344 *made the first contact:* Ventura Corceiro and Schmidt, 2004, p. 1.

344n *An industrial accident:* Ibid., p. 3.

345 *Germany's largest single source:* Chin, 2007, p. 11. Leo Lucassen, *The Immigrant Threat: The Integration of Old and New Migrants in Western Europe since 1850* (University of Illinois, 205), p. 146.

345 *three-day journey:* Jennifer Miller, *Turkish Guest Workers in Germany: Hidden Lives and Contested Borders* (University of Toronto, 2018), p. 64.

345 *cheese and olives:* Ibid., p. 60.

345 *'hot-blooded':* Ibid., pp. 34–5.

346 *'We called for workers':* Seiler, 1965, p. 7.

346 *Attempts to restrict migration:* Miller, 2018, pp. 164–7.

347 *Vietnam and Ethiopia:* Chin, 2007, p. 147.

349 *'Ten Pound Poms':* James Hammerton and Alistair Thomson, *Ten Pound Poms: Australia's Invisible Migrants* (Manchester University Press, 2005), p. 32.

349n *'Pom', as an Australian moniker:* See John Simpson, 'The *Oxford English Dictionary* and its chief word detective', *BBC News Online*, 3 May 2013.

350 *Republic of Ireland:* Robert Gildea, *Empires of the Mind: The Colonial Past and the Politics of the Present* (CUP, 2019), p. 123.

350 *Italian, Spanish and Portuguese:* Gérard Noiriel, *Le Creuset Français: Histoire de l'Immigration* (Editions de Seuil, 1988), p. 414, and Alec Hargreaves, *Immigration, 'Race' and Ethnicity in Contemporary France* (Routledge, 1995), p. 11.

350 *the Monte Rosa:* Paul Arnott, *Windrush: A Ship through Time* (History Press, 2019), p. 25.

350n *In fact, the Windrush:* The figure of two-thirds of the Windrush Jamaicans being ex-servicemen comes from a confidential memorandum entitled 'Arrival in the United Kingdom of Jamaican Unemployed' sent to the British Cabinet by the Colonial Secretary, Arthur Creech-Jones on 18 June 1948, three days before the *Windrush* landed at Tilbury. Accessible at https://discovery.nationalarchives.gov.uk/details/r/D7655430. See also Ian Sanjay Patel, *We're Here Because You Were There: Immigration and the End of Empire* (Verso, 2021), p. 61.

351 *Norwegian Jews to Hamburg:* Arnott, 2019, p. 83.

351 *well-travelled Polish refugees:* Robert Winder, *Bloody Foreigners: The Story of Immigration to Britain* (Abacus, 2005), p. 335.

352 *two-minute news story:* Available on YouTube (after 46″) https://www.youtube.com/watch?v=QDH4IBeZF-M, and Amelia Gentleman, *The Windrush Betrayal: Exposing the Hostile Environment* (Guardian Faber, 2019), pp. 100–1.

352n *This was not the Windrush's first voyage:* Arnott, 2019, pp. 140, 235.

353 *surprise and disappointment:* Colin Grant, *Homecoming: Voices of the Windrush Generation* (Vintage, 2020), pp. 77–91.

353 *'no coloureds' on rental advertisements:* David Kynaston, *Modernity Britain: 1957–1962* (Bloomsbury, 2015), pp. 173–4.

354 *white people of British ancestry:* Patel, 2021, pp. 68–9.

354 *convoluted legal formulations:* Ibid., p. 78.

354 *As the law stands:* Henry Hopkinson, *Hansard*, 5 November 1954, vol. 532, col. 827.

355 *summary execution and torture:* David French, *The British Way in Counter-Insurgency: 1945–1967* (OUP, 2011), pp. 156–7.

356 *'colonisation in reverse':* The title of Louise Bennett's 1966 poem, first published in 1966, and written in Jamaican patois. Available at http://louisebennett.com/colonization-in-reverse/

356 *'we are here because':* Patel, 2021, p. 1.

357 *more than half a million Algerians:* Hargreaves, 1995, p. 15.

357n *The first three groups:* It's very hard to get a consensus on these figures, and they remain contested. See the valiant attempts of demographer Kamel

Kateb, *Européens, 'Indigènes' et Juifs en Algérie (1830–1962)* (Éditions de l'Institut National d'Études Démographiques, 2001), pp. 310–3.

358 *disrupted the labour market:* Neil McMaster, *Colonial Migrants and Racism: Algerians in France 1900–62* (Palgrave Macmillan, 1987), pp. 5–6, 189.

358 *French soldiers conscripted* Martin Evans, *Algeria: France's Undeclared War* (OUP, 2012), p. 277.

358 *known as the Paris Massacre:* Benjamin Stora, *La gangrène et l'oubli: La mémoire de la guerre d'Algérie* (Edition la découverte, 2005), pp. 93–100.

359 *described as 'unassimilable':* McMaster, 1987, p. 222.

359n *the burkini became popular:* Hortense Goulard, 'Burkini creator says controversy boosting sales', *Politico*, 23 August 2016.

360 *Algerian migrants by French racists:* McMaster, 1987, p. 205.

360 *'a state of amnesia':* Stora, 2005, p. 319.

360 *The former colonised person:* Ibid., p. 289.

362 *a place called Aztlan:* Michael E. Smith, 'The Aztlan migrations of the Nahuatl Chronicles: Myth or history?', *Ethnohistory*, 31:3 (1984), pp. 153–86.

362 *a hundred thousand Mexicans:* I've been unable to identify a reliable estimate of the increase in the population of the USA that resulted from the war and the subsequent peace treaty. Many of the new Americans were not deemed citizens, and many Native Americans were never counted. See Richard Griswold del Castillo, *The Treaty of Guadalupe Hildago: A Legacy of Conflict* (University of Oklahoma, 1990), p. 62, and Martha Menchaca, *Recovering History, Constructing Race: The Indian, Black and White Roots of Mexican Americans* (University of Texas, 2001), p. 257.

362 *as 'savage Indians':* Agreement between the United States and Mexico, 'Reciprocal Right to pursue Savage Indians across the Boundary Line', 29 July 1882, available at https://history.state.gov/historicaldocuments/frus1882/d272, and Rachel St John, *Line in the Sand: A History of the Western US–Mexico Border* (Princeton, 2011), p. 59.

362 *Geronimo, the last of the Apache:* Robert Utley, *Geronimo* (Yale, 2012), p. 257.

363 *Americans heading south:* St John, 2011, p. 153.

363 *Mexicans' innate submissiveness:* Ibid., p. 183.

363 *'a natural aptitude':* Deborah Cohen, *Braceros: Migrant Citizens and Transnational Subjects in the Postwar United States* (University of North Carolina, 2011), p. 56.

363 *'work stooping over':* Ibid., p. 99.

364 *naked Mexican men:* St John, 2011, p. 184.

364 *There were raids:* Adam Goodman, *The Deportation Machine: America's Long History of Expelling Immigrants* (Princeton, 2020), p. 45.

364 *'caravans of sorrow':* Francisco Balderrama and Raymond Rodriquez, *Decade of Betrayal: Mexican Repatriation in the 1930s* (University of New Mexico, 2006), pp. 122, 167.

364 *migrant labour agreement:* Cohen, 2011, pp. 21–2.

365 *grateful New York Times headline: New York Times*, 20 October 1942.

365 *4.5 million work contracts:* Cohen, 2011, p. 21.

365 *'like a horse; we felt degraded':* Ibid., p. 107.

365 *they'd send us in groups:* Ibid., p. 99.

366 *The influx of aliens:* Goodman, 2020, p. 48.

367 *Texas to a Mexican seaport:* Ibid., pp. 82–104.

367 *reject anyone who had soft hands:* Cohen, 2011, pp. 98–100.

367 *As a wetback, alone:* Mae Ngai, *Impossible Subjects: Illegal Aliens and the Making of Modern America* (Princeton, 2014), p. 146.

367n *There was some criticism:* Goodman, 2020, pp. 103–4.

368 *threatened patrol officers:* Kelly Lytle Hernandez, *Migra! A History of the US Border Patrol* (University of California, 2010), p. 163.

368 *'A Mexican always walks':* Ibid., p. 49.

368 *Chain-link fences:* St John, 2011, p. 204.

368 *corpses of five Mexican men:* Hernandez, 2010, p. 131.

369 *carry drugs into the USA:* Michael Dear, *Why Walls Won't Work: Repairing the US–Mexico Divide* (OUP, 2013), p. 68.

369 *strip-searching and detaining:* Hernandez, 2010, p. 208.

369 *'Apache' haircuts:* Ibid., p. 142.

369 *'one old boy had a big bushy moustache':* Ibid.

369 *'a picture in the minds of the public':* Ibid., p. 205.

369 *'they're bringing drugs':* Suzanne Gamboa, 'Donald Trump announces presidential bid by trashing Mexico, Mexicans', NBC News Online, 16 June 2015.

370 *replaced by an annual cap:* Hernandez, 2010, p. 213.

370 *Reagan granted an amnesty:* As part of the 1986 Immigration Reform and Control Act. See Section 201. Available at https://www.govinfo.gov/content/pkg/STATUTE-100/pdf/STATUTE-100-Pg3445.pdf

370 *several thousand Haitians:* Bernd Debusmann, 'Why are so many Haitians at the US–Mexico border?', BBC News Online, 24 September 2021.

371 *swum around the fence:* Austin Ramzy, 'One dead after dozens try to swim around San Diego border fence', *New York Times*, 31 October 2021.

371 *lifts and ventilation systems:* Dear, 2013, p. 174.

371 *'show me a fifty-foot wall':* Words spoken by the then Arizona governor (and future Secretary of Homeland Security) Janet Napolitano in 2005. See Marc Lacey, 'Arizona officials, fed up with US efforts, seek donations to build border fence', *New York Times*, 19 July 2011.

Index

Picture Credits